Hope and Memory

Hope and Memory

LESSONS FROM THE
TWENTIETH CENTURY

By Tzvetan Todorov

Translated by David Bellos

ATLANTIC BOOKS
LONDON

First published in English in the United States of America in 2003
by Princeton University Press, Princeton, New Jersey

License arranged by Susanna Lea Associates, Paris

Published in Great Britain in 2003
by Atlantic Books, an imprint of Grove Atlantic Ltd

Originally published in French in 2000 as *Mémoire du mal, tentation du bien: Enquête
sur le siècle* by Editions Robert Laffont

Copyright © Tzvetan Todorov 2003
Translation copyright © Princeton University Press 2003

1 2 3 4 5 6 7 8 9 10

A CIP catalogue record for this book is available from the British Library

ISBN 1 903809 47 9

Printed in Great Britain by Creative Print and Design, Wales

Atlantic Books
An imprint of Grove Atlantic Ltd
Ormond House
26–27 Boswell Street
London WC1N 3JZ

www.groveatlantic.co.uk

Contents

Abbreviations and Acronyms

AFP	Agence France-Presse
Cheka	Soviet political police, 1917–1922 (later, GPU, 1922–1934)
CNRS	Centre national de la recherche scientifique (French Science Research Council)
EU	European Union
FLN	Front de libération nationale (Algerian National Independence movement, 1954–62)
FN	Front national (French extreme right-wing party)
GIA	Groupe islamique armée (Algerian terrorist group)
FYROM	Former Yugoslav Republic of Macedonia
Gestapo	Geheime Staatspolizei (German political police, 1933–45)
gulag	Glavnoye Upravlenie Lagerey (Soviet labor camp organization)
ICC	International Criminal Court
ICTY	International Criminal Tribunal for Yugoslavia
KGB	Soviet political police, 1953–91
KLA	Kosovo Liberation Army
MSF	Médecins sans frontières
NATO	North Atlantic Treaty Organization
NGO	nongovernmental organization
NKVD	People's Commissariat for Internal Affairs, incorporating the political police, 1934–1953
NSDAP	Nationalsozialistische Deutsche Arbeiterpartei (Nazi Party)
OAS	Organisation de l'armée secrète (French settler terrorist group, Algeria 1958–60s)
OAU	Organization of African Unity
OCSE	Organization for Co-operation and Security in Europe
PCF	Parti communiste français (French Communist Party)
POW	prisoner of war
RPF	Rwandan Patriotic Front
SS	Schutzstaffel (Nazi military police)

Preface to the English Edition

THIS BOOK IS a reflection on the political history of the twentieth century; written by a European, it focuses essentially on events that took place in Europe, in particular the conflict between totalitarian and democratic systems. The original French version appeared, to some extent symbolically, at the end of the year 2000. Since then, events outside Europe — the terrorist attacks on the United States and the responses they have elicited — have dramatically altered the scene. It is difficult, today, to think about the more distant past without taking these recent events into account. Do current developments bear any resemblance to what went before? Can the lessons of the past illuminate the present? Two years after finishing the book, I would like to take the opportunity afforded by its publication in English to explore some of the possible answers to these questions. Within the limits of this preface, I can obviously not purport to give a full analysis of 9/11 and its aftermath (besides, these events have fostered so much commentary that one would be hard put to add anything really new); I shall try, however, to describe the new facts as they relate to the general framework laid out in this volume.

After the attacks on the World Trade Center and the Pentagon, many commentators declared that something radically novel had happened, and that history — if not the history of the human race, then at least modern Western history — was henceforth divided into a "before" and an "after." What is the content of this novelty? A number of inadequate answers must first be set aside. The attacks do not constitute an unprecedented onslaught of barbarism against civilization, oppression against freedom, or evil against good. Such terms, while they have high emotive power, are poor tools for description. Wars are often conducted in the name of noble ideals, and fanaticism has always been with us. Nor can we say that what is new about 9/11 is that its victims were "innocent civilians" (a misleading phrase in itself, since it implies that all one need do is put military uniforms on civilians to turn them into guilty parties). The slaughter of civilians, alas, is nothing new; it is not only a regular feature of terrorist attacks but a phenomenon common to conventional warfare at least since

World War II. Over the past half century, the United States itself has frequently caused massive civilian casualties; one need only think of Dresden, Tokyo, Hiroshima, Nagasaki, Hanoi, Phnom Penh, Baghdad, or Belgrade. Although they did at least know their countries were at war, the victims of these actions were not asked ahead of time whether they supported their governments' policies.

Some degree of novelty might be found in the fact that America was attacked on its own soil — something that had not occurred for nearly two hundred years. This novelty does not concern the act itself, only the place of its unfolding. The inhabitants of Europe's major cities, not to mention those of other continents, have long been familiar with terrorist attacks, even if they did not claim as many victims in as short a space of time or take the spectacular form of airplanes flying into skyscrapers and government buildings. Here again, however, the originality is limited: it amounts to the fact that Americans have joined the rest of the world in a common plight, that of being the potential targets of an external attack that can come at any time.

There is an aspect of 9/11 whose novelty, in my view, is more significant: the attacks showed the increasing power of individuals and small groups. In the past, only a state — and a powerful one at that — could have organized such a complex action; 9/11 was the work of a few dozen people at most. This raised the prospect of even more dramatic events: the same individuals could get hold of weapons of mass destruction — chemical, biological, or even nuclear arms. Technological progress has made it possible for private groups to build such weapons and has also made them affordable; miniaturization has made them easier to move around.

It is almost as if George Orwell had lost out to Ian Fleming in predicting the future. Instead of a world reduced to the conflict between vast totalitarian empires, as foreseen in *1984*, we have a single empire watching in shock as a megalomaniac billionaire hidden in an underground cavern dispatches kamikaze pilots to destroy targets in American cities. Today's evildoers are not states, so it is fairly easy for them to conceal themselves and avoid military reprisal: individuals do not have a territory to defend. This James Bond scenario is confirmed by what we know of the anti-American terrorists: they come from different countries and are identified with none of them: they are stateless.

Even this rise of individual power, however, is not entirely new; it was already present in the process known as globalization. Although the term is not inappropriate — contacts between the different parts of the globe have unquestionably become more numerous in recent years — it does not bring out the most important change from the point of view of the peoples involved — namely, that these contacts are less and less under the control of states. At most, states can defend their borders, but money does not stop at border crossings. By the mere click of a mouse, individuals or groups with no political legitimacy whatsoever can choose to keep their capital where it is or transfer it elsewhere, thereby provoking mass unemployment or warding off imminent catastrophe. They can cause social unrest or help to avert it. These people, too, are individuals who wield immense power, and it is not always easy to make them face up to their responsibilities.

Our vulnerability to attack by individuals and groups is related to changes in our own identities. The danger that threatens Western societies is not merely the consequence of external attack; it is conditioned by characteristic features of our own societies. This should not come as a complete surprise: the twentieth century taught us that mankind could put its own survival in jeopardy. The spectacular advances of science and technology unlocked the secrets of the material world and gave us the ability to transform it, but as a result we are threatened by nuclear explosions and global warming, the greenhouse effect and genetic mutation. Those dangers are the price we pay for technical progress. Today's new dangers are the consequence of our life-style, the very social advances on which we pride ourselves the most.

Western citizens are proud of the amount of freedom they enjoy, the absence of bureaucratic controls, their right to travel without justifying their wish to do so, the openness of their borders. They have suddenly discovered that these precious freedoms are of great benefit to terrorists. They are proud of the accessibility of information in their societies — the fact that scientific knowledge is available to all — but this also means that the web can provide anyone with formulas for the manufacture of anthrax and plastic explosives, and that would-be kamikazes, by attending ordinary flying schools, can learn how to fly aircraft into buildings. We take pride in the universal availability of news and the speed at which it circulates, but we now realize that this same news is of use to people who wish us harm, and who are just as good as we are at manipulating the media. We have invented machines to do our hard labor for us, prolonged our life expectancy through modern medicine, and built comfortable housing in which to live; all these advantages of modern civilization are sources of pride, yet they also increase our vulnerability. What would become of us if we were suddenly deprived of energy — gas or power — to say nothing of the medicines, health care, clean water, and food to which we are accustomed? Prehistoric and medieval peoples feared the elements above all else, but modern life is dependent on so many man-made commodities that human agents now represent the greatest threat.

Who are the people who perpetrated 9/11? Let us begin by distinguishing three groups: the masterminds, the operatives, and the sympathizers.

The aims of the masterminds do not seem to me to be at all novel. As with those who fomented other violent actions of this type, such as the FLN atrocities during the Algerian war or KLA actions before the bombing of Yugoslavia, the goal of the new masterminds is to exacerbate the opposition between the forces in conflict and to provoke an even more violent response from the adversary, thereby strengthening solidarity among their own people and eliminating neutrals and moderates. Thus the attacks on America follow a familiar logic: Bin Laden is involved in a quest to increase his own power, particularly in the Arabic countries. "Anti-imperialist" rhetoric was tacked on later, in an effort to ensure the sympathy of the masses in the ongoing conflict. It should be added that, from a purely political standpoint, the forecasts of Bin Laden and his lieutenants have turned out to be totally erroneous and the results of their actions have been disastrous, both for themselves and for the cause they claimed to defend. Their bases and training camps have been destroyed, the Palestinians have never been further from fulfilling their aspiration to become an autonomous state, and the population of Iraq lives under the imminent threat of U.S. firepower.

For the operatives, the religious factor seems crucial. People agree to die with greater readiness when they are firmly convinced that it is requested of them by God and will result in their being sent directly to heaven. Unlike the masterminds, who are both fanatical and calculating, the operatives are in the main true believers who are susceptible to manipulation and made into fanatics. To many of us, such fanaticism may seem incomprehensible, but in fact it can be found in virtually all traditions, whether they be official religions or not: there have always been people prepared to sacrifice their lives for an ideal in order to bring about the reign of good. We tend to forget that (as the Enlightenment philosophers put it) passions often take precedence over self-interest.

As for the sympathizers, of whom there are huge numbers in the developing world, they have yet a different kind of motivation. These are people who would never dream of taking part in terrorist attacks, yet who approve of them more or less openly. Simultaneously attracted by the wealth of the Western world and humiliated by their exclusion from it, they seethe with resentment. Moreover, they are offended by what they perceive (with some justification) as the biased and arrogant political attitudes of the West toward them or toward peoples with whom they identify. Cases in point are the Israeli-Palestinian conflict or the embargo against Iraq, which had little impact on that country's government but fatal consequences for its population.

None of these three groups is coextensive with the entity known as Islam, however much the backers of the terrorist attacks would have liked us to believe so. For the time being at least, what we are witnessing is not a "clash of civilizations." Not all Islam is warlike, any more than all forms of Christianity spawn crusades. The ideology that inspires the hard-line terrorists is not Islam per se but a curiously modern variety of Islamic fundamentalism. From what we know of these individuals, they do not come from especially poor or backward families but were comfortably well-off; all of them had lived in the West, and many had university degrees, generally in the sciences.

Reading the accounts of how preparations were made for 9/11 and the reactions it provoked, one can be struck by the mixture of two apparently incompatible ingredients. On the one hand, the terrorists had remarkable command of technology—flying airplanes, using the web to collect and exchange information, moving around and passing messages without leaving any trace. On the other hand, they were naive believers in omens, coincidences, and heavenly rewards—things we dismiss as superstitions. In a video recording of Bin Laden conversing with visitors, we learn that he instructed his companions not to discuss their dreams, for they might give away details of the attacks yet to come! It was the conjunction of superstition — indispensable for people preparing to die as martyrs — and expertise in up-to-date technology that made these terrorists particularly dangerous.

How do these neofundamentalists and their threat to democracy compare with the dangers embodied by the totalitarian states of the twentieth century? True, in both cases violence is used in the name of a hegemonic ideology, and in both cases individual freedom is repressed. To my mind, however, the differences are far more significant than the similarities: whereas now, you have the exaltation of religion and the cult of the past, earlier you had the rejection of religion and the cult of the future; whereas now you have the action of stateless individuals and the willingness to sacrifice oneself, earlier you had the actions of all-powerful states and the willingness to sacrifice the lives of others. Nor does the damage caused respectively by the terrorists and totalitarianism belong to the same scale of magnitude: thousands lost their lives at the World Trade Center, but tens of millions were killed by totalitarian regimes. Thus today's threat differs both qualitatively and quantitatively from yesterday's; it results from the perversion of identity politics (a theme that I discuss later on in this book) and from the attempt to impose largely anachronistic values through tools of the present.

The acts of aggression committed on 11 September have prompted two equally legitimate political reactions — compassion for the victims and anger against those who ordered the attack. The U.S. government justifiably wished to punish the aggressors. But who were they? Many leads pointed toward Bin Laden and his organization, but as they do not constitute a state and thus have no territory, they were difficult to hit. It was reasonable to think that any response would also need to be innovative. Instead of conducting a punitive war, instead of bombing towns or invading a country, the United States would have to find a way to freeze the financial assets of the terrorist network, infiltrate it, and abduct or execute its most dangerous members. It would have been a long and difficult campaign. Fortunately for the United States, one country — Afghanistan — declared its support of Al Qaeda, and thus a much more traditional military response became possible. In this case, the aggressors preferred to play tough guy rather than vanish into the mist — yet another example of their political incompetence. But we cannot count on the same errors being repeated in the future, and struggles against terrorist aggression may turn out to be that much more difficult to organize and sustain.

The attack on U.S. civilians and the support of its perpetrators by the Taliban regime in Afghanistan legitimized American retaliation against that country. But to say that it was legitimate is not to say that it should be a source of pride or celebration. U.S. bombing — though it did not, as might have been feared, provoke a major catastrophe — nonetheless caused the death of several thousand "innocent civilians," roughly the same number as died in the original attacks. A first series of "unnecessary" deaths was echoed by a second. The question arises: was it impossible to find a different, less lethal response? Since real life is not a scientific laboratory, all we can do is speculate.

A complementary issue added confusion to the debate: not only was the Taliban regime guilty of sheltering Al Qaeda; it was also an obscurantist force that had destroyed the Buddhas of Bamiyan and was locking women up inside their four walls and behind their burkhas. This was not presented as a *casus belli*, of course, but it made an impact on public opinion and thus made military action seem more legitimate. Throughout the world, there are innumerable government actions that arouse our ire or our strong disapproval, but if we sought to punish them all, war would never stop. Democracies would then slip from justified self-defense into what, in this book, I call "the best of intentions" — that is, the claim to be the embodiment of good and the effort to impose it on the world by any means.

In fact, the termination of the U.S. engagement in Afghanistan has not brought a halt to U.S. military action, which continues in two main forms: a (somewhat metaphorical) war on terrorism; and, as I write this, the buildup to a perfectly classical campaign against Iraq. Both need to be examined more closely.

The war on terrorism, as has often been pointed out, is not a war in the strict sense of the word but rather a long-term struggle, something like the "war" on drugs or poverty. But what, exactly, is terrorism? The *National Security Strategy of the USA*, a pamphlet published by the White House on 20 September 2002, gives one answer: "premeditated, politically motivated violence perpetrated against innocents" (§III). This definition is not entirely adequate. Any act of war is "premeditated, politically motivated violence"; and as for "innocents," as previously stated, they are targeted in traditional forms of war as well. Was the Hiroshima bomb, dropped with premeditation on a civilian population, a terrorist act? No, it was not. And this allows us to pinpoint what is missing from the *Security Strategy* definition: terrorist violence has to be committed not by a state or its government but by individuals or groups who have no legitimate mandate to use violence. The members of the police or the military, whatever massacres or murders they might commit, can never become terrorists because they are the "legitimate" users of force within a "legitimate" state.

"No cause justifies terror," the *Strategy* goes on to assert, and thus there is no such thing as a good terrorist. The assertion may well be valid in itself, but it does not say enough. Terrorism is an act of war perpetrated by people without a state; if their struggle is victorious, however, their past terrorist acts may become legitimate in retrospect. Recent history is full of such cases, and the U.S. government has had no difficulty whatsoever in working with past or present terrorists. In the early 1940s some Zionist groups in Palestine were considered to be terrorists by the British government (which then held a mandate over the territory); but after the creation of the state of Israel, they were terrorists no longer. In the 1950s the French government pursued the Algerian FLN as a terrorist group; in 1962, once independence was achieved, the former terrorists became the leaders of the state and sat at the same table as their former enemies. In the 1980s the U.S. government (among others) armed the Afghan mujaheddin so they could overthrow the pro-Soviet government of their country, which naturally regarded them as terrorists. And in Kosovo, the KLA was described as a terrorist group—until it received U.S. support, which allowed it to participate, at a later stage, in the government of the province. As has often been pointed out, one man's terrorist is another man's freedom fighter. So even if "no cause justifies terror," we clearly find some terrorists easier to get along with than others.

Furthermore, it often happens that a state reaches some specified aim without declaring war but nonetheless by force: it can be responsible for terrorist acts without actually committing them itself. This scenario fits many actions perpetrated in the past by Western governments. Secret services or their mercenaries have carried out acts that armies could not have performed openly. Even if appearances are maintained, one can hardly describe these governments as entirely innocent of terrorism.

Finally, although terrorist acts are always odious, it is worth looking into what causes them. To understand is not to justify; on the contrary, it is the best means of defense, even if it might also lead us to make some compromises. During the Algerian war, the FLN bombed cafés in Algiers frequented by young French people; though horrific and unacceptable, these attacks were the consequence — the monstrous, excessive consequence — of the French occupation and colonization of Algeria. They ceased as soon as independence was achieved. The Palestinian suicide bombers in Israel today are reprehensible, but it is difficult to prevent them without acting upon their cause, namely the occupation and colonization of Palestinian territory. Other terrorist actions do not deserve the same consideration. Today's GIA massacres in Algeria are related to a mere power struggle, and the Basque separatist outrages in Spain do not express the suffering of an oppressed population. Not to care about causes and circumstances and distinctions is to deprive oneself of any chance of eliminating terrorism.

Taking military action against a state is a very different thing from fighting terrorism. For one thing, it is much easier (all one needs to do is bomb the enemy territory). Given that links between Iraq and Al Qaeda are far from proven, one gets the feeling that attacking Iraq today, instead of hunting for the elusive Al Qaeda, is a fallback solution to reassure public opinion that something is being done. We all look for our lost key under the lamppost, rather than where we dropped it! The planned attack on Iraq has been justified by two principles, "preventive war" and "the right of interference," which have returned to the international political scene after an absence of several decades. The U.S. government itself seems to be aware of the change in argumentation, for it felt the need to explicate these principles in its recent *National Security Strategy* document.

But "preventive war" — attacking a country suspected of evil intentions — has the disadvantage of leaving a great deal of room for subjective appreciation. The aggressor justifies his action by claiming to feel threatened: history is rife with examples of this type. As it is difficult to be impartial when one is part of the conflict, a country contemplating a preventive strike will seek the approval of an international body, such as (since World War II) the UN Security Council. Although the defects of this solution are well known, it does have the advantage of submitting might to right. The new U.S. *Security Strategy* states, on the contrary, that "we will respect the values, judgments and interests of our friends and partners. Still, we will be prepared to act apart when our interests . . . require it" (§IX). In other words, UN approval is a desirable mask for the use of force but not an indispensible one. This naturally makes other countries nervous, as it is far easier for them to see how the United States might constitute a threat to Iraq than the other way around. These outside observers, moreover, cannot help noticing that the United States is a major consumer of oil and that Iraq has huge reserves of this product. But, in fact, there is no need to look for economic motives: war is its own justification; it is the crudest manifestation of power.

The doctrine of "the right of interference" was first applied during the Kosovo campaign, something I discuss at length in this book. The *National Security Strategy* spells out this doctrine as well. It begins by listing some values it considers fundamental: "freedom, democracy and free enterprise." The U.S. government then claims to be entrusted with the mission of imposing these values over the face of the globe, by force if necessary. If it succeeds in doing so, it believes, it will have improved the fate of the human race. "Today, humanity holds in its hands the opportunity to further freedom's triumph over all these foes. The United States welcomes our responsibility to lead in this great mission."

Although based on noble ideals, this agenda is frightening. History has made us all too familiar with other attempts to carry it out. In the Middle Ages and the Renaissance, the proprietors of the best religion (as they saw it) aspired to spread it throughout the world and therefore embarked on a series of crusades and religious wars. In the nineteenth century the British and the French, self-proclaimed proprietors of the best civilization, desired that all peoples should benefit from it and thus launched their colonial wars. In the twentieth century Russia, having installed a Communist regime at home, tried to export revolution to the four corners of the earth. In each case, the protagonists may have been sincerely convinced that their cause was superior to all others, and yet they brought blood and tears to the rest of the world. This is why, at other times, a different principle has been promoted in international relations: a principle that, rather than imposing the same good on all, accepts the plurality of ideals and the sovereignty of nations. Such, indeed, is the only ideal truly compatible with the idea of "democracy"—that is, the right of every people to choose its own path, provided that it does no harm to others.

Why is the plan to impose good so dangerous? Assuming that we knew what good was, in order to achieve it we should need to declare war on all who disagreed. Countless victims would strew the path to our radiant future. But the premise itself is unrealistic. Can even the word "freedom" elicit unanimous approval? In the past, as is well known, tyrants regularly claimed to be the defenders of freedom. Moreover, are we unconditionally in favor of all forms of freedom, including that of the fox in the chicken coop? And what is "free enterprise" doing in the list of universal values? Must we declare war on all countries with state economies? As for "democracy" and its underlying assumption of equal dignity for all, would we still be practicing it if we prevented other peoples from choosing their own leaders and destinies? To impose freedom on others is to oppress them; to force equality on them is to treat them as inferior. The means destroy the ends.

I spent the first twenty-four years of my life in Bulgaria, a country then under Communist dictatorship and Soviet control. It was an antidemocratic regime; my fellow citizens were deprived of basic liberties and forbidden from engaging in free enterprise and getting rich. Should the "free world" have invaded such countries to liberate them? Such, I remember, was our secret dream in 1956, as we watched the crushing of the Hungarian uprising against Soviet domination. Thinking back to those days now, I can only bless the wisdom of the American, British, and other leaders of the time, who allowed Russian tanks to do their job undisturbed. I am grateful that my family and friends (not to mention myself) were left in bondage—but alive. To take another example, I consider capital punishment to be barbaric, and doubly so when inflicted on people who are mentally retarded or who were minors at the time of their deed, yet I do not recommend declaring war on states which enforce the death penalty.

People who believe themselves to be invested with a "mission" to make "freedom" triumph over its foes have a pretty strange world view—one that belongs, incidentally, neither to the Christian tradition nor to secular humanism. Both of the latter are based on the idea that this world is irremediably imperfect (humans are tainted by original sin; their existence is an "imperfect garden"), and that no definitive triumph over evil can ever be achieved. Only millenarist heretics and revolutionary utopians have ever maintained such an illusion. "Freedom" will never completely overcome its "foes" because the human race itself represses and undermines its own aspirations toward liberty. We shall achieve a perfect world only by turning into another species.

A virtue that is imposed on others ceases to be a virtue. But is it really virtue that motivates the interventions of the great powers, and specifically the United States? It is difficult to respond in the affirmative, given that all countries are not judged by the same criteria. Iraq is certainly no more of a democracy than Afghanistan under the Taliban—but then, neither is Saudi Arabia or Pakistan. Iraq may indeed build a nuclear weapon some day, but why aren't we upset about Pakistan, India, or Israel, countries that already have it? The answer, of course, is simple: these countries are "our friends" and do not represent a threat to "us." So why talk about universal justice, when what is really at stake is our own interest? It is this impression of double standards that provokes the rest of the world's distrust. If so many people in the world today try to find hidden motives for American action, it is not because the United States fights injustice but because it does so in a highly selective manner—intervening here but not there. If these people are resentful of the United States (to the extent of applauding or even abetting the perpetrators of terrorist attacks), it is not because the American government defends peace, prosperity, and liberty for all, but because these noble ideals are perceived as a mere mask for self-serving objectives, be they material or political.

It is true that tyrannies are execrable. Many Afghans yesterday and many Iraqis today, whether they live at home or in exile, wish for foreign military intervention to rid them of their hated leaders. But should their wish be granted? Were they to come to power tomorrow, would they allow their country's destiny to be decided elsewhere? If their policies did not meet with the approval of foreign powers, would they graciously agree to be deposed? Renunciation of the use of force by the United States or the European Union would by no means imply that they had become indifferent to injustice in the rest of the world, merely that they would deal with it through methods other than war. Milosević was not put down by the bombing of Belgrade, as I recall later on in this book, but by internal opposition, discreetly aided from abroad.

The new international situation is an ironic result of the happy turn of events that brought the history of the twentieth century to a close: the fall of the Berlin Wall, the collapse of Communist regimes, the end of the totalitarian chapter. Before this, relative global stability was ensured by a balance of terror between the two superpowers. Each was free to do as it pleased in its own sphere of influence and to control its satellites, but refrained from openly attacking the other side. Today, only one superpower remains and there is nothing to contain its action; it is tempted to behave as a global policeman, using its force to impose its will — and presenting the latter as the embodiment of good. The irony, then, is that an undoubtedly positive event has produced a negative result. Democracy brought to others through the barrel of a gun is not democracy; to impose it by force is to undermine it. Other attitudes have been more effective in the past: the West won the Cold War through policies of firmness that always fell short of military action. The ideals of individual prosperity and freedom are sufficiently attractive in and of themselves; they do not need to be promoted with bombs and missiles.

Pride is not a wise counselor. People who believe themselves to be the incarnation of good have a distorted vision of the world. The absence of any obstacle to the deployment of strength is dangerous for the strong themselves: passion takes precedence over reason. "No power without limit can be legitimate," as Montesquieu wrote long ago. Political wisdom does not consist in seeking only immediate victory, nor does it require the systematic preference of "us" over "them." The past has lessons for the present, but we must be prepared to hear them. Memory — one of the main themes of this book — should not be used only to celebrate one's own heroes, to mourn one's own dead, and to stigmatize the wrongs committed by others. The United States was fortunately spared both the Nazi genocide and the Communist terror, but its history is not without dark chapters of its own—the extermination of native Americans, slavery, lynchings and discrimination against people of color, the nuclear bombs dropped on Japan—events which have shaped both today's world and American identity. We learn more from our mistakes than from our good deeds. Thanks to them, we can begin to moderate pride with humility—and to see that, very often, the best way of defending our own interests lies in not neglecting the interests of others.

Tzvetan Todorov
October 2002

Hope and Memory

The Last Hundred Years

ON 1 January 1950 I was eleven years old, sitting under what was then called the New Year's tree. The date was a round number, and I wondered if I would ever reach the even rounder number of 1 January 2000. It seemed so far off — a whole half century away! Surely I would be dead by then. But in just the blink of an eye, here we are already at the end of the century. Now the tendency is to look back, to wonder what there is to learn from the century just passed. For the celebration of the millennium I received an insane request to select the best books of the past thousand years. A thousand years is far too long a period to make any sense. But asking questions about the past century is a different matter. A hundred years is filled by three generations at most, and many people still in early middle age remember grandparents talking to us about the very earliest years of the twentieth century. A century can exist within personal and family memory. We can try to make sense of it.

I am not a "twentieth-century specialist" in the way that a historian or a sociologist or a political scientist might be. The historical facts are well known and easy enough to look up. But facts don't come with their meaning attached, and it is the meaning that interests me. I don't aim to repeat the work that historians have already done. My purpose is to think about the twentieth century as a writer concerned with understanding the age in which he lives. My personal history and my professional background have influenced my overall approach. I was born in Bulgaria and lived there until 1963, under a Communist regime; and since then I have lived in France. Professionally, I am a student of cultural, moral, and political history, with a special interest in the history of ideas.

What counted most in the twentieth century — what allows you to make sense of it — depends of course on who you are. For an African, for example, colonization and decolonization must presumably be the decisive political events of the past hundred years.

And even among Europeans (I deal principally with twentieth-century Europe, with only brief excursions to the rest of the world) a great deal of variation is possible. For some, the major long-term event was women's liberation — women's entry into public life, their control of reproduction, and the sharing of traditionally "feminine" values of private life by both sexes. Others might argue that the massive decrease in child mortality, the no less impressive increase in life expectancy, and the ensuing alteration of the demographics of Western societies must count as the most salient features of the twentieth century. Many presumably count the great strides made by technology in fields such as nuclear power, biogenetics, mass media, and electronic information systems as the major developments of the past century.

These views are all acceptable, but my own experience steers me in a different direction. For me, the central event of the century was the emergence of the unprecedented political system called *totalitarianism*, which, at its peak, ruled a substantial part of the planet. This evil has now vanished from Europe (though it lingers on in other continents), even if its legacy can still be felt. What I want to explore in this book are the lessons we can draw from the great twentieth-century conflict between totalitarianism and its enemy, democracy.

To say that the twentieth century was dominated by the fight between these two forces is to assert a set of values that not everyone shares. The problem is that Europe suffered not one but two totalitarianisms, Communism and Fascism. The two came into violent ideological and then military conflict. At different times, democratic states came more or less close to each of them. The three possible configurations of these regimes have all been tried out in different periods. First of all, Communists put all their enemies in the same basket (as capitalists), and saw liberal democracy and Fascism as moderate and extreme versions of the same evil. Then, from the mid-1930s, and to a greater extent during the Second World War, the map changed: the democratic and Communist blocs joined together in an antifascist alliance. Finally, a few years before the outbreak of the war and once again since its end, Fascism and Communism have been seen as two variants of the same species, totalitarianism, a term first coined by and for the Italian Fascists. I will come back to the definition and delimitation of these terms, but for the present it

THE LAST HUNDRED YEARS

should be clear enough from the way I present the issue that I find the third approach the most enlightening.

This choice of totalitarianism as the major event gives a quite specific focus to the subject of this book. I talk mainly about a single continent, the one where I live, and also about a rather shortened version of the twentieth century, from 1917 to 1991 (with some consideration of the prehistory of that central period, and some questioning of the last decade of the century). In addition, I restrict myself to the public sphere alone, and will leave private life, the arts, the sciences, and technology to one side. There is always a price to be paid in the quest for meaning. It involves making choices and comparisons — and obviously other choices and comparisons could have been made in this book. The meaning that I discern does not exclude other kinds of meaning but should, ideally, complement them.

My opening hypothesis — that totalitarianism was the great innovation of the twentieth century and also its greatest evil — has one immediate consequence. We have to give up the idea, so dear to many great minds of previous ages, that progress is a continuous and cumulative process. Totalitarianism was a novelty, and it was worse than what went before. That does not mean that humanity is set on a downward trajectory. All it suggests is that history is ruled by no iron law, and maybe by no law at all.

The opposition of totalitarianism and democracy and the opposition of the two variants of totalitarianism itself, Fascism and Communism, is the first major theme of this book. But all this belongs now to the past, and only survives among us because of human memory. Memory should not be thought of as a mechanical recording of what has happened. It has many forms and functions, and we have to choose between them; it develops in stages, each of which can be distorted or disturbed; it can be possessed by different people who derive different moral attitudes from it. Is memory necessarily a good thing? Is forgetting always a curse? Does the past always help us to understand the present, or can it serve to confuse our view of the here and now? Are all uses of the past permissible? An analysis of the memories that people have of the twentieth century thus forms the second theme of this book.

Although my principal subject is the meaning of the central event of the century, I must also acknowledge the more immediate past, the period following the fall of the Berlin Wall in 1989, and examine it in the light of the lessons drawn from the analysis of what went before. Totalitarianism is now vanquished. Has the reign of good begun at last? Or are there new perils threatening liberal democracies? The example I have chosen is the Kosovo war of 1998–99. Thus, the totalitarian past, the ways in which it survives in memory, and the light it may throw on more recent events are the three movements of my inquiry.

I have interlaced my reflections on political good and evil in the twentieth century with portraits of six individuals whose lives were deeply affected by totalitarianism, but who withstood its onslaughts. The men and women I recall were not fundamentally different from other people: they were not heroes or saints, or even "righteous." They were fallible individuals facing dramatic choices in their lives; they all suffered physically but sought to pass on the fruit of their experience to others, through writing; they came close to the evil of totalitarianism but were more clearsighted than most. Through talent and eloquence they found ways of communicating what they had seen, without hectoring or sermonizing. They came from various places — Russia, Germany, France, and Italy — but they share a family resemblance. Through the different shadings that they give it, a single emotion can be felt in their works: a kind of horrified fear that does not freeze or paralyze them. They also shared a way of thinking, for which the most appropriate label would be *critical humanism*. The singular destinies of Vasily Grossman, Margarete Buber-Neumann, David Rousset, Primo Levi, Romain Gary, and Germaine Tillion help us to avoid despair.

In some distant future how will the twentieth century be recalled? As "the century of Stalin and Hitler"? That would grant those tyrants an honor they do not deserve, glorifying the perpetrators of great crimes. It would be a pity to reproduce the errors of the past in that way. For myself, I hope that what will be remembered of this dark period are the few luminous figures who in their dramatic lives kept their heads and their senses and who never stopped believing, in spite of everything, that actual human beings provide the only legitimate ideal for human aspiration.

4

What Went Wrong in the Twentieth Century

> The whole world — the whole vast space of
> the Universe — shows the passive submission
> of inanimate matter; life alone is the miracle
> of freedom.
> — *Vasily Grossman,* "The Sistine Madonna"

OUR LIBERAL DEMOCRACIES

The Great War of 1914–18 left eight and a half million dead on the battlefield, maimed another six million, and slaughtered a further ten million civilians. In the same period, Turkey caused the deaths of over one and half million Armenians; Soviet Russia, which came into being in 1917, killed five million in the ensuing civil war and in the famine of 1922, four million in the course of political repression, and another six million in the artificial famine of 1932–33. The Second World War brought about the deaths of at least thirty-five million people in Europe alone (twenty-five million of them in the Soviet Union), including the annihilation of at least six million who were Jewish, or Romany, or mentally retarded. Allied bombing of civilian targets in Germany and Japan caused several hundred thousand further deaths. To which we must add the bloody conflicts between the European powers and their colonial populations: the French in Madagascar, Indochina, and Algeria; the British in Kenya, Malaya, Cyprus; and so on.

Such are the dates and crude statistics of the major killing fields of the twentieth century. If the eighteenth century is commonly known as the "Age of Enlightenment," should we not therefore call the twentieth century the "Age of Darkness"? The recitation of the list of the massacres and miseries of the past century, with its monstrous numbers blotting out the individuals who ought to be recalled one by one, is enough to make you give up trying to

5

make sense of it. But to renounce understanding would be to lose everything.

The history of the twentieth century in Europe cannot be separated from the history of totalitarianism. The original totalitarian state, Soviet Russia, arose in the course of the Great War, and as a consequence of it, and thus bears the mark of that war very deeply. Nazi Germany followed soon after. The Second World War began with the two totalitarian states in alliance and turned into a merciless battle between them. The second half of the century was structured by the Cold War between the West and the Communist world. So the century that recently ended was dominated by the battle between totalitarianism and democracy and by the shorter struggle between the two branches of totalitarianism itself. Now that these conflicts have ceased, an overall picture emerges: it seems that, so as to put right what had previously been wrong, European nations tried one medicine, found the cure to be far worse than the malady, and so rejected it. Seen in that light, the twentieth century appears to have been an extended historical digression. The twenty-first century picks up the story as it was left at the end of the nineteenth.

Totalitarianism now belongs to the past; that particular disease has been beaten. But we need to understand what happened. As noted by Zheliu Zhelev, a former dissident who was briefly president of Bulgaria: before turning a page, you need to read it. It's a need that is an absolute necessity for those who, like myself, lived through the twentieth century. "You cannot prepare the future without clarifying the past," said Germaine Tillion in *A la recherche du vrai et du juste* (216). People who know the past from personal experience are duty bound to pass on its lessons to others. But what is the lesson of the twentieth century?

To tackle this question we need first to answer another one: what are the meanings of the terms "totalitarianism" and "democracy"?

Both terms are designations of what are now called "ideal-type constructs." What is meant by this term, first introduced in the historical domain by Max Weber, is an intellectual tool, a mental model designed to make historical reality more comprehensible — without it being necessary for there to have been any complete or perfect implementation of the construct in the real world. In other words, an "ideal-type construct" is an extrapolation that gives a sense to the underlying trend or dynamic of a political regime. Empirical reality may illustrate the "type" to a greater or lesser degree, may exhibit all or only some of its constituent elements, may do so for an entire period or only intermittently, and so on. It is important to grasp the distinction between the (ideal) model and its (concrete) applications. Some historians and sociologists still believe that they can do without conceptual tools altogether and rely exclusively on what they think is plain common sense. But "common sense" consists of nothing more or less than the abstract concepts and models wrapped up in conventional ways of saying things; as a result, commonsense commentators simply deprive themselves of any possibility of a critical understanding of their own conceptual tools. An "ideal type" is not in itself a statement of the true: its virtue lies in the degree to which it clarifies or helps us to understand empirical reality.

We are talking specifically about the political system, not about society as a whole and certainly not about specific dimensions of that society, such as its economy. It is obvious that the economic systems and social structures of political groups were completely different in Nazi Germany and the Soviet Union, and nothing much would be gained by applying the same terminology to both of them.

Modern democracy, as an ideal-type construct, relies on twin principles, both of which were first formulated by John Locke in the seventeenth century, but which were articulated more clearly in the wake of the French Revolution of 1789 (the "practical experience" of the revolutionary period required the theory to be adjusted). It is to Benjamin Constant and his *Principles of Politics* (1806) that we owe this restatement of the two basic grounds of democracy: autonomy of the individual and autonomy of the collectivity.

Autonomy of the collectivity is of course a requirement that we have inherited from the classical world, and it is contained within the very term of "democracy," which means "people power." The key questions in this respect are: do the people really hold power, or is it held by only one part of the people, or by a single individual (king or tyrant)? Does the power that is held derive solely from human agency, or is it granted by a supernatural force, such as God, the shape of the universe, or ancestral tradition? Political autonomy in this sense of the word is possessed only by a collectivity living under laws that it has made for itself and which it can modify as it wishes. Under this definition Athens was a democracy, despite the fact that its restrictive definition of "the people" excluded three-quarters of its population — women, slaves, and foreigners.

After the fall of the Roman Empire, the Christian states did not recognize political autonomy (which can also be called popular sovereignty) because they held the source of all power to be God. In the fourteenth century, however, William of Ockham went back to the early Christian principle that "God's realm was not of this world" when he declared that God was not responsible for the order and disorder of the world. Power over men, he said, belongs to men alone, and so he sided with the emperor in his struggle with the pope, who sought to combine spiritual and temporal power. From then on, the assertion of political autonomy grew ever more forceful, and it finally triumphed in the American and French Revolutions. "Every legitimate government is republican," stated Jean-Jacques Rousseau in the *Social Contract* of 1761 (II.6), adding in an important footnote: "I understand by this word . . . any government guided by the general will, which is the law"; even a monarchy could be "republican" in Rousseau's sense, provided it conformed to the fundamental principle of being governed by the "general will" of the people. In this kind of argument, "democracy," "collective autonomy," "popular sovereignty," "general will," and "republic" are closely related terms.

The French Revolution seized power from monarchs and thrust it upon the people (still defined restrictively). It did not turn out too well: terror, not freedom, reigned. Where did we go wrong? asked liberal thinkers, that is to say, those who supported the idea of popular sovereignty. What had been forgotten was the necessity of balancing collective autonomy with individual autonomy: the one does not derive from the other, they are two separate principles. John Locke had said it a century before: "The power of the society or legislative assembly constituted by [men] can never be supposed to extend further than the common good" (182). In the wake of the French Revolution, liberal minds like Sieyès, Condorcet, and Benjamin Constant realized full well that the power that had passed from the king to the people's representatives remained just as absolute (if not more so). The revolutionaries believed they were breaking away from the ancien régime, but in truth they were perpetuating one of its most damaging features. The individual aspires to autonomy no less than the collectivity, which can flourish only if the individual is protected not only from powers that lie outside his domain (such as the divine right of kings) but also from the power of the people and its representatives. That power can go so far, but no further than the limits that are set by "the common good."

"Liberal democracy" as applied to modern democratic states is thus constituted by the conjunction of two separate principles. Alternatively you can see two competing sides within liberal democracies — the "republican" and the "liberal," which Benjamin Constant called the "freedom of the Ancients" and the "freedom of the Moderns." Each has existed in the absence of the other. There was popular sovereignty without any protection for the freedom of the individual in ancient Greece; there have been monarchs ruling by divine right over societies where individual liberties were protected. What signals the birth of modernity in the political sphere is precisely the combination of these two principles.

Does this mean to say that modern democracies are states that know nothing higher than the expression of will, be it collective or individual? Could crime become legitimate if the people wished it and the individual accepted it? No. There is something higher than the general and the individual will — not the will of God, but the notion of justice. The supreme role of justice, however, is not specific to liberal democracies; it is the basic assumption of any legitimate political association and of any just state. Whatever form the association takes — tribal grouping, hereditary monarchy, or liberal democracy — it can only be legitimate if it accepts the basic purpose of ensuring the well-being of its members and the exercise of justice in their relationships with each other. Michael Kohlhaas, in the famous story by Heinrich von Kleist, does not live in a democracy, but that does not prevent him from protesting the injustice done to him or from pursuing his rights. No state can tolerate the arbitrary and selfish use of power. Like any legitimate state, democracy recognizes that the unwritten law that puts the political entity in the service of its subjects — and thereby asserts the respect that is due to them — should override the expression of the people's will just as it overrules individual autonomy. For this reason, we can describe as "crimes" some of the things that are allowed by the laws of such and such a country (for instance, the death penalty), or describe some expressions of the popular will (such as Hitler's rise to power) as "disasters."

Liberal democracies belong to the generic category of legitimate states and to the species of legitimate states that respect collective and individual autonomy. Several additional rules stand alongside the two principles (on which they depend more or less directly) and make up our image of democracy. For example, the idea of equal rights for all (and everything that ensues from this idea) substantially amplifies the autonomy of the collective. If the people are sovereign, then all its members should share in power, with no distinction between any of the constituent parts of the people. Thus in a democracy the laws are the same for all, for the rich as for the poor, for the famous as for the humble. But actual democracies can be very imperfect, even while remaining true to their ideal-type construct. Sometimes they exclude large parts of the population from taking part in political life (in France, the poor had no vote until 1848; women had no vote until 1944). Universal adult suffrage is now part of our common definition of democracy, which is why the apartheid system in South Africa could not be included. Moreover, universal suffrage is almost always used to elect representatives, not to decide directly on each issue facing the collectivity. Despite apparent exceptions (such as California "propositions," the consultations of some Swiss cantons, and French referendums), modern liberal democracies use indirect means of decision in the overwhelming majority of cases.

The autonomy of the individual is never total, for it is only exercised within a limited sphere, the domain of private life. The most effective way of ensuring it — so effective that it has become more or less synonymous with freedom and can be seen as an end in itself — is *pluralism*. Pluralism has applications in many aspects of social life, but its meaning and purpose are always the same: plurality ensures the autonomy of the individual. It has its foundation in the separation of the theological and political domains that was launched by William of Ockham. It is important to emphasize that it is a separation of the two domains, not the triumph of the one over the other. Democracy does not require citizens to cease believing in God; it requires them only to contain their beliefs within the private sphere, and to allow their fellows to hold different beliefs. Democracy is a secular system, not an atheistic one. It does not set any particular ideal for each individual life but only ensures peaceful relations between varying ideals — as long as none of them contradicts the underlying principle of justice.

Individual lives engage with different spheres, and these too must remain separated. The basic separation in this respect is between public and private life, mirroring our distinction between the collective and the individual. Benjamin Constant was well aware that the two spheres follow different rules. Just as personal autonomy does not derive from the autonomy of the collective, so the world of personal relations remains distinct from the relations that exist between people by virtue of living together in the same society. The latter dimension of human life is what the state is supposed to take charge of, more or less imperfectly; and the theoretical aim of the action of the state is justice. But that does not hold at all for personal relations where individuals become unique and irreplaceable in each others' eyes. The personal world does not rest on principles of equality and justice: it is a web of preferences and exclusions, and its highest point is love. A democratic state — and this is very revealing — does not legislate on love; ideally, it should be the reverse. "Love must always watch over justice," says Emmanuel Levinas in his account of humanism as the philosophy of democracy (108). There has to be a way of adapting impersonal law in relation to real people.

Within the public sphere there has to be a separation of the economic and political domains: it is not appropriate for those with political power also to control the economy entirely. That is why orthodox Marxism is incompatible with liberal democracy: public ownership of the means of production puts economic power in the hands of those who already possess political power. Private property, insofar as it ensures the autonomy of the individual, is in accordance with the spirit of democracy, even if it is not sufficient to ensure its triumph. On the other hand, despite conservatives' beliefs about the power of a market economy to solve social problems, a political culture entirely subservient to the economic sphere is equally alien to a true democracy.

In a democracy political life respects the pluralist principle. The individual is protected by laws from encroachments by the holders of power, as a consequence of the separation of powers on which Montesquieu first insisted. Montesquieu's *moderation* required the executive and the legislative functions of government to be kept separate, and for both to be kept separate from the judiciary. The ideal state, in his view, could take the form of a monarchy or a republic indifferently, as long as it respected the tripartition of powers, which is another name for the pluralist principle protecting the autonomy of the individual. The exercise of power is here clearly separated from the making of the laws that determine how power is to be exercised. In this view, society is not a battlefield for the different forces it contains but a law-governed state underpinned by a tacit contract to which all citizens are bound.

The same principle requires the existence of a plurality of political organizations — or parties — from among which citizens may make a free choice. Elections are organized, one party comes to power, but the other(s) retain specific rights as the "loyal opposition." This mirrors the way that in the social sphere, minorities submit to the will of the majority while also retaining the right to conduct their private lives as they please. Public associations and organizations of all kinds must also show different political allegiances — and they may, of course, claim none at all. Finally, information services — libraries, newspapers, radio, television, and so on — must also be plural, that is to say, they must not all be controlled by the same political agenda.

The pluralist system that checks political power and guarantees the autonomy of the individual has its own limits. For example, a democratic state can allow no pluralism in the legitimate use of force. The state alone disposes of an army and police force, and it represses the private use of violence, including incitement to the private use of force. Similarly, although the state prescribes no specific form of the good life, it must exclude some forms that are at variance with its own principles. People who preach the use of force, for instance, or who exercise discrimination against particular groups are punished, because they undermine the principle of equality before the law. Limitations of the pluralist principle can be extended to other domains without forfeiting the democratic structure of a society. In France, for instance, there is only one official language, and only one recognized form of high school graduation. But these are optional limitations. What is not optional are the forms of pluralism listed here.

The American and the French Revolutions in the late eighteenth century ushered in the era of liberal democracies in Europe and North America. Though many obstacles lay in their path, modern political regimes of this kind grew in strength and solidity throughout the nineteenth century. As the distinction between faith and reason grew ever clearer, so did the separation of church and state. This evolution was not to everybody's taste. Many Frenchmen continued to side with the old (prerevolutionary) order, and they often valued more highly this or that aspect of the vanished world than the world they saw before them. Modern society was indeed far from perfect. The autonomy of the individual, for all the benefits it brought, involved the loss of many traditional points of reference and created radically new kinds of poverty.

Conservative thinkers (that is, those who put a higher value on the past than on the present) made two specific criticisms of democracy. Both address real features of modern societies, whose downside is what the conservatives see most clearly. First, the loss of social cohesion. Because democratic societies are "individualistic," guaranteeing the autonomy of the individual, they sacrifice social interaction, which is the lifeblood of society itself. Public space shrinks and withers, the private sphere expands beyond imagination, and society begins to fall apart. Democratic states, the conservatives say, will soon be nothing more than collections of isolated and miserable individuals. Second, the bond of shared or common values will disappear (in conservative thinking of this kind, democracy is a "nihilistic" creed): it began with the separation of church and state, and it will end up with the loss of all common points of reference, when each person will choose his or her own values without regard for values held by others.

Both these points were endlessly repeated throughout the nineteenth century — and we should not forget that Baudelaire, Flaubert, and Ernest Renan, who are now counted among the greatest French minds of the period, despised and denigrated the idea as well as the practice of democracy. However, their critique of democracy did not give rise to any violent political action, and it seems we are dealing essentially with nostalgia for a partly imaginary past. In the later part of the century, things change: the dream of a better society becomes projected into the future instead of being cast back onto the past. This is the general context in which the totalitarian project arose. That project integrated the conservative critique of democracy — its destruction of social cohesion and the withering of common values — and proposed remedies that required radical political action.

The Ideal Type of Totalitarianism

What do we mean by a "totalitarian" regime? From Hannah Arendt to Krzysztof Pomian, historians and political scientists have spent the past century identifying and describing its characteristics. The easiest way to begin might be to compare the new notion of totalitarianism to the ideal-type construct of democracy. Its two guiding principles of the autonomy of the collectivity and the autonomy of the individual are handled differently. Totalitarian thinking simply rejects the autonomy of the individual — which was also the target of conservative criticism. In a totalitarian view the *I* of the individual must be replaced by the *we* of the group. Logically, pluralism is also discarded and replaced by its opposite, *monism*. In this respect a totalitarian state is the exact opposite of a democratic state.

Monism (which can be taken as a synonym for "totalitarian") has two complementary aspects, which are not always equally implemented. On the one hand, individual life is no longer divided between a free private sphere and a regulated public sphere; instead, everything in it, including beliefs, tastes, and affections, becomes part of a unified whole which must conform to a public standard. So the personal world vanishes inside an all-encompassing, impersonal order. Love loses its special status as a private space over which the individual has exclusive control; it can no longer seek to sway the implementation of justice. The downgrading of the individual also affects interpersonal relations. The freedom of love is incompatible with a totalitarian state.

On the other hand, a totalitarian system imposes monism in all aspects of public life so as to reach toward the ideal of an organically unified and "bonded" community. By making state dogma out of a single ideal, by requiring subjects to subscribe to it, by establishing itself as a "virtuous state," totalitarianism effectively restores the old unity of the theological and the political — it makes the pope the emperor, or the emperor pope. In a totalitarian regime, economics is subordinated to the political sphere (through nationalization or other forms of control) despite the ideological assertion (in the case of Communism) that politics depends on economics. It is also a single-party system, which is tantamount to abolishing political parties altogether, and it also takes control of all other types of public organizations and associations. Consequently, totalitarian systems, unlike conservative movements, do not favor traditional religions (save if they swear allegiance). Social unification gives form to a new social hierarchy: the masses obey party members, party members obey the nomenklatura (the party elite), and these in turn are the servants of the inner circle of leaders at whose apex sits the supreme commander, or "guide." All information services are controlled by the regime; no dissident opinion can be expressed. The totalitarian state obviously also maintains the monopoly that democratic states exercise over the legitimate use of force (so that "state," "party," and police end up being synonymous with each other).

Communism, as it was implemented by Lenin, then Stalin, and subsequently by their disciples in other countries, gives its own specific content to ideology, but it also gives it a peculiar status. The distinction between politics and ideology — between means and ends — started to lose its meaning immediately after the October Revolution of 1917. Up to that point, it had been possible to believe that revolution, party, and terror were the tools needed to create an ideal society. But once the party was in power, the separation of ends and means became impossible, and the monism that characterizes totalitarian regimes became fully apparent. Even the term of "ideocracy" becomes inappropriate because the only "idea" involved was the triumph of Communism. There was no truth of Communism that could be reached by means external to the party. It was as if the church had taken the place of God.

This peculiar position of ideology makes it a little easier to understand the persecution of the Bolshevik old guard between 1934 and 1939. It has often been asked why in that period the terror cut its broadest swath through the ranks of the most faithful and most committed. The same issue arises in Eastern Europe just after the Second World War: the purges of those years (1949–53) did not so much clear out the lukewarm or the doubters as the staunchest fighters among the Communist leadership — Kostov in Bulgaria, Laszló Rajk in Hungary, Slansky in Czechoslovakia. These men were to all appearances the Communist movement's greatest servants. Should we think of the misfortunes that befell them in terms of the sufferings of the "perfect and upright" man called Job? Or cast them in the same light as Seneca's virtuous Stoics—good and generous men beset with afflictions and sorely tried by the very gods who looked well on them? Was their persecution a mark of distinction, a privilege of Communist virtue? The question is worth pursuing because, as we now know, the Central European purges were not spontaneous events but the coordinated expressions of a single drive and intention coming from Moscow.

If the Communist regime had wanted people to follow their own individual paths toward the ideal or to make their own interpretations of the doctrine, then the old Bolsheviks who had fought with Lenin and the purged leaders of the Central European countries would have been leading candidates. But that is not what it really meant to be a committed Communist. No individual autonomy—in thought or in action—could be allowed, because only the party could be right. If all you had to do to be a good Communist was to seek the best way forward for yourself, the monist-totalitarian structure would be seriously damaged; you would have become your own legitimation, instead of receiving legitimacy from the proper authority, that is to say, from the party and its guide. No such breach in the monist fabric could be tolerated by the general secretary, who thus took on the task of eliminating or crushing any cadres suspected of wanting to think and act by their own lights. The relationship of ideology and power was very similar in Nazi Germany. Quite early on, Hitler liquidated comrades in arms of unquestionable ideological fervor and insisted on absolute fidelity not to abstract Nazi doctrine (in any case, you could hardly call *Mein Kampf* a philosophical treatise) but to power as embodied in the person of the Führer—a demand made explicit in the oath sworn by members of the SS. The concentration and personalization of power were very similar in Nazi Germany and the Soviet Union.

Totalitarianism claims to uphold and abide by the second principle of democratic states, the autonomy of the collective, together with its consequences, but in fact it empties the principle of its content. On paper, the sovereignty of the people is respected, but in practice the "general will" is hijacked to benefit the leadership group, which uses elections as plebiscites (with a single candidate standing, collecting 99 percent of the votes cast). All are held to be equal before the law, but in truth the law is not applied to members of the inner circles of power, and it offers no protection to opponents of the regime, who are subjected to arbitrary persecution. The ideal of equality is proclaimed, but in fact totalitarian society is riddled with complex hierarchies and levels of privilege. Members of some social groups have specific rights, but members of other groups do not have the right to a passport, to walk down particular streets, to use "special" shops, to send their children to special schools, and to use holiday resorts. Such discrepancy between official discourse and reality — the fictitious, illusory nature of the way the world is represented — became one of the salient features of Stalinist society.

In this respect, the real differences between democracy and totalitarianism were effectively masked. On the other hand, a degree of genuine continuity exists between the two types of regime in respect of foreign policy and international relations. Liberal democracy is primarily concerned with the internal workings of a given state and does not really determine the conduct of foreign affairs. In the nineteenth century, international relations operated in what earlier centuries had termed a "state of nature," an arena where might countered might, with no reference to right. In that period, the democratic states with the most advanced internal societies — France and Britain — were also at the forefront of colonial expansion, and each sought world domination. They renounced military conquest in the twentieth century and sought instead to gain economic influence over the greatest possible area. Totalitarian states acted no differently in their early stages: at each opportunity, they annexed territories or whole countries, and, like the democratic nations, they cloaked their imperialist policies in declarations of generosity. Of course, the regimes that they installed in annexed lands were of a different type: totalitarian dictatorship is quite different from colonial domination.

This new kind of state arose in Europe in the wake of the Great War — first in Russia, then in Italy, and lastly, in 1933, in Germany.

Even from the schematic exposition of the two types of regime given so far, the reader can surely deduce that my own preference is for democracy. However, I must point out another significant difference between the two systems that may explain, in part, why my own preference is not shared by all. Totalitarianism holds out the hope of plenitude, harmony, and happiness. The promise has not been kept so far, to be sure, but the promise remains, and people can still tell themselves that next time it will come out right and salvation will be at hand. Liberal democracy offers no such prospect, all it guarantees is that each individual will be allowed to seek his or her own happiness, harmony, and plenitude. At best it provides citizens with peace and order, gives them a role in the conduct of public affairs, and ensures fairness in their relations with each other and with the state. But it certainly does not promise them salvation. Autonomy means having the right to seek for yourself; but finding is a different matter. Kant seemed to believe that people would positively appreciate leaving behind "the status of child, in which [they] remain by their own fault," but to be honest, it is by no means obvious that everyone prefers being an adult to remaining a child.

The promise of happiness for all allows us to identify the family to which totalitarian doctrine intrinsically belongs: in theory, totalitarianism is a form of utopianism, and, in the long context of European history, utopian thinking is a form of millenarism, of which it constitutes the atheist version.

Millenarism was a heretical form of Christianity that promised its believers that they would gain salvation in this world, without waiting for the hereafter. Christ's original message made a clear separation between the two spheres, which was why Saint Paul could assert that "there is neither Jew nor Greek, there is neither bond nor free, there is neither male nor female; for ye are all one in Christ Jesus" (Epistle of Saint Paul to the Galatians, 3.28) without undermining in any way the real differences between masters, slaves, women, men, Jews, Greeks and so forth, since the unity and equality of all people would arise only in the City of God, and religion did not propose any changes to the order of the secular world. It is true that when Catholicism became a state religion, it broke this rule by concerning itself with the affairs of this world; but it never promised salvation in this life.

That promise was made, however, by Christian millenarians from the end of the thirteenth century on. Segarelli, for instance, declared that the Day of Judgment was nigh, and that there would first be a millennium, a reign of a thousand years that would begin with the return of the Messiah. His disciples thus thought that it was time to rid the rich of their possessions and to create perfect equality on earth. In the fifteenth century, the

Taborites (a radical sect in Bohemia) believed that Christ's return was imminent, and that his kingdom on earth would be a millennium of equality and abundance — for which it was time to prepare. In the following century, Thomas Münzer led a millenarist revolt in Germany, denouncing the wealth of princes and of the church, and inciting the peasants to rob them so as to speed the arrival of the Heavenly Kingdom on earth.

Utopianism differs from medieval and Protestant millenarism in that it seeks to build a perfect society by man's efforts alone, without reference to God, and is thus twice removed from original Christian doctrine. Utopianism takes its name from Thomas More's *Utopia*, which was an intellectual construction, an image of an ideal society. Utopias can have many functions, as tools for thinking, or as modes of criticizing existing societies; but only *utopianism* seeks to bring utopia to the real world. Christian millenarism called for the use of force to anticipate God's action on earth; utopianism is also inseparable from constraint and violence, because it seeks to install perfection in the here and now while acknowledging that men themselves are imperfect. The Russian philosopher of religion, Semyon Frank, noted in 1941 that "utopianism, which presupposes that the social order can be made to embody goodness, tends intrinsically toward despotism" (92). Totalitarian doctrines are instances of utopianism (the only known instances in the twentieth century) and, by the same token, variants of millenarism — and that means that they belong, as do all doctrines of salvation, to the field of religion. It is, of course, no coincidence that this Godless religion prospered in a period marked by the decline of Christianity.

All the same, the origins of totalitarian utopianism are quite paradoxical for a religion. They lie in a doctrine that was developed before the rise of totalitarian states, before the twentieth century, and which seems at first glance to have absolutely nothing in common with religion. We must now turn to this earlier ideology, which we shall call scientism.

SCIENTISM AND HUMANISM

Scientism as a doctrine starts from the hypothesis that the real world is an entirely coherent structure. It follows that the world is transparent, that it can be known entirely and without residue by the human mind. The task of acquiring such knowledge is delegated to the requisite praxis, called science. No fragment of the material or spiritual world, of the animate or inanimate domain, can ultimately resist the grasp of science.

This basic postulate has one obvious consequence. If human science can indeed unravel all the secrets of nature, if it can identify all the causes of all facts and all beings, then it should be possible to modify the processes involved and to steer them in a more desirable direction. Science is a tool of knowledge, but it underpins *techne*, a tool for changing the world. We are all familiar with this kind of derivation — as in the story of early man, who first discovers that fire is hot, then learns to control it, and so comes to heat his own home, changing forever his "natural" climate. More recently, men grasped that some cows gave more milk than others and that some seeds gave more wheat per acre, so they superimposed "artificial selection" on to natural selection. There is no contradiction here between an entirely determined universe, which rules out freedom of action, and the free will of the scientist-technician, which presupposes freedom. On the contrary: if the transparency of the real includes the human world, then there is nothing to stop us from imagining how to create "new man," a human species without the blemishes of the original strain. The logic of livestock breeding ought to work for humankind as well. Alain Besançon sums up the cult of science thus: "[K]nowledge opens the gateway to salvation" (119).

To what end should the transformation of humankind be directed? Who is authorized to identify and understand both the imperfections of the present, and the kind of perfection to which we might aspire? The answers were easy in the initial examples. It went without saying that people wanted to be warm and to eat their fill. What is good for people is good, absolutely. But what is the position when it is a question of changing *humankind* itself? Scientism has its own answer — namely, that henceforth science alone will provide the solution. The ends of humankind and of the world become a secondary effect, an automatic by-product of the search for knowledge — so automatic, in fact, that followers of the cult of science often don't bother to formulate them. In his famous eleventh thesis on Feuerbach, Marx merely asserts that "the philosophers have only *interpreted* the world, in various ways; the point, however, is to *change* it" (245). So not only does *techne* (transformation of the world) follow on directly from knowledge (interpretation of the world), but the nature of the transformation doesn't even deserve mentioning, because it is the ineluctable product of knowledge. The French historian Hippolyte Taine put it more explicitly some decades later: "Science seeks only the truth but in the end it discovers an ethics" (110).

The notion that social and individual ideals are the products of science has another important consequence. If the will alone sets ultimate ends, then each of us must allow that one man's choice of ends may not coincide with his neighbor's; as a result, forms of tolerance, compromise, and accommodation ought to be necessary. Many different concepts of the good life could in principle coexist. But scientific results are not like that: in science, wrong ideas are discarded without mercy; no one would even think of requesting a little more tolerance for hypotheses that have been refuted. There is no room for more than one version of scientific truth; errors are many, but the truth is one, and so pluralism becomes an irrelevant concept. If the ideal is the result of demonstration and not of an opinion, then it has to be accepted without protest.

Scientism derives from the existence of scientific practice, but it is not itself scientific. Its basic postulate—the complete transparency of the real—cannot be proved; the same is true of its implementation in the construction of ultimate ends through the process of knowledge. From start to finish, the cult of science requires an act of faith ("faith in reason," in Ernest Renan's phrase), which is why it belongs not to the family of the sciences but to the family of religions. To prove this, you only have to look at the attitude taken by totalitarian societies toward their own political objectives: whereas the general rule in scientific activity is to be as open as possible to criticism, totalitarian societies require blind submission and the silencing of all and any objections—just as religions do.

It has to be emphasized that scientism is not science but a world view that grew, funguslike, on the trunk of science. That is why totalitarian systems can embrace the cult of science and still not foster the development of scientific research. There is a very good reason for this: science requires submission to the quest for truth, not submission to dogma. Communists and Nazis thus backed off from the search for new knowledge: the latter denounced

"Jewish science" (and did without Einstein's physics), and the former repudiated "bourgeois biology" (and jettisoned Mendel's genetics). Challenging Lyssenko's biology, Pavlov's psychology, or Marr's linguistics in the USSR could take you straight to the gulag. That was how these two societies turned themselves into scientific backwaters. Anyway, totalitarians don't really need cutting-edge science to carry out their greatest misdeeds: firearms, poison gas, and truncheons aren't made by geniuses. All the same, a real connection to science existed in these systems, but it had undergone a mutation: it had become "possible" to grasp the universe in its totality and to seek to improve it in a no less "total" manner. This mutation, related to the birth of science, transformed timeless human evil into a new, surprising, and specifically modern form of evil. It ushered in a radically new chapter in the history of humanity that could be entitled "What Went Wrong in the Twentieth Century."

The monism of totalitarian regimes comes from the same axiom of the cult of science. Because there is only one rational way of grasping the entire universe, there is no reason to maintain artificial distinctions such as those between different social groups, between the different spheres of individual life (public and private), or between different opinions. Truth is one, and so should the human world be.

What is the historical place of the cult of science? Within the French tradition, its origins lie in the work of René Descartes. His first step was to exclude from the field of rational knowledge everything related to God; but "on matters where we are not instructed by divine faith," he wrote, total knowledge was possible provided its truth was "established by scrutiny," that is to say, by reason and will alone (*Selected Writings*, 188–89). Consequently man may "acquire absolute mastery over all [his] passions" and think of himself also as a master of nature, "in some sense like unto God" (*Selected Writings*, 238). Armed with such knowledge, a single "architect" could in principle reconfigure the organization of nations and their relationships to citizens (Descartes did not regard this as desirable but as possible). Lastly, in Descartes's thinking, the direction of such change would be guided by the search for knowledge alone, and the common good would flow automatically from the works of philosophers: "[T]he truth which they contain, being highly clear and certain, will take away all ground of dispute and thus dispose men's minds to gentleness and concord" (*Meditations*, 122–23).

Descartes's ideas were elaborated and systematized by the "materialist" philosophers of the seventeenth and eighteenth centuries. Let's follow nature in all things instead of hobbling ourselves with moral rules, said Diderot with a touch of irony: that presupposes, first, that we know what nature is (and who but men of science can provide us with such knowledge?) and, second, that we obey the precepts that follow automatically from such knowledge. However, scientism entered the political field most significantly in the wake of the French Revolution of 1789, for the new state was held to be founded not on arbitrary traditions but on the rule of reason. Such was the prestige of science throughout the nineteenth century that its cult flourished among all kinds of thinkers — both friends and foes of the Revolution — who all hoped to replace a collapsing religion with the rule of science. The utopian philosopher Henri de Saint-Simon can be found alongside positivists such as Auguste Comte and dilettante conservatives like Arthur de Gobineau among the propagators of the cult of science, together with erudite historians like Renan and Taine, who were both critics of democratic government and opinion leaders for the liberal intelligentsia. In this period the two main variants of the cult also emerge: the cult of historical science, represented most powerfully by Karl Marx, and the cult of biological science, of which Gobineau may be seen as a representative figure.

The cult of science thus belongs indisputably to modernity, if we understand by this word any doctrine asserting that the laws of society come neither from God nor from tradition but from human volition; and the cult also obviously implies the existence of science as a form of knowledge acquired by human reason alone, rather than by mechanical transmission down the generations. But despite what so many fashionable thinkers continue to proclaim, scientism is not the ineluctable end product or the hidden truth of all forms of modernity; totalitarianism, although it was inspired by the principles of the cult, is not the secret and fatal destiny of democracy. What these thinkers forget is that there is more than one strand of thought within modernity: neither the principle of self-reliance, nor the egalitarian ideal, nor the requirement of autonomy, nor rationalism leads automatically, of itself, toward totalitarianism. Scientism is constantly opposed by other doctrines that can also claim to be part of modernity in the broad sense. This conflict sets science-cult thinkers against people who can be considered to be the philosophers of democracy—that is, humanists—in a particularly revealing way.

Humanists do not accept the initial postulate of the complete transparency of the real and thus reject the idea that it is possible to know the universe without residue. Montesquieu, an eighteenth-century standard-bearer of humanism, raised two objections. First, with respect to any fragment of the universe, what is now called the "principle of precaution" must apply. The universe, he says, may of course be coherent in a way that is in principle discoverable; but principle and practice are very far apart. Concretely, the causes of a phenomenon are so varied and their interactions are so complex that we can never be sure of what we know; and as long as there is doubt, it is better to refrain from radical and irreversible action (which is not to say we should refrain from all action). Second, and more fundamentally, no knowledge can ever be claimed to be absolute and definitive, for the very claim deprives it of the status of knowledge and turns it into an act of faith. The ambitions of all utopian thinking were thus spiked from the start by Montesquieu's humanism, which, by disallowing the global transparency of the real, permits only local and provisional improvement. Both the cult of science and humanist thinking aspire to universality—but not to the same kind of universality. Scientism is based on the universality of reason, and it assumes that the solutions devised by science are by definition appropriate for all men, even if they cause suffering or even death to some. Humanism, on the other hand, asserts the universality of the human: all human beings have the same rights and deserve the same respect, whether or not they live in the same ways.

There is more to this. The human world is not just a part of the universe; it is also a singular world in its own right. Its specific difference is that human beings are aware of being themselves, and thus able to detach themselves from their own being and to act against the grain of the forces they experience. "Man, as a physical being, is, like other bodies, governed by invariable laws. As an intelligent being, he incessantly transgresses the laws established by God and changes those which he himself has established," wrote Montesquieu (*Spirit of Laws*, 101). Alexis de Tocqueville, when his friend Gobineau argued that individuals obey the laws of their own race, responded that "human societies, like persons, become something worthwhile only through the use of their liberty" (309). To believe you can know a man in his entirety is not to know men at all. Even our knowledge of animals is imperfect: today's milking cow could be sterile tomorrow. But our knowledge of men must always be incomplete, given that men are animals endowed with freedom. We can never know what they will do tomorrow.

There is also a logical contortion involved in trying to derive what should be from what is. What can be observed most easily in the world of human action is not right, but might, with the stronger preying on the weaker. But might is not right. To those who try to deduce right from might, Rousseau's rejoinder in *The Social Contract* remains entirely pertinent: "One could use a more consistent method, but not one more favorable to Tyrants" (1.§2). So, to decide on the direction of change, it is not enough to observe and analyze facts, tasks for which science is well suited; we must also appeal to aims that are the objects of free choice, which presupposes arguments for and against. Ideals can never be true or false; they can only be of a higher or lower kind.

The major criticism that Rousseau made of the Enlightenment's cult-of-science contemporaries can be summed up thus: knowledge does not make morals, and educated people are not necessarily good. (Of course, Rousseau was also a man of the Enlightenment, but in a much deeper sense than Voltaire or Helvetius.) As he put it in one of his more memorable expressions: "We can be men without being scholars" (*Émile*, 290). To come back to political systems: true democracy is democracy for all, not just for the learned or educated. Rousseau's politics implies not knowledge of the truth but freedom (autonomy) of the will. He favors pluralism, not monism, because not just error but also human desire is many.

The project of democracy, grounded in humanist thinking, does not lead to paradise on earth. It does not disregard the evil that is in man and in the world, nor does it simply resign itself to their existence; but it does not assert as an axiomatic belief that such evil can be eradicated once and for all. Montaigne said: "Good and ill are of one substance with our life" (*Essays*, 1237); and Rousseau declared that "good and evil flow from the same spring" ("Lettre sur la vertu," 325). Good and ill are "of one substance" with human life because they are the fruits of our freedom, of our ability to choose at every point between several courses of action. Their common source is human sociability and human incompleteness, for these make us need other people to guarantee our sense of existing. But our need of others can be satisfied in two ways. We can cherish other people and seek to make them happy; or else we can subjugate and humiliate them so as to enjoy power over them. Humanists understand and accept the inseparability of good and evil and thus abandon the very idea of a global, definitive solution to human problems: in this view, men cannot be freed from the evil that is in them unless they are "freed" from their very humanity. It would be vain to hope that some better political system or more effective technology could provide a once-and-for-all solution to the suffering of humankind.

Lastly, scientism and humanism take opposite views of the aims of human societies. The former, by evacuating all subjectivity from its vision, takes no account of the contingency of individual wills; the aims of society should derive from the observation of impersonal processes that characterize all humanity, if not the universe in its entirety. Nature, the world, and humanity give the orders; individuals submit to them. In a humanist view, on the other hand, individuals are not to be reduced to mere means. Such reductiveness, according to Kant, is admissible when done partially and temporarily, in order to reach an intermediate objective; but the ultimate aim always remains specific human beings — all of humanity, but seen one by one, as people.

THE BIRTH OF TOTALITARIAN DOCTRINE

Since time immemorial men have used violence to impose good. The French Revolution had no need of a science-based justification to legitimate The Terror of 1793–94; and so we can see that the use of force is not intrinsically linked to the cult of science. At a particular point in history, however, a conjunction occurred bringing together several preexisting strands: revolutionary ardor, implying the use of force; the millenarian dream of building an earthly paradise here and now; and the pseudoscientific doctrine asserting that complete knowledge of the human species was about to become available. The moment of this meeting marks the birth of totalitarian ideology. Even when power is acquired by peaceful means (as was Hitler's, unlike Mussolini's or Lenin's), the idea of creating a new society of new men and of solving all problems once and for all through an inevitable revolution always remains the basis of totalitarian societies. People can subscribe to the cult of science without being millenarists and without approving the use of violence (many of today's technocrats would fit this category); others may be revolutionaries without subscribing to the cult of science (and a whole group of early twentieth-century poets who called for a cataclysm belong to this category). But only when the three strands of violence, millenarism, and the cult of science come together can we talk of totalitarianism proper.

Neither revolutionary violence nor millenarian dreams lead to totalitarianism of and by themselves. The intellectual premises of totalitarianism are only fully established when these strands are wound together with a drive toward the total mastery of the universe propelled not just by scientific thinking but more precisely by scientism. With its forerunners in Cartesian radicalism and eighteenth-century materialism, the cult of science reaches its zenith in the nineteenth century, and that is when the totalitarian project first emerged. (We are speaking here exclusively of the ideological roots of totalitarianism, and not of its many other sources in the economic, social, and party-political domains.)

When do we find the first sketches of a genuinely totalitarian society? Marx and Gobineau both published their main works around the middle of the nineteenth century, but neither of them offer a detailed map of a future society (Gobineau, moreover, far from being utopian, foresees only decline). The theoretical and fictional works of Chernishevsky, which were so inspirational for Lenin, date from the 1860s: *The Anthropological Principle in Philosophy* came out in 1860, and the didactic novel *What Is to Be Done?* was published in 1863. Nechaiev's *Revolutionary Catechism*, which actually deals more with revolutionary practice than with the creation of a new society, was drafted in 1869 and published in 1871. One of the most revealing but least-known texts in this connection is Ernest Renan's third *Dialogue philosophique*, which dates from 1871. In it, a character called Théoctiste lays out for probably the very first time the main features of a totalitarian state.

First of all, Théoctiste says, the ultimate ends of society cannot be derived from the demands of individuals, but only from the requirements of the whole species, if not from the entirety of the living world. The great law of life is simply the "will to exist," which is more powerful than all the laws and conventions made by man. This law of life means that the stronger defeat and rule over the weaker. From this point of view, the fate of individuals is unimportant; people may be disposed of for a higher purpose. "The sacrifice of a living being for a purpose set by nature is legitimate." Now, because the laws of nature must be followed, the first task is to know what those laws are, says Renan's character, and that task must be entrusted to scholars. But as scholars come to acquire such knowledge, they also quite naturally acquire power. "The elite of intelligent beings, masters of the most important secrets of the world, would dominate the world through the powerful tools it would have at its disposal, and would impose the reign of the greatest reason possible." The world would be ruled not by philosopher-kings but by "positivist tyrants." However, they would not be obliged to follow the natural order of the universe once they had unlocked its secrets. Their job would be quite the opposite, in fact, and, like any technician, they would further nature's work by improving the species. "Science works on from where nature left off." The species must be perfected, and a new man must be created with greater intellectual and physical abilities. If necessary, substandard examples of humanity would be eliminated.

A state established on these principles would be contrary to democracy on every point. Its aim would not be to give power to all but to restrict it to the best; far from fostering equality, it would promote supermen. Freedom of the individual, tolerance, and cooperation would have no role, because the truth would be available — and the truth is one. It requires submission, not debate. "The great work would be done by science and not by democracy." This is an argument in favor of the efficiency of this new state — and it would be more efficient than a democratic system with its constant need to consult, to understand, to persuade. Renan's contrast between science and democracy might seem surprising, but it is also very revealing. Science and democracy are fruits of the same branch; they both owe their existence to the casting off of the yoke of tradition and the assertion of autonomy. But if science is transformed from a way of learning about the world into a pattern for society and a fount of ideals (in other words, a cult), then it comes into conflict with democracy. Searching for truth must not be confused with seeking good.

Théoctiste imagines that the new scientific state would need the right tools to run smoothly and that a necessary one would be terror. The trouble with the old religion-based tyrannies, he says, is that they could only threaten to send their subjects to hell for disobeying, and that wasn't nearly powerful enough. In any case, now that people have stopped believing in hellfire and devils, they think they can do what they like. This gap has to be plugged "not with a chimerical hell of unproven reality, but with a real hell." Setting up a death camp that would send shivers into every spine and instill unconditional obedience in all would be justified by the fact that it would serve the good of the species. "The being in possession of scientific knowledge would put unlimited terror in the service of truth." To put its terror policies into practice, the government of Renan's future scientific state would use a corps of specially trained men — "obedient robots unable to feel moral revulsion and prepared for any level of ferocity." Fifty years later, in his proposal to establish the Soviet Secret Police, Dzerzhinsky called for a force made up of "determined comrades — solid, hard men without pity" (quoted in Courtois, 57).

As for foreign policy, Renan imagines that the ruling sages would try to develop an absolute weapon that would ensure the immediate destruction of a large proportion of its enemies' population, and, once they had done so, they would easily acquire universal domination. "When some of reason's elite come to possess the means of destroying the planet, they would have sovereignty; this elite would rule by absolute terror, since they would have the existence of all in their hands." Intellectual power would thus give rise to material power.

We have to concede that the main features of Renan's utopia

accurately predict, point for point, the shape of utopias that would be set up more than half a century later. Renan's forecast is especially close to the Nazi project, which also had a biological pretext for its plan to create "new men." What's more, the French scholar conceived of his utopia coming into being not in France, but in Germany, which he saw as a country "showing little regard for equality or even for the dignity of the individual." All the same, Renan's utopia is not far removed from Communist society either, even if the similarity is less overt. Communism may have used the rhetoric of egalitarianism, but it did not implement it by any means. In practice, the leadership role given to the party, and the requirement of absolute submission to the leadership within the party, made Communism just as much a cult of superman as any other totalitarian system. Despite the egalitarian slogans, daily life under Communism was rigidly hierarchical.

The cult of science combined with utopian thinking is integral to the totalitarian project. But can we be sure that democracy is entirely untainted by this cult? As a matter of fact, scientism is present in democracy, as one strand among others. Whenever we believe we have cracked the secrets of the world and that we ought to change it in some way that springs directly from our knowledge of its secrets — whether in physics, biology, or economics — then we too fall into the cult of science, irrespective of the political system under which we live. Overreliance on science actually happens rather often in democratic countries. When political decisions are presented as the ineluctable effects of economic laws promulgated by experts, or of natural laws that only medical or biological researchers can understand fully, then we are the prey of the cult of science. Politicians naturally prefer to take cover behind experts. However, there will always be a fundamental difference between democracy and totalitarianism as long as this kind of subservience to the cult of science stops short of being an all-embracing, utopian plan for an immediately realizable perfect society. To turn the tables on Renan, we should rather say that the "great work" is to be done by democracy, not by science. Instead of society serving science, science should be at the service of society. That is also why democracy does not preach revolution, does not use terror, and generally favors pluralism over monism.

It is indeed fortunate for us all that modern democracies do not

30

aspire to bring perfection to this world or to improve the human race — for unlike the mere apprentice sorcerers that were the totalitarian systems of the twentieth century, modern democracies would now be capable of going a long way down that road. They possess unrivaled means of surveillance and control, they command weapons that can indeed destroy the planet, and there are scientists within them who are close to mastering the genetic code and thus to being able to produce new species, quite literally. Compared with genetic manipulation, the crude tools of reeducation and terror used by the Communists to create "new man," or the Nazis' recourse to birth control policy and the elimination of allegedly inferior "races" and individuals, now seem prehistoric.

If it turns its back on utopianism, does democracy have to also abandon all hope of a better world? Not at all. Democracy is not necessarily conservative; it does not have to resign itself to accepting the world as it is. There is no reason at all to be trapped in the logic of the excluded middle, which totalitarians tried to impose on people's minds: you do not have to choose between giving up all ideals and accepting any means whatsoever to achieve an ideal. Democracy also seeks to replace what is with what should be — but it does not claim that rationality alone can deduce what should be from what is. Lenin was a monist and therefore considered economics to be wholly dependent on politics. In a democracy, economic and political power are independent of each other, but that does not mean they have to be isolated. Economic forces try to make political agents dependent on them; politicians, in their turn, can and must place limits on economic agents, in the name of their society's ideals. A democratic utopia has a right to exist, provided that no one tries to make it come true in the here and now by the use of force.

What do people need? The citizens of democratic states, or at least their spokespersons, have often believed that people seek only to satisfy their immediate wishes and their material needs — greater comfort, more facilities, increased leisure. In this respect, totalitarian strategists have had much stronger anthropological and psychological insights. It is certainly true that people need comfort and convenience, but, at a less overt but actually more fundamental level, they also need goods that the material world cannot provide. People want their life to have a sense: they want their existence to have its allotted place in the order of the universe, and they want some way of connecting themselves to the absolute. Unlike democracy, totalitarianism claims to meet these deeper needs, and for that reason it was freely chosen by the peoples involved. We must not forget that Lenin, Stalin, and Hitler were wished for and loved by the masses.

Democracies put their own existence in jeopardy if they neglect the human need for transcendence. But how can we prevent the need for transcendence from opening the door once again to catastrophes of the kind that twentieth-century totalitarian systems brought with them? Not by ignoring human aspirations, but by separating them quite firmly from the public sphere. The absolute may not move comfortably along the corridors of power, but it cannot be expected simply to go away. Christ's original message was quite clear. When he said, "My kingdom is not of this world," he did not mean that his kingdom does not exist; he meant to say that his kingdom is not to be found in public institutions but in people's hearts and minds. For the many centuries when Christianity became and remained a state religion, this message was, so to speak, bracketed out. Today, people's relationship to transcendence is no less necessary than it ever was, but to ward off any future totalitarian aberration, it must be kept out of political life; a new Jerusalem should never be built in this land, but it should bring inner light to the lives of all. Ecstasy can be found in the contemplation of a work of art or a natural landscape; it can be found in philosophical speculation or in hearing a child laugh. Democracy does not meet our need for salvation and for the absolute; but it cannot allow itself to forget that those needs exist.

War As the Truth of Life

Totalitarian ideology takes its basic premise about human society from the modern cult of science—namely, that war is the rule of life, which is always a fight to the death. It simplifies and rigidifies Darwinian notions of natural selection and the survival of the fittest, and applies them to human society. The laws of social evolution are similarly expressed in sub-Darwinian language: the class struggle, the war of the sexes, racial conflict, national wars. In totalitarian thinking, no social group can avoid being ruled by its "will to exist" (in Renan's phrase) or by the conflicts to which that inevitably gives rise. Just like later ideologists of race, Karl Marx used the language of Darwinian natural history in his preface to *Capital*: "The evolution of the economic formation of society is viewed as a process of natural history" (137); and it is no coincidence, as Hannah Arendt reminded us, that Engels called his friend "the Darwin of history." However, it was Lenin and Hitler who most obviously took from Darwin their idea of the "struggle for life" and of conflict as the general law of life and of history. All life is political, and politics is war. Alain Besançon notes that Lenin's admiration for Clausewitz did not stop him from turning the latter's famous maxim on its head, contending that "Politics is the continuation of war by other means."

The idea that war is the natural state of man has ancient origins (the dictum *homo homini lupus* dates back to Roman times), and it certainly did not first arise in Darwin or in the writings of his vulgarizers. In totalitarian thinking, however, it is presented as an irrefutable truth, with all the prestige of a scientific discovery; and again we see that totalitarianism owes its very existence to the cult of science. Henceforth the world is divided into two: us and them, friend and foe — be they two classes, two races, or what have you — locked in mortal combat. The best thing to do, once this truth is accepted, is to put ourselves on nature's side, to "work on from where nature left off," as Renan said, and to complement natural selection with artificial selection. The gas chambers of Auschwitz and the elimination of the kulaks are already implicit in such thinking. The very vocabulary of Lenin and Hitler was perfectly explicit in this respect. The enemy is first dehumanized by terms like "vermin," "snake," or "jackal"; this makes his elimination more acceptable. "The enemies of liberty must be exterminated without mercy," said Lenin; there has to be "a bloody war of extermination" to "put down the counter-revolutionary rabble." Totalitarianism is always Manichaean, dividing the world into two mutually exclusive parties, the good and the bad, aiming to annihilate the latter.

Putting these principles into everyday practice necessarily involves the use of generalized terror in domestic policy. Lenin inaugurated it at the start of the Soviet state, and he made no apology when defending the use of terror: "We have to state explicitly that terror is in principle and politically correct, and that what underpins it and makes it legitimate is its necessity" (*Sob. Soch.*, 39:405). In Communist countries the "dictatorship of the proletariat" became a cover term for police terror: that is to say, mass murder, torture, and threats of physical violence, together with that most convenient institution known as the concentration camp. (All totalitarian states have used camps.) Life in the camps is both imprisonment and torture, for they are punishment camps, and the inmates are never certain that they will ever get out. Other forms of terror reign over the rest of the country. Constant and ubiquitous surveillance means that acts of insubordination or of mere nonconformity may be denounced, and perpetrators punished by deportation, by being thrown out of their jobs or apartments, by withdrawal of their and their children's right to enroll at a university or to travel overseas, and so on. The list of possible sanctions is infinite.

Terror is not an optional feature but a basic and integral part of totalitarian societies. It is therefore pointless to study such states without reference to terror, as various "revisionist" schools of history have tried to do, as if the tensions in these societies ran along classical lines. The link became quite obvious in 1989: as soon as terror was suspended (when the police and the military were not ordered to fire on demonstrators), the Communist totalitarian states tumbled like a house of cards.

In the foreign domain, terror takes on its familiar face of war (or its milder face of Cold War); all alliances are necessarily provisional. The aim remains domination; the means are those appropriate to the circumstances. Ultimately, the totalitarian framework justifies violence in many different ways. First, violence is the law of life and of survival. But, second, it is the right of the possessors of scientific truth. Why get bogged down in discussion when you know where to go and what to do?

It is essential for totalitarian societies to divide humanity into two mutually exclusive halves. They have no place for neutrality: the lukewarm are opponents, opponents are enemies. Because it treats "difference" as "opposition," totalitarianism is radically impervious to otherness — that is, it denies the existence of a *thou* that is comparable to an *I* if not interchangeable with it, while also remaining irreducibly distinct from it. Totalitarian thinking — which is far more widespread than totalitarian states — could indeed be defined as a mind-set that gives no legitimate

place to otherness and plurality. Its slogan could well be this pearl
of wisdom from Simone de Beauvoir: "Truth is one, error is many.
It is therefore no coincidence if the right wing claims to be pluralist" (1539). But it would not be right to play the same game in
reverse and to assert that the left is necessarily totalitarian. The
style of thought revealed by Beauvoir's remark extends the principle of war to civil life, and it makes the internal enemy no less
deserving of death than the foreign foe. In this respect totalitarianism runs counter to universalism, which favors the ideal of
peace.

This point is worth some attention. It is often said that Communism is based on a universalist ideology, and this alleged fact
makes it difficult to bring it together with Nazism under the single heading of "totalitarian," since Nazism was explicitly anti-
universalist. Raymond Aron, one of the staunchest and clearest
opponents of Communist thinking and politics, asserted in his
classic analysis of the issue that one of the two totalitarian ideologies was "universal and humanitarian," the other "nationalis-
tic, racial, and anything but humane." This allowed him to talk
of the "noble aspirations" of the Communist dream, of the Communists' "belief in universal and humanitarian values," of their
will "inspired by a humanitarian ideal" (*Democracy and Totalitarianism*, 197, 198).

There is a real problem here. Is Aron talking about the Communist ideal in the most general sense — Communism as it can be
found at various historical moments, consisting of the very Christian aspiration toward justice, equality, and fraternity? If he is,
then it is hard to see how he can consider it sufficient to describe
the regime and the policies that came out of the October Revolution as "Communist." Or is he really talking about the Soviet
state set up by Lenin? If that is the case, then, quite bafflingly,
Aron sees it exactly and exclusively as its own propaganda would
have us see it. After all, what was special about Leninism was
that it broke with Marxist and socialist traditions by abandoning
all ambitions of universalism. (Lenin denounced traditionalists of
this kind as "social democrat," even as "social traitors," and its
successors as "social Fascists.") Victory, for Lenin, involved the
physical elimination of a part of the population specified for the
purposes of the struggle as "the bourgeois" or as "the enemy."

Communism seeks the happiness of humanity but only once

35

the "bad guys" have been separated out from it, and that is what Nazism envisaged too. How is it possible to believe in the universal validity of the doctrine when it asserts that it is based on struggle, violence, permanent revolution, hatred, dictatorship, and war? It justifies itself on the grounds that the proletariat is the majority and the bourgeoisie the minority — but that already takes us a long way away from universal ideals. But Lenin's other great contribution to the theory of Communism is the leading role of the party in controlling the proletarian masses: and so even the argument for the greatest good of the majority cannot stand. Lenin would surely have been greatly amused by Aron's attempt to present him as a humanist.

Aron's words were written in 1958 and it may well be that even someone as clear-sighted as he lacked relevant knowledge not only of how Communism was implemented when it was in power but also of its political program. Nonetheless, in the same pages of *Democracy and Totalitarianism*, Aron describes Soviet Communists as "a party which grants itself the right to use violence against all its enemies, in a land where, to begin with, it was in a minority." So how then does he come to see this inevitable and systematic use of violence as an instance of "universal humanitarian values"? It seems that the Cold War context of his writing forced him to take Soviet propaganda more seriously than it deserved and to turn a blind eye to various features of Communist ideology that he was in fact perfectly able to discern.

All this rather undermines Aron's comparison of the two totalitarian regimes. He comes to the conclusion that "whatever the similarities, the difference [between Nazism and Communism] is fundamental." One of the two demonstrates "a will to build a new regime and maybe a new kind of man, by any means"; the other, "a literally diabolical will to destroy a pseudo-race." This difference really derives only from Aron's tendentious presentation of the two regimes: he focuses on the Soviet's self-proclaimed aims but on the Nazis' actual methods. Such comparison between ends and means are not justifiable. Hitler wanted to destroy the Jewish pseudo-race to purify his people and to produce a better Aryan race (the "new man") and, it goes without saying, a new kind of regime. To call this diabolical does not help us to understand it. Conversely, Stalin reckoned it was necessary, in order to achieve his aims, to destroy the pseudo-class of the kulaks whom he deliberately sent to their deaths by firing squad and famine. That is what "by any means" means. The ideals of both regimes jettison universal ambitions: Hitler wanted to create a nation, and eventually a whole world, free of Jews; Stalin clamored for a society without classes, that is to say, without the bourgeois. In both cases, one segment of humanity was written off. The only real difference lies in the techniques used to achieve these identical policy aims.

So when Aron asserts the specificity of Hitler's rule by declaring in his conclusion that "no other head of state in modern history ever decided in cold blood to organize the industrial extermination of six million of his fellow-men," we have to answer him with the fact that in 1932–33, a head of state called Joseph Stalin did decide in cold blood to organize — not in an industrial manner, but in a no less brutal one — the extermination of six million of his fellow men, the farmers and peasants of the Ukraine, the Caucasus, and Kazakhstan. Actually, Aron does not seem to have been aware of these massacres, the greatest ever carried out by the Soviet authorities.

We must therefore stress that the renunciation of universalism is no less characteristic of Communism, which professes universal ideals, than it is of Nazism, which, from its origins in nationalist movements, openly declares its own particularism. The point is that the "international" in Communist propaganda does not mean "universal." In practice Communism was as "particularist" as Nazism, since it explicitly asserted that its stated ideal did not extend to the whole of humanity. "Transnational" did not mean "transclass," and the elimination of one part of humanity was always the precondition. Kaganovich, one of Stalin's henchmen, put it very clearly: "You must think of humanity as one great body, but one that requires constant surgery. Need I remind you that surgery cannot be performed without cutting membranes, without destroying tissues, without the spilling of blood?" (quoted by Kahan, 309). The only real difference is that in one case the division of humanity is "horizontal," based on national frontiers, and in the other it is "vertical," between the different layers of a single society: national and racial war for Nazism, and the class struggle for Communism.

Even this distinction is hardly fundamental. Shortly after the October Revolution, and in any case after Lenin's death in 1924, the interests of world revolution became increasingly indistinguishable from the interests of its incarnation in Soviet Russia. What was good for the one was good for the other, and vice versa. This equation made internationalist aims merge with the interests of a single country. The Komintern, allegedly the expression of international revolution, was simultaneously the agent of the Russian intelligence services as well as a tool of Soviet expansionism and of its drive toward hegemony. Komintern cadres who failed to grasp this unification of functions soon ended up in the gulag or in front of a firing squad. Soviet internationalism was indistinguishable from the defense of national interests abroad. The Second World War allowed this truth to be seen in full light: just like imperial Russia in times gone by, Soviet Russia annexed immense areas previously belonging to its western neighbors — in Romania (Bessarabia), in Poland, and in Finland (the area known as Eastern Karelia) — as well as entire states (Estonia, Lithuania, Latvia simply disappeared), all the better to set them on the fast track to socialism. During the war, whole ethnic groups and nations were redefined as "class enemies" by Stalin and were therefore oppressed, deported, or eradicated. The same drift, more or less, happened in Nazi Germany, where racial genocide merged with "class genocide" in the elimination of specific *kinds* of Poles and Russians.

I should add that Aron himself changed his view on this. In the "Epilogue" to his memoirs of 1983 — a text that should be seen as his political testament — he wrote this: "Communism is no less hateful to me than Nazism was. The argument that I once used to distinguish class messianism from race messianism no longer impresses me very much. The apparent universality of the former has become, in the last analysis, an illusion. . . . It sanctifies conflicts or wars rather than preserving, across frontiers, the fragile links of a common faith" (471).

Democracy and the humanist thinking that underlies it are entirely in opposition to totalitarianism, in the sense that they really do constitute a universalist creed. The principle of universalism is at its weakest in foreign relations, where democratic countries continue to rely on force even if they no longer have recourse to war, at least in principle, because the form of domination now sought is primarily economic. But in the domestic arena universalism is inescapable, because all policy is conducted in the name of the collectivity and for the benefit of all. This gives rise to an unending search for the common good and also to the need for each constituency within the social body to sacrifice some of its interests — for democratic politics is the art of compromise. In a democracy conflicts are not solved by the elimination of one of the opposing sides; instead, oppositions (which must arise in any human grouping) are turned into complementarities. Far from preventing the recognition of otherness, universalism actually fosters it. What really undermines respect for the other is when difference is treated as opposition and as hostility — a path leading directly to totalitarianism. In the latter system, where the distant ideal is one of universal peace and harmony, the means of reaching it include the physical elimination of all who stand in the way. The initial victory of the revolution can never be sufficient: in Stalin's view, the class struggle would only get more intense as time went by, even in the homeland of Communism, which was of course also surrounded by external enemies.

The grammar of humanism has three persons: *I*, who exercises his or her autonomy; *thou*, who is equivalent to an *I* but totally distinct from *me* (each *thou* can also be an *I*, and vice versa), and who may be in turn (or even at the same time) my colleague, my competitor, my counselor, the object of my love, and so forth; and *they*, who form the community to which an *I* belongs, beyond one-to-one relationships, and which is, in the last analysis, the whole of humanity, all of whose members are entitled to equal dignity. But the grammar of totalitarianism has only two persons: *us*, among whom the distinctions between individual *I*s have been suppressed; and *them*, the enemies who must be fought, not to say slaughtered. In a distant future, when utopia will have been made real on earth, *they* will be nothing more than slaves (in Nazi ideology) or they will have ceased to exist (in the Communist vision, which will then have a grammar with only one person).

The paradox of totalitarian ideology is that, in making unity its supreme ideal, it ultimately returns to the same vision as that of democracy's conservative critics. For such critics, democracy's great flaw was the nihilistic individualism that it fostered. By imposing a single rule on a whole society and by requiring every one in it to obey the party's directives, totalitarian states make individualism impossible; and by drawing its values from the cult of science and by making them obligatory, totalitarianism is supposed to eradicate nihilism as well.

The Two-Edged Knife

Totalitarian ideology is a complex construction and (to borrow a phrase from Dostoyevsky) like a knife with two edges. It seeks to reconcile demands that are ultimately incompatible. This makes it vulnerable, because one day the contradictions will pull too hard on each other and bring down the whole house of cards; but it also gives totalitarianism a special strength, because, in the interim, its divergent principles allow it to appeal more widely, and it can stop up a breach in one area by invoking a contradictory value. Overall, however, there are three main fault lines within totalitarian ideology.

The first tension arises from the elementary philosophical opposition between determinism and free will. The totalitarian view is that everything that happens in the world is the result of inflexible causality (social and historic causality for one kind of totalitarianism, biological causality for the other). Everything that happens has to happen, because everything is determined by irreversible causes. On the other hand, the future is in our own hands: we have an ideal, and we must do everything necessary to realize that ideal. We are ready to sweep away the past so as to build a better world and even a better kind of man. The cult of science dissolves the contradiction between determinism and free will by introducing a third term, that of "scientific" knowledge. If the world is entirely knowable, if historical materialism does indeed show us the real laws of all societies, and if biology reveals the truth of all living things, then we who possess this knowledge not only have the power to explain existing forms of society and of life, but we also have the power to transform them in the direction we choose. That is how *techne*, which lies in the domain of the will, can claim to have the authority of science, which in itself seeks only to lay bare what is determined.

This tension is less easy to dissipate, however, when the desired object of knowledge is not a self-repeating cycle of human societies but univocal history moving toward a single end. If you take this teleological view and also believe that the future course of human history is ineluctably determined from the outset, then how can you justify making sacrifices in order to accelerate it along a path already set? Communists and Nazis alike claimed to know the destination to which history was leading them—but they intervened in the most active way possible (in a "revolution") to alter its path.

The second major ambiguity in the philosophical premises of totalitarianism relates to the question of modernity. Totalitarianism is simultaneously antimodern (as its fatalism shows) and archmodern (as illustrated by its activism). In placing the interests of the group above those of the person and social values above individual ones, totalitarianism harks back to traditional societies and in that respect must be counted as conservative and antimodern. In addition, and despite the egalitarian rhetoric of Soviet Russia, totalitarian societies are as hierarchical as any traditional society. The cult of the supreme leader is another characteristic of both totalitarian and of premodern societies. On the other hand, totalitarian societies are also in favor of many things that we customarily consider to be modern, notably industrialization, globalization, and technical innovation. Communist Russia industrialized at breakneck speed; Hitler was the herald of the "people's car" and built the first autobahns. So we can see that the modernizing aspirations of these regimes were not exclusively directed toward improving military effectiveness. It seems that in totalitarian systems relationships with *things* take the place that relationships with *persons* would have had in a traditional or premodern society.

This fracture was particularly acute in Nazism, which draped itself in a mantle of Gothic traditions, Nordic gods, ancient Germanic customs, and nature, over which men have no power. The simultaneously modern and antimodern stance of Nazism allowed it to attract support from people who would otherwise have remained miles apart—ranging from believers in biological determinism and eugenics to people like Martin Heidegger who dreamed only of freeing the world from the reign of *techne*.

Although it was less visible in Soviet Russia, where "progress" was the official aim, the same tension between modernizing and antimodern tendencies existed. Even Lenin's famous formula, "Communism = electrification + all power to the soviets," betrays this duality. On the one hand, the Communist state was an

41

industrial society in which economic factors played the major role; but it was also the opposite, that is to say, a society ruled by a moral, ideological, and theological ideal, and prepared to sacrifice efficiency on the altar of its self-image. Electrification and the power of the soviets can lead in opposite directions. Should a good engineer get sacked because he is not a good Communist? Or should electrification be carried out by competent technicians even if they are not party members? Both answers held sway at different times when it was not possible to avoid the question. I remember my father facing this problem again and again. He ran a library information service, and his dilemma was between hiring people who could read Western languages (and who must thus have had a bourgeois education, since that was the only way they could have learned French, English, German, etc.), and taking on good Communists who could read only Bulgarian and, at most, Russian. He chose the first solution and lost his job because of it.

All the same, there is a feature common to the two prongs of the dilemma, which makes it more manageable. Neither "electrification" nor "power to the soviets" makes the individual the ultimate aim of our actions; the aim is either on a level above the individual (the people, the proletariat, the party) or below it (technology, industrialization). This is probably the most striking feature of totalitarian regimes, historically speaking: from the beginning of the twentieth century they stood against the rising tide of individualism, and they exploited all the frustrations borne on the crest of that wave.

The third central ambiguity of totalitarianism relates to the place of ideology, and on this theoreticians remain divided. The pioneers in the field, such as Raymond Aron, see totalitarian regimes as ideocracies, as states legitimated by their ideologies, where ideological correctness is the supreme criterion; power is but the instrument, in this analysis, and the aim is a political ideal. Other theorists, many of whom were dissidents from Eastern bloc countries, take a quite different view, at least as far as Communism is concerned. Cornelius Castoriadis for instance, claims that Communist ideology was just a facade, and that in practice Soviet power served no aim other than its own increase; in this analysis, there was no ideocracy, only a "stratocracy" — power for power's sake, the will to will.

To clarify this point, a brief digression on the history of the Communist variant of the totalitarian state seems necessary. Because the Nazi state lasted only twelve years before it was swept away by the Allied victory, Communism, which lasted for seventy-four, and which died of "natural" causes, not by war or revolution, offers a much richer object of analysis.

It is customary to periodize the history of Soviet Russia by the reigns of its all-powerful "guides," and we follow the custom. The main divisions are between the era of Lenin (1917–24); the Stalin period (to 1953); the era of Khrushchev (forced out in 1964); and the Brezhnev period (died 1982). What is also obvious is that the main structural changes in the regime do not fit this periodization.

The first big change was in the role of terror. Lenin initiated it, and Stalin maintained it, at higher and lower levels of intensity at different times. But after Stalin's death there was a change not in the level of terror but in its nature. Mass executions were suspended, many of the gulags were closed, and torture and deportation were abandoned in favor of bureaucratic penalties and pressure within the professions. There were still plenty of acts of persecution and even new measures such as the use of psychiatric hospitals for political prisoners, but the victims were individuals, not whole categories of people. Admittedly, people had by then learned the lessons of terror, and every wisp of revolt had long been smashed. And, of course, the Khrushchev years were still very far from offering "bourgeois" legality or individual freedom; surveillance was universal, and the law offered no protection to the individual from arbitrary acts by the authorities. Nonetheless, what the "thaw" made possible was the emergence of the dissidents — people who expressed their hostility to the state more or less openly. Under Lenin and Stalin, that could not have happened; dissidents were immediately annihilated. Under Khrushchev, they were "only" kept under surveillance, oppressed, and, at the worst, sent to a camp or to a psychiatric ward.

The second modification has already been mentioned: the submerging of the internationalist ideal under an imperialistic, nationalist foreign policy (masked by the unchanging rhetoric of internationalism). The third change, by far the most important, was similarly obscured by the language of propaganda. After Stalin's death, the ideology of Communism becomes an increasingly empty shell. Nobody really believed in the millenarist promise of universal salvation any more, and the collectivist ideal was mentioned less often. Idealism was replaced by the usual accompaniments of the lust for power — the pursuit of wealth, of privilege, and of personal interests. In place of the Bolshevik old guard and fanatical believers in the Communist creed came self-serving bureaucrats and cynical careerists.

There is always a gulf between doctrine and reality, but the ways in which it was handled before and after the sea change I've described were quite different. Under Lenin and Stalin, when a disparity between language and reality was noticed, people sought to change reality. Lenin imposed the Soviet republic, Stalin collectivized the land and industrialized the country. No matter the price in human suffering and economic disaster, the main objective was to implement a program and thus to reduce the gap between theory and practice, between representation and reality. After Stalin's death the gap between language and world was no smaller, but efforts were made not to reduce it, but to mask it. From then on, official language began to lead an entirely independent life of its own, unrelated to the real world. Economic planners became less concerned with carrying out the plan than with fiddling the figures so as to benefit personally from their "success." Soviet Russia became a kingdom of camouflage, a state made of smoke and mirrors. Communist ideology was supposed to be in charge, but, save for a few exceptions, the only rule was the lust for power and personal advantage. Exactly the same change came over the other Communist countries in the Eastern bloc, with some variations related to different national contexts.

As a former citizen of a totalitarian country, I can bear personal witness to this. In the 1950s, the period that I can recall, ideology was in nearly all cases a complete sham — yet it was also indispensable. We lived in a pseudo-ideocracy. My friends and I felt we were living in a world of lies, where words designating ideals — peace, freedom, equality, prosperity — had come to mean their opposites. Despite this, official ideology remained a reasonably coherent rhetorical machine that allowed a few remaining fanatics to survive and gave the majority (consisting of conformists) a way of rationalizing the situation in which they found themselves. And everyone was a conformist, at least for part of the time. So ideology was necessary, and it had to be this ideology and not another, even if it was most often a means rather than an end. The importance of the masking effect of ideology cannot be overestimated. I should add that on the whole we preferred to deal with sincere and "honest" Communists rather than with cynics whose only loyalty was to authority. The fact that they had made a personal choice to believe, and were not just bowing down to the party, proved they had not entirely abandoned their individual autonomy; paradoxically, their commitment to Communism could serve as a rampart against the arbitrary use of power.

The change in the role of ideology, from a central to a merely superficial aspect of the regime, also explains another disparity. Official slogans declared that all individual interests and the interests of all individuals were secondary to the interests of the collectivity. But ordinary citizens of totalitarian countries saw a quite different reality—a reign of unrestrained personal interests, with each seeking his own best advantage. The "common interest" was just wrapping paper. Totalitarianism offers a critique of individualism in the name of an organic community, but it actually created something that completely contradicted its professed aims, for it ended up producing "masses" made of juxtaposed individuals, devoid of any positive public allegiance. When the ideological facade crumpled in 1989 or 1991, it was plain to see: outside the tiny fraction of former dissidents, Soviet citizens knew no rule save that of selfishness.

The last, and lesser, change happened in the 1970s, under Brezhnev, and it was but a small twist to the monist basis of totalitarianism. The twin spheres of public and private life were once again permitted to be distinct. It became possible to lead a private life that was independent of public norms (which remained dependent on ideology); people could henceforth choose more or less freely how they dressed, where they went on vacation, or where to travel abroad.

These observations on the history of Communist totalitarianism, alongside the comparison with Nazism, allow us to identify the hard core of totalitarianism itself and to hierarchize its characteristics. It requires an initial phase of revolution, which overcomes all resistance and eliminates all real and imaginary internal opposition. It then constitutes itself around the suppression of individual autonomy and freedom, and subjects all to an absolute

45

authority through the use of terror or repression. Finally, there are the consequences of this chosen principle — struggle as the law of life, the equivalence of difference and opposition, and the rejection of political and economic pluralism.

On the other hand, some other aspects of a totalitarian regime, including some of its most visible features, can be removed without altering the "ideal-type construct" of totalitarianism — mass terror, for instance, which was only necessary during the transitional phase (even though the "transition" lasted for half of the life of the USSR). Even more strikingly, scientism can cease to be the motor of policy. Although it was essential during the initial phase, once its destructive work was done, it could be turned into a mere facade.

These progressive transformations of the totalitarian regime were accelerated, multiplied, and intensified by Gorbachev in the period of perestroika and glasnost, and they allowed it to die a peaceful death, much as Spain was able to manage a transition from the Franco regime to a modern society after 1975. However, the damage done by Communism was far more profound, and it continues to hamper the countries of the old Eastern bloc. The Cold War, which set democracy and totalitarianism against each other after the end of the Second World War, thus ended with the unconditional defeat of one of the parties. This defeat was not the result of external intervention (as it was for Nazi Germany) but of the collapse of the totalitarian system in itself.

The end of the story could seem quite hopeful, because it supports the view that a political system that suppresses and scorns individual freedom to that extent must eventually collapse. Seventy-four years is far too long a time for a person, but it is merely a moment in history. Communism died for a whole set of political, economic, and social reasons, but also because of a change in the mentalities of both ordinary people and the leadership. Everyone had come to aspire to forms of the good life that the Communist regime could not provide — personal safety and peace, material plenty, and individual freedom. These values were hampered by totalitarianism but fostered by democracy. Of course, democracy does not offer collective salvation nor does it promise happiness on earth; but it does guarantee that there won't be a knock on the door before dawn and that men in gray uniforms won't take you off for interrogation. The prospect of arrest is not

46

really attractive even to party cadres with all their special privileges. In addition, democratic regimes keep the store shelves full, and we should not be so foolish as to despise people who would rather have this particular side effect of "capitalism" than the shortages endemic to Communist societies.

The collapse of the Communist system, however, has not brought the citizens of Eastern Europe or of the former USSR the happiness they expected. The party had usurped the authority of the state, and as a result the fall of Communism made it plain that there was no state any longer. Having no state is far worse than having a bad one: its absence creates an open house for brute force and for a terrifying rising tide of crime. Much the same could be said of all the values of the public sphere: tainted by the fraudulent uses made of them under Communism, they have become unusable today. That's what Adam Michnik meant when he joked that "The worst thing about Communism is what comes after." The regime had corrupted political institutions, but also, as we discovered only after its fall, it had ravaged the environment, the economy, and human souls. Children will perforce pay for the errors of their parents for many years to come. And there is a high price to pay for the freedom that has recently been won. Comfortable habits, economic routines, a basic level of amenity (at least equal to the bed and board you get in prison without even asking) have all had to be given up. Citizens of these recently de-Communized countries sometimes wonder whether the life of a free pauper really is better than the life of a well-treated slave. No one can be sure that these peoples are near the end of their sufferings. Only one thing is sure, but it tips the scale: totalitarian society does not bring salvation.

The Achievement of Vasily Grossman

It was a somber century but it was not devoid of light. Particular individuals who lived through it can light the way on our journey through hell.

The first figure in our portrait gallery is Vasily Grossman, one of the greatest writers of the twentieth century. A Russian speaker, a Soviet citizen, and a Jew, Grossman's two posthumous masterpieces, *Life and Fate* and *Forever Flowing*, offer an extraordinary analysis of totalitarian society. That analysis was made in complete isolation, without access to any literature on the subject, without public or even private debate, yet it reveals the same truths as those sought by historians — the underlying meaning of events.

Grossman's own life and fate are puzzling. He is the only Soviet writer known to have undergone a complete metamorphosis, switching from subservience to revolt, from blindness to clear sight. Why was he the only one? He began as a timidly orthodox servant of the regime, and yet in later years he dared take on the issue of the totalitarian state in all its complexity. The two writers to whom he seems most comparable are the two Soviet Nobel Prize winners, Pasternak (whom Grossman held in low esteem) and Solzhenitsyn (whom he admired). But Pasternak, who had long been an eminent Soviet writer before he published *Dr. Zhivago* in 1958 (in the West), did not focus his novel on the totalitarian system itself. As for Solzhenitsyn, who certainly did tackle the camps and the everyday use of terror, he was a literary beginner with nothing to lose, so to speak, when he published *One Day in the Life of Ivan Denisovich* in 1962 (in Moscow). Grossman is the only example, or at least the most significant, of an established and leading Soviet writer changing his spots completely. The slave in him died, and a free man arose. How did such an unusual destiny come about?

Vasily Semeonovich Grossman was born in 1905 in Berdichev, one of the main Jewish centers of the Ukraine. His parents, though not rich themselves, both came from comfortable families. They separated shortly after the birth of the child. Vasily spent two years (1910–12) in Geneva with his mother, who in later years earned her living as a French teacher; Vasily kept up his French for the rest of his life. He completed his secondary education in Kiev, thanks to support from an uncle in medical practice, and went to Moscow in 1923 to study chemistry. He got through his degree without much passion, it seems, and started work in a mine in 1930. But another kind of life beckoned: he realized that he wanted to be a writer. At the beginning it all seemed easy. His first stories were published, readers liked them, and so he gave up chemistry in 1934 to become a writer full-time.

During the first period of his career, from 1930 to 1941, Grossman's aim was to become a professional writer and to be accepted as such by his peers. His first published stories won the favor of Maxim Gorky, which was an immense help, but they were also appreciated by more marginal figures such as Isaak Babel and Mikhail Bulgakov. He wrote short stories, a novel, and reportage (*ocherki*). Grossman called himself a Marxist, but his humanist side made his friends tease him for being a *menshevik*, that is, something like a social democrat. Grossman never joined the party; his fictional characters are for the most part ordinary people deeply attached to Soviet values.

The profession of letters in Soviet society offered an enviable but dangerous career. Writers had great privileges and high salaries. As members of the Writers' Union, they received larger apartments and holiday homes by the Black Sea. But for being known, respected, and privileged, Soviet writers were also the objects of envy, and thus vulnerable to threat. At the same time, of course, they had to earn what they were getting for free by producing literary works of use to the state. The overlap between what suited the state and what fitted the talent of a given writer was sometimes wafer-thin.

The 1930s were turbulent times in the Soviet Union. Grossman knew what was going on because ill winds blew very close to home — and to survive, he had to keep his head down. His cousin Nadia was arrested in 1933 (she worked at the International Trades Union Organization and had been a great help to Grossman at the start of his literary career); and it was at

49

Nadia's that Grossman stayed on his visits to Moscow. He took it on the chin and made no effort to get his cousin released. In 1937 two of his best friends were arrested and deported. They were both novelists and, like Grossman, connected to an informal writers' group called Pereval. Once again, Grossman held his tongue. In 1938 the uncle that had paid for his secondary education was arrested in Berdichev and put to death. And still Grossman held his breath. Only the year before, he had signed a petition calling for the death penalty for the defendants in the show trial that put many of the old Bolshevik leadership (including Bukharin) in the dock. Finally, when his wife was arrested and imprisoned — for being the ex-wife of an "enemy of the people" — Grossman did at last make a move. He went to see Yezhov, the head of the political police and got his wife out of the NKVD prison. But her ex-husband, a former friend of Grossman's, got not a word of support from the writer and was executed in prison.

Incidents such as these were the order of the day in the Soviet Union's inner circles in the 1930s. Betrayal and submission were basic survival mechanisms. Grossman was not proud of this part of his life. A couple of stories that he wrote toward the end of that decade (but not published for many years thereafter) provide a glimpse of his mood in those black years. "The Young Woman and the Old" and "A Few Sad Days" are shot through with the painful awareness of human weakness. He had already seen something equally terrible that he could not speak about for many more years: in 1931, as he was catching the train at Berdichev after a visit to family members, he saw starving men and women in rags wandering between the tracks. A woman came up to his window and begged in a barely audible voice: "Give me bread! Bread!" Grossman did not respond.

War broke out in 1941 and it seems to have come as a relief. Grossman threw himself into the defense of the motherland, for he could now give the state what it demanded of him without having to lie to himself. As he said of one of the characters of *Life and Fate*: "He was certain that he was not only fighting the Germans, but fighting for a free Russia: certain that a victory over Hitler would be a victory over the death camps where his father, his mother and his sisters had perished" (316). Grossman became the Soviet Union's most celebrated war correspondent.

He was at the battle for Moscow, at Stalingrad, in the Ukraine, in Poland, and he got to Berlin in 1945. He showed exemplary courage throughout. His reports, sketches, and essays were written for the Red Army newspaper, but they were reprinted in many other journals in Russia and abroad. (In March 1945 the PCF published a selection of his pieces on Stalingrad, under a title — *Choses Vues* [Things seen] — borrowed from Victor Hugo.) Grossman's reporting focused on the fate of ordinary people, bringing out their dignity and heroism. But he also suffered a terrible personal tragedy himself during the war years. In 1944 he learned that his mother had been murdered by *Einsatzgruppen* (extermination commandos) when the German army marched into Berdichev in 1941.

Before the end of the war Grossman began a long novel, under the working title of *Stalingrad*. He finished it in 1949 and in the meantime had become one of the most respected writers in the Soviet Union. But the novel itself ran into publishing problems, for it was not quite in accordance with the rules of the day. Its main character, Strum (who reappears in *Life and Fate*), was a Jew, and that was looked down upon; moreover, the novel's other heroes were ordinary citizens, not commissars, who alone were supposed to embody the Communist Party spirit. Grossman wrote to Stalin to ask him to release the work. (It's hard now to imagine a monolithic state centralized to that degree, with the general secretary ruling on magazines' publishing schedules.) Some strings were eventually pulled in the right direction, and the novel appeared in 1952 under the title *For a Good Cause* (*Za pravoe delo*).

At first the book was treated as a great work of Soviet literature. Then toward the end of 1952 and the spring of 1953, the attacks began, unleashed by especially servile critics, jealous writers, or overzealous bureaucrats. What had been praised was now blamed, and Grossman was stunned. After accepting all the censors' recommendations, he found that his ten years' work on the novel was denigrated. It was then that he took the ultimate step for which he would never forgive himself. The campaign against "cosmopolitans" (a euphemism for Jews) was then at its height, and the Doctors' Plot (allegedly, Jewish doctors had tried to poison Stalin and other dignitaries) had just been "unmasked." Grossman was unfortunate enough to find himself at a meeting of the staff of *Pravda* where a letter was being drafted requesting harsh punishment of the guilty so as to spare the "good" Jews. Grossman "told himself that it was worth condemning a few so as to save that unfortunate race, and so, like most of the people present, he signed" (Lipkin, 40). He did not forget the experience when he wrote *Life and Fate*, where the same thing happens to Strum. This closes the second period of Grossman's career, 1941–52.

Stalin's death in 1953 marks the break. We can only guess what went on in Grossman's mind at that time. His best friend, Semyon Lipkin, recalls that at this time Grossman took to heart Chekhov's assertion that "it was time for all of us to get rid of the slave that lived inside our heart" (Lipkin, 66). The totalitarian system did not collapse, but the terror became markedly less severe. The camp gates opened, and ghosts emerged after fifteen or twenty years' incarceration. Arbitrary arrests and executions ceased, and Khrushchev's "thaw" set in. Grossman realized that he was no longer under threat of death, and he decided to make no compromises henceforth.

Grossman's personal crisis occurred in 1954, when he wrote nothing. But in 1955, he exploded with writerly energy: he revised and transformed what was to be have been part II of his Stalingrad novel and turned it into *Life and Fate* as we know it now. He also wrote the first draft of a shorter work, half story and half essay, called *Forever Flowing* (*Vse Techet*); and composed an even shorter, denser distillation of the same thematic material in "The Sistine Madonna" (from which all the epigraphs of this book are taken). In 1956 he broke with another kind of falsehood by leaving his wife and starting a new life with the woman he loved.

Grossman finished *Life and Fate* in 1960 and submitted it for publication, an act that in retrospect seems as naive as it was bold. By no stretch of the imagination could a book of that kind have been published in the totalitarian USSR, even under Khrushchev. The inevitable happened: the cowardly editors of the review to which Grossman had sent his manuscript washed their hands as fast as they could by forwarding the thing posthaste to the KGB. The political police called on Grossman in February 1961. It was a sign of the times that they did not arrest the author, only the manuscript—including each and every

scrap, draft, and copy of it, so that it could never be recon-
structed. (Grossman lived in a world without photocopy machines, not to mention word processors or diskettes.) Stalin had
writers arrested and killed; Khrushchev left the writers alone but
locked up the products of their minds.

Grossman was upset but not dejected. He felt not the slightest
temptation to recant and indulged in the pleasures of raging
protest — to no effect. In February 1962 he wrote a long letter to
Khrushchev, expressing no regrets for what he had put into his
novel and demanding reparation. The general secretary did not
reply directly, but in July 1962 Grossman was summoned to see
Suslov, head of the party's ideology section. Suslov did not
threaten Grossman with deportation, but scolded him in a pater-
nalistic way, urging him to go back to writing good Soviet stuff,
just like he did before.

Grossman died of cancer in 1964 without ever having been
arrested or deported, but also without knowing if his writings
would ever be published. Waking up in a hospital bed a few
weeks before his death, Grossman asked the friend who was
caring for him: "Last night I was taken to interrogation. . . .
Tell me, I didn't betray anyone, did I?" (Berzer, 251). He published almost nothing during the last twelve years of his life.
After the confiscation of *Life and Fate*, he barely had enough
time left to write a revised version of *Forever Flowing*, which he
did not even try to publish, and a few short pieces, the most significant of which is "Dobro vam!" (All the best!), based on
travels in Armenia. Grossman's main work thus first appeared
long after his death, and not in Russia: *Forever Flowing* in
Frankfurt in 1970, *Life and Fate* in Lausanne in 1980.

Grossman's life does not explain why it was he, rather than
another, who managed to metamorphose from an official writer
into a dissident. It is tempting to speculate that it was because
he underwent an equal metamorphosis in reassuming his identity as a Jew. Grossman came from an entirely assimilated Jewish family whose sole language was Russian. When he recreates
his childhood in *Life and Fate* — where it is "loaned" to the
character Viktor Strum — he has the physicist's mother say this:
"I never used to feel I was a Jew; as a child my circle of friends
were all Russian; my favorite poets were Pushkin and
Nekrasov" (86). When she has the opportunity to emigrate, she

53

says: "I'll never leave Russia — I'd rather drown myself" (86). And her son has the same views: "Never, before the war, had Viktor thought about the fact that he was a Jew, that his mother was a Jew" (94). These statements take on fuller meaning when we remember the systematic persecution — ranging from everyday discrimination to murderous pogroms — to which Jews were subjected under the tsars. Like many other urbanized and assimilated Jews, the Grossmans were attracted by the Revolution and by the new Soviet order, which abolished the pariah-status that the Russian Empire had forced upon them. The Soviets stigmatized anti-Semitism and proclaimed universal equality.

Hitler's role was to remind these assimilated Jews who thought of themselves as Russian and Soviet that they would remain forever Jewish. They were willing to take on this new-old identity not so much because their religion and ethnicity mattered to them as to express solidarity with those who were in peril and pain. In the letter she wrote from the ghetto a few hours before dying, Strum's mother says: "But now, during these terrible days, my heart has become filled with a maternal tenderness toward the Jewish people" (87). The same holds for Grossman himself, who immortalized his mother's fate in the novel. All of Berdichev's Jews were shot — about ten thousand on 5 September, 1941, the remaining twenty thousand on 15 September. Grossman's mother was in the second group. But unlike Strum's mother in the novel, she never managed to send a letter to her son, who only learned the truth when the Ukraine was reconquered by the Red Army (but he must have suspected it long before). Grossman was all the more affected by this loss for having failed to do anything to get his mother out of Berdichev between the outbreak of war and the occupation of the Ukraine two weeks later.

But that was not all. As he traveled with the Red Army into the liberated areas of western Russia in 1944, he saw traces of mass murders. He was with the vanguard that stumbled across the ruins of Treblinka in Poland. He spent days investigating, questioning witnesses and the camp guards who had been arrested, and shortly after, published the very first account of an extermination camp: "The Treblinka Hell."

Meanwhile, the Soviet government saw that it could make use of the universal sympathy aroused by the martyrdom of the

Jews. As early as August 1941, it set up a Jewish Antifascist Committee, whose task was to give Jews abroad a sense of solidarity with the Soviet war effort. The committee asked the two best-known Jewish Soviet writers of the day, Ilya Ehrenburg and Vasily Grossman, to compile a "Black Book" of eyewitness accounts of the Nazis' persecution and annihilation of Soviet Jewry. Grossman threw himself energetically into this task, commissioning and collecting articles, redrafting some of them, as well as investigating matters for himself.

But once the war was won, things changed again in the Soviet Union. It was no longer permissible to stress the special sufferings of the Jews; and, as the Cold War congealed relations with the former Allies, references to the international solidarity of the Jewish community became suspect. Publication of the "Black Book" was deferred, then canceled. A condensed version, for which Albert Einstein had originally written a preface, eventually appeared in the United States, but the full version did not come out until 1980 — in Israel. As national socialism (Grossman's term) became ever more overt in the Soviet Union, anti-Semitism reemerged with it. Yiddish-language publishing houses were shut down, the Jewish Antifascist Committees were dissolved, the more prominent Jewish personalities were arrested and executed. The Doctors' Plot was "unraveled" — and then it was proposed that all Soviet Jews be deported to some place in the Soviet Far East.

In the face of the persecution of the Jews, Grossman could no longer forget his own Jewishness, even if he stumbled on occasions, as when he signed the letter in 1952. Henceforth, Jewishness became one of the main themes of his writing. Viktor Strum, the central figure of both *For a Good Cause* and *Life and Fate*, is a Jew; and Hitler's genocide of the Jews is one of the main subjects of the latter novel. Grossman also ceased to turn a blind eye to Russian and Ukrainian anti-Semitism, to which significant passages are devoted in *Life and Fate* and "Dobro vam!" (All the best!). However, the Jewish dimension of Grossman's writing, which cannot be excluded from any fair description of his achievement, does not by itself account fully for the writer's complete conversion from a Soviet celebrity into a dissident.

The inadequacy of the "Jewish identity" explanation can be

seen from the chronology: Grossman learned of the shocking
fact that he belonged to a people destined for extermination between 1941 and 1945, but it was not until 1953–54 that his
conversion occurred. It was Hitler who caused Grossman to discover his Jewishness, but opposition to Hitler was perfectly admissible in the Soviet Union. The timing of Grossman's
conversion, as well as what he turned into, strongly suggests
that the change had little to do with the brutal reminder of his
Jewishness. Stalin, not Hitler, was at the root of Grossman's
conversion, which consisted essentially of the realization that the
universally detested Hitler had been barely worse than the idol
of the Soviet world, Joseph Stalin. Although he too was anti-
Semitic, Stalin's greatest sin was not the persecution of the Jews.
What led Grossman to convert were events not directly related
to the discovery of his own Jewish identity: the rejection and
then the release of his novel, *For a Good Cause*, the hostility he
encountered on publication, the compromises that these attacks
led him to make, and finally Stalin's death.

Grossman himself would not have wanted his conduct to be
explained by his ethnic identity. He always thought of himself as
a member of a single community, the human race, and attributed all the rest of identity to the ways in which individuals
come to belong to that larger world. In the discussions over the
editing of the "Black Book," he took a line rather different from
that of his coeditor, Ilya Ehrenburg. Transcripts of the meetings
show that Grossman tried to avoid excessive repetition of the
word "Jew": Jewish victims, he said, should be treated as
human beings, not as members of a separate nation. They
should be identified as Jews on first mention, he said, but thereafter recognized as individuals belonging to the human race
(Garrard and Garrard, 205). He makes the same point on a
broader front in *Life and Fate*, echoing the humanist thinkers of
the French Enlightenment but quoting a Russian: "Chekhov said
something no one in Russia had ever said. He said that first of
all we are human beings — and only secondly are we bishops,
Russians, shopkeepers, Tartars, workers" (283). Grossman was
suspicious of any kind of nationalism, including that of the "national minorities," the habitual targets of persecution by the
great nations. As he says of the Armenians, in "All the Best!":

"The nationalism of a small country can lose its humane and noble foundation with insidious ease" (158).

This is why Grossman, without forgetting that he was Jewish, sought thereafter to share his bitter experience with the victims of other persecutions, not just with Jews. *Life and Fate* only became possible through this movement from the particular to the general, and through that to another particular. Because he had suffered deeply and directly from Hitler's outrages, Grossman became equipped to understand the Soviet world. Nazism speaks the truth of Communism; the *Lagers* made it possible to know the secrets of the gulag. And that was not the end of it. In the travel notes on Armenia that he wrote in 1962, he reports that an old Armenian thanked him for having written long before of the persecution of his people. "He spoke of his compassion and love for the Jewish women and children murdered in the gas chambers of Auschwitz. . . . He would have liked a child of the long-suffering Armenian nation to write about the Jews" ("Dobro vam!" 220). In that way, the experience of suffering would help others.

It can be no coincidence that Grossman the Jew took an interest not only in the massacres of the Armenians and of Ukrainian peasants but also in the slaughter of the Japanese population. The inhabitants of Hiroshima and Nagasaki were wiped out not by a totalitarian regime but by a great democratic nation declaring its attachment to humanist ideals. Grossman did his homework on the science of nuclear fission (Strum, in *Life and Fate*, is a physicist who makes a discovery related to nuclear explosion; Grossman was, of course, a trained chemist). In 1953 he wrote a short story about Hiroshima, imagining the minds of the men who dropped the bomb, and the minds of the victims. "Neither the little boy nor his grandma, nor hundreds of others with their mothers and grannies, understood why it fell to them to pay for Pearl Harbor and Auschwitz" ("Avel," 18).

Can Grossman's personality, as deduced from his work, explain his metamorphosis? Two characteristics stand out from the start: Grossman's attachment to ordinary folk, and his preference for the truth. Although he came from a cultured background and pursued an intellectual career, he makes clear in all his works that he prefers the common man (maintaining an anti-intellectual and Christian tradition that goes back at least as far as the *Imitation of Christ* but survives as well in Jean-Jacques Rousseau). Wealth, culture, even talent do not suffice to guarantee the worth of a human being, in Grossman's view. "Among the gifted, the talented, and even, sometimes, among the great geniuses of mathematics, poetry, music, sculpture, and painting, there are many whose hearts are empty, weak, mean, indulgent, gluttonous, servile, greedy, jealous — mollusks and slugs who give birth to pearls when their consciences are disturbed and irritated" ("Dobro vam!" 215–16).

One of Grossman's last stories, "Phosphorus," returns to this theme. It tells the story of a group of friends, all of whom are brilliant in their fields: one is a mathematician, another a musician of genius, a third has made discoveries in paleontology, the fourth runs an immense factory, and the fifth — Grossman — is a well-known writer. Only one of them, Krugliak, is not a success, but he is more attentive to others. Years pass, the old friends all win glittering prizes, except Krugliak, who gets sentenced to ten years' hard labor. When he's released from the camp, he goes back to his middling life — but he remains the best of the bunch, the only one who helps others in need.

Grossman's taste for truth was no less marked, and it attracted the attention of his contemporaries: it even provoked a revealing reaction from Maxim Gorky, in the early 1930s. In his evaluation of the first works of the young Grossman, Gorky wrote to the publisher: "Naturalism is inappropriate for Soviet reality and merely distorts it. The author says: 'I have written the truth.' But he should have addressed two questions: Which truth? and Why? . . . Both the material and the author would gain if the author asked himself: Why am I writing? Which truth am I confirming? Which truth do I wish to see triumph?" (Garrard and Garrard, 106).

For Gorky, the grand master of socialist realism (i.e., of propaganda literature) at that time, truthfulness was not a sufficient criterion. In his view there were many truths, not all of which were suitable; in the political circumstances of the 1930s, that meant one thing only — namely that the truth should be told only if it serves the Soviet State. Or you could take it one step further: that the truth *is* what is useful to the party. Clearly, the

novice writer whose manuscript he reviewed had been guided by
a different precept.

In the letter Grossman wrote to Khrushchev thirty years
later, he continued to invoke the criterion of truthfulness: "I
have written in my book what I believed, and continue to believe, to be the truth, I have written only what I have thought,
felt and suffered" (Lipkin, 75). That was why, despite the confiscation of the manuscript, Grossman would not retract or alter
a single sentence. In any case, his critics did not accuse him of
lying; they claimed only that such truths did no service to the
state. Moreover, the method used to keep him silent — locking
away the manuscript — served only to underline that he was telling the truth: lies would have been refuted. Grossman concluded: "I continue to believe that I have told the truth, that I
wrote my book in the love of humankind, with pity for humankind, with confidence in humankind. I ask that my book be set
free" (Lipkin, 79).

His request was not met, of course. Suslov's condescending
explanation was of the same metal as Gorky's earlier comment:
not all truths are fit for the telling. "Sincerity is not the only requirement for a contemporary work of literature"; utility, obviously enough, was just as important. Grossman's book, Suslov
implied, would do more harm to Soviet society than Pasternak's
Zhivago — maybe as much harm as the atomic bombs that the
enemies of the Soviet Union had trained on it. Neither truth nor
freedom was an independent value. "We do not understand freedom the way they do in capitalist countries — as the right to do
anything you feel like, without any regard to the interests of society. . . . Our Soviet writers must only produce what is needed
and useful for society" (Garrard and Garrard, 358). The logic is
recognizably Orwellian.

These aspects of Grossman's character formed the basis of his
new, dissident personality. But before the decisive change could
take place, he had to go through the long, slow process of coming to terms with the death of his mother.

After Grossman's death an envelope was found among his papers, containing two photographs and two letters. One photograph showed Grossman as a child with his mother. The other
was taken by an SS officer somewhere in the Soviet Union,

showing a gully filled with the naked bodies of dead women. That must have been how Grossman's mother's life ended. Both letters are from Grossman to his mother, but they have bizarre dates on them: 15 September, 1950 and 15 September, 1961, respectively nine and twenty years after the slaughter. Grossman wrote to her as if she had still been alive. In the first letter, dating from the time when publication of the first part of his novel had been blocked, he tells her how he had learned of her death — in January 1944, but also, in a prophetic dream, from September 1941. In the dream, he enters a room he knew was hers, sees an empty armchair, with a scarf that had been his mother's draped over it. In the letter, Grossman declares his unaltered love for his mother, and his unwavering pain: he cannot manage to visualize her dying.

The second letter, written when he was in trouble with the publication of what would become *Life and Fate*, is even more upsetting. Again, he writes directly to his mother, he confirms that she is still alive in him and that he loves her more every day. He tells her that *Life and Fate* is dedicated to her, and that the book expresses the feelings and thoughts that she had inspired in him — pity of her fate, admiration of her example. What does that mean to him — the fate of the Russians, or of women, or of Jews? "For me, you are humanity, and your terrible fate is the fate and destiny of humanity in this inhumane time" (Garrard and Garrard, 353). At the same time, his mother embodies the attitude that he admires in the face of sorrow and evil. She had been able to love others, with all their flaws and foibles; she had always been affectionate and generous; the hatred that had pursued her had not filled her with hate. The massacre of the Jews was thus the starting point of Grossman's conversion, but it started him on a path that led him to open his heart to all others, to comprehend and love all human beings. Finding the meaning of his mother's fate gave him surprising strength: "I do not fear anything because your love is with me, and because my love is with you forever" (Garrard and Garrard, 353). Grossman's mother became his "inner witness," giving him strength and courage. The certainty of her love made him feel invulnerable and allowed him to love others. The books that he wrote after this realization are but the translation of a state of mind that Grossman discovered in his mother by imagining himself in her shoes to the last moment of life. Then Stalin's death freed the writer from fear. The next day, so to speak, he arose a different man.

We can now look more closely at Grossman's analysis of totalitarianism. Its main features were far from obvious to a Soviet citizen of the 1930s, 1940s, or 1950s. The worst sufferings in everyday life came from shortages, lack of living space, and the difficulty of getting around. But economic hardship was only a consequence of the structure of the regime. What oppressed Soviet citizens in addition was fear aroused by stories of executions, deportations, and torture; the arrogance of the nomenklatura (the Soviet elite); the unceasing and unbelievable propaganda; and, perhaps most of all, the way that informing on acquaintances and groveling before authority had become normal practice. But those are the external characteristics of life under Communism, not definitions of its principles.

Totalitarian society, in Grossman's view, basically requires the submission of the individual. Such a society aspires not to the welfare of the individual people who constitute it but to the flourishing of an abstract entity that can be called the state, but which is also not entirely distinct from the party, or indeed from the police. At the same time, individuals have to cease seeing themselves as the sources of their own actions; they have to renounce their own autonomy; and they must bow to the impersonal laws of history that are spelled out by the authorities and to directives issued by the various branches of government. From this perspective, Grossman says, "the underlying principle of the state [Lenin] built was the absence of freedom" (*Forever Flowing*, 228).

Marxist theory, the ideological basis for the Communist regime, gives no place to the freedom of the individual. But the Soviet state extended the principle into areas undreamed of by Marx by adding the political requirements of the regime to the constraints of history and economics. "Freedom was destroyed not only in politics and public life, but on the farms — in the right to sow freely and freely reap. Freedom was overcome in poetry and philosophy, in shoemaking, in choice of reading matter, in changing one's residence, in the working condition of factory workers. . . . [Everything] was determined wholly by the will of the state" (*Forever Flowing*, 230–31). The lack of liberty

61

affected all realms of life, including the search for truth, and that turned science into a branch of the propaganda ministry. Consequently, Soviet Russia rejected Einstein's "so-called theory of relativity" (*Life and Fate*, 453).

The terror was not an irrational aberration but an essential tool for keeping the people in a state of submission. It would be a misjudgment of the period and the regime, Grossman says in *Forever Flowing*, to see it only as the "meaningless expressions of uncontrolled, unlimited power in the hands of a cruel man" (230). Terror was necessary to crush all trace of individual independence. "After all, nonfreedom shed that blood in order to destroy freedom": such was the aim (230). The state's police reversed Tolstoy's principle that no one in the world was guilty. "We Chekists have put forward a more advanced thesis: 'No one in the world is innocent,'" says the character Katsenelenbogen in *Life and Fate* (635). Everyone is guilty of wanting to remain an individual, acting in accordance with his or her free will and in the service of others' happiness. Seen in this way, terror is legitimate, and thus the gulag became the symbol of the regime, since its sole purpose was to make people submit to the state. At the same time, the camps reveal the hidden truth of the whole regime. In *Forever Flowing*, a released prisoner reflects, as he walks around Leningrad, that "barbed wire was no longer necessary, that life outside the barbed wire had been assimilated in its inner essence into life in camp" (63).

Where should we look for the origin of the totalitarian vision? Contemporary enemies of totalitarianism prefer to cast it as far away as possible from their own tradition. For the Russian Solzhenitsyn, it can only be an import from the West; for the German Ernst Nolte, it has to have an Asian source, or just possibly a French one. Grossman, who feels as Russian as a Russian can be, and heir to a great literary tradition, wonders first whether the fault does not lie in a specifically Russian taste for submission, even for enslavement. But he draws back from this explanation. "Nor have the Russians alone come to know this road. There are more than a few peoples in the world who either distantly and vaguely or closely and clearly have experienced through harsh fate the bitterness of the Russian path" (*Forever Flowing*, 217). All that can be said is that in Russia and in many other places there is a tendency to think of mind and body, abstract and concrete, the everyday and the sublime, as radically separate entities, and that this can foster the rise of a totalitarian system. Enslavement of the body is more easily accepted when you believe that the soul is quite independent of it.

The first totalitarian state was born in Russia in 1917, and its midwife was V. I. Lenin. That much is certain, and one of Grossman's constant themes is that Yezhov and Beria (the heads of the political police) cannot be separated from Stalin as head of state; and that Stalin cannot be separated from Lenin, who set up the main structural features of the regime. Lenin's primary characteristic was to subordinate all action to a single goal, that of victory at any price. It was Machiavellian to excess, with the end justifying the means, in the absence of any transcendent value. "In a dispute Lenin was not trying to arrive at the truth. He wanted to win" (*Forever Flowing*, 202). He was like the surgeon who trusted nothing but his scalpel, in Kaganovich's story, and who didn't hesitate to cut into living tissue to achieve his aim. Because war was the truth of life, there was no reason not to practice it; and war against domestic enemies is called terror.

The continuity from Lenin to Stalin does not mean that the latter did not try anything new. First, he promoted the idea of the nation within the USSR. From the start, the regime that emerged from the October Revolution had lost any universalist aspiration, since it required the submission, and indeed the liquidation, of its class enemies, "the Russian aristocracy and the industrial and commercial bourgeoisie" (*Life and Fate*, 664). From the start, too, the revolutionary process was indissoluble from the fate of a single country, Russia. In this sense, Grossman writes, Lenin was unwittingly "creating the great nationalism of the twentieth century" (*Life and Fate*, 402). In the early years, however, the national project was masked by the promotion of world revolution. Under Stalin, it became systematized and was turned into the theory of "socialism in one country" (*Life and Fate*, 402). The truth of international socialism is thus revealed as national socialism: without ceasing to be socialism, its aims merge with those of the nation.

The identification of the regime with the nation is what allowed the Russians to pull together during Hitler's invasion. They may have been only moderately happy with the regime, but they arose as one man to repulse the invader and to defend the fatherland. It was the "Great Patriotic War" (which is still the official Russian term for World War II), and its symbolic leaders were Alexander Nevski and Peter the Great more than Marx and Engels. The victory at Stalingrad was one consequence of nationalist socialism openly espoused. But another consequence was the spreading persecution, in the war years, of the national minorities that lived within the borders of the USSR, since it was suddenly remembered that they were hereditary enemies of the Russians. The Kalmuks, the Crimean Tatars, the Chechens, the Balkars, the Bulgars, and the Russianized Greeks of the Black Sea coast were thus deported to the frozen tundra of Siberia. Shortly thereafter began the persecution of another minority — the Jews.

The second twist that Stalin gave to the Communist regime was the replacement of men of conviction who had reached positions of command by their own efforts with others who were entirely subservient to central power. First-generation Bolsheviks had dreamed of turning reality into utopia and were quite prepared to use terror to achieve this; they were energetic, courageous, selfless, but also brutal, impatient, and lacking in concern for individual lives. It was these men who crushed every expression of freedom. But there came a point when these Communist cadres became a liability, and, in a perfectly rational way, Stalin organized the Great Terror to get rid of them.

The new team that settled in after the end of the war at every level of the power structure was not made up of "selfless campaigners" or "barefoot apostles" but of men with a taste for dachas, cars, and the good life. Their enemy was not the liberty, which had in any case been done away with, but the revolution. The initial utopian dream, the idea of a perfect society, ceased to be an aim because it became clear that it was only a means — a means of seizing power, of keeping hold of it, and of strengthening it until it came to occupy the role and function of the state. "The people who created [this state] had conceived of it as a means to the realization of their ideals. But it turned out that their dreams, their ideals were merely a means, a tool, of the great and dread State" (Forever Flowing, 193). There was no longer any room for idealists, for people acting out of their own convictions, even if they were strictly Communist convictions. Because the original ideology was not abandoned, however, the Stalinist period also ushered in the reign of hypocrisy. Language served not to describe the world or to prompt its transformation but only to hide things. A "gigantic charade" was played out as everything became a show: electors pretended to vote, managers pretended to manage, trades unions mimicked the actions of real unions, writers pretended to express their real feelings, and the peasants pretended to slave away at their fields. Only in the theater could you see shows that were not pretending to be something else! To bring off an achievement of that ilk, it was better to use pliant and servile minds and to crush any still capable of independent thought.

Although this view of totalitarian society is based on the observation of Soviet Russia, many of these features were common to Nazi Germany as well. German Fascism was similarly grounded on the denial of liberty, and it treated people as inert matter, in line with other pseudoscientific doctrines of the period. "Fascism has rejected the concept of a separate individuality, the concept of 'a man,' and operates only with vast aggregates" (*Life and Fate*, 94). Like Communism, it also holds that war is the truth of human relations. And like Communism too, but even more explicitly, it combines the socialist idea (submission of the individual) with the national idea (the cult of unlimited power). It came after Communism and must have been influenced by it. "The European preachers of nationalist revolutions saw and understood the flame in the East. First the Italians, and then the Germans, proceeded to develop the concept of national socialism in their own ways" (*Forever Flowing*, 216). Lastly, the regimes made the same use of terror, which allowed Grossman to speak of "the identical creaking of the barbed wire stretched around the Siberian taiga and around Auschwitz" (218).

Life and Fate deals with the similarity between the Communist and Nazi branches of totalitarianism in a grand, almost Dostoyevskian scene in a German camp, where the old Bolshevik Mostovskoy confronts Liss, a high-ranking Gestapo officer and Himmler's personal representative, who tries to persuade him that the two totalitarian regimes are mirror images of each other. In addition to the common features we have already listed, Liss points out that the economic systems of the

Nazi and Communist states are not as different as they seem. "Our capitalists are not the masters. The State gives them their plan" (401). Moreover, the two states have common enemies: "The German Communists we've sent to camps are the same ones you sent to camps in 1937" (398). As for the persecution of the Jews, Liss suggests that "tomorrow you may make use of our experience yourselves" (399). But the borrowings were not all one way. "It was the Roehm purge[1] that gave Stalin the idea for the purge of the Party in 37" (402–3). The likenesses hardly prevent conflict between the two countries but they make the war paradoxical. "If you should conquer, then we shall perish only to live in your victory . . . through losing the war we shall win the war — and continue our development in a different form" (397). Mostovskoy is disturbed but not convinced.

Can this parallel be maintained even in the face of Nazism's greatest crime, the extermination of the Jews? Grossman is well aware of the tragedy through the fate of his own mother. Nevertheless, he sets it against the Communist regime's horrific massacre of Ukrainian peasantry in the early 1930s. It came about in three stages. First, farmland was collectivized and the kulaks (farmers earning more than minimal incomes) had their land seized. They were stigmatized, many were arrested, and some of them (the proportion varied from area to area) were given a summary trial and executed. The second stage involved the deportation of all surviving kulaks and their families to uninhabited areas of Siberia. They were packed into cattle trucks, taking up to fifty days to reach their destinations; many died en route. They were dumped in the middle of nowhere, with just a few basic hand-tools. They had to build their own houses, clear their own land, sow, and reap. Only a small portion of them survived such trials.

The major disaster did not take place in Siberia but on fertile Ukrainian soil. With the more enterprising peasants either dead or deported, a fearful downward spiral began. Harvest yields declined dramatically, while party members claimed that all was

[1] Also known as the Night of the Long Knives, the Röhm purge of 30 June–1 July, 1934 involved the slaughter of about 150 high-ranking Storm Troopers (SA) by the SS, on orders from Hitler. The aim was to eliminate a rival power base in the emerging Nazi state. [DB]

going well. The peasants left on the land were unable to supply the quantities of grain required by the state, so the authorities sent zealots to seize all the peasants' reserves of food and, as a punishment, forbade them from making food purchases in the towns. So the countryfolk fell back first on what was left of their stores, then they ate their seed corn, their seed potatoes, and their livestock. When winter came, they fell upon acorns; with those gone, all they had were cats, dogs, rats, snakes, ants, and earthworms. By the spring, the famine spread far and wide. People went mad with hunger before they died of it. They tried to flee, but the police sent them back; cannibalism broke out. "Deaths from starvation mowed down the village. First the children, then the old people, then those of middle age. At first they dug graves and buried them, and then as things got worse they stopped. Dead people lay there in the yards, and in the end they remained right in their huts. Things fell silent. The whole village died" (*Forever Flowing*, 160). Current estimates put the number of victims of this tragedy at over six million.

There are many differences between the extermination of the Ukrainian peasants and the extermination of the Jews, but there are also some similarities. First, and strangely, both crimes took place in the same area: the *Einsatzgruppen* of the SS — the mobile murder units — operated in precisely those parts of the Ukraine that had suffered the great famine. (Grossman briefly mentions a closer link between the two crimes: Ukrainian irregular forces used by the Germans to speed up the murder of the Jews were mostly composed of survivors of the famine, and they thought they were taking revenge on Russians and Bolsheviks, which is what they assumed the Jews to be.) Second, the victims of the Nazis and the victims of the Bolsheviks were equally passive, equally unable to resist the power of a totalitarian state. Both peasants and Jews were being punished for what they were, not for what they had done. "One thing I am certain of: it's terrible to kill somebody simply because he's a Jew," says Viktor Strum in *Life and Fate* (578). And that is what Hitler did. "But then we have the same principle: what matters is whether or not you're the son of an aristocrat, the son of a merchant, the son of a kulak" (578). The violence is the same, whatever the criterion of exclusion happens to be. "It moves from continent to continent, and sometimes it takes a class form and then it is transformed into a racial form . . . but as an entity its total quantity is constant" (*Forever Flowing*, 240).

To make their jobs easier, murderers always convince themselves that their victims are not human beings, that they are members of an inferior species and thus do not deserve to live. Anna Sergeyevna, a character in *Forever Flowing* who had taken part in the liquidation of the kulaks, puts it this way: "I could see then how people were being tortured and how badly they were being treated! But what I said to myself at the time was: 'They are not human beings, they are kulaks.' . . . In order to massacre them, it was necessary to proclaim that kulaks are not human beings. Just as the Germans proclaimed that Jews are not human beings. Thus did Lenin and Stalin: kulaks are not human beings" (144–45). But they are human beings, all of them. However, people who kill the human inside themselves in order to exterminate others do indeed cease to behave as human beings.

Grossman shows equal emotion and feels equal compassion for the victims of both totalitarian regimes. In *Life and Fate*, Viktor's mother, Anna Semyonovna, is shot by the SS, like Grossman's own mother; Anna's friend Sofya Osipovna Levinton perishes in a gas chamber. In *Forever Flowing*, the gentle Masha dies in the gulag, far from her husband and child, whereas Ganna and Grishka, the wife and son of Vasily Timofeyevich, starve to death. One set of deaths is cruel and speedy, the other cruel and slow, but the victims are all equally entitled to pity and remembrance.

In alliance with the Western democracies, Stalin triumphed over Hitler and drew immense prestige from a victory that allowed people to forget, or at least to minimize, his own crimes in the murderous 1930s. Some people even took the view that victory provided a retrospective justification for the Terror: if Stalin had not crushed his internal enemies, would he have been able to win against the external one? But once the war had been won, Liss's predictions began to become true. It was Russia's turn to impose itself on the Eastern European nations and to deport entire populations. Russia also reopened its camps to accommodate not just German POWs, but Soviet POWs who had just been released — from the German camps! And now it was also Russia's turn to attack the Jews, as it developed a plan to send them into yet another exile — a plan suspended only because of the tyrant's death in 1953. The two totalitarian regimes were not like each other in all respects, but each was as bad as the other.

Grossman offers more than a critical analysis of totalitarianism, although that is the underlying thread of his writing. He sees the enslavement and degradation of the individual as the source of the evil in totalitarianism; this leads him to see the individual as his own guiding value. By "individual" Grossman means both a source of action (the autonomous self) and a target of action (the finality of the other). To put it in other words, Grossman's values are *freedom* and *kindness*. "The reflection of the universe in someone's consciousness is the foundation of his or her power, but life only becomes happiness, is only endowed with freedom and meaning when someone exists as a whole world that has never been repeated in all eternity. Only then can they experience the joy of freedom and kindness, finding in others what they have already found in themselves" (*Life and Fate*, 555). Why freedom and kindness should be values can be explained by the uniqueness of each individual. These thoughts are prompted in the novel by Sofya Osipovna's agony in the gas chamber and by the fate of an unknown child called David who clings desperately to her to the end. "'I've become a mother, she thought. That was her last thought" (*Life and Fate*, 554).

Grossman stands in the tradition of the Russian novelists of the nineteenth century. His characters, like Dostoyevsky's, engage in great philosophical debates; and the structure of *Life and Fate* is loosely based on that of Tolstoy's *War and Peace*. Ideologically, however, the model to which Grossman admitted to feeling closest was Chekhov, because it was Chekhov who brought into Russian literature a new kind of humanism based on the ideas of freedom and loving kindness. Freedom is to be taken in the broadest sense — the individual's right to act as an autonomous subject. In the words of Ivan Grigoryevich, one of Grossman's stand-ins in *Forever Flowing*: "I used to think freedom was freedom of speech, freedom of the press, freedom of conscience. But freedom is the whole life of everyone. Here is what it amounts to: you have to have the right to sow what you wish to, to make shoes or coats, to bake into bread the flour ground from the grain you have sown, and to sell it or not sell it as you wish; for the lathe-operator, the steelworker, and the artist it's a matter of being able to live as you wish and work as you wish and not as they order you to" (99). Humankind is distinguished from matter and from other animals by its ability to choose its own fate, since humans have consciousness; only in death do human beings quit the realm of freedom for the domain of necessity. For that reason, not everything real is rational, if by "rational" is meant not the possibility of knowledge but the ultimate justifiability of things. Everything that stands in the way of freedom in this world is contrary to that higher rationality.

It should be comforting to know that the instinct for freedom is part of humanity's biological nature, for that would suggest that political regimes based on the systematic suppression of individual liberty cannot last very long. Even totalitarian states failed to mutate the species so as to eradicate its yearning for freedom. "Man's fate may make him a slave, but his nature remains unchanged. Man's innate yearning for freedom can be suppressed but never destroyed," says Grossman in *Life and Fate* (216); and the point is proved, he says, by the history of the twentieth century, in spite of the rapid development of formidable tools of oppression in the hands of modern states. But that is only half comforting. The trend of biological evolution ("The whole evolution of the living world has been a movement from a lesser to a greater degree of freedom"; *Life and Fate*, 690) does not necessarily determine the history of humankind. Modern states have more power than those of our ancestors. Are we more free than they were?

Freedom is the first humanist value; kindness is the second. A single person is not a whole person: ["I]ndividualism is not the same as humanity" (*Life and Fate*, 281), for people then become the sole targets of their own actions and not just their source. The highest form of a relationship with another is simple kindness, an act or token by which we make another person happy.

Grossman's concept of loving kindness is at odds with doctrines of the general good, which are all irreparably flawed, in his view, by the value they place in abstractions. But people do not commit evil for evil's sake; they do it believing they are acting for the general good (but are obliged to make others suffer meanwhile). This argument is given its most elaborate exposition in *Life and Fate* by the "holy Fool" Ikonnikov, a prisoner in a German concentration camp who writes a short treatise on the whole issue. "Even Herod did not shed blood in the name of evil; he shed blood in the name of his particular good" (405). Insofar as the pursuit of the good disregards the individuals who should profit from it, it becomes the same as the pursuit of evil. Human suffering derives more often, in fact, from the pursuit of good than from the intention to do evil. "Whenever we see the dawn of an eternal good . . . the blood of old people and children is always shed" (406). This rule holds for ancient religions as well as for modern doctrines of salvation, such as Communism. Projects aiming to eradicate evil so as to usher in a reign of universal good are best left alone.

It was Chekhov who taught Grossman that "grand progressive ideas" should be put to one side. "Let's begin with man; let's be kind and attentive to the individual man — whether he's a bishop, a peasant, an industrial magnate, a convict in the Sakhalin Islands or a waiter in a restaurant" (*Life and Fate*, 283). If we always bear in mind that individuals cannot be reduced to an abstract entity, we may avoid misdirecting our good intentions toward the pursuit of universal good. As Emmanuel Levinas wrote in his interpretation of Grossman, "the 'small kindness' from one person to his fellowman is lost and deformed as soon as it seeks organization and universality and system, as soon as it opts for doctrine, a treatise of politics and theology, a Party, State or even a Church" (Levinas, 230). The truly just do not seek good in this world but practice kindness. They give help to the injured, even if they are enemies, they hide Jews being hunted, they pass on letters from prisoners. There is a scene in *Life and Fate* that serves as an example of the birth of loving kindness: a Russian woman gives a crust of bread to a German prisoner who expects to be lynched. Such kindness is embodied most emblematically in maternal love. That's what Sofya Osipovna discovers at the very end of her life, when she becomes a mother through an act of kindness; and at the start of every life, there is woman. "Everything in a woman — her tenderness, her concern, her passion, her motherliness — constitutes the bread and water of life" (*Forever Flowing*, 115).

However, you can't just say that men and women are drawn

by their very nature toward freedom and kindness, and leave it at that. Whatever their nature may be, human beings are also the subjects of fate and of history, and in twentieth-century continental Europe, history came dressed in the garb of totalitarianism. The system did not recognize the rights of individuals and suppressed their freedom: individuals living under such rule ceased to be good or kind. The pursuit of the general good was their excuse for harsh and selfish behavior. An example: Grishka is a jolly fellow who likes to spend his evenings dancing and singing, but he spends his days hounding the starving Ukrainian peasants to their deaths (*Forever Flowing*). Ten years later, the survivors of these massacres rejoice in their turn as they see the Jews suffer[2] and are able to grab their houses and possessions. "Gloating spite" (*Life and Fate*, 81) is also part of human interaction.

One unforgettable chapter of *Forever Flowing* portrays a gallery of different Judases. Each has been guilty of baseness — by informing on someone, or by spreading false rumors, or through betrayal — but each has his own good excuse. In a totalitarian society, "everyone is guilty" and "everyone is innocent" can co-exist. The Judases accepted as self-evident that the state was more powerful than they were, so they willingly gave up their freedom and thus ensured the state's victory. Yet they did not cease to be humans, to love those close to them, to enjoy good music and great books, to advance scientific knowledge. They were people who "wished no one harm, yet throughout their lives . . . did harm to others" (246). History can be just as powerful as human nature in determining the course of an individual life.

What should we conclude from all this? On the one hand, Grossman leads us toward a conclusion that he does not spell out. What he had learned from rubbing shoulders with some of the vilest murderers on earth was that you cannot get rid of such people by declaring them to be different from others, nor can you do it by blaming it on their backgrounds, or by calling them mad. "It is not the creatures themselves that should fill us with horror," he said of the Treblinka assassins, "but the state that caused them to crawl out of their holes and made them

---

[2] It was popularly believed that Jews had a special role in running the Soviet state. [DB]

useful, indispensable and irreplaceable" ("The Treblinka Hell," 388). It's not "the Germans" or "the Russians" who are bad, it's Nazism and Communism that are rotten. What has to be fought is a regime, and ordinary kindness is not up to such a task. Human virtue is too weak to cure all ills, and the only way to make totalitarianism impossible is to set a different political structure against it. Justice and democracy may have emerged from kindness and love but have grown far apart from simple virtues; all the same, democracy and justice are the only political forces that can stop totalitarianism, by arms if necessary, and make it possible to exercise kindness and freedom.

There's no point making too sharp a distinction between good and bad people. "Good men and bad men alike are capable of weakness" (*Life and Fate*, 840). The distinction should rather be made between people's understanding of their own actions: between bad and good conscience, between memories of successes and of failures. Nothing is ever gained once and for all. "Every hour, every day, year in year out, he must struggle to be a man, struggle for his right to be pure and kind. He must do this with humility" (*Life and Fate*, 841). In the unending struggle for freedom and kindness, the presence of an "inner witness" — the memory of a being who embodies love — can be a great help.

Vasily Grossman took strength from just such an inner witness, and he used it to resurrect himself and to write magnificent works. But his inner eye probably failed to bring him peace or serenity. These are the feelings that went through him after he had surveyed the grounds of Treblinka: "It seems the heart must surely burst under the weight of sorrow, grief and pain that is beyond human endurance" ("The Treblinka Hell," 407). And at the very end of his life, visiting a quaint Armenian village, Grossman confesses: "The dreadful, inextinguishable anxiety of the human soul can't be calmed, can't be fled; silent sunsets over the countryside are as powerless to soothe it as the lapping of the eternal sea, or even the sweet town of Dilidjan" ("Dobro vam!" 194).

Two of a Kind

> The humanity of humans meets its fate, and in
> each age that fate is special and distinct from
> previous ages. The only common feature
> is that it is invariably heavy.
> — *Vasily Grossman, "The Sistine Madonna"*

PEAS IN A POD

The use of the terms "totalitarian" and "totalitarianism" implies that a number of historically distinct states that thought of themselves as opposites actually belonged to the same species. But it is not clear how many varieties the species had. Does the Communist variety include only the Russian type, Bolshevism (irrespective of its subsequent cloning in Eastern Europe), or more specifically Stalinism, the extreme phase of Bolshevism? Does the Fascist variety extend only to the Nazi regime, or to a wider family of Fascist states? If so, does Franco's Spain belong to it?

Whatever the answers, the mere act of comparing Nazism and Communism arouses powerful negative emotions. There are several reasons for these reactions. The main one is not really political. Nobody likes being used as a mere example of a historical generalization. Because almost everything that has to do with totalitarian regimes involves suffering, not discomfort but real pain is aroused. The comparison of Nazism and Communism is often downright offensive to the individuals involved. We would not be so unfeeling as to tell someone who has just lost a child that his pain is much the same as that of many other unfortunate parents. It's a point worth emphasizing: for each of us, our own experience is unique, and more intense than anybody else's. Appropriating other people's pasts to support ideas and arguments quite alien to the meaning they had for the people concerned may seem to many an example of intolerable intellectual arrogance.

Similarly, anyone involved in mystical experience rejects any comparison of it on principle and may rule out even talking about it. Mystical experiences must remain inexpressible and un-representable, incomprehensible and unknowable, because they are holy. We can respect this attitude, but as it relates to the private sphere it does not concern us directly. In public issues, far from ruling out uniqueness the tool of comparison is the only means by which singularity can be established. How can you claim that a phenomenon is unique if it has never been likened to anything else?

The second reason for resisting comparison is just as comprehensible but no less inappropriate in this context. For most people the German variety of Fascism, Nazism, especially its macabre institution of the extermination camps, is the incarnation of ultimate evil. This gloomy eminence means that anything compared with Nazism is instantly associated with the notion of absolute evil. Depending on your point of view, such comparisons acquire one of two opposite meanings: for people close to Nazism, the comparison looks like something of an excuse; for people close to Communism, it looks like an accusation. Things are actually rather more complicated, because there were murderers and victims in both camps. With the passing of time, we are less and less involved with the actual protagonists, but there are groups whose national or ideological positions cause them to identify, albeit unconsciously, with one or the other side. This results in four typical reactions to comparisons between the *Lager* and the gulag, in which one set of murderers ends up quite close to the victims of the other side:

A. Nazi murderers are for the comparison, since it offers them an excuse.

B. Nazi victims are against the comparison, since they see it as an excuse.

C. Communist murderers are against the comparison, since they see it as an accusation.

D. Communist victims are for the comparison, since they see it as an accusation.

There are, of course, exceptions to these psychopolitical determinations, and I will come back to them. But as a first, approximate observation we can say that it is much easier to guess what opinion a person has of a comparison between Nazism and Communism if we know with which of the four groups he or she

75

identifies (consciously or unconsciously). For example, Soviet dissidents and opponents of the Communist system in the final decades of its life found the comparison quite natural. Zheliu Zhelev (mentioned in Chapter 1) was an unknown researcher in history and politics when he began to attack the Communist regime in Bulgaria by writing a book called *Fascism*, dealing with Western European politics of the 1930s. The official censors understood the subtext straight away: the book was banned, and Zhelev lost his job. When he republished the book in 1989, after the fall of the Communist regimes, Zhelev, who could now call a spade a spade, wrote a new preface in which he referred to the "perfect matching of the two varieties of totalitarianism, the Fascist one and our own Communist one." If a distinction had to be made, it would be in favor of Fascism, he says: "Not only did the Fascist regimes end sooner, but they began later, which proves that they were but pale imitations plagiarizing the real, authentic, perfect, and complete totalitarian system" (Zhelev, 15).

People who feel close to Communist ideas or authorities in Eastern and Western Europe are opposed to making the comparison, as are those who identify with the Jewish or Romany victims of Hitler. Sometimes the two kinds of opposition merge with each other (for easily grasped historical reasons, some people have been both on the side of the Jews and in favor of Communism). Germans, for their part, can identify with both types of attitude that Nazism arouses, and, as the recent *Historikerstreit* has shown, they may stress either the sameness of the two regimes or their difference.

We can understand and even accept these kinds of resistance on the personal level (after all, who wants to belong to the family of Satan?), but we cannot allow them to stand in the way of historical research or political theory. Comparison is an indispensable tool of knowledge in these disciplines, and it necessarily produces observations of similarity and difference. The pursuit of knowledge has no respect for dogma, and it cannot proceed by treating each event in isolation (even if people who experienced the event may wish to treat it as unique). Moral judgment should also proceed from the knowledge thus gained and not precede it. That seems to be the current consensus among the historians and sociologists who have dealt with this question extensively already; it also seems to be the general view of European society. It is the view on which the following pages are based.

None of this necessarily proves that "totalitarianism" as such exists. Concepts do not exist in nature, waiting to be discovered. No concept can be said to be "true"; it can only have greater or lesser utility. If "totalitarianism" helps to delineate the essential features of Communism and Nazism, then its use is justified; but if all it encapsulates are incidental or superficial features of the two regimes, then it can be dispensed with. What remains to be shown are the respects in which the comparison is illuminating, and those in which it is not.

Joint study of the two systems can be justified, first of all, in terms of a global typology of political regimes. Totalitarianism is significantly different from democracy, and it is also quite unlike the tyrannies of earlier times. Let me just list here the main distinctive features of totalitarianism that have already been discussed: its need for an initial revolutionary phase; its transformation of collective autonomy into a mere facade; its rejection of personal autonomy; its preference for monism over pluralism, on every level; war as the rule of life; root-and-branch elimination of difference as a collective aim, with the ensuing systematic destruction of a part of the population; generalized terror; collectivization at every level. These features are both common to all totalitarian regimes and essential to each of them.

The comparison is also justified in historical terms. The history of the first half of the twentieth century cannot be understood outside the complex intertwining of the two regimes. It would be an exaggeration to say that Nazism was just a reaction to Bolshevism. Such a claim would also undervalue the importance of local traditions — it is no coincidence that Renan imagined that his utopian society would arise in Germany, nor is it by chance that Tocqueville predicted that Gobineau's book on the inequality of the races would be most widely read in that same country. Nonetheless the closeness of the interaction — both in emulation and in conflict — between the two totalitarian regimes is plain to see, taking place behind the scenes (when Germany took up the Russian idea of the concentration camp) or out in the open, as with the German-Soviet Nonaggression Pact of 1939.

Totalitarianism was at its apogee in Europe between August 1939 and June 1941 when Germany and the USSR entered into several treaties that allowed them to carve up the continent. During this two-year period, the Soviet Union occupied the Baltic states and parts of Romania, Poland, and Finland. With the exception of the United Kingdom, the rest of Europe came under Nazi control, either through annexation, military occupation, or pliant governments in alliance with Germany. A few traditionally neutral nations survived through policies basically favorable to Hitler. If the Führer had been content with this and had striven to consolidate and make sense of these acquisitions, then today's Europe would probably still be run by Hitler's heirs.

Both totalitarian regimes were based on the same critique of liberal democracy and individual autonomy; and both were fired by revulsion at the carnage of the First World War.

Finally, we must state that the Nazi and Soviet regimes can be known and analyzed rationally. I emphasize this because it is something that others have denied. Why should we be unwilling to look at totalitarian regimes with the tools of reason? Perhaps because we value reason highly and thus feel uneasy about granting any kind of rationality to actions we deem abominable. Calling Hitler's or Stalin's criminal acts "mad," "paranoid," "irrational," or "diabolical" serves primarily to put up a barrier between them and us, so as to afford us unconscious protection against their evil. We expel them from humanity by saying: "They must have been mad to do that! A normal human being like me could never do such a thing!" It's a strategy that helps to stop us from feeling threatened by those acts.

But reason may serve evil as well as good: it is infinitely pliable and may be the means of any end. As Benjamin Constant observed in the early nineteenth century, "In the name of infallible reason, Christians have been fed to the lions, and Jews burned on the pyre" (*Religion*, 592). A case in point: Stalin decided to starve the peasant population of the country's most fertile region. The decision was a logical deduction of ideas that Stalin held about the nature of the Soviet state, about the role that peasants should play in it, and about his own role as head of state. It was entirely compatible with the policies of violent social transformation initiated by Lenin just after the Revolution. So there is no reason to talk of irrationality in this case. The same was true of Hitler's extermination of the Jews, which was similarly logically consistent with the Nazi leader's plan for a transformation of society. But the representations, images, beliefs, and convictions that ground such actions are neither rational nor irrational; they are only to a greater or lesser degree just, accurate, revealing, or suggestive. Interpretations of the world are not ever either true or logical in themselves; they differ from each other in degree but not in nature.

I therefore disagree with Raymond Aron on this point as well. In *Democracy and Totalitarianism* he asserted that "the undertaking itself [of exterminating Jews] was as unreasonable in relation to the aims of the war as was the great purge in relation to the goals of the Soviet regime" (203). But it is Aron's claim that is actually irrational. He puts himself in the place of Stalin and Hitler and chooses what seem to him to be rational aims, instead of observing what the aims of Hitler and Stalin really were. The actions he refers to were perhaps not really to the advantage of the Nazi or the Soviet states; but there is no a priori reason to suppose that the actions of the heads of those states were intended to serve such a purpose. From inside the view that Hitler and Stalin had of the world, and starting from the aims that they set themselves, their choices were perfectly rational, alas — no more and no less rational than the choices we make every day to reach our own aims, even if the means used are infinitely less criminal. In fact, in other writings Aron gives a lucid analysis of the rationality of these apparently mindless campaigns.

There is no need to introduce a special category to account for these and only these actions, just as there is no need to invoke "absolute evil" — an evil qualitatively different from all other historical examples, an evil indulged in for its own sake, as if prompted by the devil himself. Totalitarian evil is extreme, but it is not "absolute" — for, even here, the old Socratic adage that no one seeks evil remains valid (but we must complement Socrates by saying that an aspiration to do good can also lead us to do evil things to our fellow men). All actions, even the worst of them, have their reason. Montesquieu wrote in 1721: "No one is a villain *gratis*; there is always a determining motive, and that motive is always an interested one" (*Persian Letters*, Letter 84, 200). This does not mean that all of history can be explained; but it does mean that we should not abandon reason as a tool of analysis.

Members of the NKVD and the SS who put "enemies" to death did so in the belief that they were serving the right cause and acting rationally. As Rony Brauman said, such people do not act in response to the pangs of "some dark thirst for evil" but "from a sense of duty and an unwavering respect for the law and for hierarchy" (*Le Débat*, 144). In his own eyes and those of his comrades, a perpetrator of an evil act always sees himself as a force for good. Even Hitler, whom we now see as the incarnation of pure evil, never claimed to be such. On the path to hell, you will only find good intentions. Seen in terms of individual psychological motivations, what went wrong in the twentieth century was hardly anything new, and not in any way specific to the past hundred years. What was new was the political structure of totalitarianism and the mind-set of scientism that underpinned it: those were the factors that made otherwise ordinary dispositions produce far more catastrophic results than ever before. And the individuals who either chose to do or not to do evil were not different kinds of human being. It is just that one group allowed its feelings of humanity to wither, and the other did not.

The reasoning that led to criminal actions may or may not be shared by others. The significant distinction is between acts whose rationality is purely subjective, existing only in the mind of the individual subject, and those whose rationality is intersubjective, that is, capable of being accepted by contemporaries or by later historians of the period. Only the second kind of rationality can make actions legitimate. Hitler's deductions were not irrational from his point of view: they were based on indisputable evidence — for instance, the observation that a high proportion of the early Bolshevik leaders were Jews. But his deductions cannot be shared, because they run counter to the universal moral feelings of the human race.

The need to provide the population at large with an enemy which must then be expropriated and enslaved is comprehensible in terms of the logic of state power, but by itself the extermination of an internal enemy does not strengthen the power of the state. What the state loses is easier to see: competent and loyal servants, free and efficient labor (a severe loss in times of war). And because these acts do not meet the expectations of people who have not yet fully assimilated the logic of totalitarian power, they have to be kept secret or else disguised. Whereas the *Kristallnacht* riots (when German synagogues were burned down) were widely publicized, the "final solution" remained a state secret. In Russia, similarly, rivals and open opponents were fought off in public; but for the trials of high-ranking Communists, confessions had to be extorted, or, rather, the defendants were required to admit to imaginary crimes in order to be found guilty.

This no doubt explains why people are often reluctant to talk of rationality in this context. But even if the person who holds supreme power acts outside of the traditional logic of the state, he does not necessarily act outside of all rationality. The good that he seeks has changed but has not simply disappeared. The actions to which Aron refers are not "unreasonable" even if they are unthinkable inside the logic of a nontotalitarian state. That is because the Communist project subjects all individual wills to the will of the party embodied in its leader; any assertion of an alternative legitimacy distinct from the power of the leader has to be annihilated. This requirement explains the apparent absurdity of the Moscow show trials, which killed off staunch Communists in the name of Communism.

I think the same holds true of the extermination of the Jews, which was certainly the Nazis' greatest crime. At a particular moment in the war, the extermination of the Jews became an overriding priority for Hitler. There is a similarity in decisions made by Stalin and Hitler that suggests the existence of this alternative logic. It is well known that Hitler reallocated military trains so as to maintain the supply of Jewish victims to the death camps; what is less well known is that Stalin set aside 40,000 rail cars and 120,000 NKVD men to deport the Chechens, the Ingush, and the Crimean Tatars to Siberia in February 1944 when the Red Army was terribly short of men and matériel. Madness? Not really. Both leaders were pursuing their overriding priorities, which derived directly from their political programs.

Whatever the incidental reasons for these historical acts, it is worth emphasizing that they were committed by specific individuals and were not just emanations of the abstract logic of totalitarianism. The Nazi state collapsed when Hitler died, and so no real comparison can be made, but we may imagine that had Göring been in charge of Nazi Germany, then the concentration camps would have run just the same, but the extermination camps would have been stopped. The argument is better illustrated by Russian history. Terror was initiated by Lenin as soon as the Revolution emerged victorious, and it was maintained, with periods of particular intensity, until the death of Stalin. However, there were no murders of high-ranking officials until the assassination of Kirov in 1934 and none after the death of Beria in 1953. Leaders who lost power before or after these dates were allowed to go into retirement (in some cases, under house arrest) and were not asked to confess to imaginary crimes.

The Great Purge and the genocide of the Jews were therefore

81

inseparable from the volition of two individuals, Stalin and Hitler. But that still does not make them irrational acts. On this point I accept Aron's view that "the intervention, not of the personality cult, but of a particular personality" (*Democracy*, 202) was essential. Aron takes as axiomatic that individual freedom is inalienable, and that all actions therefore result to some degree from the will of the perpetrator. This interpretation also implies that we have to pay attention to the motives of people like Stalin and Hitler—not so as to put "intentional" explanations over "functional" ones, in the language of a long-standing debate, but so as to stop ourselves from assuming that these two terms are mutually exclusive.

These especially heinous crimes were imagined and committed by individual subjects. However, the totalitarian context was by no means incidental to them. The system allowed power to become concentrated in the hands of a single individual enjoying total immunity. Stalin needed to get rid of the Bolshevik old guard and to bring terror to every level of social life so as to perfect the regime whose servant he was. Hitler remained loyal to his dream, which was not only to restore German power but also to rid the earth of the Jews. Nonetheless, the structure of totalitarianism allowed these criminal projects to be implemented and to result in the deaths of millions of people.

APPLES AND ORANGES

The family resemblance between Nazism and Communism is indisputable, and justifies not only the legitimate comparison we are making between them but also our treatment of them as two varieties of a single species, totalitarianism. But they were also significantly different from each other, and this has important repercussions—on the typology of political regimes as well as on our understanding of the historical processes at work in the twentieth century.

One way of broaching the question of the difference between Nazism and Communism is to say that their realities were much closer to each other than the images they projected of themselves. There is always a gap between the party's program as it appears in newspapers and propaganda sheets and the reality of daily life under a totalitarian regime, but the gap was much larger in Soviet Russia than in Nazi Germany. The Nazi program was closer to the truth of Nazism than the Communist program was to the reality of the Soviet regime. That can serve as a first major difference. Communist ideology was much more removed from reality than Nazi ideology, and it was therefore a much greater incitement to violence and eventually necessitated elaborate and tedious camouflage to hide the gap between the world and its representation. The Soviet regime was much more untruthful, illusory, and theatrical than the Nazi regime.

Soviet propaganda proclaimed that Communist ideology sought only peace, whereas the Nazis had opted for war. In fact, Soviet and Nazi policy aims were identical — both sought imperial expansion. In this respect Nazi ideology describes the Communist world more accurately than Communist ideology. Granted, the policy was not pursued with equal energy by the two states. Even if the Ribbentrop-Molotov pact encouraged him to do so, Hitler, not Stalin, actually started the Second World War.

Communism calls for a transnational ideal of peace, and it also calls for equality between men. Communist society, though, was anything but egalitarian. As in democracies, some people became richer than others, or were more successful, or rose to greater influence; but the Soviet regime also fostered a system of privileges and castes reminiscent of feudal England or prerevolutionary France. Margarete Buber-Neumann, a sharp-eyed observer of Soviet realities in the 1930s, was astonished to discover that the holiday resorts for ministry employees were divided into no less than five different levels of "luxury" for the different ranks of the bureaucratic hierarchy. A few years later she found such social stratification reproduced in her prison camp, with different food rations for each of the four categories of prisoner. Communist ideology did not openly promote the idea of "supermen" yet, in the country itself, everything was so structured as to produce veneration for the powerful. A particular caste made up of the high-ranking party officials and military and political police officers constituted a "new class," which enjoyed freedom and power that mere mortals could not even dream of acquiring. Similarly, the cult of the *vozhd'* (guide) was much more distant from the egalitarian program of Communism than was the cult of the Führer from the explicitly hierarchical slogans of the Nazi regime.

The disjunction of theory and practice under Communism explains one major difference between the two regimes that has frequently been pointed out. The inmates of Nazi camps knew why they were there, but the political deportees in the USSR — who considered themselves to be good Communists — did not understand their fate. That is what produced the pathetic plight of those (rather few) Communist leaders who pleaded with Stalin to save them and then asked for forgiveness from the hand that was smiting them. They still loved the party even as it punished them. As the party was always right, they sentenced themselves to death.

On the other hand, the Communist program spoke the truth of Nazism at a different level. The NSDAP did indeed proclaim it would restore traditional values and the natural order of things, giving individuals proper roots in the community: it sought to be much more antimodern than did Communism. In practice, though, mass society, modernization, and industrialization freed people from traditional identities and turned them into nameless members of the crowd. The revolution wrought by Nazism was barely more conservative than the Communist revolution — which is why the final stage of the battle in Germany was between Nazis and conservatives.

It is often said that the Nazi program was antagonistic to the Enlightenment, whereas Communism claimed direct descent from eighteenth-century rational philosophy. But this is an oversimplification. The "Enlightenment" was not a homogenous school of thought. It included materialists like Helvetius, as well as critics of materialism, like Jean-Jacques Rousseau; it had a scientistic strain (submitting everything to the rule of necessity) as well as a humanistic strain (where human beings were defined by their freedom). The cult of science was just as central to Nazism as it was to Communism (and on this point the Nazis, Hitler included, had to mask their intellectual antecedents), and both were equally hostile to the humanist tradition. For that reason the difference between the two is better measured by the respective sizes of the gap between theory and practice than it is by any gap between the practices of the two regimes. That said, only Nazi ideology had recourse to the romantic tradition or to mystical invocations of the earth, the dead, and pagan or medieval legends; Communism itself had no truck with such things (though that does not mean that they were entirely absent from the minds of some of its supporters).

Fascism and Nazism are, of course, traditionally seen as right-wing movements, whereas Communism sets itself on the left; and the two parties did indeed find support among social classes that have traditionally seen themselves as "right" and "left" respectively. But we must look for the facts beneath these words. The meaning of the opposition between left and right has changed progressively over the past two centuries to such an extent that it has at times become quite imponderable. It would be too easy to say that "left" means to be on the side of the poor and down-trodden and "right" refers to support for wealthy exploiters; but this simple-minded distribution is hardly applicable to twentieth-century Europe. The first reason for this is the rise of a middle class, which in many countries became more numerous than all the others put together. The second reason is that the right also appeals to the poor; Hitler had popular support, and, to take a contemporary French example, Le Pen's Front national has on occasions been the leading party among working-class voters. Third, Communists when in power are both in a position of dominance and also "on the left."

Nor can we say that "left" means the defense of individual freedoms, whereas "right" refers to the maintenance of law and order and of a strong and centralized state. The very terms, which ultimately derive from the conflict of "Liberals" like Benjamin Constant against "Ultras" like Bonald in the years following the French Revolution, are no longer very suitable. The state has become not just the sole legitimate user of force but also the source of an individual's benefits and protections (it has become a welfare state). In Europe, it is no longer seen as antithetical to individual liberty, since it guarantees it. Individuals' liberty may itself become a threat to others around them — and constraining that liberty may also become a "left-wing" measure. There are no longer any oppositions between left and right as fundamental as the conflict between autonomy and heteronomy, or between acting in accordance with the general will against acting in accordance with tradition. All contemporary democratic political parties grant sovereign power to the people through universal adult suffrage, and they differ among themselves only in the relative mix of conservatism and reformism that they call for — and that mix is often more dependent on whether the party is in power than on political principles.

This does not mean that the left-right distinction has lost all meaning, only that its sense is relative and changeable. In all democratic societies there are polarities — between reform and conservatism, equality and hierarchy, freedom and authority — and there is no reason for the tensions between these poles to disappear, since the positions themselves are fully compatible with the basic postulates of these societies. These polarities are all real dimensions of the human condition, and any one of the poles can be turned into an ideal. As we have seen, the principles of individual and collective autonomy can themselves come into conflict with each other, just as freedom and equality can.

So there's a long future ahead for left-wing and right-wing political formations that make simultaneous or successive use of these oppositions or of others of the same kind; political life in every country will go on being structured by the great left-right divide, not because of any ideological gulf between them (for there is none), but because the pluralist principle can only be maintained by alternation, so that every citizen can make a choice. Consensus is not sufficient to maintain political life in a democracy: an individual must be able to choose between at least two different blends of democratic ingredients and between two different teams. This need corresponds to an ancient if unconscious rule of human society, which imposes a formal framework on rivalry, so as to channel personal ambitions and resentments into common structures.

However important the left-right opposition may be in the internal political cultures of the democracies, it seems to us to be secondary to the opposition between democracy and totalitarianism, which constitutes the very structure of the history of continental Europe in the twentieth century and has played a no less fundamental role in the minds of individuals. This opposition puts on one side the bloc of extremist regimes, whether they be "left" or "right," and on the other side, moderate regimes, which may be governed by left-wing or right-wing parliamentary parties. That does not prevent the two extreme regimes from attacking each other, in words or deeds, as they are fighting for the same space; nor does it prevent the "moderate" left and right from maintaining their rivalry.

There is therefore not much to be gained from setting "right-wing" Nazism against "left-wing" Communism. It is much more important to see both of them as "extreme," as totalitarian and not democratic. As early as 1931, Semyon Frank wrote an essay entitled "Beyond Right and Left" where he foresaw that the growing similarity between the "reds" and the "blacks" would justify their being grouped together in a single category (58). The radical difference claimed by the Nazis' and Communists' programs was not borne out in practice. On the other hand, the two regimes did have quite different genealogies. Communism saw itself as the logical conclusion of ideas first preached by Christianity, whereas Nazism had no respect for that tradition and saw itself rather as the heir of paganism. The former claimed to be the victory of those who had been slaves, the latter set itself up as the victory of the masters, and so on.

The policy of annihilation of "inferior races," in particular of Jews, is often seen as the most striking singularity of the Nazi regime. Let us see how specific it was. The killing of the Jews was not unique in terms of the number of its victims — just as many died as a result of Stalin's artificially created famine in 1932–33. Nor was it unique because its victims died not because of what they had done but because of who they were, "guilty" for the mere fact of belonging to a specific group. The same has been true at particular times for members of particular social classes: men, women, children, and old folk who were considered "bourgeois," "kulaks," or even "peasants" perished simply because they belonged to those social groups, not because they had done anything. The entire class was deemed unfit to live; Grossman was right about that. Nor does the singularity of the genocide lie in the overall decision and planning of the extermination by the highest authorities of the state — that happened on the Soviet side, too. It does not lie either in the fact that the Germans were a highly civilized people living in the middle of Europe, as has sometimes been suggested. Culture does not necessarily produce virtue, as Rousseau told us long ago; we should no longer be surprised when civilized peoples behave in immoral ways. So what is special about the killing of the Jews?

The specificity of the Nazi crime lies in the policy of murder. The idea that ultimate harmony can only be achieved by the elimination of one part of humanity is present in both Nazi and Communist programs. It takes an even more radical form under Communism, which postulated the complete and utter suppression of hostile classes; whereas the Nazis wanted to eliminate specific "races" (Jews) while reducing others (Slavs) to slavery. But in reality the scales are tipped the other way. Although the numbers of dead were approximately equal, the Nazis' systematic destruction of the Jews and other groups deemed undeserving of life has no real parallel. To put it in a nutshell: Kolyma and the Solovki gulags were the Russian equivalent of Buchenwald and Dachau, but there never was a Treblinka in the Soviet Union.

Only in Nazi extermination camps did putting people to death become an aim in itself. Nazi ideologues, had they sought to justify the extermination camps, would have invoked higher aims — to promote the happiness of the German people, of the "Aryan race," or even of all humanity once it had been so "cleansed." But even granted such long-term aims, the concrete action undertaken by the executioners had one and only one end in itself: killing. Which was why special camps were set up to proceed with mass murder: Treblinka, Sobibór, Belzec, Chełmno, and the special "murder sections" in concentration camps like Auschwitz and Majdanek.

The majority of those who died in the USSR did so from a different logic. Death was not an aim in itself, but either a punishment or a tool of terror or else an insignificant accident or loss. Inmates of the gulag died after three months from exhaustion, cold, or disease. No one bothered even to notice — prisoners were negligible entities and would, in any case, soon be replaced. Peasants could be allowed to die of hunger because that was a precondition for the collectivization of agriculture, of the submission of Ukraine to Russia, of the country to the city. Death had no meaning here, it was just that life was cheap. Class enemies certainly had to be eliminated, but that task was going to be achieved primarily by history and by nature (in the form of the frozen Siberian tundra). Nazis treated life just as cheaply in the concentration camps where they used forced labor; but in the extermination camps, death was an end in itself. So despite the similarities between their programs, each of the two regimes had its own specific features in this respect.

Nonetheless we should recall that the Soviet side also perpetrated acts comparable to the extermination of the Jews, although none of these crimes killed as many people as famine, cold, and mistreatment. The crimes referred to here are the mass shootings of social and ethnic groups — executions not of individuals, but of whole categories of people. In July 1937 it was declared to be necessary to liquidate the kulaks once and for all (even if they were by then ex-kulaks). Their deaths were not motivated at an individual level, but by a quota system (about one out of four); around 200,000 people were executed.

The same kind of logic applied to the officers of the Polish army who had been taken prisoner after the occupation of part of Poland in 1939. The group had a social identity (they were officers, and therefore enemies of the proletariat) and a national identity — as Poles, they were potentially enemies of Russia. On 5 March, 1940 the Politburo decided their fate: all were to be shot in the back of the neck. In all, 21,900 men were executed, including the 4,400 shot in Katyn forest. Even in the context of Soviet Russia, Stalin seemed to be aware of the exceptional nature of this decision, and he made every member of the Politburo sign the resolution, so that none could ever say they had not known or were not party to the decision. This kind of systematic execution, which the Soviet authorities long denied ever having carried out, is similar to the Nazi genocide, but it was on a much more limited scale. The Nazis murdered two and half million Polish Jews.

There is another way of understanding the specificity of the genocide of the Jews. It differed from the other great massacres under totalitarian systems by the nature of its victims. The Jews, their religion, and their traditions had played a central role in European history, in some respects comparable with the role played by ancient Greece, over an even longer period. That doesn't make it any less of a crime to murder a Ukrainian peasant, but it does suggest that the project to weed out and eliminate the Jewish ingredient in European — and human — identity has a larger historical import than other extermination campaigns that aimed "only" to murder a given set of people.

The massacres and genocides that occurred within the Communist world are also central to the history of Communism, but in a different way — not in terms of the victim groups that they singled out (which varied through time and by region, as there was nothing as specific as anti-Semitism), but in terms of the perpetrators. Granted, anti-Semitism is closely linked to the history of Christianity, and therefore to the history of Europe, in ways that obviously fall far short of the Nazi genocide. However, the Communist enterprise was a catastrophic conclusion and a wicked travesty of the basic tendencies of the same history — its egalitarian utopia, Christian millenarianism, belief in free will, rationalism, and the praise of science.

Alongside official ideology and the actual practice of individuals, we also have to consider the ways in which people imagine themselves. In this respect the differences are especially wide. A Communist has a quite different self-image from that of a Nazi, and vice versa. This difference has to be taken into account; it is not enough to say that each resembles the other in some "objective" sense. It is an irreducible opposition at the level of lived experience, and that is why a former militant — a former believer, that is — cannot be persuaded that he is like his or her sworn enemy. Within the domain of individual memory, such self-images remain entirely legitimate; but the opposition becomes less and less legitimate as we move away from memory and enter the domain of history.

One conclusion seems clear to me: a comparison of the two regimes is a fruitful exercise, but it does not provide a key that opens all the doors. The same is true of the very concept of totalitarianism. More specifically, I would say that the concept is more useful as a generic than as a specific notion. What I mean is that labeling Communist and Fascist regimes "totalitarian" only suggests their most general features — features that are far from superficial, of course, but nonetheless falling short of a full or adequate description. These broad characteristics serve to reveal and to set the major dimensions of the regimes, but they cannot do more; other variables need to be brought in. On both sides, the structure of the state tended toward unification, but bureaucracy did not play the same role in each, nor did the cult of the leader mean the same thing when applied to Hitler and to Stalin (or even when applied to Lenin, Stalin, and Brezhnev). On both sides terror was present and the camp system flourished, but although the stories of their inmates all have a family resemblance, the functions of the camps were not exactly the same. This list of differences could be extended ad infinitum. On the other hand it is very enlightening to call these regimes "totalitarian" to distinguish them from what they were not. They were not democratic, they did not foster an individualistic society, or humanist philosophy; and they were not at all like conservative regimes or military dictatorships either.

The Reckoning

What judgments can be made of the two varieties of totalitarianism? We must first separate the regimes from their protagonists. Like many other people I consider both regimes equally execrable. The direct victims of both number many millions; it would be in bad taste to rank the regimes by their "scores." A hungry, freezing, louse-infested, and beaten-up concentration camp prisoner hardly cares to know whether the camp is a Soviet or a German one, since all suffering is alike. The Nazis' extermination of their victims has no direct equivalent on the Soviet side — but it was all the same a horrible act to starve millions of people to death within the space of a year.

This overall judgment has to be varied depending on time and place. For example, Nazi dictatorship in Poland was vastly more murderous than Soviet dictatorship; but in Bulgaria the reverse was true. Throughout the harshest pro-Fascist period in Bulgaria, from 1939 to 1944, there were 357 executions, all types of victim included; but in the single year 1944–45, as Bulgaria entered the Soviet sphere of influence, 2,700 people were killed by the new regime.

From a historical point of view, Communism has the central position. It lasted longer, beginning much earlier and ending much later than Nazism; it spread more widely, to almost every continent, and was not confined to the European theater; and it killed an even greater number of people. It is also more important to condemn it from our present perspective: it has a greater power to confuse and to seduce, and unmasking its imposture is more urgent. But there is an obvious imbalance in the way the two regimes are officially described. The Nazi regime is universally abhorred (save by a few marginal groups), whereas Communism (in France, in its Trotskyist variant) still enjoys wide respect. Antifascism is obligatory, whereas anti-Communism remains suspect in many European countries. In contemporary France and Germany, Holocaust denial is an offense punishable by law, whereas denying Communist crimes — indeed, praising the ideology that commanded them — remains perfectly legitimate.

Because of the way Communism ended, by a "natural death" rather than by military defeat, Communist leaders have never been tried, none of them has asked forgiveness, and their uncountably many victims have never been compensated. It would be desirable for the balance to righted, at least on the symbolic and ideological levels, not to mask or to minimize Nazi horrors, but to remember also the horrors of Communism, which are just as close to us.

Let us now turn to the protagonists. Here again we have to make distinctions between those in power and those in the opposition, and between leaders and grass-roots militants. Judgments will vary: they will not be the same for decision makers and for their operatives, who were, for the most part, conformists and careerists (just like most people in a democratic regime), swept along by a raging totalitarian storm.

In countries where Communists never took power (this does not arise for Nazism) there were no crimes to speak of, and we may even be tempted to sympathize with militants who sought only to help the downtrodden and to struggle for greater social justice, freedom, and peace. Those ideals are not specifically Communist ones, however, and were shared by a number of other social and religious movements. What is specific to Communism is not its aim of ultimate harmony, but the means chosen to reach it — the submission of personal choices to the choices of the party, the exclusion of a part of the population (class enemies), the revolutionary putsch and the dictatorship of the proletariat, the abolition of private property and of individual liberty. It also required unconditional support of the Soviet Union and of other Communist states, which were taken to be incarnations of justice, peace, and the good life. These choices were an integral part of what it meant to be a Communist. It is only possible to deny that fact out of voluntary ignorance, or as an intentional travesty.

The Communist masquerade was so powerful that ex-Communists whose eyes had been opened often turned into firm and outspoken anti-Communists. Such turnarounds are much less common among Nazis, whose political program was a relatively accurate description of practice (their own, but also of Soviet practice). And that is why ex-Communists understandably enjoy a stock of sympathy that has never been available to ex-Nazis.

The Achievement of Margarete
Buber-Neumann

Brest-Litovsk, 8 February, 1940, early afternoon. Officers of the
Soviet political police, the NKVD, lead twenty-eight men and
two women prisoners to the bridge over the River Bug. At this
point in time, the Bug does not flow through Poland, as it has
become the border between two totalitarian empires. Germany
controls all Poland west of the Bug, and the Soviet Union all to
the east of it. The two women and two of the men who are sick
have been taken by truck from the rail station at Brest-Litovsk
and dropped at the bridge; the other men have come all the way
from the station on foot. Three days earlier, the NKVD had put
them on the train, under close guard, in Moscow; and a month
before being brought together in Moscow, they had all begun
their journeys much further east, in Soviet prisons and camps.
All the prisoners are long-standing Communists or left-wing socialists; they are also all German or Austrian; some of them are
Jews who had emigrated to the USSR in the 1930s to escape
persecution by the Nazis. They had all been arrested and deported to the east not long after arriving in the Soviet Union.

So they stand there by the bridge, in the freezing cold. They
see a German soldier come over from the other side, and as he
approaches they make out his uniform. It's the steel-gray uniform of an SS officer. The Soviet officer salutes the German with
military decorum, and then the two of them check over the
manifest. There's no escaping what will happen next: Stalin's
police will hand thirty German and Austrian émigrés over to
Hitler's police. Three of the men panic—a Hungarian Jew, an
old Communist who is also a German teacher, and a working-
class lad from Dresden who got mixed up in a clash with the
Nazis and had been sentenced in absentia by a German court.
They all know that for them the SS means death. They begin to
protest and to argue, but the NKVD men hustle them onto the
bridge until their German colleagues can take over. Half an

hour later it's all finished. The prisoners of Stalin are now Hitler's.

One of the two women on the bridge that day was Margarete Buber-Neumann, and she is the one who has preserved the memory of this scene (*Under Two Dictators*, 166).

The Ribbentrop-Molotov pact made the years between 1939 and 1941 an idyll of friendship between the two great dictatorships. As a token of good faith, the Soviet government agreed to "release" political émigrés from its camps and prisons so as to return them to Nazi Germany. About a thousand people, including probably more than three hundred Jews, were thus expelled from the USSR at that time. We do not know what happened to each and every one of them, but the overall picture is quite clear: some were shot, some died in concentration camps, and some — bitterly disappointed by the Soviet Union — converted to Nazism. At that point in history you would have had to be blind not to see the close relationship between Nazism and Communism.

Margarete Buber-Neumann, our only witness of the Brest-Litovsk scene, was born in 1901, in Potsdam, Berlin's royal and military twin city. Grete Thüring's parents were modest middle class people of peasant origin, but they held radically different attitudes: her father admired Prussian military discipline and was of monarchical and nationalist persuasion, whereas her mother held liberal views and was sympathetic to socialist ideas. Grete and her two sisters joined the Wandervögel (literally, "migrant birds"), a nonpolitical, unconventional, scoutlike youth organization (its motto was "Inner truthfulness, outer purity"). As the Great War brought much suffering in its wake, former Wandervögelers sought out socially responsible tasks. On leaving school, Grete trained as an infant teacher and then got her first job. She read and admired the more or less socialist works of August Bebel, Leonhard Frank, and Rosa Luxemburg; and in 1921 she joined the Young Communists. By 1926 she had become a party member, and from 1928 she worked for one of its institutions, the German-language news review published by the Komintern under the title of *Inprekor*.

What was it that persuaded people to become Communists in Weimar Germany? Buber-Neumann often asked herself that question and came up with the following answer. "Conversion" starts with the best of intentions: a love of liberty, that is to say, a rejection of purely conventional prejudices in favor of social commitment, free love, and Bohemianism (which in those days seemed to go together naturally enough); a belief in the equality of all people, whatever their ethnicity, class, or gender; a love of your fellows, a passion for justice, and an awareness of the sufferings of others. If you share all those hopes, then when you open your eyes and look at the world around, you can only be struck by the yawning gulf between dreams and reality. "In my case, compassion turned into a profound feeling of social guilt" (*Révolution mondiale*, 74). A young person of that sort thus feels that he or she needs to improve the world, especially on behalf of its poorest people — and that was precisely the policy aim of the Communist Party.

Once among others of like mind the novice convert acquires several benefits. A sense of community replaces the feeling of isolation that is the fate of all in an individualistic society. You suddenly become associated with thousands of other people who share the same values and who are now your comrades and your "brothers." "WE was a word we saw in very large capital letters" (*Plädoyer*, 37). The curse of loneliness is banished by the sense of belonging to a collective movement. A second benefit is certainty: instead of struggling with doubt, going back and forth, and changing your mind all the time, you now know the right answer to every question. "Suddenly, everything seemed wonderfully easy to understand" (*Révolution mondiale*, 74). As a system of thought claiming the status of science, Communist ideology does not just explain what is but also lights the path toward the ideal. Common sense tells us that progress is preferable to stagnation; and the USSR was the land of progress. The prospect of happiness that it offered was guaranteed by science; and so it became irresistible.

The sunny and positive image that the Communist movement projects binds the convert ever more tightly to it; along with the psychological advantages that the movement provided, it led new members to take the next step, to abandon personal judgment and accept party discipline. That was when converts learned the difference between mere sentimentality in their attachment to the cause of the downtrodden and their love of justice — and the efficiency of organized struggle. "Idealists,

95

reformers, and friends of humanity were quickly made to look ridiculous, then they were scorned, and in the end they were even persecuted by the party. What it wanted was something quite different — unconditional loyalty and the permanent renunciation of personal opinion. It wanted us to be 'faithful to the general line,' as they called it, and to submit to iron discipline" (*Plädoyer*, 34–35). The new member has now learned to distinguish means and ends — or, at least, to separate distant ends from immediate ones. He or she now grants that some actions that contradict the compassion at the root of his or her allegiance may be necessary, because they serve the ultimate goal that has been set by the party. Individual autonomy is laid on the altar of the collective autonomy that the future will bring. At this point German Communists and German Nazis — both of them opposition groups, fighting the establishment but also fighting each other, on the streets — unwittingly took on common features. By laying aside personal judgment and will, by swearing loyalty to a party and to its leader, two groups that had been utterly opposed to each other (one motivated by universal generosity, the other by the defense of its own interests) came to resemble each other. And at the same point in time, the political strategies of the two parties also began to converge.

It is striking how the reasons for joining the Communist Party given by Buber-Neumann resemble religious conversion, which provides many of the same benefits: it offers a creed with elevated ideals, the sense of belonging to a community, and the reassurance of dogma — with loyalty to the party taking the place of blind submission to the church. On the other hand, of course, Communist dogma claimed to be scientific. "Faith in science played a huge role in the light that shone forth in the 1920s from the lay religion of Communism" (*Révolution*, 70). Marx's and Engels's hypotheses about economics, history, and society become articles of faith beyond discussion. In later years, when she lived in the Soviet Union, Buber-Neumann would discover that the same situation held for all other sciences. A friend who was a psychologist complained to her that "we're forced to swallow [Pavlov's] doctrine whole, as if it weren't science at all, but an article of political faith" (*Potsdam*, 388). We can thus see why the Communist regime was so harsh in its persecution of the representatives of Christianity, even though the fundamentals of the two doctrines were not in contradiction: other religions were seen as direct competitors, and there was room for only one God.

Private life as distinct from public life disappears once inside the Communist faith. Grete quickly learned that lesson, to her own cost. In 1920, moving in Jewish left-wing circles, she met Rafael Buber, Martin Buber's son. She lived with him, and as soon as she was twenty-one and legally entitled to do so, she married him. The couple soon had two daughters. The Bubers separated in 1925; one of the reasons for their estrangement was that Rafael had moved away from the party. Grete raised the children by herself until 1928, when a court order awarded custody to her mother-in-law. From 1928 to 1934, she could only see her daughters twice a year; and from 1934 to 1945, she had no contact with them at all. She didn't see them again until 1947. "On joining the party, a Communist had to abandon private life," she says in her autobiography (*Potsdam*, 115).

In 1929 she met Heinz Neumann and moved in with him (she never married him, but some years later she added his name to hers). Neumann was then one of the leaders of the German Communist Party. The son of a wealthy and liberal Jewish family, Neumann rejected all ethnic identity and considered himself to be a citizen of the world. He had joined the party at the age of eighteen, in 1920, and with his brilliant mind he soon became one of its most active propagandists and eventually a leading figure, second only to Thaelmann. Like many intellectuals, he was drawn to radical thinking, and he had no time for compromise or moderation. He learned Russian quickly, gained the approval of Soviet comrades, in particular of Stalin, who treated him as one of his trusties. But Neumann was a man of convictions, not a servant of higher authority, and his radical mind led him to advocate open struggle against the Nazis and against the Social Democrats. In the 1930s, however, Soviet policy toward the Nazis underwent a change, and Neumann's intransigence was no longer appropriate. He was summoned to Moscow in 1932, and he took Grete along with him. Neumann's violent anti-Nazism was now seen as "deviationist"; his criticism of the official party line also brought him dangerously close to the Trotskyists, who were convinced that Stalin had betrayed the Revolution. Nonetheless, Stalin remained on cordial

97

terms with Neumann and even had the couple spend their vacations with him on the Black Sea coast. In her autobiography, Buber-Neumann tells of almost comical scenes during this interlude.

But Neumann could not now go back to Germany. The Komintern sent him to Spain in 1933, and then, at the end of that year, to Switzerland, and finally broke off all contact with him. Heinz and Grete got to Zürich without any documents, and without a penny. They eked out a living for a few months, until Heinz was arrested, quite by chance. His true identity was established; Nazi Germany demanded his extradition, so as to try him, but the Swiss turned down the request, though they kept him in detention. Then the Soviet Union offered to give him asylum, and the couple returned to Moscow, via Le Havre, in 1935. They were put up once again at the Hotel Lux, used exclusively for foreign Communists, but the whole atmosphere had changed. Nobody asked them round for a meal; their old friends were either dead, or too afraid to mix with people of such uncertain status. The show trials were at their height. Heinz and Grete worked for the Komintern's foreign-language publications. One day, Dimitrov, the new boss of the Komintern, called Neumann into his office and asked him to write a book praising the new political line in favor of "popular fronts" — provided he begin it with a thoroughgoing self-criticism. Neumann refused, since he did not wish to write what he did not think. In so doing he signed his own death warrant. The party did not need courageous individuals acting out of conviction; it wanted submissive creatures prepared to change their opinions whenever necessary.

Neumann had a tragic end. He realized ever more keenly that the Soviet Union was a bloody dictatorship quite unrelated to the ideals for which he thought he had been fighting. During the trials he was outraged to hear old Bolsheviks making abject confessions of their "errors" and "treachery" and denouncing their best friends. He told Grete: "I guarantee you that if they drag me into the box for a show trial, I'll find the strength to shout 'Down with Stalin!'! Nobody will be able to stop me!" (*Revolution*, 371). They spent the last months of their lives in the Hotel Lux listening to the footfalls in the corridor, waiting for people to be arrested. It was also the period of their greatest love — as if their political passion had first to fade to let their amorous feelings reach full bloom. The last letter Heinz ever wrote to his wife consists exclusively of all the terms of endearment he ever used for her — and there were more than forty of them! In the night of 26–27 April 1937, the footsteps in the corridor stopped in front of the Neumanns' door. Heinz was arrested, and all he had time to say to Grete was: "Cry then. There's enough to cry about now" (*Under Two Dictators*, 5). He was sentenced to death and shot on 26 November 1937 — but it took more than fifty years for Neumann's precise fate to come to light. The intention had been to have him star in another show trial that never took place. Neumann never had an opportunity to shout out his defiant truth for the world to hear.

Up to this point Margarete Buber-Neumann's public life had been entirely subordinated to Heinz's career, and, in her own words, she had been no more than an "accessory." But Heinz's arrest gave her a new life for which she accepted responsibility. Living with a Communist leader hadn't obliged her to close her eyes to everything around her, but it hadn't prompted her to examine things too closely. When she had visited Russia in 1932, she had not been aware of the famine that was ravaging a large part of the country. All the same, she had seen a hugely long line snaking out of the Moscow post office and had been surprised to learn that the people waiting were all trying to mail bread to relatives. She had also been surprised by the general indifference to political events, as well as by the social injustice and the hierarchy of privileges to be found in the "home of socialism." She also came to realize that the public stance of internationalism was just a rhetorical facade designed to mask the privileged position of the Russians: a better word for it would have been "patriotism." But from 1937 there was nothing to stop her from seeing the world as it was.

Between Neumann's arrest and her own, on 19 June 1938, Buber-Neumann lived through a terrible time which she considered, in retrospect, to have been even worse than her years in the gulag. "The year between my husband's arrest and my own detention was the most atrocious year of my life" (*Plädoyer*, 128). The first months were spent standing in line at the gates of Moscow's prisons, trying to find out where Neumann was so she could send him a little money. She was finally told he was in the Lyubyanka, but in December the prison refused to accept her money. "Neumann? Not here any more," they said (in fact, he had already been shot). Buber-Neumann's passport was confiscated and her work permit was withdrawn, so she had no means whatever of supporting herself. She avoided starvation by selling books and clothes at the flea market. She jumped every time she heard footsteps approaching. She requested permission to leave for France to join her sister Babette Gross, the partner of Willi Münzenberg, formerly a leading figure in the Komintern, but was turned down. It was almost a relief to be arrested at last. She had become one of those German Communists that Vasily Grossman mentions, first persecuted by Hitler, and then by Stalin.

Buber-Neumann spent six months in custody before being sentenced to five years' deportation to a camp, on the vaguely formulated charge of being "a socially dangerous element." She arrived at Karaganda camp, deep in the steppes of Kazakhstan, not far from the Chinese border, in early 1939. It was a huge camp, twice the size of Denmark, with a population of around 170,000 inmates. Surveillance was not very harsh, but escape was unthinkable — there was nothing but desert for hundreds of miles in each direction. Political prisoners were few in number and they were terrorized by the criminals. Hygiene was lamentable; everyone was infested with lice and bugs. But the worst of it all was the way food was allocated by the camp authorities in proportion to work done. Prisoners worked in the fields or in the mines and had to fulfill set "norms." If they failed to reach the norm, their food ration was reduced, from what was at best a meager fare of soup and bread (save for the trusties). The less food prisoners got, the less work they could do; and the less they worked, the less they were fed. Progressively smaller rations brought death from exhaustion and starvation within a few months. Buber-Neumann only survived because a sympathetic doctor among the prisoners gave her a certificate stating that she was "unsuited to heavy labor."

One year later, in early 1940, Buber-Neumann was summoned to the camp commandant's office and was told that she would be leaving. A long journey took her to a Moscow prison, where she had far better conditions — clean linen, hot water, and adequate food. It seemed to be set up so that she and her new comrades in misfortune, all of them women prisoners of German or Austrian nationality, would be restored to presentable form before being sent on elsewhere. But where would they be sent? Not one of these old Communists (or partners of old Communists) imagined for a moment that they would be returned to Hitler. Even when the group — now including men — was put on the west-bound train, they all thought they were on their way to freedom in a neutral country. The truth did not dawn until 8 February, 1940, when they saw the SS officer crossing the bridge over the Bug to collect them at Brest-Litovsk.

Thus began the second episode in Buber-Neumann's life as a concentration camp prisoner. After six months in a prison, she was sent to the women's camp, Ravensbrück, without sentence or a specified term. She did not get out of it until April 1945. To begin with, living conditions were tolerable: the camp was clean, the food was adequate, and there was no hard labor. Things got worse after 1942 and by the end of the war they were as bad as in Karaganda. In 1944 the Germans began to make "selections" of the weak, sick, and aged, who were then exterminated. From the beginning, though, all inmates were subjected to mental and physical torture, which, Buber-Neumann realized, undermined and profoundly corrupted them all: in the end, they all came to adopt the values of the SS camp guards as their own. "Christian morality declares that suffering ennobles the sufferer. That can only be a very qualified truth. Life in a concentration camp showed the opposite to be true more often than not. I think that nothing is more demoralizing than suffering, excessive suffering coupled with humiliation such as comes to men and women in concentration camps. That is true of individuals and probably of whole peoples" (*Under Two Dictators*, 214). Buber-Neumann's illnesses and punishments (she spent fifteen weeks altogether in the isolation cell) brought her near to death several times.

On top of the persecution she suffered at the hands of the SS, Buber-Neumann also had to undergo persecution from the large group of German and Czech Communists in the camp, many of whom held positions of power. She was interrogated as soon as she got to Ravensbrück; and her stories of the Soviet camps resulted in her being ostracized as a "Trotskyist." The die-hard Communists did not see people as individuals but only as representatives of a category. For them, Buber-Neumann clearly belonged to the "enemies of the Soviet Union."

Fortunately Buber-Neumann also met other kinds of inmates. In her first year at Ravensbrück, she got to know Milena Jesenská, a Czech journalist who had been Franz Kafka's lover, and who had been sent to the camp for antifascist activities. The two women became very close friends until Milena's death in 1944. Inka, a Czech Communist who had been a medical student, disobeyed the party line and struck up a friendship with Buber-Neumann; later on, she saved Grete's life by stealing medicines that she needed. She was also befriended by non-Communist French deportees, including Germaine Tillion, Anise Postel-Vinay, and Geneviève de Gaulle. None of them knew if they would ever get out alive; so they told each other what ought to be handed on so that their suffering should never be forgotten. For a whole sequence of Sundays, Buber-Neumann told her French friends what she had experienced in Soviet camps, with Postel-Vinay acting as interpreter for those whose command of German was not adequate (as for Germaine Tillion, she kept up her comrades' spirits by recounting her comical adventures as an ethnologist in Algeria).

In April 1945 the Red Army drew near to Ravensbrück. The camp authorities freed many of the prisoners, including Buber-Neumann. To avoid Soviet checkpoints, she walked westward, and, after a couple of months of wandering through the ruined landscape of Germany, she ended up at her grandfather's farm. A new life was about to begin.

After seven years of prison and *Lager*, Buber-Neumann was once again free, but nothing could be the same as before. Her father had died during the war, but not before disinheriting her and her sister Babette — for being Communists! Grete settled in Frankfurt and tried to go back to her original career as a school teacher — but the U.S. military administration would not let her, as she was already too old. She was asked to talk about her experiences at local Social Democrat youth meetings, but she was warned to talk only about the Nazi camps, not about the Soviet ones. She got back in touch with her two daughters, now grown women living in Jerusalem — but they, she discovered, were ardent admirers of the Soviet Union, the victor of the war against Nazi Germany. Buber-Neumann's biography was a heavy burden to bear.

In early 1946 she was invited to stay with Olof Achberg, a Swedish millionaire who had known Münzenberg and his prewar network and had remained sympathetic to Communism. He was prepared to help the old Komintern stalwart, as long as she said nothing about Soviet camps. The quiet of the Swedish capital suited Buber-Neumann; her protector found her a flat and an office job. And that was where she found her new vocation.

During their Ravensbrück years, Milena and Grete had planned to write a book entitled *The Age of the Concentration Camps* in which they would narrate their joint experience of the two totalitarian systems. But now that Milena was no longer alive, Buber-Neumann resolved to take on that task alone, as a duty toward her friend, and toward all those people who, in one camp or another, had told her, Don't forget me, tell my story to everyone! Buber-Neumann suffered survivor guilt — as did many former inmates — until she had got down to this labor; every night, she had nightmares of camp life. As she began to write, she found, little by little, that her guilt was assuaged. Her new vocation was to be an exemplary, not to say unique, witness of the inhumanity of both kinds of totalitarianism. The amazing vitality of this simple and modest woman — a reward, so to speak, for her long years of camp life — allowed her to become a memoirist and a historian. She went on to write books that fought against ever present evil, to address very varied audiences, to be a witness.

Her first work, entitled *Prisoner of Stalin and Hitler*, which recounts her life from 1938 to 1945, was first published in Swedish in 1948, and shortly after in the original German. The immediate result of this book was that she lost her job and flat in Stockholm, since her wealthy protector was outraged by such anti-Soviet propaganda. So Buber-Neumann went back to Germany. Later that year, the book appeared in English in shortened form as *Under Two Dictators* (Gollancz, 1949), but in French, only the first part, concerning Siberia, was published at that time. The second episode, about Ravensbrück, did not appear for another forty years.

What was new about Buber-Neumann's book was that it set in parallel an experience of both Communist and Nazi systems. On each of these two subjects there were already plenty of books appealing to captive audiences — there was no lack of antifascist or of anti-Communist testimony. What was important in Buber-Neumann, and what disturbed its readership (or, less frequently, aroused its enthusiasm) was the continuity that she showed between the two systems. The closeness was made obvious on two distinct levels — first, by their contiguity, as evidenced by Buber-Neumann's own life or by the NKVD and SS officers saluting each other on the bridge over the Bug; and, second, by their similarity, as evidenced by the description of daily life in Karaganda and in Ravensbrück.

In her historical and autobiographical writing, Buber-Neumann comments on the many connections and analogies between the two political systems, prior to her own experience of the camps. Radek, the head of the Komintern, urged German Communists to collaborate with the National Socialists as early as 1923. The Night of the Long Knives (an internal Nazi Party purge) and the Reichstag fire gave Stalin the idea of using Kirov's murder as a pretext for "cleansing" the party and for making his dictatorship even harsher than before (Buber-Neumann's view of this is identical to that of Vasily Grossman, though she could not have known it). Soviet leaders like Mikoyan and even Stalin had told Heinz Neumann how much they admired Hitler's successes. As for the hold of the police state over the people, Buber-Neumann observes that the Nazis were a step behind Stalin: in Germany, the terror controlled only a part of the population (Jews, active oppositionists), whereas in the Soviet Union everyone felt the impact of the terror in their daily lives. But the comparisons are particularly telling when Buber-Neumann analyzes camp life as she knew it.

Comparisons can be made on several levels. In the first place, concentration camps have similar roles and functions in both systems — to exercise political terror, and to provide the state with cheap and biddable labor. "The two camp systems emerged from very different political and metapolitical situations, but we must not forget that they ended up achieving the same identical ends." That is why they should be denounced equally — and absolutely. "My hatred for German concentration camps is no greater and no smaller than my hatred for the camps of Stalin the dictator" ("Qui est pire?" 244). That said, comparison shows similarities and differences between the two.

In practice, political prisoners of both sides (as well as the "racial" prisoners of the Nazis) lived under the brutal and ruthless control of common criminals. (There were some exceptions, such as Buchenwald, which was run on a day-to-day basis by German Communists.) On both sides, beatings and punishments were common. In Germany, infants born in the camps were killed; in Russia they were not, but were separated from their mothers a little later. The strict orderliness of the German camps was very different from the muddle of the Russian ones, but it is not easy to know which was preferable. "I still wonder which was worse: the lice-infested wattle hut at Birma camp, or this nightmarish orderliness" (*Ravensbrück*, 53). In the Russian camps, as opposed to the German ones, there were almost no real enemies of the regime. In later years David Rousset, who was a political deportee at Buchenwald, said: "We were all guilty. Our strength lay in our guilt" (*Sur la guerre*). But the proportion of political prisoners fell progressively as more and more prisoners without any history of opposition were crammed in — Jews, Romi, and "asocials."

The Soviet Union had no gas chambers or extermination camps. That is a significant difference, but it hardly makes Russian camps nice places to be. Intentionally engineered hunger to punish "inadequate" output, diseases spread by vermin and left untreated, and the bitter Siberian cold killed people more slowly than Zyklon-B, but left them no less dead. "It is hard to know which is less humanitarian — gassing people in five minutes, or taking three months to crush them with hunger," said Buber-Neumann when called as a witness at the trial of David Rousset (Rousset, *Pour la vérité*, 183). The significant difference is more in the role which the slayings played in the overall programs of the two regimes. Ironically, it was the Soviets, whose theoretical framework stressed social and historical processes, who allowed "natural selection" to run its course: in the gulag, hunger, cold, and sickness drove the weak to the wall. The Nazis, on the other hand, who claimed to believe in the pseudo-Darwinian doctrine of the "survival of the fittest," used "artificial selection" at Auschwitz and also at Ravensbrück: the SS, their doctors, and guards decided on which prisoners should die and which should be saved. The Soviets sacrificed human lives as if they were worthless, but the Nazis were overcome by a kind of "murder madness" ("Qui est pire?" 241).

The main difference that Buber-Neumann stresses is related to the opposing ideologies of the two regimes. The Soviets treated their camp populations like *slaves*, whilst the Nazis treated them as *subhuman*. The Soviet Union had two reasons for the camps: to maintain political terror, and to provide free and pliant labor for mines, factories, and agriculture. The latter reason was quite essential, as the gulags were expected to play a major role in the Soviet economy. It differed from the slavery system of ancient societies insofar as the Soviet Union's huge population seemed to provide an inexhaustible supply of labor. Camp authorities therefore took no care of their inmates, did not bother to feed them properly, or to clothe them adequately, or to treat them when they were ill. When they died, others would take their place. In addition, the political and economic functions of the gulag were camouflaged by propaganda intended for Western visitors (which no one in the Soviet Union believed) according to which the aim of the camps was to reeducate people with wrong ideas and to transform them into fully fledged Soviet citizens.

German camps also fulfilled the terror function for the population at large, but to begin with they had no comparable economic role. It was only in the later stages of the war that the camps began to provide a steady supply of labor. On the other hand, they served to humiliate and to corrupt individuals, as if their aim was to reduce people to the status of animals. "The main function was not to foster slave labor," writes Buber-Neumann, "but to exercise systematic torture and degradation" (*Plädoyer*, 224). Furthermore, and this is a quite striking difference, it was in Nazi camps but not in Soviet gulags that human beings were used as guinea pigs in medical experiments. At Ravensbrück, for example, there was a group of Polish girls whose legs were covered with horrible scars. They had been inoculated with bacilli so that the progress of the diseases could be observed. It was because the Jews, the Romi, and the Slavs, alongside the sick and the old, were regarded as subhuman — as incompletely human — that they had to die, without any reference to their possible economic use.

Buber-Neumann did not write her book solely to get over her nightmares. She also considered it to be a weapon in the fight against the still-triumphant totalitarian regime of Soviet Communism. She wanted her exemplary experience to open the eyes of people who had not seen what she had seen; and to do that she needed to tell her tale as simply and truthfully as possible. Such was her duty at that time. Communism was not worse than Nazism, but it wasn't any better either. "One of these dictatorships has now been destroyed," Buber wrote in the preface to *Under Two Dictators*, "and its victims rescued from prison and concentration camp. The other one still exists, and millions of people are still suffering in its prisons and concentration camps" (xii). So rather than just indulge in reminiscences of her past sufferings, Buber-Neumann used her remaining strength to fight the still unvanquished evil of the Communist totalitarian regime.

She was not the only one to do so. Victor Kravchenko's *I Chose Freedom* came out in 1946 and made a great impact on Western readers. Kravchenko was a political refugee from the Soviet Union, and in his book he told of his life in Russia and of the misdeeds of the Soviet regime. The French Communist weekly *Les Lettres françaises* (edited by Louis Aragon) ran a character-assassination campaign against Kravchenko — a liar, they said, because he claimed that concentration camps were rife in the USSR. Kravchenko in his turn sued the magazine for libel. He called a score of witnesses who had lived in the USSR, and one of them was Margarete Buber-Neumann, whose own book was soon to be published in French. The case was heard in early 1949.

A mere slip of a woman, Buber-Neumann told of her imprisonment under Stalin as well as Hitler, and her evidence caused quite a stir. The lawyers for *Les Lettres françaises*, led by Joë Nordmann, used traditional Communist tactics by seeking to invalidate not what Buber-Neumann said but what she was. But Kravchenko won, and the case went to appeal. Before the second hearing, Nordmann's team came up with a letter signed by four Czech Communists who had been imprisoned at Ravensbrück. They accused Buber-Neumann of having been an informer for the SS and the Gestapo at the camp. The libel didn't stand up for long since other former Ravensbrück inmates (French and Norwegian) gave contradictory evidence to the court. Kravchenko won the case a second time at the appeal.

But there was one detail in this episode that upset Buber-Neumann deeply. One of the signatories of the libelous letter was Inka, the young Communist doctor who had saved Buber-Neumann's life at Ravensbrück. How could that individual have testified against her? Had Inka been tortured? Or had Grete simply been wrong about what sort of a person Inka was? Neither hypothesis was easy to entertain. Buber-Neumann didn't know which to believe.

The real truth behind the letter was not revealed for many years. The Communist public relations machine had geared itself up for a damage-limitation exercise over the Kravchenko book. That was why it started looking for other former Ravensbrück inmates in Czechoslovakia. Two of those they found were obedient Communists who wrote what was needed without any fuss. Inka, however, was in the hospital following the birth of her first child. The comrades went to see her to explain that Kravchenko and Buber-Neumann were conducting an anti-Soviet smear campaign. They appealed to her sense of duty as a Communist, and under that pressure, and so as to get them out of the hospital ward, Inka signed the letter. But she did not forget what she had done. Time went by, the baby grew into a young man, and in 1967 Inka made her first visit to the USSR. She was dismayed by what she saw. She took part in the Prague Spring of 1968 and was expelled from the Czech Communist Party the following year. That was when she read Buber-Neumann's *Révolution mondiale*, and it made a great impression. She now had only one wish—to see Grete once again so as to explain her cowardly act.

It took a long time for that wish to be fulfilled. But in 1986, Inka was allowed to go to Paris for a reunion of former Ravensbrück inmates. Alas, Buber-Neumann was too old to travel and did not attend. But their mutual friend Anise Postel-Vinay took the risky step of driving the visa-less Inka over the German border to see Buber-Neumann in Frankfurt-am-Main (for old Resistance fighters that was hardly a major adventure, but it was illegal all the same). Inka wanted Grete to assuage the ineradicable and painful memory of the worst offense she had ever committed. But there was to be no deliverance from guilt. Buber-Neumann greeted her old friends warmly, but she had no idea what letter they were talking about. Her memory had begun to fail—not from political manipulation, but from physical decline and old age. So the human truth behind the letter

could never be told. Inka never ceased to be plagued by remorse. "She cannot unwrite the letter now" (*Plädoyer*, 182–83;
with thanks to Anise Postel-Vinay).

In 1949, the Kravchenko trial had attracted wide international attention, and Buber-Neumann's testimony did not go un-
noticed. Her name became well known, and *Under Two
Dictators* was quickly translated into eleven languages. In 1950,
she appeared at the stand again, as a witness for David Rousset,
the plaintiff in another libel case against *Les Lettres françaises*.
In the meantime, she had started a libel case of her own against
Emil Carlbach, a former Buchenwald inmate. Carlbach had
launched a smear campaign against Buber-Neumann in the East
German press, alleging that she was a former Trotskyist who
had become an American spy. She claimed she had been unjustly
persecuted in the USSR and then handed over by the NKVD to
the SS, despite being a Communist at the time. But the real
truth, according to Carlbach, was that she was already a Gestapo agent — as were all the Trotskyists! — who had luckily been
spotted by the ever vigilant Soviet police and handed back to
her masters, the Gestapo, who still had use for her. The case
was won by Buber-Neumann, though it took until 1952 to get a
verdict. Even then Communist media didn't stop repeating the
same libels (*Plädoyer*, 53–63; see also Schafraneck).

Over the following years, Buber-Neumann gave many public
lectures on her own life and on her understanding of the Communist world. She was an enthusiastic member of the international Congress for Cultural Freedom, which aimed to act as a
counterweight to Soviet propaganda and was led most notably
by former members of Willy Münzenberg's network, such as Arthur Koestler and Manès Sperber. She also ran a Committee for
the Liberation of Victims of Totalitarian Arbitrariness and welcomed the emergence of the dissident movement in Eastern Europe. In 1957 she published a further volume of her
autobiography, covering the period 1901–37, under the title
Von Potsdam nach Moskau. Stationen eines Irrwegs (From Potsdam to Moscow: Stages on the wrong road) — a remarkable
book (yet to be translated into English) which makes it easier to
understand how people became Communists in the interwar
years.

In 1963 Buber-Neumann kept the second of the two promises

she had made to Milena Jesenská at Ravensbrück. She published a book about Milena, which marked a new phase in writing about the concentration camps, since it focuses not on the author's own experience but on that of another person. Meeting Milena had changed Buber-Neumann's life, to such an extent that led her to write the following astounding sentence: "I thank my fate for having sent me to Ravensbrück and thus to have allowed me to meet Milena" (*Ravensbrück*, 40). Her attachment to Milena had had a high price. When Milena died, Buber-Neumann felt her life had lost all meaning, and for a time she even lost her appetite for freedom. When she settled down to writing the life of Milena, twenty years later, Buber-Neumann did not rely solely on memory, but she researched what her friend's life had been before they met. She achieved the effect she sought. Milena's is no longer a forgotten name, the obscure addressee of Franz Kafka's love letters. Thanks to Buber-Neumann she has become a real person, an author in her own right, and the model of a generous friend.

Buber-Neumann's subsequent works were more historical than testimonial. In *Kreigsschauplätze der Weltrevolution* (Theaters of the world revolution) (1967) and in *Der Kommunistische Untergrund* (The Communist underground) (1970), she analyzes the history of the international Communist movement between the two world wars. But she returned to testimonial literature in her last writings. *Die Erloschene Flamme* (The extinguished flame) is a set of portraits of people she had known, and *Freiheit du bist wieder mein . . .* (Freedom, you are mine again . . .) is the last volume of her autobiography, covering the period 1946–51. She also worked for radio and television in the 1950s and 1960s, but after 1968 she had to put up with onslaughts from the "New Left," which was no keener than the old on being reminded how close Stalin had been to Hitler.

Buber-Neumann died in November 1989, a few days after the fall of the Berlin Wall. In our eyes, today, she was the outstanding witness of the totalitarian evil that dominated European political life in the twentieth century. What made her such a model of testimony — "exceptional," in the words of Albert Béguin in 1949, "an absolute witness" according to Alain Brossat, writing in 1999 — was, first of all, the life that she lived, but, perhaps more important, the attitude that she took to it. She was upstanding and rigorous, and in her memoirs she tells only what she saw and learned at first hand. She puts facts before opinions, she does not glorify her own role in things, nor does she always put herself in center stage. She respects nuance in a world of conflict between absolute truths; and she makes her journey to hell and back not entirely bleak. Her books even give the reader reasons to place a little more trust in human resilience, because they show us a former deportee with a sense of humor, a commitment to fairness, and a good ear for the art of storytelling. Buber-Neumann herself did not sink into despair in the camp because she remained attentive to the signs of human goodness, however infrequent they may have been. What she best liked to recall of the months that she spent in the punishment cells in Karaganda was not the hunger or the nights spent fighting off lice and bugs, but the cigarettes that a comrade in misfortune rolled for her, and the songs that he sang.

Alongside her exemplary fate and the high quality of her testimony, the most impressive thing about Buber-Neumann is the simple fact that she survived seven years of camp life in often quite atrocious conditions. How did she do it? She gave several answers to that question. She had excellent health at the start of her ordeal; she came from a family accustomed to hard work; and her earlier life in the Communist underground had taught her not to trust appearances. She managed to remain curious about the world and about people, and it is this, combined with her astounding recall of details, that makes her books so remarkable. She also retained an interest in spiritual life, and that is what helped her escape from the dreadful material life to which she was subjected day and night. But above all else, it was probably Buber-Neumann's gift for friendship and companionship that allowed her to survive. "Knowing you were needed by another human being was what gave you the greatest strength in the camp" (*Plädoyer*, 124). In that respect, she was lucky: "I've always found people who needed me" (*Ravensbrück*, 73). The prime friend and "needer" was Milena.

In all the people she came across, Buber-Neumann knew how to separate the individual from the ideological or sociological class that he or she was supposed to incarnate. It's an observation she made even before the war — any two Communists belonging to different factions only need to spend a short while

111

talking to each other for them to discover that, despite being sworn enemies with nothing but scorn for their opponent, they have lots in common and can be friends. Or, to take another example: a Paris hotelkeeper who refused on principle to allow children to stay, but who gurgled with delight the first time a real baby turned up. Buber-Neumann turned this observation into a personal rule: political commitment does not occupy the entire space of an individual's being; people's own history is only rarely in phase with social, political, and national history. When she saw Allied bombers appear in the sky over Ravensbrück, she was overjoyed, since Germany's defeat would hasten the collapse of Nazism—but she could not stop herself thinking about all the non-Fascist Germans on whom the incendiary bombs would fall just the same (*Ravensbrück*, 110). After the war she carried on refusing to equate people with the jobs they did—even when, one evening, the chief guard at Ravensbrück, Langefeld, came knocking at her door in Frankfurt.

Heinz Neumann has a special place in Buber-Neumann's books. In retrospect, she could see his weaknesses and his mistakes, and she rejected all his ideas and acts. All the same, for eight unforgettable years, he had been the love of her life. The fanatical Communist and dogmatic Stalinist had also been a loving and vulnerable human being. Buber-Neumann was able to maintain an unyielding stand on ideas and regimes while remembering that they only manifest themselves through human beings worthy and capable of love. So Buber-Neumann's clearheadedness about bad ideas sits alongside considerable fidelity to people who held them. That was the last lesson taught us by a woman whose life story is inseparable from a history of the twentieth century.

Preserving the Past

The Madonna has lived everything through us,
for she is within us, her son is within us.

It seems to me that this Madonna is the most
atheistic expression of life, of the human
without divine participation.
— *Vasily Grossman*, "The Sistine Madonna"

THE CONTROL OF MEMORY

The totalitarian regimes of the twentieth century sought to
achieve total control of memory. Such a dangerous ambition had
never been thought of before. Admittedly, rough and ready stabs
at steering collective memory were made in earlier ages through
the destruction of documents and public monuments. To take a
fairly distant case in point, the Aztec emperor Itzcoatl (early fifteenth century) destroyed all the stelae and codices in his domain
so as to remake Aztec traditions to his own liking. A hundred
years later, the Spanish conquerors of South America made great
efforts to uproot and put to the flame anything that bore witness
to the former grandeur of the vanquished. Because they were not
totalitarian, however, Aztecs and conquistadors attacked only the
official repositories of memory, and they let many other forms of
remembrance survive, in oral narratives and poetry, for instance.
But the tyrants of the twentieth century realized that mastery of
information was the key to the conquest of peoples and lands.
They sought to capture memory systematically and to bring even
its most secret repositories under control. Their plans did not always work out, but there can be little doubt that all trace of some
past events (by definition, we cannot know which) have been utterly destroyed.

There are innumerable well-known examples of attempts to
control memory. "The entire history of the brief 'millennial Reich'

can be reread as a war against memory," wrote Primo Levi (*The Drowned and the Saved*, 31); the same could be said of the USSR or of Communist China. One of the most widespread techniques used in all these societies to thwart the free circulation of knowledge could be called *wiping out the evidence*. From summer 1942, and to a greater extent after Stalingrad, the Nazis began unburying old corpses so as to cremate them. Inside their camps, they built huge incinerators for this purpose. Next, the witnesses and operatives of the massacres were eliminated. So nothing but dust remained. The Communist regimes were not so concerned to eliminate every trace, since they believed they would be in power for all eternity; vast burying grounds are to be found in the frozen wastes of the northern parts of the former USSR. Before they evacuated the camps, the SS burned all their archives and any paperwork that might incriminate them. We still don't know if the various security services of the old Soviet Union did the same when their regime fell.

A second technique was to *intimidate* people and to forbid them to seek information or to pass it on. Listening to foreign radio stations was banned in Nazi Germany and in Soviet Russia; overseas broadcasts were in any case jammed. The bans applied also to those involved in state crimes. "All SS who took part in the extermination campaign were given the strictest orders to remain silent on the matter," according to Auschwitz commandant Rudolf Höss. When the camps were shut down, many of the SS were sent to the most dangerous parts of the front. One of the major reasons why extermination camps replaced the mobile death squads (*Einsatzgruppen*) was because the latter involved far too many people for the genocide to stay secret. Higher ranks were of course kept informed, but Himmler appealed to their sense of responsibility to be the keepers of a secret on behalf of the German people, who might not be strong or hardhearted enough to bear it. Speaking to a group of SS commanders, Himmler asked his listeners to "take the secret with them to the grave," adding that the Final Solution was a glorious page of history that would never be written (*Procès*, 145). But how could a never-mentioned fact contribute to Nazi glory? Only Hitler, at the pinnacle of the leadership, dreamed of commemorating the extermination one day by placing bronze plaques on the sites of the crime.

114

In Communist countries the ban on knowing applied to huge areas of life, but it affected most especially anything to do with the gulag. People had only the vaguest intimations of what was really happening. Camp guards were put under the official secrets act and inmates who had a greater chance of getting out alive were required to swear an oath of silence or else risk another sentence. On the Solovki Islands, it is said, they shot the seagulls so they couldn't be used as carrier pigeons. When a prisoner's wife was allowed a visit, "she must sign a declaration, promising not to disclose, by even one word, after her return home, what she had seen of the camp through the barbed wire"; and the prisoner, for his part, had to sign a similar declaration "not to mention in conversation his and his fellow-prisoners' life and conditions in the camp" (Herling, 88, 89). In Bulgaria, too, prisoners freed from the camps had to sign a statement that they would never say anything about what they had seen during detention; if they did, they would be liable to a charge of "spreading false rumors," and the whole business would start up again. Many former camp inmates did not speak about what they had experienced for twenty years.

A third means of hiding reality and erasing all traces of memory was the use of *euphemism*. Under the Nazi regime there were numerous expressions for alluding to the great secret of the extermination camps. The meaning of these formulas — "final solution," "special treatment" — is now well known, but even at the time they were not terribly hard to decode ("special treatment is carried out by hanging"; Kogon, Langbein, and Rückerl, 6). As soon as their secret meaning became known, they had to be replaced by new, even more impenetrable formulas, which could also quickly become unusable — words like "evacuation," "deportation," "transportation." There were many official circulars on the proper use of these terms. The aim of such euphemisms was to prevent some kinds of reality from having an existence in the language, and thus to make it easier for operatives to carry out their tasks. Twenty years after the end of the war, Adolf Eichmann carried on using terms like "Jew-free zone," "the evacuation of all Jews to Auschwitz," "wearing myself out with all this deportation business." These expressions made the massacres more acceptable in his eyes; as he explained at his trial, it was better "to speak of this with more humanity."

The transformation of language went well beyond this handful of notorious euphemisms and constituted what the anti-Nazi philologist Victor Klemperer called LTI, *lingua tertii imperiii*, the "language of the Third Reich." On the Communist side, the whole language was similarly infected, resulting in what George Orwell called "Newspeak," a language made of fixed formulas quite disconnected from anything real.

The last main tactic used to control information and to manipulate memory is the simplest of all—lying, or, in more polite language, propaganda. The Nazi regime was considered to have had great mastery in the art of propaganda even in its early years, and the skills of Göbbels, the propaganda minister, were cited alternately with fear and admiration. But if we look at both totalitarian systems and compare them, we have to admit that the Nazis were just clumsy beginners in this domain. Significantly, every Communist Party cell had to have its "agitprop" supremo, where "agit" stands for "agitation" and means indoctrination, and "prop" is short for "propaganda."

Taking a leaf out of Potemkin's book (Catherine the Great's favorite statesman put up apparently prosperous artificial villages ahead of the empress's carriage, and dismantled them after she had passed), the Soviet security services were not at all worried about hosting foreign visitors, and the more intellectual they were, the better. Édouard Herriot, the left-wing French prime minister, visited Ukraine at the time of the famine. He met only smiling children who said they had meat pies every day. He asked to visit a church, and so the Cheka turned a warehouse that had been a church back into an appropriate stage set, where they dressed up in disguise as worshipers, and their local commander stuck on a false beard and pretended to be the priest. Herriot was hoodwinked and entirely reassured. Romain Rolland, the French novelist, also visited the Soviet Union and was taken to a camp by the sinister head of the secret police, Yagoda. He saw a show put on by the inmates, which persuaded him that "reeducation through labor" was a wonderful pedagogic experiment from which New Man might well emerge. George Bernard Shaw also visited the camps and sang their praises; as did Maxim Gorky (but he may have had other reasons for not speaking the truth). During the war, U.S. vice-president Henry Agard Wallace went to Magadan, a slave-labor camp city in Siberia, and his wildly enthusiastic report on what he saw is a stunning example of self-deception (Wallace and Steiger, *Soviet Asia Mission*, 33; see also Culver and Hyde, *American Dreamer*, 339).

The case of Jerzy Gliksman is particularly instructive. A socialist Jew from Poland, Gliksman went to the USSR in 1935 as a tourist and sympathizer. Since he had trained as a lawyer, he asked to see a reeducation camp. He was taken to Bolshevo, not far from Moscow, where he was struck with wonderment by the glowing good cheer of reeducated teenage delinquents. Five years later, he happened to be in that part of Poland that was occupied by the Red Army in execution of the Ribbentrop-Molotov nonaggression pact. That was how he got his second, involuntary, and much more extended stay in a Soviet camp, and he came away with a rather different impression. Convincing stage sets regularly fooled foreign observers (though it is true that they wanted to be fooled). The Nazis never managed to do that.

The Nazis did make a propaganda film of the Theresienstadt concentration camp, and it can be viewed at the camp museum at Terezin, in the Czech Republic. It was the most presentable of the camps, a kind of "model camp" (but its inmates were regularly "transported" to Auschwitz), and it could thus be shown to the outside world. But when we see the film today, we see it as an utter indictment of the Nazis. Their attempts to embellish the camp were crude and transparent, and what they showed is hardly cheering: the football teams play with suspicious ardor, the barracks are overcrowded, and the inmates' eyes, when the camera catches them, are desperate. The Soviets produced a similar sort of film about the Solovki Islands, and that too is a clumsy and transparent fabrication. The prisoners are obviously pretending to be keen, their smiles are self-evidently insincere. But we should think rather of the vast number of Soviet books and films that flooded the world for decades on end with their images of an achievable happiness, of a land of socialism and justice, of paradise on earth, which gave millions of people reasons to live and to hope. This image still lingers in various remote corners of the world. Under Hitler, young Germans must have been just as hoodwinked as my friends and I were when we were at school in Sofia; but outside of Germany Nazi propaganda never had anything like the impact of the Communist variety.

These techniques and more were systematically used by totalitarian regimes to ensure victory not just in the war on the ground but also in the information war. Because control of information was given high priority by Nazis and Communists, their enemies put immense effort into countering it. Spreading awareness and understanding of totalitarianism and, in particular, of its worst excess, the camp system, was, in the first place, the inmates' only survival mechanism. But that was not all: telling the world about the camps was the best means of combating them, and it was worth making sacrifices to achieve this end. That is no doubt why forced laborers in Siberia cut off their own fingers and tied them to the logs that were floated down-river: gruesome bottles cast in the sea, these messages told whomever found them by what sort of worker the log had been felled. Information that leaked out did save lives. One of the reasons why the deportations of Hungarian Jews were stopped in summer 1944 was because Vrba and Wetzler had managed to escape from Auschwitz and to pass on a message about what was going on there. Obviously, actions of this kind were extremely dangerous. Anatolii Marchenko, who had done time in the gulag, managed to publish his testimony, but it earned him a new sentence, and he ended up dying in detention.

In this context it is easy to understand why memory has acquired an aura of prestige among the enemies of totalitarianism, why even the humblest act of recollection has been assimilated to antitotalitarian resistance. (Before it was appropriated by an anti-Semitic organization, the Russian word *pamyat'*, "memory," was used as the series title for a remarkable samizdat collection when recollection of the past still counted as an act of opposition against the authorities.) Free access to the past unfettered by centralized control is one of the fundamental, inalienable freedoms of democratic countries, alongside freedom of expression and freedom of thought. It is particularly useful for the darkest episodes in those countries' own history. For instance, there is perhaps no fully adequate account of France's colonial history, but in principle no obstacle stands in the way of such an account being written. In the immediate aftermath of the Second World War, the role of Vichy was certainly presented in an attenuated and prettified manner, but nowadays the study and analysis of that period can be conducted without any political opposition. By the same token, research on the past history of totalitarian regimes is also unconstrained. Nazi crimes are amongst the best-documented facts in the history of the twentieth century. The offenses committed under Communist regimes are less prominent in collective memory, but they can hardly be said to be unknown, as they were in the years after 1945. The *Black Book of Communism*, edited by Stéphane Courtois, was a bestseller in several European countries.

All the same, the status of memory in democratic societies does not seem to be guaranteed for all time. Perhaps because of the standing of some talented writers having lived under totalitarian regimes, the valuation of memory (together with its corollary, an attack on forgetting) has been applied in recent years far beyond its original context. We often hear the liberal democracies of Western Europe and North America reproached for aiding and abetting the decline of memory and installing a reign of forgetting. As we drown in an ever growing flood of information, we are accused of being destined to evacuate it at the same speed. We have been cut off from our traditions, such critics say; we have been dumbed down by the leisure society; we have lost our spiritual curiosity and no longer know the great works of the past; and so we are condemned to the vain pleasures of the instant and to the crime of forgetting. By this argument, democratic states would be leading people along the same path as totalitarian ones — less roughly, to be sure, but actually more effectively, because their techniques provoke no resistance and make us all consenting participants in the long march to obliviousness.

When applied in such broad and general terms, however, unconditional support of memory and the ritual disparagement of forgetting themselves become problematic positions. The emotional charge of everything related to the totalitarian past is huge, and people who are subject to it mistrust all attempts at clarification, all calls for analysis prior to the making of judgments. But the stakes of memory are too high for us to allow them to be dictated by enthusiasm or anger. We must begin by acknowledging the main features of a complex field — the ways in which the past lives on in the present.

THE THREE STAGES

Past events leave two kinds of trace: "mnesic" traces in people's minds; and material ones in the outside world, such as a footprint, a vestige, a letter or a decree (for words are also facts). These kinds of traces have much in common with each other. First, they are only small parts of past events, the remainder having been lost forever; second, they are usually not voluntary traces but the result of chance events or of unconscious drives. For most historical traces, no one decided that they should survive — the great exceptions being, of course, those ancient and modern tyrants who tried to preselect what would survive them. The eruption of Vesuvius killed all living things in some of the towns and villages close to the volcano, but by the same token it preserved them under ash for all eternity; it spared other nearby towns, which as a result have been entirely lost to memory. It is the same at the individual level; whether we like it or not, we can't choose what to forget or to remember. Some memories we would rather be without, but they come back to haunt us night after night. The Greeks were well aware that memory could not be tamed by the will; according to Cicero, Themistocles, who was famous for his powers of recall, complained: "Nam memini etiam quae nolo, oblivisci non possum quae volo" (I remember even what I do not want to remember, and I cannot forget what I wish to forget; quoted in Weinrich, 25).

But if we want to make the past live on in the present, we have to work through three stages. In practice these three levels of memory-work overlap and may occur in any order; I lay them out as stages for the sake of clarity.

Establishing the Facts

Everything has to rely on this groundwork, without which we cannot even really talk about working on the past. Before asking any other questions we need to know: where did Captain Dreyfus's famous "slip" come from? And was Dreyfus a traitor or not? Was it the Germans or the Russians who gave the order to shoot in Katyn forest? Were the gas chambers of Auschwitz intended for men or for lice? This is where we must draw the line between historians and frauds. It's just the same in daily life: we have to make discriminations between reliable witnesses and mythomaniacs. In the private as in the public sphere, lies, misrepresentations, and pure fictions have to be mercilessly rooted out if we really wish to resurrect the past and not just confirm our own prejudices.

Seeking out the past does not automatically make it alive in the present. Only a few mental and material traces of what was are available to us; a process of selection, over which we have no control, has already occurred between the facts of the past and the traces they have left. But now there has to be a second selection procedure, which is conscious and voluntary: we have to choose which of the surviving traces of the past to use, which of them we judge, for one reason or another, to be worthy of perpetuation. As we make such choices, we also discriminate between traces and rank them in terms of their importance: some will seem central and others only marginal to the work of memory.

In some cases the recovery of the past may be halted at this stage. An outstanding example of this kind of memory can be seen in Serge Klarsfeld's *Memorial of the Deportation*. Nazi executioners wanted to annihilate their victims without leaving any trace: with moving simplicity, the *Memorial* lists the names of all French Jewish deportees together with their place and date of birth, and the date of their departure to the extermination camps. In this way Klarsfeld restores human dignity to the dead. Life lost out to death, but memory has won a victory here in its battle against oblivion. A monument of like kind was the publication in 1997 of documents relating to the so-called Katyn massacre, when all Polish POWs of officer rank were shot without trial in 1940 (Pikhoia and Geishtor, *Katyn*). Promoted by Aleksandr Yakovlev, the former aide to Mikhail Gorbachev, the Katyn volume establishes the facts, independently of all questions concerning the ultimate meaning of the event or the use that was made of it. Establishing the facts is a worthy end in itself.

As we have seen, in democracies no constraint should be placed on this first phase of working on the past. There should be no higher authority in the state that can say, you don't have the right to look for the truth on your own, or, people who don't accept the official version of the past will be punished. Autonomy of judgment is the very lifeblood of democracy: individuals and groups have a right to knowledge, and consequently a right to know their own history and to make it known to others, and the state has no business forbidding or permitting such actions. But when individuals or groups have experienced extreme or tragic events, their right is also a duty — the duty of remembering and bearing witness.

A minor consequence of this requirement is that it is wrong to legislate on the facts of history. Even though it was passed with the best of intentions, the recent French law making Holocaust denial an offense is inappropriate. Existing legislation allows charges of libel and of incitement to racial hatred to be brought to protect individuals affected by negationist nonsense; but law-courts are not the right places to establish historical facts, however grave.

Construction of Meaning

The difference between the first and second stages in the appropriation of the past is the same as the distinction between constituting an archive and writing history in the proper sense. In working with the past, construction of meaning has to follow the establishment of the facts. Facts, once known, have to be interpreted — they have to be fitted together, strung out along the line of cause and effect, compared with each other, distinguished from each other, and set against each other. Selection and combination are once again the primary tools. But the criteria by which we judge the writing of history are different from those that apply to the first stage of factual research. Facts are subject to the test of truthfulness (did these things take place?), and the results of the test sort historians from charlatans, and testimony from eyewash. But a different kind of distinction is needed to separate good historians from bad ones, outstanding witnesses from mediocre ones. "Truth" remains a relevant concept but with a rather different meaning. In establishing facts, we use "truth" to mean *equivalence* or *correspondence* between an assertion and the thing that happened ("4,400 Polish officers shot by NKVD troops in Katyn forest in 1940"). But in judging a work of history, we use "truth" to signify the power to unveil the underlying meaning of an event. A great work of history does not just give us reliable information; it also teaches us about the workings of human psychology and social life. Obviously, these two kinds of truth are not opposite but complementary.

This second kind of truth cannot be measured like the first. Facts can be right or wrong, but meanings are constructed by the writing subject and may change. A given interpretation may be untenable, that is, it may be refuted, but there is no absolute degree of truthfulness at the other end of the scale. Deciding whether Stalin was a genius, or a tyrant, or a warped mind is not like finding out a fact. A brilliant interpretation may be superseded some day by an even more brilliant one; no impersonal yardstick can measure the "brilliance" of any given historical interpretation. Historians are really in the same boat as novelists and poets: the only real proof that they have unveiled a deeper level of underlying meaning is their success in persuading their readers that they have done so — and that may happen in their own immediate circles or in far distant ones, it may happen in their own time or many years later. The ultimate criterion of "unveiled" truthfulness is intersubjective, not referential. All the same, the absence of absolute truth in the domain of meaning does not mean that any interpretation is as good as any other.

The construction of meaning aims to understand the past; and the wish to understand — to understand the past as well as the present — is a defining characteristic of humanity. What allows us to say it is a species-specific trait? Unlike all other animals, humans have self-awareness; that means that they are constitutionally double, since there is always a part of the human mind that is reflecting on the rest of it and thus not subject to that same reflection. This is what makes people able to act freely, and it is also the basis for the human drive toward interpretation. Humans fulfill themselves as humans by developing their powers of interpretation. The more they try to understand the world, the more they understand themselves, and the more fully human they are.

It might be thought that when the object of knowledge consists of such extreme forms of evil as the twentieth century has known, understanding is not a particularly desirable aim. Trying to understand evil could make it seem almost ordinary. Even Primo Levi, an unimpeachably scrupulous witness of history, suggested that "one cannot, what is more one must not, understand what happened [at Auschwitz], because to understand is almost to justify" (*If This Is a Man*, 395). We cannot sweep aside this warning, coming from a writer as upright as Levi was. However, it did not stop Levi himself from spending much of his life trying to understand and draw lessons from what he had experienced at Auschwitz. He often said so quite forcefully: "I think that for a nonreligious person like myself the main thing is to understand and to make others understand. And also to seek to put down the Manichaean representation of the world as black and white" (*Conversazioni*, 248). On the other hand we have to wonder for whom the warning was mainly intended. It would be perfectly justifiable if it was addressed to Levi himself or to other camp survivors, for it is not the task of victims to try to understand their executioners, just as women who have been raped are not the right people to unravel the psychology of sexual aggression. Understanding relies on some degree of identification with the perpetrator (be it partial and temporary), and that could be highly damaging for a victim.

But we are not camp survivors, and we cannot but ask ourselves whether we should hold back from even trying to understand the greatest evil. Nor can we accept without question the automatic equivalence that Levi apparently asserts between "understanding" and "justifying." The whole apparatus of modern criminal justice is based on a quite different premise. Murderers, torturers, and rapists must pay for their crimes, to be sure. But society does not only punish the criminals; it also seeks to understand why the crimes were committed and to take appropriate action to prevent their recurrence. Such an aim is not easily achieved, but the point is that the aim exists within our societies. Where poverty is seen to be a contributory factor in a crime, then the causes of poverty need to be addressed; where emotional deprivation in infancy seems to be a cause of later crimes, then greater attention needs to be paid to repressing cruelty to children. The law has not abandoned the concept of the freedom of the individual, however, and, save in cases of mental illness, it continues to recognize personal responsibility. No crime is ever the automatic consequence of a cause. Understanding evil is not to justify it, but the means of preventing it from occurring again.

A special difficulty arises when we seek both to *understand* and to *judge*. Making a judgment involves drawing a line between the judging subject and the object to be judged; whereas understanding implies recognizing our common humanity. These two types of mental action don't belong to the same field. What we seek to understand are human beings, capable of a great variety of different acts; what we seek to judge are specific acts carried out at particular times and places. The fact that all humans are made of the same stuff should not be allowed to obscure the gulf between what could have been done and what was actually done. Probably all of us are selfish; but not all of us become racists; and among racists, only the Nazis went to the extreme of racial extermination. People are all *potentially* criminal, but they are not all *actually* so, for they have not all lived the same lives. Some have been able to develop and cultivate their capacity for love, compassion, moral judgment; in others these capacities have been suppressed and killed off.

That is the difference between Pola Lifszyc, a girl living in the Warsaw ghetto who voluntarily boarded the train to Treblinka so as to stay with her mother (see Krall), and Franz Stangl, the camp commandant, whose exclusive concern was to carry out his job and not to think about its ultimate purpose (see Sereny). Some people can kill and torture, others can't, and that is why we will avoid the term "banality of evil" that Hannah Arendt used in her essays on the Eichmann trial. The evil that Eichmann and Stangl did was not ordinary, and when these men were putting thousands to death, they were not ordinary men either. There really is a difference, a quite decisive difference that justifies Primo Levi's whole career in public action and education. People may be made from the same mold, but events are singular. Those are what we must ponder and judge, because history consists of events.

Moral and legal responsibility should not be our only concern, however. We must recognize our shared humanity and question what that means. From this perspective, and even while we retain our autonomy as subjects, we must grant that there is no radical discontinuity between the self and the other (since others live in us, and we live in and through others), or between the camps' extreme form of evil and the ordinary forms of evil we encounter in everyday life. We positively need a double vision of this kind; we have to constantly switch between the role of judge, with respect to individuals, and the role of advocate with respect to the human race.

What is it exactly that we should try to understand when faced with an evil as fearful as that of the twentieth century? What we

125

need to understand are the political, social, and psychological processes that allowed it to happen. Victims whose willpower was taken from them do not require understanding of that kind. We can pity, comfort, protect, and love a woman who has been assaulted — but there is nothing much to understand about the behavior of a person subjected to an assault. The same can be said of whole peoples. There is nothing to "understand" about the sufferings of the Ukrainian peasants who were starved or the Jewish children and old folk who were thrown into gas chambers: compassion, not comprehension, is the appropriate response. But this is not true if the aim is to resist evil. In that case, it is better not to avoid the specifically political issues "by putting the spectacle of misfortune in the place of thinking about evil," as Rony Brauman says (Brauman and Sivan, 100). What we need to understand are not what people were forced to submit to, but what they sought to do — not only as perpetrators of evil, but also as fighters against evil, as resisters, and as rescuers of human lives.

Understanding is never complete, can never be absolutely "final." We are limited by the innate ability of the human species to act freely, beyond the determination of causes and beyond all probability. There is an irreducible element of mystery in human conduct — which is what makes it human. And that is true of acts with consequences at the individual level as well as acts that affect entire nations. Today's newspaper has a report about a suburban housewife who drugged her husband and two sons, cut their throats, then hanged herself. There had been no clues at all that such a tragedy was brewing in a family that everyone else thought completely contented and successful. Unthinkable, incomprehensible are the words that come to mind to describe a mother slitting the throats of her children. On a different scale, the same issue arises for the millions of deaths at Auschwitz. How can we "understand" that, or Stalin's ironhearted decision that millions of Ukrainians deserved to die? As we have seen, these macabre consequences derive from acts that were not in themselves irrational; but nothing we know about human individuals and human societies would allow us to "generate" these events, that is to say to assemble all the factors that would necessarily produce such results.

This consideration of the first two stages of the work of memory leads us to another conclusion, which is that remembering is not the opposite of forgetting. The two opposing terms are *destruction* and *preservation* (or "wiping" and "saving"): memory can only ever be the result of their interaction. It is impossible to recover all of the past — and if it were possible, it would be a terrifying thing indeed, as Borges has shown in his story "Funes the Memorious." Memory has to be a selection; only some features of an event are preserved, and others are dropped and forgotten, either straightaway or little by little. This makes it unsettling to see computers' information storage capacity described as "memory," since one of the constitutive features of human memory, forgetting, is quite absent from the electronic kind.

Preserving without making choices falls short of being memory work. What is objectionable about Nazi and Communist murderers is not that they selected those parts of the past that they wished to preserve — I'll be doing exactly the same — but that they granted themselves the right to decide what would be available to others. Paradoxically, you could say that memory, far from being its opposite, is a forgetting: a *partial* forgetting, in both senses of the word, that is indispensable to making sense of the past.

Application

The third stage in the life of the past in the present is its instrumentalization in terms of present aims, its *application* to the here and now. After *establishing* the facts and *interpreting* them, we can now *use* the past. This is what people do when they want to serve their present aims by reference to the past, and it is how politicians work too.

Professional historians do not like to admit that they have anything to do with the third stage. They prefer to consider their work done once they have thrown new light on what happened and on what it meant. It is of course possible to exclude application of historical knowledge, but I think it happens very seldom. A historian's work is hard to imagine unless it refers at some level to values, and these values determine the historian's own approach to his material. The questions and topics on which a historian focuses can only be ones that strike him or her as being useful, important, in need of urgent inquiry. Depending on the

127

aim of the study, the historian picks out from all the data that are available from archives, testimonies, and other sources those elements which seem most revealing. These must then be knitted together to support an argument and to show the lesson that can be drawn from the chosen fragment of history, even if the "moral of the tale" is not stated as explicitly as it would be in a fable. Values are everywhere, and that doesn't upset anyone. But values can't be separated from the wish not just to know the world, but to act on it, and to change it in the here and now.

Putting the past into service in the present is quite obvious in politics, but it is far from absent from activities clothed in the garb of science. The historian's trade differs from so many others in its rock-bottom criterion of truthfulness, which obliges historians to be scrupulous in gathering information; but that does not prevent the knowledge thus gained from being put to use. It is a naive illusion to believe that use can be kept out of history; to think that knowledge and its application can be insulated from each other is just a fantasy. "Superficially neutral language doesn't add anything to knowledge" wrote David Rousset when he was collecting documents on the concentration camps (*Lignes*, 206). Writing history, like any work on the past, never consists of establishing facts and nothing more. It always also involves selecting those facts that are more salient or significant than others and making connections between them. Selection and combination cannot only be directed toward truth; they must also always strive toward a good. Scholarship is obviously not the same thing as politics, but scholarship, being a human activity, has a political finality, which may be for good or bad.

In practice the three phases I have distinguished always coexist. Most often, you begin with an idea for the application of knowledge before you start impartially collecting facts. We only look to the past for examples to make some planned present action legitimate when we have just such a plan. Memory being selective by nature, there have to be criteria that allow it to choose what it retains from the great mass of information received; and those very criteria, conscious or unconscious as they may be, are most likely to be the main guide to the uses we make of the past.

TESTIMONY, HISTORY, AND COMMEMORATION

The traces of the past that live on in the present fall into a variety of different kinds of language, of which I concentrate on three: the language of *testimony*, the language of *history*, and the language of *commemoration*.

Testimony is the type of discourse that arises when we summon up memories and, by shaping them, give meaning to our life and construct our identity. Each of us is the witness of our own life, and we build our picture of it by suppressing some of its events, by retaining others, and reshaping or adjusting yet more. Such memory-work may make use of documents (material traces), but by definition it is solitary work — we owe no account for the picture we have of ourselves. There are of course risks in memory-work: intentional forgetting can lead to remorse, suppressing particular memories can cause neuroses. The beneficiary of such work is the individual: memory helps us to live a little less badly and adds to our mental comfort and sense of well-being. Nobody else has a right to tell us what image to have of our own past, even if many try to do so. In a sense, our own memories are irrefutable because they have substance by the mere fact of their existence, irrespective of their relationship to reality.

A historian is someone attached to the discipline whose aim is to recover and analyze the past; or, more generally, anyone who seeks the same end and accepts impersonal truth, not individual interest, as the ground rule of such activity. Over the past few hundred years, historians as well as philosophers have subjected such a notion of truth to far-reaching and often justified criticism, for our instruments of knowledge are blunt ones and the search for truth cannot but reflect the subjectivity of the seeker to some degree. Even making due allowance for the imperfections of historical research and researchers, however, we must still draw a line between the language of truth and the language of fiction. Otherwise it really would be the end of history.

This is very obvious if we look at things in practice. A historian may be fallible, since he or she is human, and may likewise be influenced in some degree by his or her historical and geographical circumstances. But a historian has one distinctive feature — to seek to establish as far as possible what she or he considers, in all

129

honesty, to be the truth. This is the truth of correspondence, but it is also, despite the greater difficulty of proving it, a truth of unveiling. It is not possible to be "relativistic" at this level. A historian has only to invent one fact or falsify one document to be dismissed, defrocked, and hounded out of the profession. It would be the same for a biologist or physicist who fabricates results. These aren't just less respectable scholars than others or scholars with unacceptable opinions: they are completely and irretrievably beyond the pale of scientific and scholarly endeavor. A historian who fails the test of truthfulness does not belong to the profession and can be counted at best a propagandist.

There would seem to be a complete contrast between *testimony* (of one's own life) and *history* (of the world of others), with the former serving an individual interest, and the latter serving the quest for truth. However, a witness may consider that his or her own memories merit a place in the public realm, because they may contribute not simply to his or her own development but also to the education of others. At this point there arises a "document," which may compete for public attention with historical texts proper. Historians often have reservations about testimonial literature. Not only do they attract lots of readers, but until they have been examined with the tools of historical scholarship (which often proves to be impossible), they have little truth value. Witnesses, for their part, mistrust the historians — because they weren't there, they didn't suffer physically, they were still in short pants or not even born when the events took place. This undeclared war could be settled, all the same, if we could grant that testimony, even if does not respect the criterion of truth in the way that history must, nonetheless enriches historical discourse.

The complementarity of history and testimony can be illustrated by examples taken from my investigation of daily life under extreme conditions during the German occupation of France (1940–44) (Todorov and Jacquet). History tells us that France was defeated when its army stopped fighting, causing widespread panic. More detailed histories record that on 17 June, 1940, the seventh Army Corps retreated south of Bourges and that one of its companies of Senegalese infantry spent the night in the woods before moving on the next day. But when Mme Y. B. recalled those days, she told the story quite differently. During the night, she says, the soldiers bivouacking in the woods used up all their live ammunition. The noise terrified her neighbors, who were driven out of their minds. "They spent three days and three nights hugging each other. We worried they were going to hurt themselves, suffocate each other. We separated them and put them in different rooms, but, guess what, in the evening they got back together. They just stayed in each others' arms. They had an eight-year-old niece staying with them for a holiday, they stuffed her under a mattress, so the Germans wouldn't get her. The girl was suffocating." A story of that kind, fragmentary as it is, seems to me just as eloquent and revealing of people's state of mind at that time as any historical generalization.

History books tell us that Resisters who were caught by the enemy suffered mightily. For witnesses, though, the Resistance was not a general entity, but specific groups and individuals who suffered concretely in their prison cells, from thirst, for example. "We urinated into a broken bottle and wetted our lips with the liquid," one witness recalls. Another added: "At 9 A.M. the Germans took us down to the urinals, and though they were green with mould, we licked them straight away. When the Germans saw that, they gave us a cup of water each." Details like these make abstractions more palpable; they seem to bring us much closer to the truth of the experience.

Returning deportees often found it difficult to readapt, historians tell us in a general way. Mr. R. M. remembers one specific returnee. "He had already been in hospital, in a therapeutic center, because for days and nights he had been having nightmares, remembering the torture he'd been through. He was frighteningly thin. He said almost nothing about having been deported. He didn't seem to hate Germans or the minority of Frenchmen who had cooperated with them. He had a shaved head, and he came to a dance with his girlfriend's sister, who'd had her head shaved at the Liberation. So there they were, dancing together, one shaved head with another." These two shaven heads — one shaved by the Germans as an enemy, the other shaved by the French for having had relations with the enemy — give us a snapshot of two humiliated individuals supporting each other without regard for the "sides" each was supposed to be on. This single image is as powerful as any long and reasoned argument.

That does not mean that memoirs and testimonials should always be given precedence over historical writing. The two types of approach to the past are complementary, not contradictory. To understand the inner workings of the minds of supporters of opposite ideologies, we should listen, for instance, to what former members of the collaborationist *milice* and of the Resistance have to say. But to get a grasp of the values of each of these two positions, to understand their practical consequences, the relationship between their words and their acts, we should rather turn to the works of historians. For dates, numbers, and names, we look to historical research; but for sharing the experience of the people involved, memoirs are irreplaceable. If we wish to understand the fate of the Kolyma deportees, we do not have to choose between Robert Conquest's historical analysis and the autobiography of Evgenia Ginzburg; nor do we have to choose Raul Hilberg against Primo Levi when we study Auschwitz.

The past lives in the present not only through testimonial literature and historical inquiry but also through commemoration. Like the witness, the commemorator is pursuing his or her personal interest; but in common with professional historians, celebrants operate in the public sphere and aspire to irrefutable truthfulness, as far removed as possible from the unreliability of personal accounts. Commemorative writing has sometimes been referred to as an expression of "collective memory," but as Alfred Grosser has pointed out, the term is very dubious (see *Les Identités difficiles*). Memory, in the sense of mental traces, only ever belongs to an individual; collective memory is not memory at all, but a variety of discourse used in the public arena. It serves to reflect the image that a society, or one of its constituent groups, wishes to give of itself.

Commemoration—the discourse of celebrants—can be found in obvious places: schools impart a common image of the past to children; historical movies and television documentaries offer images of the past to a broader public; and organizations like the British Legion and U.S. veterans' clubs also serve to maintain a group vision of the past. In politics, commemorative discourse can be found in speeches made at every level, from White House to Borough Hall, as well as in parliamentary debate and in newspaper articles. Commemorative discourse obviously makes use of material supplied by historians and witnesses, but it does not respect the test of truth that these latter forms must pass. It is partly a matter of pragmatic circumstance. The schoolteacher

132

knows, and pupils are there to learn; television audiences can't ask questions, and no one challenges the mayor when he's making a speech. In parliament, opposition members aren't necessarily forewarned that the prime minister is going to refer to such and such a piece of history, and as they haven't been able to check up in advance, they let the reference pass.

Historians and witnesses may easily complement each other, as I have suggested, but a fundamental difference of aims and methods between historians and celebrants makes them pretty much incompatible. This contrast needs to be stressed most especially because celebrants seek to use impersonality (they are not speaking about themselves, after all) to suggest objectivity, and thus truthfulness. But the discourse of commemoration is not objective at all. While history makes the past more complicated, commemoration makes it simpler, since it seeks most often to supply us with heroes to worship or with enemies to detest; it deals in desecration and consecration. A recent example of the effects of consecration on our knowledge of the past was the ceremonial reburying of the remains of André Malraux in the Pantheon, the French national mausoleum for the "great men" of its Republican history. The event unleashed great waves of ink from the pens of politicians and journalists, who outdid each other in singing the praises of the novelist turned minister of culture. The result was that several rather important facts about Malraux (such as his involvement with Stalinist propaganda in the 1930s) were not even mentioned, and the whole existential and ideological complexity of the person was grossly simplified. *Re*memoration is to try to grasp the truth of the past. *Com*memoration is to adapt the past to the needs of the present.

The term *revisionism* has come to mean the same thing as *negationism*, the politically motivated claim that the gas chambers in German concentration camps did not exist. It's a great pity that the term has thus been lost for a better use. Historical truth — truth unveiled — is always, fortunately, subject to revision, and every historical advance is "revisionist" in the real sense of the word. This kind of revisionism stands opposed to pious or sanctified history, which is precisely what the discourse of commemoration is made of.

Commemoration may be inevitable, but it is not the best way to make the past live on in the present: in a democracy we need

CHAPTER 3

something other than sanitized and sanctified images of the past. We can be pretty sure that commemoration serves celebrants' personal or collective interests rather than their moral elevation when it becomes so fixed in form that any deviation provokes cries of outrage. Shortly before he died in 1995, the German playwright Heiner Müller was invited to oversee the production of one of his plays in the municipal theater at Verdun, the site of a particularly bloody French victory in 1917. While there, he went to see the war memorial and answered journalists' questions on his impressions. "The artificial set that's been made out of the place leaves me cold. These memorials belong to an art of the dead, a monumental art, to be sure, but a worthless one. Real art is art made for the living" (see Sadowska-Guillon, 106–9). His statement raised the ire of the organizations responsible for the upkeep of these national shrines, and the town council of Verdun threatened to cut the theater's funding and to close it down unless it broke off all relations with Müller. I've never been to see the Verdun memorial and so I have no view of its aesthetic worth, but I know that Müller was, in principle, quite right. In our world, human values, not monuments, should be holy.

MORAL JUDGMENT

To put the past in the service of the present is an act. To judge such an act, we require it to have more than a truth of correspondence (as for historical facts) and a truth of unveiling (as for historical interpretation), for we must evaluate it in terms of good and evil, that is to say, by political and moral criteria. It is obvious that not all uses of the past are good, and no less obvious that the same past event can give rise to very different lessons. For example, in *The Forty Days of Musa Dagh* (1933) the Austrian writer Franz Werfel told the story of the Armenian genocide and of those who resisted it; one of his aims was to encourage resistance to Nazi anti-Semitism. But at much the same time, Hitler is said to have chatted over dinner about the same crime, which gave him some hope of impunity if he were to do something similar: "Who remembers the Armenian massacre nowadays?" The same event, and two quite different uses of it.

134

The first question we have to ask in this context is whether it is legitimate to make judgments about the past. In fact, historians practically never fail to do so. But are they right?

We could question the legitimacy of moral judgments about the past in several ways. If we were to believe that human beings are not at all free, that all our acts obey an iron law of necessity whether we know it or not, then it would indeed be fatuous to praise or to blame the past. An act has a moral value only insofar as it might not have been committed. For this reason physicists and biologists don't make judgments about the objects of their study, for they deal only with the realm of necessity.

Imitation of the natural sciences has been a widely shared tendency in history, anthropology, psychology, sociology, and the human sciences in general. Since the early nineteenth century scholars have tried to show that humans are affected by causes of a higher order, causes more concrete than the harmony of the cosmos or the divine intervention which justified the fatalism of antiquity. History itself, in the sense of an irreversible sequence of events — or, to say it another way, the social context — is the prime mover here. In the early 1800s, Benjamin Constant wrote: "A century is the necessary product of those that went before. A century can only ever be what it is." So it would be pointless to pass judgment on the past. "There is nothing to be censured and nothing to be praised. . . . The spirit of an age is a necessary fact, a physical fact. A physical fact can be stated but not judged" (*Œuvres complètes*, III.1, 528). A hundred years later, in 1914, Nikolay Bukharin, the theorist of Communism, claimed that "there is nothing more ridiculous . . . than the attempt to make Marx's theory an 'ethical' theory. Marx's theory knows no other natural law than that of cause and effect, and can admit no other such law" (quoted in Cohen, 167–68).

In the second half of the nineteenth century, biological causality was added to social determinism. If we act as we do because we are of a certain race, can we reasonably be held responsible? Maurice Barrès campaigned for Dreyfus to be found guilty, but he did so in a way that cast little moral blame on the alleged traitor. "We are asking this child of Sem to have the fine features of the Indo-European race. . . . If we had truly disinterested minds, we would not judge Dreyfus by French morality and

135

French laws, as if he were our equal; we would see in him a representative of a different species" (Barrès, 153, 167). For Barrès the Jewish soldier Dreyfus was more a zoological specimen than a defendant, because he displayed the behavior of a different human species that Aryans had no real right to judge. And finally, in the early years of the twentieth century, a third kind of causality was added to social and biological determinism, or else sought to supersede them as explanations for an individual's behavior — the belief that very early childhood and the infant's relationship with its parents determines the nature of unconscious drives. We do not ask our psychoanalyst for moral judgments, but for help in developing self-understanding.

What is common to these three forms of determinism (whose historical order is not entirely illogical) is that they all seek totalizing explanations that leave no space for moral judgment. If humans are like ants in all respects, then we should not judge them, but only try to explain. However, this extrapolation did not satisfy even those who laid bare the various determining forces of human existence, because they too could only admit the obvious fact that no unified causal explanation allows the actions of individuals to be predicted (or "generated"); some degree of freedom always seems to escape the grip of causality. Benjamin Constant thus added to the passage I have just quoted that even when historical circumstances determine the general trend, they still leave individuals with a wide margin of freedom. "Everything is moral for individuals, but for the masses, everything is physical. . . . Every individual is free as an individual since he or she has only to deal with himself or with forces that are no greater than his own. But as a member of a group, the individual is no longer free." An individual acting in accordance with his or her own free will performs acts that can be given a moral value. Whatever philosophical form may be given to this argument, it has to be granted that we all behave on the presupposition that all individuals have a margin of freedom, because nobody fails to judge the acts of others by a moral yardstick.

There is nonetheless another way of questioning the validity of moral judgments in historical matters. This consists not of denying their right to exist, but of recognizing their multiplicity and seeing this as proof of their arbitrariness. In Nietzsche's terms, this is called "perspectivism." If one judgment is as good as another, why bother with judgments at all, since the facts belong to the past? Morality and justice are in this argument mere masks for desire and the will to power; historians may write about these values, but there is no way of discussing them rationally. Relativists do not dispute the existence of values that are more than personal, but they always relate them to a specific time and place. Values, they say, are exclusively the product of historical and cultural circumstance.

This seems all the more plausible when we realize that we are, necessarily, always dealing with language, as we are reminded by the deconstructionists. To take one example from the many that are possible, a recent commentator asked why he should respect critics who support the Russian poet Osip Mandelstam in his conflict with Joseph Stalin when, in the language they use, each of the two parties represents the other as the devil. Similarly, since Solzhenitsyn is as intolerant as the head of the KGB, what is the value of a judgment that elevates one above the other? Soviet dissidents imprisoned in psychiatric wards treated their doctors as impostors: the language they used was thus just as intolerant as the language of the psychiatrists. Everyone makes judgments from his or her own position; such judgments are arbitrary; and so it would be better to eliminate them from discourse about the past.

I don't think this relativistic argument—even if it is quite widely expressed nowadays—should be taken completely seriously. It could only be entertained if we took the prior step of disconnecting language from the world in which the language is used. Let's say that Stalin and Mandelstam hated each other equally; but only the general secretary sent fifteen million people to the gulag, among them the poor poet, who died from exhaustion as soon as he got there. Neither Solzhenitsyn nor the other dissidents sent anyone to prison or to a lunatic asylum. Those are the reasons why most of us condemn Stalin and feel sympathy for his victims. Uttering insults is not a good action, but to inflict endless suffering by deporting people, by starving and humiliating them before having them killed, is infinitely worse.

Moreover, it is far from obvious that all values are relative. While granting that many values are culturally and historically determined, we also possess the feeling and the intuition, I believe, that other values are not so determined, and cannot be justifiably overturned by any historical or cultural specificity. That is why we have no difficulty in understanding intuitively the moral teachings of figures far distant from us in time and place, such as Buddha, Socrates, or Jesus. Some people may wish to dispute this point, but in practice we all behave in accordance with it. We do not allow human sacrifice, genocide, enslavement, or torture to be excused on grounds of the historical context in which they occur. But that obviously does not free us from seeking to understand why and how such actions seemed to be acceptable or even praiseworthy to whole nations.

Consciously or not, everyone relies on criteria that permit distinctions to be made not so much between good and evil absolutely as between more and less good, more and less evil. What are these criteria? To answer that question we must briefly discuss moral judgment itself.

Within the European tradition, the concept of good underwent substantial transformation over the centuries, and that is why it is not easy to answer our question simply; but a comparison of our moral ideas with those of the ancient world ought to make it easier to pinpoint our own, more or less conscious, criteria. In Kantian terms the first point of contrast is between the heteronomy of the ancients and the autonomy of the moderns, that is to say, the development over the centuries from submission to a law that originates elsewhere to a state where humans make the laws they live by. The ancients would have thought it absurd for men to make the law, for the law was inscribed in the order of the cosmos, or else it was God's revelation. Greeks and Hebrews alike thus held virtue to be measured by conformity to a law which came from "outside." But for modern humanity, there is no moral merit in merely submitting to the law; merit begins with freedom and can only be earned by actions which involve the exercise of free will.

The second feature that separates these two ideas of goodness involves the transition from objectivity to intersubjectivity. The ancients' ideal of the good life did not exclude relations with the other, but it did not focus on them. The classical sage withdraws from society and keeps at a distance from other people. Christianity marked the beginning of the transition. "All the Law," said Christ, hangs on the two commandments: to "love the Lord thy God" and to "love thy neighbor as thyself" (Matthew 22.37–40). God is in every person, however humble, and "inasmuch as ye have done [good] unto the least of my brethren, ye have done it unto me" (Matthew 25.40). For Saint Paul this meant that loving God was nothing other than loving one's neighbor: "[T]herefore love is the fulfilling of the law" (Romans 13.10). God manifests himself to humans through other people. The new ideal is not to excel or to perfect the self, but to exercise charity, which is necessarily an intersubjective value.

From a religious point of view the love of other beings is meritorious only insofar as it reflects or increases the love of God. However, the whole development of Western humanism from the Renaissance to the Enlightenment consisted of shedding the divine guarantee while maintaining the ideals of goodwill and charity, which it initially protected. For humanists, good exists only within human society, not in an individual seen in isolation from others. "It is only in becoming a social being that man becomes a moral being," noted Jean-Jacques Rousseau, despite his own taste for solitude (*Fragments politiques*, in *Œuvres complètes*, 3:477). In addition, the other must be put above the self. "The more his cares are consecrated to the happiness of others, (. . .) the less he will be deceived about what is good or bad" (*Émile*, 252). This is why Kant, in later years, insisted that it was not possible to switch around the elements of what he called the "moral ends" of humankind, namely "my own perfection" and "the happiness of others." Individuals who seek only their own happiness are just selfish; those who seek only the perfection of others are unbearable preachers who see the mote in the other's eye without noticing the beam in their own. We would add that to treat your neighbor as you would treat yourself is a question of justice (since we all obey the same laws), but to put your neighbor above yourself — from love or from a sense of duty — is to enter the domain of morality. That is how we should understand Levinas's reference to a "humanism of thinking-of-the-other," which is a way of saying that in the modern world a moral act is necessarily disinterested. "The only absolute value is the human possibility of giving the other priority over oneself" (Levinas, 109).

This is still not an adequate description of moral judgment. Let's imagine a public figure who sets himself up as the permanent defender of others, and as a systematic critic of his own community. The moral stock of such a person would certainly not seem very high. And why not? Well, we have long known people of that sort, from biblical prophets who lambasted their people for living sinfully to travelers who glorified distant peoples — "noble savages" — so as to criticize their own. In our own time, we have seen writers assuming the mantle of national conscience and flagellating themselves for the guilt they share for their own people's crimes: German writers who make out that Germans are the worst people on earth, Americans who see the history of the United States as an unbroken chain of imperialist aggression and racial injustice. But the position of *moral censor* also excludes any self-appointed holder from the domain of morality.

Another attitude full of good intentions similarly excludes authentically moral gestures, one that could be called *reflex compassion*. The way news is circulated nowadays makes this a universal temptation. Wars, massacres, famines, and natural disasters now unleash ubiquitous images of corpses, of wounded dying without medical assistance, of weeping adults and skeletal children, which make us shout "This must stop!" at our television screens. So we donate a bag of rice or a handful of dollars to the cause of good. Compassion is better than indifference, to be sure, but it also has secondary effects we would be better without. As Brauman says, reflex compassion turns evil into a mere misfortune, it substitutes a gush of feeling for "cold" political analysis, and in so doing it gives us all a good conscience by making us valiant victims by adoption. My brief exposition of modern ethics is therefore quite inadequate: it is not enough to say that the other must be put above the self, and it is even less satisfactory to assume the mantle of a teacher of moral lessons. We need to revisit the concept of a moral act.

The crucial episode in infantile development is the acquisition of an ability to distinguish between good and bad, to which the child is led by the pleasure it experiences from the love and attention of carers and the displeasure it feels at their absence. These affective experiences carry the seed of ethical categories: good is what is good for the infant, and, similarly, bad is what is bad for it. The significance of this first step should not be underestimated. If deprived of primary love or of the certainty that it is cared for, a child may grow up in a state of ethical atrophy and radical *nihilism*. It may turn into an adult capable of doing evil without being aware of it at all.

However, this first step in the acquisition of a moral sense, the distinction between good and bad based on love, is only a beginning. As the child grows and acquires friends of the same age, it makes a second and sometimes painful discovery. The equation of "good and bad" with "me and other" has to be broken, just as, when applied to groups, it has be disconnected from "us and them." The child learns that it is not necessarily the incarnation of good, and that others are not necessarily bad; and at that point it begins to outgrow infantile *egocentrism*.

Then and only then can the third stage commence, although there are few who manage it. The third stage involves abandoning all exclusive or definitive ways of apportioning good and bad without ceasing to make a distinction between them. In the third stage, with nihilism and egocentrism vanquished, the obstacle to be surmounted is Manichaeism. To always see evil in oneself (or in one's own group) and good in others would be just as harmful as the reverse. The fact that an action serves our own interest in no way enables us to know whether it is morally "good" or "bad."

It is now easier to grasp why we are reluctant to grant moral credit to someone who systematically excoriates his own group and favors the other, because we know instinctively that the role of moral conscience is actually quite comforting to its holder. He or she becomes the virtuous one, as the keeper of values and guide to the strait and narrow. When said by such a public figure, "We are all guilty" actually means "I'm rather less guilty than you are, because I'm the one who's saying so." Such a person cannot be accused of being ethnocentric or xenophobic — but he or she acquires a rewarding role in the community as the guardian of its values.

Merely inverting the equations of "us = good" and "the other = bad" does not allow the public scourge to rise above the domain of moral Manichaeism. The flaw in the role of permanent critic of one's own community is that it takes for granted where good and evil are to be found. You can only avoid that trap if you are able to take equal distance from your own group *and* from its opponents.

It is essential to understand that this third stage of development must be completed. Let us here recall that the underlying premise of totalitarianism is the simplified division of the world into good people and bad people, people to be promoted and those to be eliminated. Auschwitz and Kolyma represent extreme but logical extensions of the initial black-and-white division of the world, and we too are tainted with it whenever we see perpetrators of evil only as enemies to be overcome and put down. If we have to become totalitarian in order to crush totalitarianism, then totalitarianism has won.

All that may be very well in abstract, but it is very hard to put into daily practice. And that is natural enough, for the illusion of a world that revolves around our own self, and the temptation to see everything in terms of black and white, are related to some of our deepest drives; most of our spontaneous reactions to adversity are prompted by them. And so it is hardly surprising that the same illusions and temptations are to be found in various ideological movements of our recent history.

MASTER NARRATIVES

We have our criteria, but we now have to find to what we should apply them. The facts of the past do not come raw; they always reach us as part of a story.

The historical narrative of an act that is not morally neutral is always slanted, toward good or toward evil; and it always involves at least two protagonists, the subject (or actor) and the object (or acted-upon). There are thus four roles in any historical narrative with an ethical dimension: benefactor, beneficiary, malefactor, and victim. At first sight only two of these roles — benefactor and malefactor — are marked for value, while the other two, being passive, seem morally neutral. In reality, however, the passive roles, by the fact of being connected to the active ones, have moral connotations. To be the beneficiary of an act is less glorious than being its agent, because the fact of receiving constitutes a mark of our own need or powerlessness; to be the victim of a misdeed, on the other hand, is more respectable than being its agent. In this distribution we can already see the two main forms of historical narration: the heroic narrative, which lauds the triumph of "our side." and the victim narrative, which relates its sufferings.

Why put victims alongside the heroes whom we all admire? Is there anything pleasant about being a victim? Surely not. But although nobody wants to be a victim in the present, many would like to have been one in the past. Victim status is indeed something to which people aspire. Families are full of people playing victim so as to give others the far less enviable role of persecutor. Victimhood gives you grounds to complain, to protest, to make demands, and others just have to respond, or else cut off relations entirely. It is also more advantageous to remain in the victim role than to obtain reparation for the ill that has been done (if there ever was real harm caused), because reparation is once and for all, whereas a victim can rely on the recognition and attention that his status provides more or less indefinitely. At another level entirely, we can see how powerful victim-stories are in the passion of Christ, the keystone of the Christian religion.

What works for individuals works even better for groups. If some community can claim convincingly to have been the victim of injustice in the past, then it acquires an inexhaustible line of credit in the present. If in that society groups and not only individuals are granted rights, then such a victim community can make good use of its status; and the greater the past offense, the greater are the rights in the present. Members of the group don't have to struggle to acquire privileges, they have them automatically, just by belonging to the formerly underprivileged. And that gives rise to rivalry for the status of the "most unfavored," in a mirror image of the international competition for "most-favored nation" status.

African Americans provide a classic example of such a development. They protest the indisputable injustices of slavery and racial discrimination but have no intention of losing the lasting moral and political advantages that the history of their community gives them. Louis Farrakhan, the leader of the "Nation of Islam," took this position to an outrageous extreme when he declared: "What's six million dead Jews, outside America? The black holocaust was a hundred times worse than the Jewish holocaust." Victims beware! Your sympathy card can be trumped! But we may well doubt the desirability of what Chaumont calls "victim rivalry." It has been convincingly argued that many of the problems of the African American community derive not from current discrimination but from its inability to overcome the traumas of its past history, and from the consequent temptation, as Shelby Steele puts it, "to exploit their own past suffering as a source of power and privilege" (118).

The rewards of victimhood don't need to be material ones. The debt to be paid is symbolic; tangible reparations would be trivial, for the advantages granted to members of groups enjoying victim status are of a different order. As the French Jewish writer Alain Finkielkraut quickly realized when he was young: "Others had suffered and I, because I was their descendant, harvested all the moral advantage. . . . Lineage made me genocide's huckster, the witness and practically its victim. . . . With this sort of investiture, any other title seemed wretched or ridiculous to me" (11–12).

Of the four roles in moral historical narratives, then, two can be filled to personal advantage (the beneficent hero, the innocent victim), and two bring no advantage (the malefactor and the passive beneficiary). When we identify our own group with one of the positive roles in its past history, we gratify ourselves by so doing; and we may also be gratified by giving to others the role of passive beneficiary of heroic actions, or else of perpetrator of evil ones. To describe the past in this way obviously produces no moral benefit for whoever indulges in such ritual and agreeable behavior.

History has always been written by the victors. What you used to win by winning was a right over the past, but in the twentieth century people have campaigned for a history of the losers, the victims, the subjected, and the vanquished, to take its rightful place alongside the victors' history. On historical grounds, the claim is absolutely legitimate, since it invites us to learn about whole aspects of the past that had previously been neglected. In ethical terms, however, to identify with victims does not make us more meritorious. There really is no moral difference between identification with the bomber pilots who ended the Second World War and identification with the passive population that suffered nuclear annihilation, since in both cases we place ourselves in the position of the "good" and the "innocent."

The only chance we might have of climbing a moral rung would be to recognize the evil in ourselves and to struggle against it. You gain no direct benefit from discussing the evil that your "own side" might have done, or the help it may have gained from the heroic actions of the "other side," just as you draw no gratification from seeing the other side as victim or benefactor — but that is the only way you can undertake a critical examination of your own collective identity, the only way you can put the perfection of the self and the happiness of others above your own interests, and thus be engaged in moral action when studying the past. Revisiting historical episodes in which one's own group was neither 100 percent heroic nor the complete victim would be an act of higher moral value for writers of historical narratives. No moral benefit can accrue from always identifying with the "right side" of history; it can only arise when writing history makes the writer more aware of the weaknesses and wrong turns of his or her own community. Morality is by definition disinterested.

As my classification of roles and their moral effects may seem rather abstract, I would like to give some concrete examples in order to explore whether or not it is true that people gain pleasure from adopting the two roles of hero and victim.

For Russians, 9 May, 1945 is the date of their final victory over Nazism and the end of a war in which they lost more than twenty-five million dead. Most Russians are therefore perfectly happy to take part in commemorations of their own heroic role. For Central Europeans, however, the same date symbolizes the start of Soviet rule, marking not their liberation but their enslavement.

The events of the past have indeterminate meanings, and they acquire firm value only through present action. The French see 8 May, 1945 as a day to be proud of, because French generals stood alongside American, British, and Soviet representatives at the signing of the German surrender. But during celebrations of 8 May people do not like to recall that it is also the anniversary of the massacre at Sétif, in Algeria. The Algerians had naively thought that as France had at last freed itself from the Germans, they would now be able to free themselves from the French. But at the end of the war France saw itself as a world power under threat and was more determined than ever to hang on to its global empire. Their initial defeat in 1940 was what made the French so unyielding toward the Algerians, and they put down a pro-independence demonstration in the town of Sétif with uncommon violence. The number of dead and wounded has never been established: estimates range from 1,500 to 45,000.

The same configuration can be illustrated by another episode in modern history (on which I will say more later), the dropping of atomic bombs on Hiroshima and Nagasaki, and the controversy aroused by plans to exhibit *Enola Gay* (the aircraft that dropped the bomb on Hiroshima) at the Smithsonian. John Dower, an

American specialist in modern Japanese history, has written with insight about the sharp difference between American and Japanese presentations of the episode, even while both sides acknowledge and use exactly the same well-established facts.

Americans conventionally provide "a triumphal or heroic narrative in which the A-bombs represent the coup de grace administered to an aggressive, fanatical and savage enemy"; for the Japanese, however, the dominant story is a "victim narrative" in which "atomic bombs symbolize a specific form of suffering — rather like the Holocaust for the Jews" (Dower, "Three Narratives," 65, 66). The Hiroshima museum is itself entirely given over to the victim role; there is not the slightest mention of the Japanese government's possible responsibility for starting and pursuing the war, or for the inhuman treatment of POWs and civilians by Japanese soldiers. Each year, 1.5 million people visit the Hiroshima museum in its grand park, which also contains a memorial to the 176,964 victims of the bomb. However, a memorial to the 20,000 Korean forced laborers who were in Hiroshima and who died just the same as the Japanese has been erected elsewhere, outside the sanctified grounds. Hiroshima was a mainly military town before the war, but there is nothing to recall the 1938 Nanking Massacre, carried out mostly by troops from the Hiroshima garrison of the Japanese army, who slaughtered around 300,000 Chinese. So we can see that American partisans of the "heroic narrative" and Japanese defenders of the "victim story" are equally happy to promote their "own side."

The difference between the two stories came to the boil in 1995, during the commemoration of the fiftieth anniversary of the atomic bomb. The aircraft that dropped the bomb on Hiroshima, *Enola Gay*, was supposed to be the centerpiece of a Washington, D.C., exhibition designed to present the event in all its complexity. But war veterans and other patriotic groups raised political support to campaign against the exhibition, which they considered offensive because it did not show the United States exclusively as hero and benefactor triumphing over Japanese militarism but suggested that America was responsible for a massacre that could not be entirely justified.

How can you write a narrative of history without identifying with either hero or victim? John Dower's study of U.S. and Japanese reactions to the Hiroshima anniversary might be a model to follow. He divides it into three parts: "Hiroshima as Victimization" (for the Japanese approach); "Hiroshima as Triumph" (for the U.S. reaction); and "Hiroshima as Tragedy."

Happiness does not make the news, and idylls rarely figure in history books. History tends toward the grave, and toward tragedy, where good and evil are never entirely separate from one another. The Second World War (unlike the First) might look like an exception, since Hitler was indisputably the face of evil, and every battle to defeat him was thus in the service of good. But to argue along those lines we have to accept that ends justify means, and that it is permissible to imitate the enemy in order to overcome it. Until 1942 the British and American governments considered attacks on civilians as barbarous acts; but from then on, they used the same tactics. In February 1945, forty thousand civilians died in the fire-bombing of Dresden; and in March, the Tokyo blitz slaughtered one hundred thousand. (Hiroshima and Nagasaki were still to come.) The soldiers who did these things, Dower argues, "became heroes with the blood of women and children on their hands, and in this regard protagonists in a tragic rather than triumphal narrative" (Dower, "Three Narratives," 95). Former victims copied earlier acts of atrocity.

What is tragedy? Not just a story of suffering and wretchedness, not just the absence of good, out of which a victim story can also be made. Tragedy is the impossibility of good: a place whence every path leads to tears and to death. The Allied cause was, unarguably, a better cause than the Nazis' or the Japanese, and the war against them was just and necessary; but it brought about miseries that cannot be dismissed with a wave of the hand on the grounds that they happened to "them" not to "us." A carbonized bowl of rice and peas that belonged to a twelve-year-old girl who was vaporized by the Hiroshima bomb can have almost as much weight as the flying fortress called *Enola Gay*. In fact, it was the plan to display the bowl, on loan from the Hiroshima Museum, which made the whole Washington project unacceptable to U.S. veterans. If you are brave enough to think simultaneously of the bomber crew and of the bowl, then you cannot avoid seeing history as tragedy.

The Achievement of David Rousset

David Rousset was born in France in 1912 and died in 1997. Before the war he campaigned for the Socialist Party, and then became involved in Trotskyist circles. He was arrested in April 1943 as a resister, deported to Buchenwald, and freed in April 1945. He returned to France, and brought out two books which had great impact. *The Other Kingdom*, which won the Renaudot Prize in 1946, is simultaneously a narrative and an analysis of the Nazi camp system; and *Les Jours de notre mort* (The days of our death) (1947) is a polyphonic fiction composed of many different narratives of deportation. These two works brought into the French language a new adjective, *concentrationnaire*, to describe the camp regime, but they also forged an image of what deportation had been like for political prisoners that remained dominant in France for many years. Thereafter, Rousset went into politics and was elected to the French parliament, and he also wrote several more books on history and politics.

What was exceptional about Rousset was not that he had been an activist, a deportee, a survivor, or a witness, but that in 1949, of all the victims of Nazi repression, he alone fought on against the concentration camps that were still in existence. On 12 November 1949 he published an appeal to all former inmates of Nazi camps to take part in an investigation of the still-extant concentration camps, including Soviet camps. It had a quite shattering effect. There were a lot of Communists among French camp survivors, and they were torn between conflicting loyalties; many of the federations of former prisoners split in two. Rousset eventually won the support of other ex-deportees, but it was he who had taken the initiative and acted selflessly. It was a courageous act for which Rousset came under immediate and violent attack. His old friends abandoned him — even Emil Künder, his old comrade from Buchenwald, the German Communist to whom Rousset had dedicated *Les Jours de notre mort*. Former friends crossed the street so as not to have to acknowledge Rousset's existence. Communist journals, notably *Les Lettres françaises*, heaped insults on him;

Rousset sued for libel (Margarete Buber-Neumann was one of the witnesses for the prosecution) and won. Other former friends from the left wing repudiated him. In 1950 Sartre and Merleau-Ponty published in *Les Temps Modernes* a piece entitled "Les Jours de notre vie" (The days of our life) by which they broke off all relations with their comrade. "The truth is that experience, even of something as absolute as the horror of the concentration camps, cannot determine a political position," they wrote, so as to justify their refusal to condemn the Soviet Union—thereby providing us with a striking example of the political irresponsibility that was characteristic of French intellectuals of the period.

Rousset did not lose heart and persisted in his campaign. In January 1950, in the same month as the publication of Sartre's attack, he and a group of other former deportees founded an International Commission against Concentration Camp Regimes, which aimed to investigate all continuing concentration camps, wherever they might be. The founders' political, religious, and philosophical backgrounds were varied; what brought them together was their shared experience of Nazi camps and their common conviction that the most urgent task at hand in the world they lived in was to ensure that all other camps of that kind would cease to exist. The Soviet authorities did not give permission for the commission to investigate within the USSR, so the commission held a mock trial in Brussels in 1951 where an international panel (Germaine Tillion was the French representative) assessed the current state of knowledge of the Soviet camp system. Rousset acted as counsel for the prosecution.

The commission was very active for a decade. Rousset had unwittingly invented the idea of NGOs (nongovernmental organizations), which bring pressure to bear on governments by mobilizing public opinion, while remaining entirely outside of official structures. With its rigid division of the world into two opposing camps, the 1950s were not kind to "humanitarian" groups, as they would be called today. But that did not stop Rousset, and his commission got down to work. Its first task was to establish reliable facts. To that end, thousands of witnesses were interviewed, and their stories were analyzed and compared; the commission also collected, translated, and published relevant documents. Once this groundwork was done, public action could be undertaken, through questions to governments, legal suits, and press releases. What Rousset built was something like a forerunner of Amnesty International, and his many campaigns brought results, especially in "capitalist" countries.

Rousset gave twelve years of his life to this selfless task, though the labors of the commission members were doubly burdensome. Since the organization had no external funding, it was staffed by volunteers who had to earn their livings some other way; meetings were held in members' kitchens or backrooms. On top of this, of course, they were given regular drubbings by high-profile commentators in the "progressive" media, who accused them of being U.S. agents, enemies of peace, and barefaced liars. The only way of carrying on was to treat insults and lies as a duck treats rain, to let old friends turn their backs, and to accept support from people you would not otherwise value very much. As Germaine Tillion recalled fifty years later: "To defend Justice and Truth sometimes you have to face great suffering, perhaps even death (though with the profound and uninterrupted support that comes from thus remaining close to those that are close to you). A different form of courage is needed when Truth and Justice require us also to face up to those who *are* close to us—our comrades, our friends. . . . David Rousset possessed both forms of courage" (*A la recherche du vrai*, 217).

Understandably enough, there were moments when even the staunchest were gnawed by doubt and tempted to give up a hopeless struggle. Like anyone else, Rousset and his friends were "permanently paralyzed by emotions of affection and hatred, which conjured up any number of subtle ways of justifying cowardice out of the ambiguousness of things" (*Lignes*, 221). If they persisted nonetheless, it was because their painful experiences of deportation had marked them at the deepest level of their being, and they did not have to ask for whom the concentration camp bell tolled: it tolled for them (203). So, despite all the troubles it brought them, working for the commission made them feel that they were performing "the cleanest and the most necessary task since the last war" (205). Let us recall that the sole means of fighting against concentration camps at this period was to bring pressure to bear on totalitarian governments from the outside.

Rousset could have simply taken care of himself by devoting the rest of his life to recollecting the past, nursing his wounds, and keeping aflame the coals of resentment against those who had so grievously hurt him. But he chose to put care for others above care for himself by using past experience as a reason for action in the present, in a context he could only grasp by analogy, from the outside, since he was not a direct participant in it. That was how he understood his duty as a former deportee; and, most important, that was why he sought the cooperation primarily of other ex-deportees. "You cannot refuse the role of judge," he told them. "As political deportees, your most important task has to be that of judge. . . . Other people, people who never were in a camp, can say they can't imagine what it was like, they can claim they're not competent to judge. But we're all specialists, we're professionals. It's the price we have to pay for having been granted life beyond the camp" (Copfermann, 199). Investigating present-day concentration camps is the duty of all camp survivors. Contradicting Sartre and Merleau-Ponty, Rousset insisted that the right political choice was grounded in that essential experience — an experience that injected camp survivors with what Rousset called "a mad passion for truth and justice."

That choice necessarily involved making comparisons between Nazi and Soviet camp systems. Rousset was aware of the risks of doing that. Some of the differences were irreducible. There had never been any extermination camps in the USSR. Treblinka left you speechless and overwhelmed with pity for its victims, but it was not a basis from which you could extrapolate or construct any general argument; it provided no grounds for present action. But the camp system itself was common to the two regimes and despite real differences between them, comparison of the two types of concentration camp regime remained entirely justifiable. The comparative method was Rousset's essential tool; it led him from the known to the exploration of the unknown, and thus to understanding.

This raised a second question. Would it not have been even more justifiable to make the generalization broader by assimilating the suffering of camp inmates to "the universal wailing of humanity throughout the ages," to all kinds of misfortune and injustice? One risk of using the comparative method is of watering down the specificity of an experience through analogies with everything else. The result would be paralysis, because such universal analogizing would make the task of the campaigner impossibly huge; it would also be a fundamental mistake to see the camps as just one among many injustices in the world. They represent the greatest degradation of humanity in the history of the twentieth century. As Rousset said at his trial: "The misery of the camps has no common measure with any other misfortune" (*Pour la vérité*, 244). Rousset is making a generalization, but a limited one. He does not evacuate the specificity of the facts, but puts the facts in relation to each other. "No common measure" does not mean "no relation." The seed of the extreme can be found in the ordinary, but we must not forget the difference between the seed and the fruit.

Rousset's constant concern was to maintain the right balance between keeping a scale of values and crimes, on the one hand, and not dismissing topical injustices simply because they looked trivial alongside absolute evil. So he denounced hypocritical parallels, between the gulag and the fate of blacks in the southern United States, for instance, but would not keep silent about torture in Algeria on the pretext that the evil of the camps was incommensurably worse. His commission published the results of its inquiries into Soviet and Chinese labor camps, but it also published reports on Spanish and Greek prisons, on detention in Tunisia and torture in Algeria. The report on Algerian prisons — by a group of former deportees, including Germaine Tillion and Louis Martin-Chauffier — shows that it is necessary to be critical of one's own country even when it is not under a totalitarian regime.

How did Rousset become capable of such meritorious action? What were the elements which prepared him for such an exceptional life? In Rousset's own book, *Les Jours de notre mort*, we find many of the answers.

What strikes the modern reader of this book is the amount of political debate in it. Rousset tried to reconstruct the political positions adopted by the entire range of deportees, and all the conflicts between them. Other survivor-narratives focus on daily life in the camps and on the details of individual experience. Rousset does provide that also (for instance, in his account of the journey from the French assembly point at Drancy to Buchenwald), but that was not his main concern. Like courtiers in one of Shakespeare's history plays, Rousset's characters never stop making speeches. Though they may seem tedious nowadays, they underline Rousset's real purpose in writing: not to entertain, not to moralize or to philosophize, but to give a political analysis of an experience which for him had been essentially political. His Communist colleagues in the camp spent their time dreaming of a society free from barbarity, which they

152

would help to build after their release. Rousset did not have exactly the same dream, but he had no reservations about telling his German captors that he had always "fought against capitalists. We have to get rid of them and of their system. When the war is over, we have to build a united, planned economy in Europe, within the framework of genuine peoples' democracies" (*Les Jours*, 2:108–9).

Rousset's attitude as a deportee was framed from the start by this political program. Nowadays we have grown accustomed to thinking that once the huge initial hurdles had been overcome, the bravest of the camp inmates were motivated above all by the wish to bear witness, to struggle against oblivion, to preserve the record of the cruelty of the perpetrators and of the humanity of their victims. But that would not have been enough for David Rousset. He needed to do more than remember, reiterate, regurgitate, or resuscitate the past. What he sought was an understanding that would form the basis for action. "Since Buchenwald, uninterruptedly, I had been trying to understand, to observe with care . . . and to get as close I could to the German Communists, so as to lay the ground, through cordial cohabitation and utterly sincere appreciation on a daily basis, for a postwar situation that would be conducive to a shared political objective. The experience of the camps ought to provide both sides with reasons for wanting to build a socialist United States of Europe" (*Les Jours*, 2:78–79). The key words here are: understand, political, and provide.

So from the time of his deportation on, Rousset believed that his own experience, however unpleasant, should not be isolated from others, nor be treated as a monument: on the contrary, it had to be instrumentalized and applied to a political purpose. In the camp, therefore, his first duty was to do everything he could to understand. As he wrote in later years: "The dilemma was simple but imperative. Whether to submit to mere fortune, or else to understand and to take action. Action is not always possible. But you can always reach understanding" (as quoted by Bensaïd, *Lignes*, 127). Primo Levi tells us that the SS told prisoners "Here there is no why." But Rousset never stopped asking: why?

A striking feature of the basically political vision of *Les Jours de notre mort* is what we might call Rousset's dissolution of the categories by which collectivities are normally designated in conventional political analysis. Rousset does not go in at all for the black-and-white of guards and prisoners or the two-term analysis of perpetrators and victims. In the world he depicts there were infinitely many levels and layers; and there were fierce struggles for power between different groups of prisoners. People from different countries did not behave in the same way; nor did people from different social backgrounds. Political beliefs also interfered with social categories: Communists were never confused with Trotskyists, and they were themselves quite separate from "bourgeois" democrats. Behavior was also considerably affected by the amount of time spent in the camp. So the result was a camp population made up like a mosaic of varieties of attitudes that could not be classified in any simple way. "White wasn't always white and black wasn't always black" is how Rousset's biographer sums it up (Copferman, 15).

Some prisoners resigned themselves to their lot, did what they were told, and whatever else was necessary to cope with hunger, cold, and fatigue. They constituted what Rousset called "camp fodder"—men who had adapted to the demands of the world of the concentration camp. Nobody was safe from that fate, and Rousset, who often rose above it, knew that he could only too easily succumb. He would have preferred to have unselfish relations with his comrades; but he realized that when he gave up his tobacco ration to a friendly *kapo*, he suddenly found his bread and soup ration increased. "I ate it. I was so hungry! But I really resented being hungry to that extent. I would have given anything to avoid the experience" (*Les Jours*, 2:299).

Other prisoners accepted their submission and were keen to prove that submission was unavoidable; and as soon as they gained any power, they tried to force their comrades to behave as they had done. "To justify themselves they sought to destroy the dignity of others, to give a grand demonstration that men cannot resist, to prove that you just needed the right conditions to topple all values." But one of them suspected that was not the only answer. "Is there something in man that is not shit? he wondered. He must have found the suspicion unbearable" (*Les Jours*, 2:176). He needed to see that everyone else was like him. "To see himself . . . absorbed in the same hopelessness, with all links to others severed, and to deny the final, ultimate shred of solidarity was a victory for such a man, a complete justification of his own suicide, of the only suicide that really matters, a suicide which blasphemes life" (2:305).

What were the forms of dignity that some tried to destroy and others clung to at any cost? Its simplest expression could be just keeping clean, that is to say, refusing to let yourself go or to give way to fatigue. "To keep clean in spite of the conditions was to save a shred of dignity, and was thus a way of resisting" (*Les Jours*, 2:12). Or else it might involve maintaining respect for work well done, to prove the worker's own excellence. Other prisoners saw dignity in taking an eye for an eye, a tooth for a tooth. "The Russian restored his own dignity by killing" (2:287). Men who belonged to a Resistance organization possessed a dignity that would outlive them. Others chose to give meaning to their lives by taking care of others. "Hewitt found his own form of resistance, which was a decision to sacrifice himself for others. In order to live he needed to feel he was useful, to be sure he was fulfilling a human function" (1:121–22). And then there were those who resisted by teaching comrades Mozart's chamber music, thereby adding a spark of beauty to their lives. "I played for them one Sunday evening. . . . They made an admirable audience. I was happy" (2:260).

One of Rousset's recurrent concerns was to undo national stereotypes, especially the obviously tempting view of Germans as "nothing but Nazis." He could not accept that equation, if only because the camps also housed many members of the German anti-Nazi resistance. But the camp guards were also not all made of the same cloth. One *Kommandoführer* refused to hit the prisoners, and even to keep watch over them; and when he left the camp, he gave the prisoners his best wishes for a speedy return home. (His was a most unusual case; straight after describing it, Rousset adds: "There were also brutes") (*Les Jours*, 2:108). But another *Meister* left his subordinates a slice of bread every day, and a third "smuggled in tomatoes and fruit" (2:266). Rousset concluded that "most of them were not Nazis. They were fed up with terror and war. But they did not know which way to go. . . . They had lost confidence in themselves and in others. They were desperate, and obedient" (2:109). What was true of the Germans was also true of Russians, French, and Poles.

The Communists, with whom Rousset was in touch every

day, also refused to believe that nationality determined character. However, the Communists' disregard of nationality as a determining factor was only a stepping-stone to the acceptance of another equally rigid form of social and political determinism. Bad behavior by a prisoner was not to be accounted for by the fact that he was Russian or Ukrainian, the Communists explained, but because he was "a common criminal" or "a kulak" or "a Fascist stooge" (1:121). In their eyes the world was divided into two mutually exclusive halves: whoever was not pro-Soviet was necessarily in cahoots with the Nazis. "The Warsaw uprising was carried out by Polish Fascists on behalf of their paymasters in London" (2:143).

Rousset parted company with his comrades on this point, and it was a decisive one. He did not want to substitute one kind of determinism for another, nor to pile one upon the other. He had realized that human beings are never fully accounted for by the category to which they belong; that individuals can also wish, choose, and act either in accordance with the forces that control them, or in opposition to them. The exercise of liberty is what makes people so different from each other; if all of us only ever obeyed the iron law of necessity, then we would all be as alike as two cans of beans.

That is what Rousset saw as the main change that his camp experience made to him, and he regarded it as a precious acquisition. "I had always been passionately interested in ideas. But who in our world gave a damn for ideas? Maybe at Buchenwald, but not the guys in the transports! I learned to watch how people without any ideas managed to live. I found them fascinating, and the most abject of them often had surprising qualities. I realized that ideas are not indispensable to human existence, and the world manages without them" (*Les Jours*, 2:229). Rousset didn't give up his love of ideas, but from then on he put people above them.

He came back to the same point years later, in the autobiography he wrote with Émile Copferman. Before his arrest, he says, he lived in a world of books and abstractions — "revolution," "socialism," "humanity." During his captivity he suffered cruelly from being deprived of reading matter. But he began to find a remedy which he came to cherish dearly: taking an interest in individual people. "It was the start of an outstanding experiment which was immensely rewarding for me. . . . I had no access to books. But I began to discover men" (Copferman, 65). Rousset didn't value people *instead of* books; on his release, in fact, he threw himself back into reading and writing. But he now put people *above* books. He had gone into the camp with all the prejudices of a militant intellectual, as he says, but he managed to overcome the dangerous habit of living through abstractions; he realized that he could no longer reduce the suffering of individuals to instances of some category or other. Only categories can be condemned in absolute terms (e.g., Nazism is evil); individuals may also be judged, but only in relative terms. "Some of them turned into bloodthirsty beasts, but what had made them rotten was the system itself" (*Les Jours*, 2:267).

Within a concentration camp there were two opposing forces, even if there were also many intermediate positions between them. On one side were the SS, whose conduct sought to prove that humanity was not of a piece, but made up of two radically different species, masters and slaves, those who act and those who are acted on — by fear, hunger, and instinct. The masters achieve their ends if and when the slaves themselves believe they are of a different essence, if they themselves abandon all forms of protest, give up any wish to bear witness, renounce all attempts to share any kind of feeling with the SS.

On the other side, there are the resisters — more numerous by far than those who belonged to Resistance organizations. Resisters carried on acting on their own behalf, at least in part as free and responsible subjects, and consequently rejected the idea that humanity was divided in two, the free and the entirely captive. "The civilians and the military thought of us as animal excrement. In their eyes there was nothing human about us." But men who resisted asserted the unity of the species. Rousset said of his comrade Emil Künder that the greatest service he performed was "to impose us on others as human beings" (*Les Jours*, 2:68). Rousset's overall conclusion is that the unity of men is achieved by asserting the inner freedom that all human beings possess. "Abject and frightening as we were, we nonetheless carried off a victory that goes far beyond us and which is a victory for the whole of the human collectivity. We never gave up the struggle, we never recanted. . . . We never believed in the final disaster of humanity" (2:685).

David Rousset is in many ways an unusual figure among camp survivors. I never knew him personally and I do not know what he was like in daily life. (His close friends have told me that his private life was in keeping with his public image.) In any case, his books are free of the atmosphere of anguish that is characteristic of many other survivor narratives. He had seen and had faced horror, to be sure, but he had also managed to extract some benefit from it. More than anyone else, Rousset put what he learned into practice. His experience of concentration camps gave him the means to struggle against still-extant camps and to prevent any new ones coming into existence. The lesson he learned was a political one, and it defined a position within the public sphere; but paradoxically, Rousset's politics were based on his faith in the autonomous subject. To put it another way: Rousset's ideal for the collectivity consisted of freedom for the individual. This discovery explains Rousset's conduct after his release: it was what made him choose truth over loyalty to an organization. "You can't let your class, your party, or your state choose between truth and falsehood for you. Your ultimate court of appeal is you, yourself" (*Lignes*, 222).

So he was able to get through camp without being terribly damaged by it; indeed, he profited from the discovery that it imposed upon him, that people matter more than ideas, and that even the most restricted existence still remains a human life. Rousset says that he learned the secret from Emil Künder, the old German Communist whom he admired. The secret was to live in the present, and not to treat the present exclusively as deprivation in comparison to a better past. "What had allowed him to survive many years in this hell was the decision he had taken one day to live in this other kingdom, casting out any unhealthy nostalgia for the past" (*Les Jours*, 2:87). Rousset learned the trick for himself — how not to give way to longings for distant times and people, how to keep his eyes open to what was around him, how to take pleasure in being alive, even under such demeaning conditions, how to accept the present and the people it provides. "This new taste for the animal behavior of my fellow humans was what prevented me from dying of mental starvation. Quite to the contrary, it seemed to enrich me" (2:229).

That must be the most enlivening experience that anyone ever brought back from the camps of death.

The Uses of Memory

> It was she who walked barefoot and stepped
> lightly over the trembling soil of Treblinka, from
> the marshalling yard to the gas chamber.
>
> Yes, that is her. I saw her in 1930 at Konotop
> station, she came up to the carriage of the
> express, her face was dark with pain, she raised
> her wondrous eyes and said voicelessly, with
> only her lips moving: "Bread . . ."
> — *Vasily Grossman, "The Sistine Madonna"*

THE FRYING PAN AND THE FIRE

At the turn of a century, Europeans, and perhaps the French most
of all, seem obsessed by a cult of memory. Possessed by nostalgia
for an age now irrevocably past, we revere its relics and indulge
in magic rituals that are supposed to keep it alive. A new museum
opens every day of the year, somewhere in Europe. All the everyday activities of yesteryear — lacemaking, chestnut harvesting,
donkey breeding, and millinery — have their own *écomusées*. And
our calendars are so full of memorial days for the remarkable
events of the past that there's almost no room left for anything
more to happen in the future!

There's nothing natural about this compulsive concern for the
past, which cries out for interpretation. The cult of memory does
not always serve good causes. As the distinguished French historian Jacques Le Goff pointed out, "commemoration of the past
reached its peak in Nazi Germany and Fascist Italy" (158); we
could add that the commemorative tide was just as high in Stalinist Russia, where carefully selected events in the historical record
were used to comfort national pride and to prop up flagging ideological faith. That's not about to happen in Western democracies.
So is the fashion for commemoration a symptom of the health of
peaceful societies in which, thank goodness, nothing much ever

happens? In the 1990s, history happened every day in the Balkans, but who wanted to live there? Or is it nostalgia for the lost era of Europe's global power? Or should we simply be pleased that the younger generation can learn from the experience of its elders?

Unfortunately, positive effects do not always flow directly from obsession with the past — quite the opposite, in fact. In France, hardly a week of the 1990s went by without a TV film, a documentary, or a debate on the Second World War, dealing with either the heroism of one or another group, or the rise of Nazism, or the persecution and genocide of the Jews. Yet an extreme right-wing party with an explicitly racist ideology deriving in part from the Nazi program (but without the Nazis' plans for extermination, it must be said) scored up to 15 percent of the popular vote in presidential and parliamentary elections, and, in a few constituencies, it even reached an absolute majority. Similar trends have been seen in several other European countries. Meditating on the purpose of the Holocaust Museum in Washington, Philip Gourevitch observed that "there is every reason to believe that exposure to barbarism is *not* an antidote against it" (*Behold Now Behemoth*, 62). How far can we generalize this observation?

The absence of automatic effect first struck me at the time of the trial of Klaus Barbie for crimes against humanity. This was the first prosecution of its kind in France. The defendant was the former head of the Gestapo in Lyon, and the aim of the trial was not so much to punish him for crimes committed forty years earlier as to educate the French by reminding them of the horrors that resulted from a policy of racial discrimination. The trial was widely featured in all the media, and nobody could escape the lesson in virtue that was being given. But during the trial, in June 1987, a gang of youngsters in Nice beat a Tunisian-born laborer to death. When they were arrested, the hoodlums told the police: "We're racists, we are. We don't like Arabs." The father of one of the boys was quite happy to declare that he understood and approved his son's motives.

Such "mis-fires" of memory don't just happen in France, of course. All over the world, even while it has never been so widely denounced in the unparalleled flow of information we now enjoy, evil continues to wreak havoc. What I would like to argue here is that "memory," without further definition, is neither good nor bad in itself. The benefits we might wish to derive from it can be neutralized or even confiscated. There are several ways in which we can forfeit the value of the past. They relate to the uses we make of the past and to the manner in which we reminisce. Let us begin with the latter. We can fall into the frying pan by making the past *sacred* and thus isolating it completely from the present; and we can fall into the fire by making it *trivial*, by seeing the present exclusively through the lens of the past.

To assert that an event is singular, or unique, or specific is not the same thing as saying that it is sacred. The two claims are not at all synonymous. I begin with an example that is familiar to everyone, the extermination of European Jewry during the Second World War, and the memory of it that has been preserved. It is perfectly legitimate to describe the Nazis' attempt to exterminate the Jews as a singular and specific event, but we must also specify what we mean by that description. In terms of values, all human lives are equally precious, and when victims are counted in millions, it is pointless, to say the least, to try to establish hierarchies in martyrdom. (One of Woody Allen's characters quips that, in matters of genocide, "records are there to be beaten.") When they exceed a certain level, crimes of this kind, however specific they may be, seem to dissolve into the unmitigated horror they provoke and the absolute condemnation they deserve. And this is just as true for the extermination of Native Americans, the enslavement of Africans, and the terrors of the gulag as it is for the genocide of the Jews. The life and dignity of a man, woman, or child means the same, irrespective of race, nationality, or culture. The destruction of preliterate nations is no less despicable than the extermination of the people of the Book.

We have a dangerous tendency of attributing greater significance to actions that concern us more directly. As each of us necessarily forms the center of our respective worlds, so we see what comes closest to us as most important. The Japanese writer Kenzaburo Oe, for example, considers the Hiroshima bomb "the cruelest days in human history" (*Hiroshima Notes*, 79), "the most dreadful conditions ever suffered by mankind" (16), "the most merciless human doom of the twentieth century," and so forth (29). The debate on specificity is not a question of historical facts: the uniqueness of every event is unarguably obvious at the literal level. What is specific and also merits examination is, of course, the meaning of an event. We have already looked at what made the Nazis' killing of the Jews a singular event — the explicitly formulated aim of systematically exterminating a people indissociably connected to the historical identity of Europe.

But this specificity, established through a set of comparisons and a precise historical context, is sometimes understood to mean *sacred*. Putting aside the oddness of sanctifying the annihilation of one's own people, the equivalence asserted between the specific and the sacred is far from obvious. Sanctification is a mark of restriction, by definition; it places its object in a separate category and makes it untouchable (and words that refer to it, especially if they are not proper names, like "genocide" or "totalitarian," become similarly "sacrilegious"). But just because the events of the past are unique, just because each one has a specific meaning, does not forbid us from making connections between them and other events. The opposite would be nearer the truth: the specificity of events does not require their isolation but their interconnection. The more such links can be made, the more the event becomes particular (or singular). God is sacred — but God is held to be an ubiquitous and absolute presence, and not particular, as are all facts located in a specific time and place.

If the singularity of the genocide of the Jews is understood in this new, sanctified way, that is to say, if it is held to be without relation to all other past, present, or future events, then it would justify us in denouncing the comparisons that are made in various quarters, and could legitimate our opposing all and any attempts to understand or to represent it (claims that the genocide is "incomprehensible," "unspeakable," "unsayable," and so on really mean "you must not . . ."). But such an approach would automatically prevent us from learning any lessons from the event and would close off all "application." It would be paradoxical, to say the least, if we asserted that the past should be a lesson for the present, and at the same time that it has no connection with the present. Things that are sanctified in this way are not much use to us in our real lives. The sanctified past may be kept in quarantine if we so wish it, it can remain a memory that guides us in our actions, but to adopt that approach does not allow the past to make its proper contribution to an understanding of the human race or its future.

The past can thus become a veil obscuring the present and an excuse for holding back. In the spring of 1994, Philip Gourevitch went to Washington to attend White House press briefings on the Rwandan genocide. The United States had decided not to intervene, so the briefings were vague and evasive. Because the two buildings happen to be close to each other, Gourevitch also wandered into the Holocaust Museum and saw hundreds of lapel badges and clips in the gift boutique with logos that declared "Never Again!" "Always Remember!" "Let Us Not Forget," and so forth. But these appeals to memory had no impact on the way in which current events in Rwanda were being voluntarily forgotten; in their own way, they made it easier to take no notice.

More recently, in January 2000, many heads of state gathered in Stockholm to commemorate the genocide of the Jews. Not one of them saw fit to use the occasion to make a public protest (as David Rousset had done fifty years before, and as they were being asked to do by a petition) against the crimes being committed against its own people by the totalitarian regime of North Korea. The petition pointed out that there were still dozens of concentration camps flourishing in North Korea, and that between one million and three million people had died there of hunger in the preceding five years.

Sanctifying the past is one danger; but the opposite process, whereby present events lose all their specificity through unwarranted parallels with the past, is just as bad. Evil as extreme as that of the twentieth century is easily turned into a rhetorical weapon; but whenever we have recourse to those verbal forms, we betray the specificity of the past event, and, more seriously, we almost certainly misunderstand the present. As Rousset said, the evil of the camps was not just more intense than any other; it also had a different meaning: the killing grounds of Auschwitz and Kolyma revealed the truth of unprecedented ideologies and political systems.

So when we call a shit a Nazi, we forfeit the lesson of Auschwitz. Hitler's name is most frequently taken in vain in almost every context—even while the genocide of the Jews is supposed to be unique. In 1956 Western governments thought they had found Hitler's reincarnation in Nasser, who had had the cheek to nationalize the Suez Canal. Since then, the dead Führer has never stopped returning to life: the U.S. government uses his name to describe its enemies when it needs the support of the international community (Saddam Hussein has been called a "new Hitler," just like Slobodan Milošević). The hate-figures themselves return the compliment (less effectively) by calling the West "Fascist" and "Nazi."

In the Middle East these comparisons have become small change. On one side, Arab leaders from Nasser to Arafat are represented with Hitler's moustache; and on the other, Arab media accuse this or that Israeli politician of behaving like the Nazi leader. The insult also works inside each camp: according to the French newspaper *Le Monde*, one U.S. web-site opposed to the Oslo peace agreements showed Ehud Barak in a Nazi uniform unrolling a Palestinian flag and saying "I'll finish the job for you, *mein Führer!*" (*Le Monde*, 16–17 July, 2000). We even find paradoxical combinations of the two processes of sanctification and trivialization: the Holocaust Museum in Washington refused entry to Yasser Arafat on the grounds that he was "a reincarnation of Hitler" (*Le Monde*, 21 January, 1988).

To sum up: the slogans that we have heard on Paris streets since 1968 calling the riot police "Nazis" are as unjustified as the recent claims of the current leader of the Russian Communist Party, Gennady Zyuganov, that Boris Yeltsin and his team were committing genocide against their own people. "No bomb, no Auschwitz can be compared to the crematorium that the reformers have set alight in our lands," he said (quoted in *Le Monde*, 27 November, 1998). Such purely rhetorical projections of the past onto the present hardly help to make it comprehensible; in fact, they make it more difficult to see it for what it is. To say that the Russian president Vladimir Putin is walking in Stalin's footsteps obstructs our attempts to know who Stalin was and who Putin will be.

SERVING PURPOSES

Memory can be sterilized by the way it is handled. A sanctified past brings nothing to mind but itself; a trivialized past reminds us of anything and everything. But even if we avoid the frying pan and the fire, the services we ask the past to do for us are not all equally advisable.

Individuals and groups alike need to recall the past to assert their own identities. Both are of course also defined by their actions in the present and their projects for the future, but they cannot actually do without reference to the past. Without a sense of our own identity, we feel threatened in our very being, and may be paralyzed. The requirement of identity is perfectly legitimate — people need to know who they are and to what group they belong. Knowing that you are a Catholic, or a Communist, or a Scotsman, or a longshoreman allows your own existence to be recognized, it tells you that you are not nobody, that you are not in danger of being swallowed up by the void. So if we learn something about the past that forces us to reinterpret the image that we had of ourselves and of our own circle, we have to modify not just an isolated aspect of our selves, but our very identity. If you have seen an Alzheimer patient, then you've seen memory loss destroying identity.

There is nothing wrong with a need for identity, although it would be more correct to consider identity multiple rather than singular, variable rather than fixed. However, people and groups exist among other people and groups. It is therefore not enough to assert that each has the right to exist: self-assertion can impact in different ways on the lives of others. Actions that strengthen the identities of individuals and groups may well be useful to those who undertake them, but they have no moral value in themselves. Moral value can be attached only to actions that benefit others. Identity politics are quite distinct from a morality based on otherness.

Let us now return to the main roles we identified in historical narrative. To assess the moral value of those who make the past live again in the present, we have to ask on whom they project themselves, with which actor or group of actors in the historical narrative they identify themselves.

First, we cannot rely on people to choose only "positive" characters as models of behavior; "bad" figures can also be attractive if their example offers us some advantage. In every crime there is a criminal and a victim, but nothing ensures that people who reflect on the past will always side with the victims. As Germaine Tillion warned us: "The crazy world of the Nazis is very suitable for stimulating sadomasochistic fantasies" (*La Traversée*). The story of a massacre may elicit compassion — but it may also give satisfaction to sadists and voyeurs, whose emotions are not alien to human nature. The Kielce pogrom of 1946, for instance, imitated the violence of the Second World War, which had shown just how easy it was to commit murder (Bensoussan, 146). Hitler, it is said, recalled the Armenian genocide in a paradoxical way — hoping that the genocide of the Jews would be forgotten just as quickly. Stalin used the same kind of reasoning when he signed the old Bolsheviks' death warrants. In the presence of Molotov and Yezhov, he asked who would remember any of that rabble ten or twenty years after. "Nobody. Who now knows the names of the Boyars that Ivan the Terrible got rid of? Nobody" (quoted in Glover, 328). Stalin and Hitler were fortunately wrong, and memory has vanquished the oblivion they sought to impose. But the point is that, in their references to the past, they identified not with the victim but with the perpetrator.

Let us suppose, though, that we have chosen to identify ourselves with the "good" side. That does not prevent us from being victims in one context and perpetrators in another. As Primo Levi said: "An oppressed person can become an oppressor. And often does" (*Conversazioni*, 247). Or as Margarete Buber-Neumann reminds us, suffering does not make its victim noble. Albert Camus was one of the first to make the connection between the Second World War and the war in Algeria, where the French army played an opposite role. "The facts are there, as obvious and ugly as reality: in Algeria we are doing what we blamed the Germans for doing to us" (*Actuelles*, 128). In 1958, even while memories of the Second World War and its atrocities were still fresh, the French began to use torture as a systematic tool in Algeria. Reviewing Henri Alleg's famous exposé of the issue, *La Question*, Jean-Paul Sartre commented: "In 1943, in the Gestapo's Paris HQ in Rue Lauriston, French people screamed with fear and pain, and all France heard their cries. The outcome of the war was not sure at that time, and we did not want to think about the future. Only one thing seemed completely impossible — that men would ever be made to scream like that in the name of France. But the impossible can always happen. Now, in 1958, in Algiers, torture is being used regularly, systematically. Everybody knows . . . but nobody talks about it" (Sartre, 72).

Alas, there is nothing particularly French about the inability to learn the right lessons from the past. We could even coin a maxim, in the manner of a classical moralist: we never learn from

166

other people's mistakes. By "we" I mean to say any collective entity, be it a nation, a class, or a faction, to which we belong or with which we identify ourselves. So if I may return to the example of France in Algeria, I would say that the French learned very little from the story of the crimes committed by the Germans during the Second World War. If the victims of 1944 turned into the perpetrators of 1958, it is because they were not on the side of the perpetrators in 1944.

People may identify with the victim of past crimes and draw the conclusion that history allows or even obliges them to take up an aggressive attitude in the present. It is after all the basic structure of revenge — hurt suffered justifies hitting back. But what makes this different from revenge is that the former victim that has become an aggressor makes a victim of some party that has nothing to do with the original aggressor. This occurs in tragic cases of cruelty to children whose parents were themselves battered or abused as children. Twenty, thirty, or forty years later, the abused child who is now an adult visits his own child with the same torments, often without grasping any connection between the events.

To some degree, this situation is similar to the politics of memory practiced nowadays in Israel. Without going into detail on a topic that many others have explored, we may note that nowhere else in the world is the memory of the genocide of the Jews more present (and there are obvious reasons for that); yet Israel's policy toward its neighbors, and particularly toward the Palestinians, is not irreproachable in respect of the right of others to existence and dignity. Past experience has not automatically handed down a lesson that might be of benefit to these others; on the contrary, it is invoked to justify policies which put the victims' descendants and their compatriots in the opposite role, making Palestinians, in Edward Said's expression, "the victims' victims" (*Le Monde*, 27 May 1998). But there is nothing inevitable about this. Israeli Supreme Court Judge Landau decided that, in view of the Jews' long history of suffering, it was legitimate to use torture on Palestinian prisoners to protect Israeli civilians and combat terrorism; but in the same country, Professor Leibovitz, referring to the same past history, reached the opposite conclusion, namely that torture should be opposed by all possible means. Neither of these

167

lessons can be judged in terms of its relationship to the past; they can only be judged in the light of our present moral and political beliefs.

The continuing violence in present-day Algeria, insofar as it involves two opposing factions of the same people, constitutes another variant. The Algerian massacres are, of course, examples of the criminalization of religious fanatics whose faith has become a mere facade, and they also illustrate the cruelty of revenge (since each outrage seems to respond to another). But it is also the fruit of an older history — the long-term effect of 120 years of violence perpetrated by French colonizers on colonized Algerians. The slaughter of the war of conquest, the systematic humiliation of the native population during peacetime, and the brutality of the war that led to independence have all left deep scars that cannot be quickly healed. As with battered children who turn into adult bruisers, violence done to nations can engender similar violence years or decades later. Evil does not vanish from history as soon as its perpetrator has been dealt with. The brutalities of the Algerian war, just like Hitler's crimes, still spread evil in the world of today.

What Memory Is For

If the forms and functions of memory can be so easily misapplied, would it not be better to forget the past? In some cases, maybe it would. In a democracy, people have a legitimate right to recover the past as they please, but memory should never be imposed on them as a duty. It would be horribly cruel to keep on reminding someone of the most painful parts of his or her own past: the right to forget exists as well. Euphrosinia Kersnovskaïa concludes her amazing illustrated account of twelve years in the gulag with an address to her mother: "You asked me to write the sad story of these 'years of apprenticeship.' I've carried out your last wish. But would it not have been better for it all to have sunk into oblivion?" (Kersnovskaïa, 253). In *Writing or Life*, Jorge Semprun tells us how at a particular moment in his life he was virtually saved by being able to forget his time in the concentration camp.

In the public sphere too, forgetting may be preferred to remembering. Amerigo Vespucci, the explorer of the American continent, has this story to tell us. After describing the relations between Europeans and the native population, which alternated between cooperation and hostility, he notes that groups of natives were often at war with each other. Why so? "I could not learn from them why they make war since they do not have private property, or command empires or kingdoms, and have no notion of greed. . . . When we asked them to tell us the cause, the only reason they could give . . . was that they wish to avenge the death of their ancestors: in sum, a bestial thing" (Vespucci, 34). If this is correct, should we not wish that these peoples had forgotten their hatred a little so as to live in peace, had allowed their resentments to subside and found better uses for the energy they wasted in war? But that would be to wish these people to be different from what they were.

The opening paragraphs of the Edict of Nantes are worth mentioning here. The edict was issued in 1598 and its purpose was to put an end to the religious wars that had been tearing France apart. The French king, Henri IV, declared "that the memory of all things having taken place on one side and on the other from the beginning of March 1585 to the date of our accession to the throne, and of all things having taken place during and on account of the earlier troubles, be extinguished and put to rest, as a thing null and void; and it shall not be allowed or permitted to our crown prosecutors nor to any other public or private person, at any time or for any reason, to mention them or make a suit or charge relating to them in any court or jurisdiction whatsoever. . . . We forbid all our subjects of every rank and station to renew the memory of these things" (Cottret, 363).

Closer to us in time, though, is the opposite example of Paul Déroulède, a poet who founded the French League of Patriots and held strong militaristic beliefs. His calls to the French to never forget their defeat of 1870 and to keep the hatred of Germany alive paved the way for the First World War and the slaughter of Verdun. Plutarch once said that politics may be defined as the art of making hatred less eternal — that is to say, of subordinating the past to the present. But the war cries of the enemies of forgetting — Déroulède, Péguy, Barrès, and many others — had their impact and were a factor in the outbreak of the First World War. In the 1920s the memory of the humiliating

169

Treaty of Versailles gave Hitler what he needed to persuade his compatriots to get ready for the Second World War. Slogans like "Don't Forgive, Don't Forget," which are often heard nowadays, are hardly indicative of civilization's progress.

If remembering the past leads to death, surely forgetting is preferable? In Brussels, in 1988, a group of Israelis and Palestinians sat at the same table on the explicit understanding that "just to start talking, we have to put the past in parentheses" (*Give Peace a Chance*, Brussels Congress, March 1988), and they were surely right about that. If the past is to rule the present, then neither the Jews, nor the Christians, nor the Muslims are going to give up their claims on Jerusalem. In Northern Ireland, both extremist parties were determined neither to forgive nor forget and until very recently continued to add names to the long list of the victims of the troubles, with each assassination prompting a revenge killing. All that is presumably why Winston Churchill called one day for an act of forgetting once the horrors of the Second World War were over. He only forgot that forgetting cannot be achieved by an act, either of the will or of parliament.

The genocides of the middle part of the twentieth century, from Stalin's massacres to those of Pol Pot, were carried out in the name of the future; totalitarianism needed to eliminate the "unsuitable elements" to create "new man." More recent slaughters, however, have been perpetrated in the name of the past. In Rwanda, the Hutus' campaign against the Tutsis was pursued as revenge for the humiliations the latter had inflicted on them in previous decades; the wars in Yugoslavia were laced with reproaches for massacres suffered by each and every party years or centuries before; in Algeria, the crimes of today are made all the easier by the fact that the crimes of yesteryear have not been forgotten. The recollection of violence past feeds violence in the present: it is a mechanism of revenge.

Revenge is not highly valued these days, and people do not often claim it as their motive. But when it is masked in the dress of justice, revenge is far from alien to us. That often becomes clear when a death occurs. We frequently see the parents of abused and murdered children calling for the guilty to suffer the heaviest penalty, that is to say, capital punishment. Something similar occurred recently in the cases brought against French Health Ministry officials for having failed to prevent HIV-contaminated blood being administered to hemophiliacs: the parents of the victims wanted the officials to be found guilty of murder, so that their sentences would be as close as possible to their children's fate.

But there is a double distinction to be made between justice and revenge. First, vengeance means responding to an individual act by another, broadly comparable, individual act: you killed my son, I kill yours. Justice, on the other hand, pits a general law against an individual act, and the very nature of the lawcourts makes it clear that it is not a matter of an individual taking revenge. Revenge, like forgiveness, is a personal thing; justice is impersonal, because the law makes no distinction between persons. Sentences, moreover, are not reflections of the crime but proportionate to sentences for other crimes — that is to say, penalties are not directly motivated by the offense but form a system. A judgment heals the fracture in the social order by confirming the reach of the law (written or, in the case of crimes against humanity, unwritten) and therefore the health of the social order itself. But criminal law does not compensate the victim for the hurt that has been suffered; what matters in this respect is not whether justice has been applied leniently or harshly but the fact that it has been exercised.

Revenge is a violent response to violence and in turn provokes more violence: evil goes on increasing, not diminishing. There are a thousand examples of this infernal cycle, from the *Oresteia* to Sicilian vendettas. But we all know that the only way Montagues and Capulets will ever bury the hatchet is when one of them voluntarily renounces an act of vengeance instead of carrying it out. Revenge has the further disadvantage of giving avengers a good conscience and of never prompting them to question the evil in their own hearts. The moral issue is displaced by physical reparation. Justice, on the other hand, has the disadvantage of being abstract and depersonalized — but it is the only chance we have of reducing violence.

The same could be said of capital punishment, which is a legalized form of revenge, and which is still used in many non-European countries, including the United States. Many studies of the issue have all reached the same conclusion, that capital punishment is a purely retributive form of justice (the killer must be killed) and has no preventative function, despite the claims of its supporters. In his essay on capital punishment, Albert Camus quoted the revealing fact that 170 of the 250 men hanged in England in the earlier part of the twentieth century had themselves attended a hanging (see Camus with Koestler). Firsthand experience of the death penalty had thus affected their behavior not at all. The relationship of capital punishment to personal vengeance is underlined by the fact that in some U.S. states victims' relatives are now allowed to attend the execution of the perpetrator.

The death penalty is not just an ineffective weapon in the fight against crime; it also has a negative effect on any society that uses it. Like other forms of vengeance, it creates the illusion that evil can be got rid of in the person of the guilty party. Second, the irreversible and definitive form of this punishment implies that the criminal is incapable of change. For Rousseau perfectibility was the very definition of the human: unlike other animals, human beings are not totally determined by their "nature" and are capable of change by acts of free will. This concept of humanity lies at the root of democratic rule, which respects and protects the autonomy of the individual. We may therefore question whether states that continue to make wide use of the death penalty can really be considered part of the democratic world.

Keeping alive the memory of harm that has been done to us can lead to acts of revenge, but forgetting can also have dire effects. A quite illuminating parallel can be made between the social and the psychological. Psychoanalysis makes memory a central issue, because it holds that neuroses are caused by a memory disorder called repression. Repression is the process by which the subject excludes from active memory various facts or events that occurred in infancy and have become unbearable, for one reason or another. The analytic cure involves the recovery of the repressed memories. But what use will these memories be once they are brought back to consciousness? During the period of their suppression these memories remained active forces that prevented the subject from living fully; once recovered, they can be put back in their rightful place. The aim of analysis, according to the French historian Pierre Nora, "is not to stifle you with the eternal regurgitation of your past, but rather to free you from it" (*Le Monde*, 29 November 1994). Mourning constitutes another way of disabling memory. To begin with, we refuse to admit the reality of the loss we have suffered, but little by little, without ceasing to treasure the memory of the deceased, we alter the status of the images attached to him or her, and pain is slowly assuaged by a sense of distance. Broadly speaking, we do not believe that the past should rule the present.

In public life, similarly, recalling the past does not provide its own justification. To be useful, it has to go through a process of transformation, and just like a personal memory, it has to be worked through (*durchgearbeitet*, in Freud's terminology). In this case, the transformation consists in going from the particular case to general maxim—a principle of justice, a political ideal, or a moral rule—which must be legitimate in itself and not just because it relates to a cherished memory. The singularity of facts does not prevent their lessons from being universal. For example: the saving of Bulgaria's Jews during the Second World War was a unique event, unlike any other; but it nonetheless bears a meaning and a lesson for everybody, then and now (see my *Fragility of Goodness*). Memory of the past can be useful to us if it hastens the reign of justice, in the most general sense—and that means that the particular must be subordinated to the abstract precept. The criminal justice system, as we have seen, is based on the generalization of particular offenses; it is embodied in impersonal laws applied by a judge acting on behalf of anonymous authority ("the crown" or "the republic") and by jurors who are not personally acquainted with the accused or with the victim. This has to be so for justice to exist: it would not be justice if it were applied by the actual victims of the offense. Deindividualization, if I may coin such a term, is a precondition for the rule of law.

The right use of memory is one that serves a right cause, not one that merely reproduces the past. The libel cases pursued by Viktor Kravchenko and David Rousset were perfect examples. Their detractors, opposed to their campaigns against concentration camps, had not forgotten their own past experience: Pierre Daix, Marie-Claude Vaillant-Couturier, and all the others who appeared for the defense had lived through the hell of Mauthausen or Auschwitz, and they had perfect recall of the camps. Their refusal to join the struggle against the gulag wasn't the result of a lapse of memory; it came from an ideological parti pris. Vaillant-Couturier, a Communist member of parliament, declared that she would not even consider the question since she knew that "there are no concentration camps in the Soviet Union"

(Rousset, *Pour la vérité*, 194). Which is how former deportees became real negationists — more dangerous even than those who today deny the existence of Hitler's gas chambers, because, at the time of the trial, the Soviet camps still existed, and the only available means of fighting against them was to denounce them in public. Daix's memory was no less accurate than Rousset's, but what makes the latter's preferable is that it served to defend democracy, not totalitarianism. It is otiose to ask whether we need to know the truth about the past, because there can only be one answer: yes. But it is not so straightforward when it comes to the ends to which we put the recollection of the past. Those ends are to be judged in terms of values, not according to their fidelity to a memory of the past.

Everyone has a right to affirm identity. There's no reason to be ashamed of finding your own folk better company than strangers. If your mother or your child has been a victim of violence, then the memory of such suffering affects you more than the death of people you have never met, and you keep that memory alive with greater vigor. But there is greater dignity and merit in moving on from your own misfortunes and those of your close relatives to the misfortunes of others. A French Jewish writer, André Schwarz-Bart, wrote a remarkable novel about the genocide of the Jews, *The Last of the Just*, and then devoted himself to the world of black slaves. When he was asked to account for this change, he replied: "A great rabbi was once asked: 'Why is the stork, whose name in Jewish [*sic*] is *hassida*, meaning loving, because it loves its own, why is it classified as an unclean bird?' The rabbi replied: 'Because it gives its love only to its own'" (quoted by Grosser, *Crime*, 239)

In 1957, a French official, Paul Teitgen, who happened to be a camp survivor, resigned his post as a senior administrator in the city of Algiers. Why? Because the marks he saw on the bodies of tortured Algerian prisoners looked just like those he had seen on his own skin after the Gestapo had dealt with him in the cellars of Nancy.

Georges Jeanclos was an extraordinary sculptor who made a profound study of Jewish traditions in search of his own inspiration. In 1960 he produced *Galut* (meaning "exile" or "destruction" in Hebrew), otherwise entitled *Hiroshima*, a sculpture expressing with unforgettable power a tragedy that happened in a faraway place. On a trip to Guatemala, Jeanclos became aware of the immense suffering of its people, and commemorated it in a miniature but overwhelming monument to human misery, *Guatemala City* (1982). In the same year, in response to the dramatic events in Beirut, he made *Sabra and Chatila*, a composition consisting of a half of a male body supporting a female trunk. In an interview, he said: "It's always the same story, ever since the Holocaust" (quoted in Sojcher, 99).

Ritual commemoration, when it only confirms a negative image of the other in the past or a positive image of the self, is ineffective as a tool of public education, and, what is worse, it is an easy way of giving us all a good conscience while averting our eyes from present emergencies. Strident cries of "Never Again!" in the wake of the First World War did nothing to avert the Second World War. Today's constant and detailed recapitulations of the sufferings and heroism of the various parties in that conflict may make us wary of Hitler or Pétain, but they also make us blind to current dangers — for they are not aimed at the same groups and are not of the same kind. Denouncing the failings of someone under the Vichy regime makes you look like a stalwart fighter for memory and justice, but it involves not the slightest risk of obliging you to face up to your responsibilities for contemporary misfortunes. It can be very gratifying to commemorate the victims of past crimes, but getting involved with the victims of today is much trickier.

It is often said nowadays that there is no statute of limitations on the rights of memory, and that we should all be fighters on its side. But when we hear such appeals against forgetting and for the "duty of memory," we should realize that we are not being asked to undertake any recovery of memory — through the establishment of facts or through their interpretation. Nothing and nobody stands in the way of such work in democratic states like those in which we live. What we are being invited to undertake is the defense of a particular selection of facts that allow its protagonists to maintain their status as heroes, victims, or teachers of moral lessons, against any other selection that might give them less gratifying roles. That is why we should avoid "falling into the trap of the 'duty of memory,'" to quote Paul Ricœur (*Le Monde*, 15 June 2000), and devote ourselves rather to the work of memory.

If we do not want the past to return, we have to do more than recite it. George Santayana's old adage that those who forget the past are condemned to repeat it (in *The Life of Reason*, 1922) is misleading because it implies that those who remember the past are likely to avoid its mistakes. The historical past, like the natural order, has no intrinsic meaning, and by itself it produces no values at all. Meaning and value only come from human subjects questioning and judging the past, or the nature of things. The same historical fact, as we have seen, can be interpreted in opposite ways and support mutually contradictory policies.

All the same, the past can make a contribution to the constitution of collective and individual identities, and it can support the development of values, ideals, and principles. But to allow the past to serve in that way, we have to subject our own values, ideals, and principles to rational examination and to the test of debate; we must not seek to impose our ideals just because they happen to be ours. The relationship of the past to values is essential, but it is also limited. The past may enrich our principles of action in the present, but it does not provide the meaning of the present. Today's forms of racism, xenophobia, and exclusion are not identical to those of 1950, 1900, or 1800, and they do not affect the same people. Sanctifying the past robs it of all effectiveness in the present; but if we simply assimilate the present to the past, we blind ourselves to the nature of both past and present, and this in its turn leads to injustice. It is hard to find the path that skirts the pitfalls of sanctification and of trivialization, that leads us neither to serve only our own interest nor to give lessons only to others. But that strait and narrow path does exist.

The Achievement of Primo Levi

The Nazis' attempt to hide the crimes they committed in the concentration and extermination camps was a total failure; as I have said, there can be few episodes of modern history that are better documented. Many camp survivors felt they had a mission to bear witness, and many did so, some of them as soon as they were free, and others after a lapse of forty or even fifty years. All these testimonies are moving, many are also full of meaning. But one above all other witnesses has gained worldwide recognition and fame through writing, and that is Primo Levi.

Levi, born 1919, was an Italian Jew deported to Auschwitz in February 1944. He got out barely alive just over a year later. His first work of testimony, *If This Is a Man* (titled *Survival in Auschwitz* in the United States) was published in Italy in 1947 and prompted little interest at the time. Over the following years, Levi pursued two careers, as an industrial chemist and as a writer (Grossman was also a chemist, but Levi carried on working until normal retirement age). Some but not all of his other books deal with his camp experiences: *The Truce* (titled *The Awakening* in the United States) tells the story of how he got out of Auschwitz and back to Italy; *If Not Now, When?* is a novel about the Jewish Resistance; *The Periodic Table* contains passages about the camps; and he also wrote some shorter texts on the same general topic, collected in *Moments of Reprieve*. As time went by Levi's first book gradually acquired the status of a classic. After he took his retirement, Levi was led to return ever more frequently to what he had lived through at Auschwitz, in interviews and then in a long essay, *The Drowned and the Saved*. Levi died in 1987.

Primo Levi is admired nowadays to such a degree that he is not far short of an icon — an outcome he would have scarcely appreciated. His work and fate have prompted many interpretations. I have written about him elsewhere, so here I would like to concentrate on a single, central question that preoccupied

Levi in his writing about the camps, and that is the question of evil.

The attitude that Levi adopted toward perpetrators of evil can be summarized as: no forgiveness, no revenge, but justice. No forgiveness: "I am not inclined to forgive. . . . I never forgave our enemies of that time, nor do I feel I can forgive their imitators . . . because I know of no human act that can erase a crime" (*Drowned and Saved*, 137). No revenge: "I was not interested in revenge . . . it was fine with me that the very just hangings should be handled by others, professionals" (*Drowned and Saved*, 168). Why did Levi make these choices?

First, you can only forgive what you have suffered yourself: to forgive on behalf of others is presumptuous, to say the least. That is why murder — and genocide is mass murder — is by definition unforgivable. The dead man's family may decide to cease hating the murderer, but it cannot speak for the deceased. Forgiveness, it would seem, is essentially of use to the forgiver, who can then live on in peace; but we have no right to make forgiveness a general requirement. Legal pardons — amnesties — are just as questionable if they are awarded ahead of any trial and relate to serious crimes like murder, torture, deportation, or enslavement: they are tantamount to a suspension of justice in the name of supposedly higher considerations, such as the avoidance of civil war. Forgiveness is a personal decision, whereas crime always goes beyond the private sphere. An offense or crime not only damages the individual victim; it also shatters or at least unsettles the social order, which relies on notions of justice and retribution. When one individual pardons another, he or she decides to cease resenting the offense that has been done; but such forgiveness in no way repairs the damage done to the social order.

The temptation of revenge is just as dubious. Revenge, Levi points out, settles nothing, but only adds another layer of violence to the violence already done. The additional layer does not stop violence; it merely lays the ground for new explosions in the future. "From violence only violence is born, following a pendular action that, as time goes by, rather than dying down, becomes more frenzied" (*Drowned and Saved*, 200). As we have seen, examples are legion.

The most difficult question about evil is not that of punish-

ment, in Levi's view; he spends much more time on the problem
of how to judge evil. In *The Drowned and the Saved* the chapter on "The Memory of the Offense" is followed by one entitled
"The Gray Zone." This is Levi's own term for all the people
who cannot be classified simply as either "inmates" or
"guards." Indeed, in the German *Lager* as in the Russian gulag
the higher echelons of the SS or the NKVD employed many
prisoners whom they thus raised above the mass while keeping
them far below themselves. There were *kapos* usually picked
from the criminal inmates; there were the technical and medical
orderlies, the skilled workers, and other workers with specific
jobs to do. Such was Levi's own situation. He probably owed
his survival to the fact that he was put to work as a chemist and
not as an unqualified laborer. Such people belong to two categories at once; and despite the great differences between them they
were all simultaneously abused and privileged.

Levi uses the idea of the "gray band" on an even broader
canvas. He tells how one day a usually merciless and cruel SS
suddenly felt compassion for one of his victims: "That single
and immediately erased instant of pity is certainly not enough to
absolve Mühsfeld. It is enough however to place him too, although at the extreme boundary, within the gray band"
(*Drowned and Saved*, 58). On the other hand, even people who
remained ordinary prisoners were not exempt from selfish behavior that harmed their fellowmen, and so they too belonged
to the "gray zone," on the opposite edge. In other words, the
gray zone actually covered the entirety of the camp population
in one way or another. In his head-on campaign against Manichaeism, Levi clung above all else to this concept. In an interview about *The Drowned and The Saved*, he said: "The central
chapter, the most important one in the book, is the one entitled
'The Gray Zone'" (*Conversazioni*, 247). And people who disagree with Levi know that this is the key element of his thought
that they have to engage.

A possible misunderstanding connected to this idea must be
dealt with straight away. What Levi implies, without always
stating it explicitly, is that human actions need to be situated
and examined on both a legal and an anthropological (or psychological) level, and that neither should be dropped in favor of
the other. Or in his own words: "I don't mean that we are all

equal. Because we are not all equal before God, for believers, or before the law, for nonbelievers. We are not all equal, we are guilty to different degrees. But we are all made of the same stuff" (*Conversazioni*, 247).

Respecting the legal dimension implies that humans are always considered to be free agents, and consequently responsible for their acts. In this sense it is not permissible to muddy the distinction between perpetrators and victims. Levi protested vehemently against artists like Liliana Cavani, whose film *The Night Porter* claimed to deal with life in a concentration camp and intentionally blurs the borderline between guards and prisoners. Levi quoted Cavani's words, "We are all victims or murderers and we accept these roles voluntarily," to disagree most firmly: "I do not know, and it does not much interest me to know, whether in my depths there lurks a murderer, but I do know that I was a guiltless victim and I was not a murderer. I know that murderers existed . . . and that to confuse them with their victims is a moral disease or an aesthetic affectation or else a sinister sign of complicity" (*Drowned and Saved*, 48–49).

Levi was similarly irritated by the depiction of criminals as incarnations of absolute evil. He reacted negatively to another film, Pasolini's *Salo or the 120 Days of Sodom*, which overlays the history of Mussolini's last republic with reminiscences of the Marquis de Sade. "I disliked this film greatly, it seemed to me to be the work of a man without hope. . . . Things were not like that. Such total barbarity did not exist. There was a huge gray zone. It even included almost everybody. At that time we were all gray" (*Conversazioni*, 251). There was not one group of wholly white and another of wholly black. "There is no doubt about it, every one of us can potentially turn into a monster" (*Conversazioni*, 250). What Levi meant was that people cannot be divided into two mutually exclusive categories of angels and demons; but that does not make the crimes committed any less heinous. These two reactions to films might seem contradictory, but they are not. Both extremes were equally unacceptable — saying that everyone was equally gray (Cavani) and saying there was no gray zone at all (Pasolini).

This is largely why Levi seems so different from most other modern writers and public figures who regularly refer to one or another recent catastrophe. Alongside such barrel-voiced preachers whose confidence in their own rightness is grounded in the exploits, misfortunes, or crimes of their own folk, Primo Levi seems to embody humility. He does not shout but speaks *sotto voce* ("I don't like to raise my voice," he said in an interview); he weighs up the pros and the cons, he recalls the exceptions, and seeks out the reasons for his own reactions. He neither gives shattering explanations of past history nor adopts the tone of a prophet with a direct line to the holy. Facing the extreme, he remains human, all too human. And when he does speak of evil, the source of the offense, he does not point an accusing finger at others, but subjects himself to intense and never indulgent scrutiny.

In *The Drowned and the Saved* Levi narrates at some length the story of Chaim Rumkowski, the elder of the Łodz ghetto. Rumkowski was intoxicated by the paltry power that the Germans gave him, and he tried to act like a virtual monarch — which, given the awful conditions of life in the ghetto, was grotesque and pathetic. But instead of laughing at Rumkowski or waxing indignant, Levi uses the story to meditate on the corrupting effects of power on those who hold it. Rumkowski failed to stand up to it; but are we sure we would be stronger than he was? "How would each of us behave if driven by necessity and at the same time lured by seduction?" (*Drowned and Saved*, 68). The pointing finger turns away from Rumkowski and toward Levi himself: Rumkowski's tragedy is ours too. "We too are so dazzled by power and prestige as to forget our essential fragility. Willingly or not, we come to terms with power, forgetting that we are all in the ghetto . . . and that close by the train is waiting" (69).

A few pages later Levi tells a personal story. One day, when everyone in the camp was very thirsty, he found some water and shared it with his closest friend but not with other comrades. Looking back on this act of "us-ism" — selfishness extended to the person closest to you — he does not beat his breast. Anyone else would have done the same, and in any case he did no great harm, and killed nobody. All the same this tiny event is enough to give him "a shadow of a suspicion: that each man is his brother's Cain, that each one of us . . . has usurped his neighbor's place and lived in his stead" (*Drowned and Saved*, 81–82).

For someone with a moral conscience this conclusion is frightening. Is there really no barrier between evil and ourselves? Evil is extreme; but not one of us is impervious to it. These two statements side by side are enough to drive even the best will in the world to despair. But are we dealing with the same kind of evil in both cases? Levi sought with great care and no doubt also great anguish to find where a gap or divide might be located. The search mattered to him not just in abstract terms but for keeping his own life going. The dilemma could be put as a choice between two conceptions of evil. On the one side, we could believe in the existence of absolute evil, of an evil that is an end in itself, evil that you do to serve the devil, as Christians would say; the kind of evil that makes someone cut up a child into little pieces or to torture someone to death. Only some people encounter this kind of evil. On the other hand, we could believe that the only evil that exists is ordinary, common, banal evil, the kind that derives from giving preference to the self, like Cain over Abel; in some extreme circumstances such as war, military or totalitarian dictatorships, and natural disasters, ordinary evil can have extraordinary consequences. In this second case, we do not need to imagine a devil.

Levi devotes a chapter of *The Drowned and the Saved* to "Useless Violence" (echoing Grossman's phrase, "alogical violence," in "The Treblinka Hell"). "Useful" violence is only too easy to see: it arises when an individual who cannot achieve his or her aims by peaceful means feels sufficiently self-confident to use force. In such cases violence is no more than a brutal means — a convenient shortcut — to reaching the good, of the individual or of the community. But in the world of the camps Levi observed all sorts of actions that seemed to exemplify "useless violence." Why, for example, were no latrines or even a drop of water provided in the cattle trucks taking the deportees to the camps? Why were inmates made to strip naked so often? Why were they not given spoons but obliged to lap up their gruel like dogs? Why make the yard assemblies last for hours? Why insist on the so-called beds being made and remade to perfection? Why were the dying brought to the camps — people who would have passed on in any case in a few days? Why make the inmates perform useless work? Why treat human beings as raw materials — metal, fibers, phosphates — when if they had been allowed to live they could have produced far greater added value?

What is at stake in the issue I raised earlier about the rationality of evil now becomes clearer. If it can be shown that the latter kind of violence is truly useless, then evil of that kind really would be of a radically different nature from the evil with which we are all familiar, and there would be a wall between such absolute evil and ourselves; but if that cannot be shown, then such evil might well be found in any of us. Levi hesitates on this issue and does not give a final judgment. As he examines what he has described, however, he has to allow on each occasion that an action that at first sight seemed "useless" turns out to have had its own rationality on some level. It was logical to dehumanize camp inmates because the Nazis assumed from the start that the inmates were subhuman. It was logical to make enemies suffer because their suffering consolidated the Nazis' strength and proved their superiority. It was logical to require obedience to absurd commands because it proved that submission required no justification. It was logical to show superior strength because the aim of the entire operation was to achieve absolute superiority. In sum: if we grant that it is logical and useful to seek one's own advantage, then we should not be surprised by "the joy in your neighbor's misfortune" (*Drowned and Saved*, 107).

Levi often refers to John Donne's line about no man being an island — "ask not for whom the bell tolls, it tolls for thee." The truth of the connectedness of all to all is confirmed in a ghastly way by camp life, where an individual can assert himself just as much by putting others down and by doing them harm as by raising himself up and doing himself good. Humanity is one, but individuals are ranked relative to each other, so that the abasement of one constitutes the greatness of another. Knowledge of a misfortune contributes directly to the happiness of those that observe it from the outside — unless they see the victims as extensions of themselves, in which case the misfortune of others immediately becomes their own. Good and evil thus flow from the same spring, as Rousseau said, from the continuity between *I* and *other*, between ourselves and other people. We enjoy the happiness and the misfortune of others for the same reason, the fact that they are not really separate from us. The only real difference lies in the nature of the individual's relationship with those others. The other's misfortune gives us pleasure when we compare ourselves to that other while remaining outsiders; his or her happiness similarly gives us pleasure when we consider the other as an extension of ourselves. We suffer from others' misfortunes by contiguity; we take pleasure in them because we are not different from others.

Can we hope for a change in this state of affairs? What could be done to make such a change take place? Levi was skeptical about the position of Jean Améry, another camp survivor turned writer who had decided to "hit back": "Those who 'trade blows' with the entire world . . . pay a very high price for it because they are sure to be defeated" (*Drowned and Saved*, 136). Levi chose a different course, the path of reason and discussion; but fighting the whole world with argument is not necessarily less prone to failure. You can carry on resisting, indeed you must, but without any certainty of success. Every which way can seem a dead end. Liana Millu, a survivor of Birkenau whom Levi befriended, found that the writer's attitude grew ever bleaker as the years went by. Levi's first book, *Survival in Auschwitz*, told of a particular evil; his last work, *The Drowned and the Saved*, sees evil creeping slyly into every cranny.

Once again we have to ask whether yesterday's evil is the same as today's. History is always singular, and nothing ever happens twice in exactly the same way; for a generation at least, the memory of Europe's past crimes prevented the return of the same evil. But that was little consolation for Levi. The next crime would come disguised as something else, and then the game would be up. As long as what we see coming is not Fascism but nationalism or religious fanaticism, our guard will be down. A suspicion took hold of Levi: Auschwitz served no purpose, and human history will resume its horrifying path.

Huge slaughters keep happening, mostly outside Europe. Between 1975 and 1979, Pol Pot's Communist regime in Cambodia eliminated everyone not inclined to support its plan to create a new man. The number of dead is not easy to establish, but it was probably about one and a half million people—about one in every seven Cambodians. Levi knew it was genocide: "It is our own fault if we know so little about it. It's our fault, because we could have been better readers, we could have known more. . . . We didn't do so out of mental laziness, and because we prefer a quiet life" (*Conversazioni*, 246).

Fifty years after Auschwitz and seven years after Levi's death, the Hutus of Rwanda began murdering the Tutsis in the hundreds of thousands. Yolande Mukagasana described the slaughter of members of his own family, and then added: "Anyone who is not strong enough to read this gives himself away as an accomplice of the Rwandan genocide. . . . Whoever prefers not to learn about the agony of the Rwandan people is the murderers' accomplice. The world will not give up violence until it agrees to learn about its need for violence" (107). Mukagasana is not asking for much — she does not ask us to exercise justice, or even to take sides, but only to take the trouble to read and listen. But that is not nothing. Extreme evil is common; ordinary evil is ubiquitous. Fighting evil in the whole world is impossible, and universal compassion equally so, except for saints. "If we had to and were able to suffer the suffering of everyone, we could not live," wrote Primo Levi (*Drowned and Saved*, 56). And those who would be saints may lose their lives. So to keep ourselves alive, we choose the objects of our compassion according to circumstances, pitying some and forgetting others.

Levi found that truth particularly hard to accept. Forty years of thinking about Auschwitz taught him that the real culprits, apart from a number of individuals with direct responsibility, were the indifference and apathy of the German people. Save for a few exceptions, the Germans as a whole allowed themselves not to know for as long as possible; and when ignorance ceased to be an option, they kept their heads down. So how can we justify our own voluntary ignorance today, and our choice of doing nothing? Is that not tantamount to complicity in new disasters, no less painful for being different from past ones? The distinction Levi made between the "anthropological" and "legal" dimensions of human action is of little help here. If we only take care of our families and friends, then we can hope that our actions will have some effect, but that might mean behaving just like the Germans behaved during the last war. If we choose to extend our action to the whole country, however, or to the whole of humanity, how can we avoid the sense of failure?

The only choice we seem to have is between guilt and despair, a position that can obviously lead to suicide. However, that is no reason for assuming that Levi ended his own life. Several camp survivors, some of whom became well known, did commit suicide as a long-delayed conclusion to Auschwitz, but the causes of Levi's death are far from clear. Many commentators, including some of Levi's close friends, have doubted whether the writer killed himself. He left no message, and never once spoke to his friends about ending his life. An accidental death cannot be ruled out — he may not have thrown himself down the stairwell, he may have fallen in a dizzy spell. And would a chemist like Levi have chosen such an uncertain method if he had really wanted to kill himself? It will never be possible to be absolutely certain about what happened. However, even if we do assume that Levi killed himself, there is no reason to suppose that his suicide was directly connected to his experience of Auschwitz. What is for sure, though, is that suicide is in no sense a logical conclusion to Levi's thinking.

The lesson that Levi draws from his reflections is enough to make the reader despair, yet the reader emerges strengthened by Levi's books. What miracle allows this to happen? The light shines from Levi's manner of pursuing his meditations. He makes no great proclamations, trumpets no eternal truths; he writes with meticulous care for the actual words he uses, which are always clear and precise; he accepts arguments based on reason alone, and he places the search for truth and justice above ease of mind. The light doesn't come from the world that Levi describes, but from Levi himself. That a man like him has indeed lived on earth and resisted being tainted by evil offers encouragement and hope to us all. Primo Levi, or the despairing fighter: the two terms of the description are equally important. His unwillingness to be content with the bitter conclusions that he could not avoid reaching is what makes him particularly precious to us today.

CHAPTER 5

The Past in the Present

> We were afraid, we were ashamed, we were in
> pain: why had life been so horrible, are
> we not guilty of that, you and I?
>
> There has never been an age more heavy to
> bear than our own, but we did not
> allow the human in man to die.
> — *Vasily Grossman,* "The Sistine Madonna"

"Moral Correctness"

How do we use the past in the world of today? I'm going to
discuss a number of examples taken somewhat arbitrarily from
recent French history to illustrate the forms and functions of appeals to the past, beginning with examples that put the past in the
service of "moral correctness."

The term "political correctness" describes a kind of conformism current in U.S universities defining the code of verbal conduct
required for academic success. The term may be recent, but intellectual conformism obviously has a long history behind it. In the
French context, in the years following the Second World War, it
was politically correct to adopt a strongly "antifascist" position.
With a degree of guilty conscience for their behavior during the
Occupation, which De Gaulle's stand in London and the activities
of the Resistance inside France could not really override, the
French, and especially French intellectuals, stridently asserted
their antifascist commitment — *after* Fascism had been defeated.
This is what gave the Communist Party, and the left in general, its
unparalleled prestige in that period. Only a handful of voices
were raised against all forms of totalitarianism, whatever their
rhetorical camouflage, and they were clearly "politically incor-
rect." The common or garden "progressive," David Rousset commented, was "inclined to swallow any cliché provided it had the
label 'left-wing' attached to it" (*Lignes*, 196). Why was that so?

187

Because the truth is often awkward, and, when it comes to the crunch, most of us put convenience before truth. "In the West it was convenient to denounce the bourgeoisie and its crimes, and to excuse the mistakes that Stalin and his sidekicks made" (199).

Around 1975, after thirty years of economic growth and intellectual stagnation in France, political correctness began to crumble as its foundations wore away. In its place a new language of morality arose. The phenomenon is worth noting for itself, since morality as such was not highly prized and indignation could be easily provoked — often from the very proponents of the new moral discourse — by the slightest suggestion of censorship, especially if it concerned representations of sex. But when it came to sensitive issues at the center of the new moral discourse, things were different: portions of the recent past had to be seen, unambiguously, as the incarnation of evil. Anybody associated to any degree with this absolute evil was anathematized.

What is the incarnation of evil in the world of moral correctness? The answer should not be self-evident, because what is automatically associated with good and evil is not immutable and changes over time. For many centuries in Europe the identification of good and evil was the prerogative of the Christian Church. The separation of temporal and spiritual powers made no difference because the state adopted the values defined by the church. But in the latter part of the nineteenth century, the French state declared itself to be, in principle, secular, and therefore neutral with respect to competing ideologies (though in practice it exercised preferences). Artists and intellectuals of the romantic movement had dreamed of taking over the role of the priests (see Bénichou) but their hopes came to naught. The role of the priests stood vacant.

The resulting gap was a space which the state would not fill, but which various competing forces within civil society tried to occupy. These forces therefore offered icons to admire and enemies to hate. A society cannot simply give up its moral bearings at a stroke; but because the new moral forces were no longer automatically legitimated by the church or the state, they had to stake their claims in competition with others, in a permanent and daily effort. A new role of *moralizer* thus arose in the structural place formerly occupied by the priesthood, relying on persuasion to attract and retain a public hearing.

What are the features of a moralizer? The term is meant to describe public persons who pride themselves on having the ability to discern good and evil. Being a moralizer does not mean you are moral. A moral person subjects his or her own life to the criteria of good and evil, which transcend personal pleasures or satisfactions. A moralizer, on the other hand, tries to subject the lives of others to these same criteria, and profits by so doing — by putting himself on the right side of the fence. Moralizing provides the moralizer with recognition of his own existence and confirmation of his own value. And it was always thus. The man who threw the first stone at the adulterous woman took secret pleasure in his own moral superiority. A moralizer is thus close to what are called Pharisees, not so much in respect of hypocrisy or pettiness, but because they judge their fellow beings harshly. What makes a moralizer is not the content of his or her convictions, but the strategy used. A moralizer has a good conscience and is satisfied by his own self-righteousness. If a moralizer appeals to memory, and particularly to the memory of evil, then it is in order to teach a lesson to his or her contemporaries.

Good and evil can be described in abstract and general terms; but moralizing discourse is more persuasive when it takes the form of a truthful narration of facts, that is to say, when it appeals to the past. Which parts of the past are chosen for such purposes nowadays? No consensus was possible while totalitarian programs remained credible competitors with democracy. In the 1930s, for instance, totalitarians and democrats did not and could not have the same moral points of reference. After the collapse of the Fascist states, the struggle went on, since Communist utopias had not lost their appeal for large sectors of the French population. But over the past twenty-five years the conflict has subsided, and democratic principles seem to have become accepted by the broad mass. Nonetheless, this apparent harmony masks continuing disagreements, which boil down to a single proposition accepted by some and contested by others: that Nazism was worse than Communism. However, if we accept that Nazism was the greatest evil, then we have already defined and set two morally edifying narratives. The most pitiable victims are the victims of Nazism, the most admirable heroes are those who fought Nazism, in military combat or through the Resistance.

189

Nonetheless, we can easily imagine moralizers whose hierarchy of values is different (such do indeed exist).

Contemporary moralizers thus appeal to the past to praise the good and anathematize the bad. As we can see all around us, the victims are continually being commemorated and the perpetrators constantly being condemned. The prime example of the latter are, of course, the Nazis, and, for a significant proportion of the public, especially for people who consider themselves to be "on the left," the Nazis are the sole incarnation of historical evil. Every moralizer needs a way of figuring absolute evil, and so it is provided nowadays by terms like Fascism, racism, and anti-Semitism. Moralizers of the left do not put Communist crimes on the same level as Nazi crimes; they never use the word "genocide" to describe the massacres that took place in Russia, China, or Cambodia. Today's moral consciences (at least in France) demand punishment for Pinochet, a bloodthirsty dictator, but not for Castro, another bloodthirsty dictator. The ideology of Fascism and the regimes that were based on it are condemned by the vast majority of French citizens. Anyone suspected of indulgence toward such regimes or their offspring may be treated with contempt, whereas whoever denounces a Fascist sympathizer may take pride in having served the general good.

Surviving Nazi war criminals are now very few and will soon have disappeared. What remains possible, though, is to reconsider the past and to discover that people whom we previously esteemed had in fact been involved to a greater or lesser degree with Fascist or Nazi authorities during the war. There have been many spectacular examples of such posthumous denunciations (notably, questions raised about the wartime position of François Mitterrand, the former Socialist president of France). In addition, the rise of extreme right-wing movements since the 1980s has allowed a kind of updating of such retrospective accusations: just about the worst suspicion that can be entertained about a French public figure nowadays is that he or she is "playing into the hands of the far right." Identifying the enemy in historical terms thus allows the struggle to be pursued in the present. Let us now look at the forms which this struggle may take.

The first striking paradox we have to note is that antifascism only really flourished *after* the defeat of Fascism. During the life of the Third Reich, the antifascist front only existed for a brief period, from the launch of the Popular Front movement in 1935 to the German-Soviet Nonaggression Pact of 1939. After 1945, though, it became one of the major political forces in Western Europe. This strange turn derived from the guilty feelings of a large part of the population (as I mentioned earlier) working in conjunction with the clever strategy of the European Communist Parties, which asserted their leadership of a movement whose values could hardly be contested, given that disapproval of Fascism enjoyed unanimous support. Now that the French Communist Party has little influence and no real effect in the political field, the antifascist ideal persists in the area of morality.

Fascist contamination can be tracked down by our moral censors through however many layers it may take to find the damned spot, whether or not the culprit was actually aware of harboring such blackness, and irrespective of expressed intentions. A relatively recent case of such moralizing persecution was the campaign directed against the French writer Gilles Perrault for failing to denounce with adequate energy two former negationist sympathizers. Perrault, whose left-wing commitments are hardly secret, was thus made guilty at fourth remove from the crime itself—but the mud that was flung at him was just as black as if he had been a Nazi criminal himself. When Jean Clair, Jean-Philippe Domecq, and Benoît Dutertre criticized the heavily subsidized French avant-garde, they too were attacked as cryptofascists. Was Hitler not just as hostile as they are toward the avant-garde? Pierre-André Taguieff, one of the best commentators on racism and the far right in France, also found himself treated with moralizing suspicion. He seemed too close to his subject for comfort; by agreeing to public debate with open supporters of the right, he had fallen for the ploy of "dialogue." Alain Brossat, similarly, has been accused of negationism and—to cap it all—of anti-Semitism for having criticized Israel's policy toward the Palestinians.

The moralizing critics who launch these kinds of attack all use the same rhetorical tools of argumentation. With their favorite quotation from Brecht's *Resistible Rise of Arturo Ui*, "the bitch that bore [Hitler] is in heat again," they hark back to the long tradition whence their neo-antifascist commitment derives. From the same revolutionary tradition, which is effectively defunct

191

nowadays, they appropriate terms like "struggle," "resistance," and "vigilance." Their deductions often have the form of a false syllogism: X is published by A; Y is also published by A; ergo, X and Y are tarred with the same brush. Since Y may be suspected of having extreme right-wing leanings (racist views, anti-Semitic opinions, etc.), so X may be suspected too. Often the main proposition is not stated but suggested, so it cannot be either confirmed or denied. Rather than saying "X is a Nazi" (or a pillar of the Vichy regime, or a supporter of Le Pen), our moralizers snidely ask: "How can we be sure that X was not a collaborator?"

The commonest and so to speak the foundational rhetorical device of moralizing discourse is the excluded middle: whoever is not antifascist as we are may be suspected of indulgence toward Fascism. The consequence of this ploy is a systematic anathematization of the enemy. Any contact with evil is considered totally damning, and damns the entire group or collectivity concerned (for instance, Le Pen's Front national party is held to be Fascist from top to bottom). The only proper attitude toward an enemy of that sort, moralizing critics assert, is (civil) war; any attempt to introduce nuances into the argument is seen as treason.

Moralizing critics are not officially connected to the state or to its institutions, so their targets are not interrogated by the Inquisition or thrown into jail, and do not have their books burned in public. Moral correctness in France is primarily exercised in the news media, and only occasionally in the lawcourts and in books. But the power of the media should not be underestimated. It is not at all easy for those who have been accused of complicity with evil (the term "collaboration" is more likely to be used) to defend themselves in public; it is very hard to exculpate yourself from accusations based on values that have universal approval. As Taguieff says, "in modern democracies, social execution takes place in public through the widest possible broadcasting of the charges" (Tagueiff, 65). In this context, a charge is as bad as a sentence, because nobody takes any notice of the editorial correction or of the letter to the editor from a dissident reader published three weeks later in small type. A public denunciation means that the witch-hunt is open. Social ostracism and the verbal branding of the suspect may be less brutal than older forms of repression, but they are just as effective.

Nowadays it is not the writer who has become the priest, as in the impossible dream of nineteenth-century romantic poets, but the talking head. Media personalities have learned how to fashion public opinion to accord with their own convictions, through the unrivaled power of television, radio, and the press, a power that writers of past ages could not even imagine. To do this effectively in France, moralizing critics need an intellectual image and a platform—a chat show or a column—allowing them to reach and influence an audience. In the 1920s Julien Benda denounced the way in which many French intellectuals and artists were putting their talents at the disposal of highly dubious political programs. What we can see today is not that the "scribes" are betraying the "church of art," but that they have acquired vastly more power.

Can we agree nonetheless that even if they are not very admirable our Moral Consciences are necessary in order to contain and counteract a far greater evil? Not really. By blackening their enemies to excess our Moral Consciences distort them and destroy their credibility. For example, the Front national of Le Pen, however hateful its ideas may be, is not a reborn Nazi Party, nor is it a terrorist organization; it expresses many demands that have to be looked at in their own terms. Its decline in the later 1990s from the levels of support it reached in the earlier part of the decade stemmed less from what our Moral Consciences said about it than from contingencies such as a split in the leadership, the successful prosecution of Le Pen for striking an opponent, and the fall in the level of unemployment. But we should remain alert—circumstances may change again, and the danger of the far right may well return.[1]

Do our Moral Consciences truly want the far right to fade away? Over a period of years during the Mitterrand presidency, and probably at the president's prompting, it seemed as though some left-wing newspapers gave full and detailed coverage to the far right so as to make it seem more important than it really was. Who would ever have heard of the obscure writings of the negationists had it not been for the incessant publicity they got from being denounced? Some of our Moral Consciences went so far as to demand that, since the original perpetrators of Nazi crimes

---

[1] These words were written in the spring of 2000. In April 2002, the leader of the far-right National Front, Jean-Marie Le Pen, received nearly 18% of the popular vote in the first round of the French presidential election. [TT]

had been sentenced, negationists should now in their turn be prosecuted for war crimes! The reason for such overblown estimates of the threat of the far right is perfectly clear, however: the danger of a resurgence of neo-Nazi or neo-Fascist forces is absolutely essential to the survival of neo-antifascist fighters, who, if they had nothing at all to fight, would lose all the symbolic benefits of being our Moral Conscience. Just as the politicians of the left saw an advantage in the maintenance of the Front national to divide the right-wing vote, so our Moral Consciences are keen to keep the far right alive — and, in their own way, they actually help to keep it going.

As often happens when there is a firm but false symmetry between two opposing blocs, the medicine is remarkably similar to the malady. To be antiextremist to the extreme makes you an extremist too. Neo-antifascist demonstrators use slogans ("One bullet for Le Pen, a full belt for the FN!") that are as objectionable as what they are trying to fight. Or else, in the name of the fight against discrimination, you discriminate against people who hold opinions that are different from yours. If we really want to fight the French far right, calling it names won't do much good. We need to know what its ideas and arguments are, and we need to counter them with better arguments and ideas. Even that won't cause it to disappear, since its supporters are not necessarily drawn to it by ideas — they also join it in search of collective identity, personal safety, and as a way of making their protests heard.

But like must be compared with like, and racism and antiracism are really not at all similar to each other. Neo-antifascists are infinitely less dangerous than neo-Fascists, and we must not put apples and oranges into the same basket. Race-hate crimes happen every day in France, and they cause actual physical and moral suffering to their victims. Neo-antiracist excesses do no such thing. They are verbal excesses, forms of discourse that damage the standing of individuals. What is lamentable about this kind of polemic is that it strengthens the adversary instead of weakening it, and petrifies public debate instead of enlivening it.

In truth, the middle is never excluded in matters of political and existential choices. We do not have to choose between supporting murderers, on the one hand, and joining in the chorus of glee when murderers are given a lethal injection, on the other. The opposite of one evil is not necessarily good — it may be another evil. So you can disagree with public moralizers without becoming an anti-Semite, a holocaust denier, or a racist or a Fascist or a supporter of the far right. If we want to be free of the Manichaean world view dividing humanity into mutually exclusive categories of good and bad—a view akin to totalitarian doctrines—then a good way to start would be to avoid becoming Manichaean ourselves. A maxim for the twenty-first century might well be to start not by fighting evil in the name of good, but by attacking the certainties of people who claim always to know where good and evil are to be found. We should struggle not against the devil himself but against what allows the devil to live—Manichaean thinking itself.

We all condemn Nazi crimes, pity their innocent victims, and admire people who resisted. There is something reassuring about this consensus. Imagine for a moment what the world would be like if contempt for victims (as Nietszche recommended), praise for Nazis, and scorn for Resisters had triumphed! However, adopting these consensual attitudes in public does not make our morality or our politics any better. Why not?

The moral issue was raised by Plato and can also be found in the New Testament. Jesus did not just recommend us to carry out praiseworthy actions such as giving alms, praying, and fasting, but adds: "Therefore when thy doest thine alms, do not sound a trumpet before thee, as the hypocrites do in the synagogues and in the streets, that they may have glory of men. . . . They have their reward." So Jesus didn't say: Stop being righteous, stop giving alms, and steal. All he asked was that acts of goodness be done privately: "Let not thy left hand know what they right hand doeth. That thine alms may be in secret. . . . When thou prayest, enter into thy closet, and when thou hast shut thy door, pray to thy Father which is in secret" (Matthew 6.2–6). This requirement was quite alien to the classical-pagan world (whose heroes, far from avoiding fame and glory, sought it avidly), but it has now spread far beyond its original context and no longer seems specifically Christian. Kant—and also just contemporary common sense—sees moral action as necessarily disinterested. In that sense Jesus' precept has been generalized, and we all recognize that if we "have our reward," then we are not "doing alms."

It is not easy to act out of the sight of others. A true believer may do it more willingly, without a "reward," since Jesus prom-

195

ised that "Thy Father which seeth in secret shall reward thee openly" (Matthew 6.6). But what about those of us who no longer believe in a divine father seeing into the soul and settling all accounts at the end of time? Of course, we are tempted to seek external approval — but rewards provided by others deprive our action of its disinterestedness. The path of moral action is thus a lonely one, and we take it because our happiness is made of the happiness of others, and not because it leads to personal glory.

A person who puts himself publicly on the side of right, who condemns evil men, weeps for the weak, and admires the strong, adds nothing to his own worth, since moralizing never can be a moral action. Heroes do not transmit their virtue nor do victims lend their halo to those who admire them, whatever the latter may hope: there is nothing heroic about admiring a universally recognized hero. It would rather be the opposite, because self-righteousness is the enemy of action. It is, of course, perfectly normal and even praiseworthy to take pleasure in the prestige of heroes to whom we are related and to sympathize with victims who in some sense "belong to us," but when such feelings are expressed in the public sphere they acquire an additional meaning: they serve personal interest, not moral education. Ritual invocations of the good, the bad, and the victims of the past in support of one's own group may prompt the admiration of group members, but not of one's own conscience. Nor does one gain any moral boost from sticking to accepted values. Public appeals to the past are educative only when they put ourselves in question, and show us that we (or the groups with which we identify) have not always been the incarnation of goodness and strength.

Moral action is by definition individual and has to be undertaken outside of the public sphere; but political action is clearly different, and has to be judged by results, not by the motives of its proponents. A politician who improves the people's well-being is a good politician, even if the only motive for such action is a thirst for glory. The danger has a different disguise in the political field and comes under the mask of "the best of intentions." Good intentions are far more widespread than bad ones, of course; the paradox is that they are much more dangerous. The history of any part of the globe can provide innumerable examples of the fact that good intentions have created far more victims than evil ones. The slippery slope consists in seeing oneself as the incarnation of good that others must be made to accept, not just in private life but also in the public sphere. This confusion between the moral and political domains is inversely symmetrical to the muddle imposed by totalitarian regimes. Totalitarianism subjects moral choices to political objectives and deems the good to be whatever serves immediate aims, such as the victory of the revolution or the dictatorship of the party. The problem of good intentions is that they subject politics to moral choices, as if political life were conducted in a theocracy where morality had taken the place of theology. That would produce crusades in external relations (the good must be imposed on others, whether they like it or not), and in the domestic sphere it would give rise to the rule of virtue and the persecution of moral incorrectness. The legal structures of Western democracies (which are all effectively if not formally secular) are not particularly threatened by this danger, but social life is by no means fully insulated from such slippage.

Moral indifference on one side, the posture of Moral Conscience on the other — a way ahead that skirts both these dangers is not easy to find or to follow. Because of the vacuum created by the absence of any official state morality, everyone who acts in the public sphere feels the need to refer to a set of moral values illustrated, if possible, by an exemplary narrative. Lobbies and pressure groups need this even more, since they are competing with each other for greater influence. Our era of "individualism" thus prompts us to compensate for what we lack. But such appeals to historical narratives add nothing to the virtue of the people who indulge in them; and no social advantage can come from giving in to the "best of intentions." Each of us can find the means to stand up to the trend of our times; as Rousseau said, we are free to "acquiesce or resist."

HISTORY AND MYTH

In Renaissance iconology, Mnemosyne, the goddess of memory, was depicted as a woman with two faces, one turned toward the past, the other toward the present. One of her hands held a book (in which memory can read the past), the other a quill (presumably, so as to write the next chapters). The work of memory thus respects two requirements — fidelity to the past, utility in the pres-

197

ent. But what if these two requirements come into conflict with each other, if the truthful restitution of the facts of the past could do harm in the present?

Such conflicts can arise, as we can see in two recent "affairs" about individuals generally seen as heroes. Artur London, who was born in Czechoslovakia and died in 1986, was a Komintern official in the 1930s, and fought in the Spanish Civil War. He married a French woman, became one of the leaders of the Communist Resistance inside occupied France, and was deported to Mauthausen concentration camp. He returned to Western Europe at the end of the war, then went back to Prague in 1948 and became deputy foreign minister. He was arrested in 1951 in the so-called Slansky plot, and sentenced to life imprisonment (most of his codefendants were executed). In 1955 he was released and rehabilitated, and he moved back to France in 1963. In 1968 he published *The Confession*, which relates his life in prison. Costa-Gavras made a film of it, starring Yves Montand, and brought London's story to a worldwide audience.

In 1996 Karel Bartosek, a Czech historian who has lived in France since 1982, published *Les Aveux des archives*, a study of the relations between the French and Czechoslovak Communist Parties, which draws for the most part on archives in Prague that had recently become accessible. Bartosek himself had suffered "repression" after the Soviet invasion of Czechoslovakia in 1968: he spent six months in jail, was then thrown out of academic work and became a laborer; later, he was stripped of his Czech nationality and expelled from the country. One chapter of Bartosek's book deals with the Artur London case, and it prompted noisy polemics in the press. There were two issues: some people, especially the former comrades of the deceased revolutionary, accused Bartosek of having misrepresented the precise details of London's biography; others, mostly historians and journalists, were concerned with the proper role of historical research in contemporary society.

What Bartosek was reproached with in the latter debate can be summed up thus: whatever the true facts may be about the life of London or anyone else of that kind, only what it is useful to know should be made public. The fullest version of this argument was given in *Le Monde* in December 1996. It contended that because "the far right is on the prowl in our cities," it was necessary to keep the flame of antifascism burning bright, to carry on calling heroes heroes, and to proclaim "that the Republican struggle against Franco in 1936 was the good fight, . . . that Artur and Lise London remain the indestructible symbols of authentic Communist passion," alongside Jean Moulin, the French Resistance leader who was killed by the Nazis, and who was "the pure archangel of our national revolution." From this point of view it was clearly necessary also to heap scorn and contempt on people like Bartosek who, while claiming to be only historians, cast aspersions on "any exceptional figure," showed that "heroes are an illusion," and promoted "hatred of heroes and saints." Historians of that kind, *Le Monde* concluded, merely help the far right in its campaign against "moral feeling" in general and civic commitment in particular.

The vast majority of professional historians in France rejected this vision of the role of history, which boiled down to saying that some truths are not for the telling (*Le Monde* published their collective letter in support of Bartosek). But the attitude of the original article in *Le Monde* does have famous precedents in France. The first was perhaps the declaration by Maurice Barrès that Captain Dreyfus had to be found guilty even if he was innocent, because the alternative would discredit the French army. "Even if the client of counsel for the defense were innocent, the pro-Dreyfus faction would still be criminal" (Barrès, *Scènes*, 138). Another famous precedent was provided by Jean-Paul Sartre who was opposed to revealing anything about Soviet concentration camps in the early 1950s. He may not have actually said it, but there is a well-known formula attributed to him that "we must not dampen the hopes of Billancourt" (that is, of the French working class — Billancourt was the site of a huge automobile works) by letting it know that the "land of socialism" was not yet paradise on earth. At that time people also claimed that leaking facts on the Soviet camps would harm the cause of peace, play into the hands of American imperialism, and so forth.

If we adopt this position, then historians have no obligation to the truth, only an obligation to the good. They serve as a particular variety of propagandist. This would be a defensible position if we were convinced that what exists is not facts but only verbal representations. Such historians would then be no different from celebrants. And that would lead to the complete collapse of all true scholarship, which presupposes that knowledge is something other than a mere projection of the will.

But even if we adopt the pragmatic stance of Barrès, Sartre, and their contemporary disciples, we must question whether such disrespect for the truth is even compatible with the causes it supports. When the cheating that had taken place in the Dreyfus trial was finally uncovered, it brought the anti-Dreyfusard faction into permanent discredit in France. In the long run, Communist lies did terminal damage to the attractiveness of Communist ideals. Would it be effective, nowadays, to fight the far right while leaving it with the monopoly on truth in this or that respect? Moral correctness really is dangerous because white lies always end up being found out, undermining the very positions they were designed to promote. Even the voluntary suppression of awkward facts does immense harm once the cover is blown, and instead of serving a noble cause, it may well discredit that cause entirely. We should not forget what happened over the Katyn massacre. For more than forty-five years the Soviets sought to keep their own image clean by accusing the Nazis of having perpetrated the murder of many thousands of Polish officers. When the truth was finally discovered, it dealt a fatal blow to the credibility of all official statements coming from Soviet authorities.

Politicians and historians have different roles to play. Politicians aim to influence the minds of citizens, and, though not at all obliged to lie, they can legitimately choose to say one thing rather than another, so as to prompt the reaction they seek. In 1940 Charles de Gaulle had no interest in reminding the French of their weaknesses and cowardice in the past; to arouse them to resistance against the Germans, it was rather better to remind them of Joan of Arc. But historians do not aim to increase the supply of holy images, or to enhance the cult of saints and heroes, or to wash the feet of "archangels." A historian tries to get closer to the truth with the means at his disposal.

That is why history is always, in a sense, sacrilegious. We would be punished for slighting sacred things. Historians, however, always desecrate the public sphere; they turn religious objects into profane ones. History is the contrary of idolatry, and by its very nature it contributes to the "disenchantment of the world," which Max Weber saw as an essential feature of modernity. Maybe in very grave circumstances—say, during the Nazi occupation of France—it would have been legitimate not to deal with those chapters of history whose lessons might dishearten the public; but that release from historical duty does not permit the historian to claim that attempts at propaganda are the same thing as real historical research.

In 1969, as in 1940, Charles de Gaulle believed that France "does not need truth. What she should be given is hope, cohesion, and purpose" (quoted in Brauman, *Éloge*, 53). For broadly similar reasons, historical research on the Vichy regime was not encouraged in France in the postwar period. Only when German and American historians looked at the recent French past dispassionately did French public opinion accept that Vichy had not been the "shield" against greater German pillage that it claimed to have been. But even if the recent rise of the far right in France is worrying, our present circumstances can hardly be described as very grave.

So what verdict should we reach about the historical role of a character like Artur London? What Bartosek discovered in the archives were many previously unknown aspects of London's life. Born in 1915, London went to Moscow in 1934 where he was on the permanent staff of the Komintern. He went to Spain in 1937–38 with the International Brigade, not as a combatant but as head of the East European section of the Servicio de investigación militar. This military police unit reporting to the Soviet political police "purged" the Republican Army of its unreliable elements. After the war, in Switzerland and then in France, London was a member of the Czech intelligence service and of the political police. Oddly enough, he wrote the first report denouncing the American Communist Noel Field, who would in his turn be used in the trial of London. None of these aspects of London's work gets a mention in *The Confession*.

Disclosures of this kind produce a bad impression nowadays, and it is not surprising that London's friends and family, supported by a handful of historians, raised protests. They contended that the man they had known, even if he had been a professional revolutionary with strong political convictions, had not been a spy or a policeman. London had been a man of courage and generosity, with high ideals, which he demonstrated in the difficult circumstances of underground life and deportation.

One of the lessons of this dispute is that we should choose not between the two sides but listen to both of them. That is what London's friends admit implicitly in their attempts to justify his involvement in espionage: "It happened in the context of the Cold War, and was subordinated to utter fidelity to an international ideal." Men like London really did believe that the end justified any means. They were not cynics who filled their pockets with taxpayers' money, but "idealists" who believed that Communism was the best possible state for the human race. To hasten the coming of Communism (even if they all accepted that it would take a very long time), they were prepared to do anything needed — even to "purge" their own team, undertake espionage, spread false rumors, forge papers, and hound people to suffering and death. For them, ethics was entirely subjected to politics, which was indeed Communist doctrine. As Jacques Rossi, another former Komintern official, has recently reminded us, Lenin considered that "what is ethical is what serves the interests of the proletariat" (*Le Monde*, 19 March 1999).

The stories of the Communist leaders of this period have an unmistakably and powerfully tragic quality. Heinz Neumann has already provided one illustration. In an appendix, Bartosek reprinted the testamentary letters of the eleven Czech leaders who were to be hanged as a result of the Slansky trial. These immensely touching documents show that on the very eve of their execution, after terrible physical and moral torture, and even while they knew very well that they had never committed any crime, these men had lost none of their confidence and faith in the same ideals. Noel Field offered another example of the same persistence and fidelity. After his release from prison in 1954, he refused to return to the United States, and dragged out the rest of his life in the "socialist camp"; far from being broken by the torture he had undergone, he carried on proclaiming his unwavering loyalty to the party. Nikolay Bukharin, similarly, having been sentenced to death after going through interrogation, humiliation, and torture before the trial, wrote a personal letter to Stalin reassuring the general secretary of his love and fidelity — to Stalin, to the party, to the Revolution, to Communism. And instead of reproaching Stalin for the injustice done to him, Bukharin asks for forgiveness: "Adieu until the end of time, and harbor no resentment toward the miserable person that I am" (quoted in *Le Débat* 107, 166).

The wave of trials of party leaders in the period 1949–53 is obviously a subject worthy of historical investigation, but it should not be allowed to mask the fact that the vast majority of people accused of political crimes in countries under Soviet control at that time were non-Communists. Bartosek's statistics make that crystal clear: "For the entire period 1948–1954, Communists make up 0.1% of those convicted, 5% of those sentenced to death, and 1% of those actually executed." These figures underline the unfairness of presenting Artur London as an *exemplary* victim of Communist power; what's worse is that they explain why Communist authorities might have thought it useful to have people believe that London was the exemplary victim. In fact, the first major wave of oppression dealt with people who could be accused of having connived with the Nazis (during the occupation and partial annexation of Czechoslovakia); the second wave dealt with whoever seemed insufficiently keen on collaborating with the new Communist regime; and only the third and much the smallest wave concerned Communist leaders.

After his release and rehabilitation London remained just as much a committed Communist as before. So maybe what had happened to him was just Stalin's fault, or the fault of corrupt or incompetent policemen. Intentionally or not, *The Confession* actually served Communist interests. So it is only natural if people of London's kind, if they are still alive, or their former friends and relatives, find contemporary historical research baffling and unacceptable. They are witnesses, and they do not see the same things as historians do. Both groups may be right, but if so, they are right about different things. Warmhearted and charismatic individuals may also have been steely agents of repression (I met some such in Bulgaria). In human history, the perpetrators of evil do not always look like monsters.

The second major debate of this kind concerned two celebrated figures of the French Resistance, Lucie and Raymond Aubrac. Insinuations had been made about their real role during the Occupation, and in order to lay them to rest once and for all, the couple asked a French daily newspaper, *Libération*, to organize a panel discussion of their case. Several well-known historians took part, as did the Aubracs themselves; the aim was to establish the facts once and for all. But the panel turned out to be a disappointment for the Resistance fighters.

The historians on the panel were able to demonstrate that the recent insinuations about the Aubracs' role were groundless. At the same time, they could not but point out that the Aubracs' own accounts of their actions over the course of the years had not been entirely reliable. At various times Raymond Aubrac had offered different versions of the same events; Lucie Aubrac admitted she had taken a few liberties with historical accuracy to make her story more lively and instructive. As members of the Resistance, the Aubracs were beyond reproach; but as witnesses, they fell short of perfection. This conclusion thus prompted a debate not dissimilar to the quarrel over Bartosek and Artur London: was it useful to darken even slightly the shining image of the hero? Why try at all costs to smash idols? Would it not have been better to keep these necessary myths whole and entire? Lucie Aubrac, in her own conclusion to the panel discussion, described historians as "supposedly serious gentlemen . . . whose traditional tools of study are facts, dates, and the analyses and conclusions that follow logically from them . . . specialists who store up only the cold and naked truth." She for her part was a witness and "primarily a teacher," defending "the honor of the Resistance"; "by every means available — through books, films, documentaries — I shall go on broadcasting the value and the glory of the Resistance." The Aubracs' position seemed to many to be quite upsetting. What this aging couple had put themselves through resembled a public execution. It almost seemed as if the entire inheritance of the Resistance was under threat.

The Aubrac case reminds us once again of the distinction that has to be made between testimony, commemoration, and history. The same requirements do not apply to each. We require testimony only to be sincere, and we should not take a witness to task for human fallibility. Commemoration is quite explicitly dependent on contemporary needs, and it takes from the past only what serves the present. But history surely cannot abandon its commitment to "the cold and naked truth."

The Resistance specialists on the Aubrac panel found it hard to give up this last point. François Bédarida spoke of the historian's right to "patiently reconstitute the chain of actual events" and insisted on the historian's "duty of truth"; to be effective and legitimate, "a politics of memory has to be grounded on a work of truth." Jean-Pierre Azéma rejected any indulgence in political correctness "on the frequently alleged pretext of the specificity of this or that issue," even if it involved the genocide of the Jews or the class struggle; historians, he said, "should never, in any way, allow their work to serve the interests of any particular memory" (*Libération*, 9 July 1997). Henry Rousso also came out against the idea of "necessary myths" and the concept of "truths that are better not said." The aim of history, he concluded, was to lead to knowledge, not to faith. "Transmission of the past must not be reduced to the passive cult of heroes and victims" (Rousso, 138).

Paradoxically, it is more difficult nowadays to do historical research on "good guys" than on "bad guys" in recent French history. Contrary to what might be expected (and contrary to the claims of some ill-informed non-French writers), there is no problem nowadays about denouncing the squalid behavior of the Vichy regime or of its supporters: there are innumerable books on the subject, and newspapers are keen to scoop up any new revelation. On the other hand, it is much more difficult to do or to publish research on yesterday's heroes, be they Communist or Gaullist. Their contemporary worshipers are quick to take offense; when they threaten to sue for libel, publishing houses lose their nerve. Those who took part in those dramatic events or witnessed them directly feel hurt. How dare people question their vision of the facts, when they are the ones who suffered physically? But former members of the Resistance, whose action in the past was admirable, cannot be allowed a monopoly on its interpretation in the present. Their wish to make their own version of history sacrosanct does no great service to knowledge, nor does it serve action in the present. To quote Henry Rousso again: "Historians and former Resisters who think they can write a history of the Resistance that maintains entirely its edifying value are making a big mistake" (136). Historians are no strangers to the world of values, and the vast majority of current historians prefer the values of the Resistance to the values of Nazism, but their overriding value remains the unwavering and steadfast pursuit of the truth.

HISTORY AND THE LAW

The cult of memory does not always serve history well; nor does the law when instead of providing a source of documents for analysis by historians it becomes a showcase of historical knowledge. Recent trials for crimes against humanity in France were supposed to reawaken the nation's memory. But I must question, as did Simone Veil,[2] whether the lawcourts really were the only available tool for keeping memory alive. On the one hand, using the law to set an example or to teach a lesson can be seen as an abuse; on the other, there are many other places where memory is kept alive. The past is remembered through political action, through the school syllabus, by the media, and in history books. The D-Day landing of 1944 was given a spectacular commemoration in 1994, and it remains alive in everyone's memory. Do we really need a trial as well to remember it better?

It is also far from obvious that lawcourts can do a better job of teaching history in an accurate and nuanced way than books by specialists. For instance, when Klaus Barbie, "the Butcher of Lyons," was tried for crimes against humanity, the court allowed as evidence his acts of torture of members of the Resistance as well as of civilians and Jews. This was not strictly legal, as there is a difference between war crimes and crimes against humanity; nor did it do any service to history, since the Resistance also used torture against captured Gestapo officers. Moreover, after 1944 the French Army used torture systematically in Algeria, and no one has ever been convicted of crimes against humanity on those grounds. Finally, by putting a German policeman in the dock for the first trial of this kind in France, the courts downplayed the involvement of the French in Nazi policies; many of the witnesses accused the French *milice* of having been even worse than the Germans.

The historical significance of Barbie's acts was also muddied by the use of witnesses like Marie-Claude Vaillant-Couturier, a survivor of Ravensbrück and Auschwitz who had taken a leading role in the postwar struggle to suppress the truth about Soviet gulags. A similar cloud hung over the trial of Paul Touvier because the plaintiffs were represented by Joë Nordmann, who had served for many years as legal counsel to the French Communist Party. He had been particularly aggressive on behalf of his clients in the Kravchenko and Rousset trials in 1948 and 1949, where

[2] A camp survivor and French politician who introduced more liberal abortion laws as a cabinet minister, and became the first president of the European Parliament. [DB]

his task was to demonstrate the nonexistence of concentration camps in the Soviet Union. Is it possible to denounce one set of camps and to defend another set? Is that what "memory" is to be used for? It is true that at the Nuremberg trials Stalin's representatives sat in judgment over Hitler's colleagues: a particularly obscene situation, since the judges were guilty of crimes as horrible as those of the accused.

The third French trial for crimes against humanity took place in Bordeaux in the winter of 1997–98, and it will probably remain the last one dealing with matters arising from the Second World War. The charges against Maurice Papon for having materially assisted in deporting Jews to Germany while he was a town hall official in Bordeaux during the Occupation were first laid in 1981. It was an exceptional event in every way. The case took no less than seventeen years to reach the courts, and the hearings dragged out over six months. It attracted wide attention, with several pages devoted to it each day by many newspapers, intense television coverage, and ten or more books on the case published during or just after the trial. So what lessons can be learned from the Papon affair?

As an external observer I do not have much to say on the legal side of the case. Nor am I familiar with the huge pile of documentary evidence — 6,300 items were submitted to the court, and that's not counting all the evidence that was disallowed. It seems beyond argument that Papon committed a moral fault in failing to dissociate himself more clearly from the policies of Pétain's *État français*, and in failing to show more compassion for his victims. But did he fail in what some people call "a duty to disobey"? Such a claim can only be entertained by people who like playing hero when the danger is over. Anyway, morality is not the same thing as the law. Did Papon commit an offense against the law as well as an offense against morality? It all depends on how much power to maneuver Papon really had, and on what he imagined would happen to the people he put on the trains. The difficulty of reaching a judgment of these two factors was reflected in the court's final decision: ten years' jail for being an accessory to illegal arrests and arbitrary imprisonment (he was found not guilty of murder). The verdict fell halfway between the maximum sentence, which might seem the only appropriate one for such a crime, and acquittal.

The Papon case would have attracted far less public attention if the accused had been seen only as an individual on trial for his crimes. But it was generally taken to be an exercise in public education, directed especially toward the younger generation: it was supposed to teach them that the anti-Jewish policies of Vichy France had contributed to the Nazis' "final solution"; and also that a public official blindly pursuing professional advancement could become an accessory to crimes against humanity. But did the Papon trial really achieve its pedagogic aim?

The first major risk of the trial is that it would serve only as an example of scapegoating — by making Papon take the rap for the whole of the Vichy regime, even for the existence of Auschwitz. If the real target had been the Vichy regime, then every person who held an official position at or above Papon's level in the Vichy hierarchy should have been charged. Not only was that course not taken, it was actually agreed in advance that that there would be one trial for the Gestapo (that was the Barbie trial), one for the French *milice* (Touvier), and one for the French administration (René Bousquet or, failing him, Maurice Papon). While the Papon verdict was in deliberation, people who feared an acquittal tried to influence public opinion with the claim that "to acquit Papon would be to exonerate the Vichy regime!" The slogan really gave the game away: it was not Papon but the regime that was on trial.

Other equally important principles of the law were treated in similarly cavalier fashion. The highest courts of the land introduced several changes to the law on crimes against humanity so as to make it fit first Barbie, then Touvier, and then Papon. When the judge released Papon from custody pending trial, the plaintiffs' protests suggested that they had entirely forgotten the principle that a defendant is innocent until proved guilty. One commentator, Pierre Nora, asked what teachings could possibly come from a trial if the defendant's case is deemed lost from the start. Nor can one believe that the jury deliberated without external pressure: long before the verdict was given, every organ of the respectable media and every political figure of every party had already declared Papon guilty. From that point of view the main lesson of the trial was that, in France, the law remains a tool of politics.

Can the trial be seen nonetheless as a history lesson? Not

really. Maybe some teenagers heard about the sufferings of Jews during the Occupation for the first time because of the trial. But it is no secret that lawcourts make poor classrooms. The law deals with a kind of truth that has only two forms — guilty and innocent, black and white, yes and no; but the questions set by history rarely have simple answers of that kind. In effect, the Papon trial put in the place of the balanced and complex vision of the Vichy regime that scholars had constructed over the preceding twenty-five years two simplified, but altogether more easily remembered, caricatures: the view that Pétain's regime acted as a shield against the German invaders, and thus protected the French from an even worse fate; and the view that holds Vichy to have been a Fascist regime that collaborated actively in the extermination of the Jews. The difference in the respective aims of history and law permeated every aspect of procedure. The court disallowed some items of documentary evidence, whereas no historian could ever take such an action; it also insisted on the use of the spoken word alone, as the law requires, which meant that none of the participants was allowed to use notes. Can you imagine a historian working without writing anything down?

Since Greece and Rome lawcourts have always been closely associated with theater. Like a good play, a good trial is one that leaves a strong impression on its audience. The Papon trial was no exception. Counsel for the prosecution requested the presence of the press and the suppression of adjournments so as to ensure the unity of action; the emotional temperature was raised by slide projections of child victims on giant screens; and tension was released with *coups de théâtre*. All fair play in a court of law; but amateur dramatics are unrelated to the historian's quest for fairness and the (always approximate) truth.

Opinion polls showed that overall the French were satisfied that the Papon trial had taken place. But that does not mean that the French had made great advances in civic education; nor should the satisfaction registered be seen necessarily as an entirely positive thing. On the contrary, it may be more appropriate to be concerned about such a tidal wave of self-congratulation. Unanimous condemnation of this figure from a bygone age when the majority of French people alive today were not even born, of a figure with whom nobody could identify, meant that the French could wallow in self-righteousness and comfort themselves with the fact that the bad guys are always the others. As for civic education, the results were really meager, when you note that surveys conducted at exactly the same time revealed that 48 percent of the population considered themselves at least "somewhat racist"!

A parallel episode is worthy of mention here. The trial of Maurice Papon in 1997 for crimes against humanity committed in 1942 coincided with the hearings of the International Criminal Court (ICC) on the genocide in Rwanda that had taken place much more recently, in 1994. The French defense minister would not allow members of the French armed forces to give evidence in this court, because, he said, it was just a "show trial." The French government subsequently changed its position, but the mere fact that such a prohibition could be issued speaks volumes. What it says, in effect, is that we are happy to prosecute crimes against humanity provided they took place at least fifty years ago and provided there is no conceivable connection between the accused and ourselves. The UN adopted a similar stance; Kofi Annan, the secretary-general, put pressure on a commission of the Belgian Senate to prevent a summons being issued to General Dallaire, who had been in charge of the international peace-keeping forces in Rwanda at the time of the events. There was no denial that the events took place, only an insistence that they should not affect the policies of any government. For analogous reasons the United States has long obstructed the establishment of the International Criminal Court, seeking exemption for U.S citizens.

The Papon trial, according to Henry Rousso, "contained no pedagogical impact whatsoever" (*Hantise*, 95). Does this educational failure—the inability to draw the right lessons from the past—mean that we would do better to forget rather than to remember? Surely not. But it does mean that it would be better to leave specialists to operate in their own fields. To leave historians to establish facts and to make the initial interpretation of them. To leave schools, public service media, and parliament to teach, as they are intended to do. The courts, for their part, should be left to express the law and to apply it to individual cases. One talking head said in the course of the trial that "we mistreat our immigrants, but happily we've got the Papon trial to restore France's image." Far from compensating for present injustices, retrospective heroism seems designed to absolve us from having to deal with them, even when they are injustices for which we are responsible.

I should also like to consider here the suspension of the statute of limitation, which these trials for crimes against humanity have made topical once again. To return to the last French case, Papon was sentenced in 1998 for what he had done in 1942, that is to say fifty-six years beforehand. It is not easy to imagine that this suspension of limitation will be universally applied, and that the perpetrators of the Rwandan genocide will be tried in 2050. But the main problem is not one of imagination.

The first objection to the suspension is that it creates major difficulties for the operation of the law itself. A legal case is based on oral and written evidence. But what is the value of oral testimony given more than fifty years after the facts, when the stories told by the witnesses to themselves and to their families have long since supplanted their first impressions? That was one of the reasons why the trial of Ivan Demjanjuk, in Israel, ended in acquittal. The man was suspected of being "Ivan the Terrible," one of the cruelest of the camp guards at Treblinka. The trial showed that Demjanjuk was the wrong man, displaying the unreliability of evidence relating to the distant past. Even documentary evidence requires intuitive familiarity with the context if it is to be correctly interpreted. But such intuitive familiarity is unlikely to be a characteristic of jurors who could be Papon's grandchildren, and were not selected, in any case, for their skills as historians. We take infinite pains to establish the truth when trying a man for a single murder; why should we be less meticulous when there are thousands if not millions of victims?

There are also more general reasons for questioning whether the statute of limitations should ever be lifted. To try a man for crimes committed half a century earlier is to assume that the individual has remained like unto himself, and thus to deny the passing of time. This assumption contradicts what biology, psychology, and ordinary common sense tell us; it also runs counter to the principles of humanist philosophy on which modern secular states are grounded. Man is perfectible, said Rousseau, and that is what makes humankind different from all other species. Human beings can transform themselves; and that is why, unlike other animals, humans are responsible for their being. That does

211

not imply that everyone changes. However, to preclude such a possibility is to deny some people the right to belong to the human race — which happens to be the definition of a crime against humanity. That is also why capital punishment is barbarous: it denies some people the possibility of changing, and thus excludes them de jure from the human species before ending their lives.

The suspension of limitations makes crimes against humanity quite exceptional in the eye of the law. All crimes are subject to some limitation — save for crimes against humanity. But there is no categorical distinction that clearly separates different types of crime. It is sometimes said that crimes against humanity involve killing people not for what they have done but for what they are. But as Paul Ricœur pointed out, the killing of civilians — who are not themselves aggressors in any way — has become normal practice in modern total warfare. What personal guilt can we attribute to the inhabitants of Tokyo, Hiroshima, or Nagasaki who were annihilated in the 1945 bombings? They died because they were Japanese. War crimes are subject to the statute of limitations. To set off crimes against humanity by making them an exception to the general rule tends to make us separate them all the more from other forms of behavior and thus to make them even less comprehensible. Can we really believe that that is the best way to stop them happening again?

Those are my reasons for being opposed to maintaining the suspension of limitations in the legal arsenal. Imprescriptibility is the legal translation of eternity — and eternity has no place in human jurisprudence. The absolute, the sacred, and the eternal are not subject to the law, which deals with finite, imperfect, and relative beings. And that is why it can give amnesties and strike things off the record; that is why it dares to break the infernal cycle of revenge by putting peace first, even if such peace were an injustice in the eye of God.

Reimposing the statute of limitations certainly does not mean abandoning the idea of crimes against humanity. They are what they are, whatever the laws of the land in which they took place. A crime against humanity would then transcend any geographical boundary, but not the boundaries of time. I will come back to the forms of contemporary international law; but whatever form it takes, it needs no recourse to eternity.

The Achievement of Romain Gary

Romain Gary's last novel, *Les cerfs-volants* (The Kites), begins and ends with an enigma. On the half-title page the dedication reads: "To Memory." On the last page, the last sentence has no obvious relation to what precedes it: "I shall end this tale by inscribing once again the names of Pastor André Trocmé and of Le Chambon-sur-Lignon, because you can't do better than that." These were effectively Gary's last published words (the book appeared in 1980, shortly before the author committed suicide). Gary obviously attached great meaning to these strategically placed words, because he came back to them in his suicide note: "So what's the reason? Maybe the answer is to be found . . . in the last words of my last novel: 'you can't do better than that.' At last I've said all I have to say" (quoted in Bona, 398). What then is the message that Gary put at the head and tail of one of his most accomplished works of fiction?

Romain Gary's own adventurous life reads like a novel. He was born in 1914 in Russia, and lived as a child in Vilna and Warsaw; his mother, a nonobservant Jew, brought him to France in 1928. When France fell in June 1940, he was one of the very first to make his way to London to join the Free French and was in active service in the air force throughout the war. In 1945 he was made a Compagnon de la Libération, the highest honor that the new French government could award. From then until 1961, he was simultaneously a professional diplomat and a successful writer. He left the diplomatic service to become a full-time writer, and alongside his novels he wrote and directed movies, and also worked as a correspondent for French and U.S. magazines. Then came the "Ajar adventure": writing under that pseudonym, a fact that remained a closely guarded secret, Gary reinvented himself and scaled the hitherto unheard-of peak of winning the Goncourt Prize a second time, for *Momo* (1975). Gary was a man of many parts: he had native command of Russian and Polish, he wrote in English as well as he wrote in French, and he spent significant parts of his life in different countries. Gary was always on the move, and he used at least four pen names, of which "Romain Gary" was only one. His adventurous life has already attracted several biographies. Gary was also a master of spectacular stylistic effects, especially when writing as "Ajar"; he was a juggler of narrative forms, and a theorist of the "total novel." But what I would like to concentrate on here are the puzzling formulas of *The Kites*, taken as the words of a thinker — a thinker who wrote not philosophical treatises or political tracts, but novels and autobiographical narratives.

Gary's thinking did not change a great deal from the beginning to the end of his thirty-five-year career as a writer. He simply managed to "say what he had to say" ever more fully in the course of an œuvre that began with *European Education*, first published in London as *Forest of Anger* in 1944, and later re-translated from its 1945 French edition. Several features of this novel are striking. It was written in 1943–44 by a French airman on active duty based in the United Kingdom, but it deals with the lives of starving Polish partisans hiding in the frozen forests around Vilna, in Lithuania, something of which Gary had no direct knowledge. When Gary was not writing, he was flying bombing missions; and that makes the absence of heroics and of hatred for the enemy all the more remarkable. Already Gary's main enemy seemed to be black-and-white thinking itself. In *The Kites*, thirty-five years later, he put it thus: "Black and white, makes me sick. Gray, that's the only thing that's human."

Gary certainly doesn't turn a blind eye to Nazi atrocities in *A European Education*, and he doesn't tone down their cruelty one bit. Hangings, rapes, and torture are prominent enough. But what Gary won't do is say that the Germans are inhuman and therefore entirely different from normal beings like us. First, not all Gary's Germans are Nazis — Augustus, the old musical-toy maker, and the young soldier who deserts to join the Partisans certainly are not. But second, and most important, the Germans who carry out inhuman acts never cease to behave like human beings; they do not step outside the bounds of our nature. "Germans aren't the only thing. It's always been on the prowl, all around the human race. . . . When it gets too close, when it gets right inside you, then men become Germans. . . . even if they're Polish patriots" (*Éducation européenne*, 76). "It's not their fault either; it's not their fault if they are men" (*European Education*, 75). It would be too easy if evil were confined to Nazis. What

Gary discovered in the very time of war was much more devastating than that. In the way they behaved, the Nazis demonstrated one aspect of all humanity, something that is in all of us. Overcoming that evil is much harder than beating the Nazis. The winners of the war, Gary saw, would be only apparently victorious. They may believe they triumphed over evil, but in fact they will become blind to the evil in themselves. Gary already knew in 1944 that people who believed that this just war would establish a reign of harmony and peace in the world were fooling themselves; he knew that it would take centuries, not years, to transform humanity, if it ever could be transformed.

This discovery did not lead Gary himself or the characters in his novel toward pacifism or moral relativism. At that moment in history, evil was represented by Nazism, and it was the overriding duty of all to fight it — and to fight without illusions. The Partisans were no saints; they had inevitably been contaminated by the evil they struggled against. They shoot the German deserter, and they shoot Augustus, because they have to. In any case, victory will bring only temporary deliverance, for humanity will carry on as before. It will keep moving like "a shapeless mass of blind and shaking potatoes" (*European Education*, 230), or like ants tirelessly transporting their twigs. "What use is it to struggle and pray, to hope and believe?" (248).

Throughout his life Gary stuck to the message of his first book, but he learned to express it with ever greater clarity. We can study the unfolding of Gary's thought by focusing on the three major figures of all moral tales: the hero, the victim, and the evildoer.

I should repeat that Gary was himself an authentic wartime hero, but he never made his own exploits into a novel. He barely mentions his war service in his autobiography, *Promise at Dawn*, and when he does so, he mostly brings out the comical and personally humiliating aspects of it. A different personal episode is worth mentioning here. In 1976–77, the Order of the Compagnons de la Libération asked Gary to write a book about its members. Gary agreed and drew up a detailed questionnaire, which he sent out to everyone who had been awarded the honor. He got about six hundred responses, started to conduct interviews, and lined up a publisher. But after a year's work on the project, he gave up. "I just could not find the right way — if there is a way — of tackling the sacrifices and the struggles of the

Compagnons," he wrote to the publisher (Larat, 52–54). Some of the thoughts inspired by the work on the Compagnons probably found their way into Gary's last novel, *The Kites* (copies were specially printed for members of the Order), but like *A European Education*, this last novel deals with episodes from the Resistance, not with the war itself. And here, too, the Resisters are not exactly portrayed as supermen: they are fighting for a just cause, to be sure, but that does not prevent them from being vain or cruel. Another German deserter, having failed in an attempt on the life of Hitler, is driven to suicide by the Resisters.

Why did Gary refuse to portray heroes? At one level, Gary felt uneasy about making books out of the suffering and death of people who had been close to him ("they didn't die in the service of high sales"). At a deeper level, he realized that the hero embodies the "masculine" values of strength, courage, self-denial, self-sacrifice (characteristics of Resistance heroes like Jean Moulin and Pierre Brossolette, the idols of the narrator of the first Ajar novel, *Gros-Câlin*). Gary is prepared to admire heroic figures, but not to forget the other side of the coin, the "macho" values that lie at the root of the greatest evils. "The last thing young people need are exemplary deaths. Incitements to heroism are just for the impotent" (*La Nuit*, 109). Heroes have to be strong, but "I'm against strong men" (235). For thousands of years the macho drive to dominate and exploit other people has been the root cause of wars, massacres, and persecutions. It may do less harm, but in Gary's view it is hardly more admirable when it is embodied in modern politicians or promoted by American writers like Jack London and Ernest Hemingway.

Victorious heroes run the special risk of believing they have emerged untainted by their fight against evil and have become the perfect embodiment of good. The Nazis were defeated, were rejected by all, and had even begun to understand that they had been the agents of evil. But the victors could easily remain blinkered, seeing evil only in "them" and failing to see it in themselves. Good conscience may do good men a great disservice, which is why Gary reached the conclusion in 1946 that "when a war is won, it's the losers, not the winners, who are liberated" (*Tulipe*, 25). The main character of the novel where this maxim is coined, a Jewish Buchenwald survivor called Tulipe hiding in Harlem, New York, follows up its logic by launching a humanitarian movement which he calls "A Prayer for the Victors" (58). Years later, David Rousset expressed the same thought when he said "Victory is where the real terror lies" (*Legacy of the Bolshevik Revolution*). Readers might have mistaken *A European Education* as a hymn to anti-Nazi warriors, but that is not a mistake you could possibly make with *Tulipe.* So it is hardly surprising that, after his initial success, Gary's second novel sank like a stone.

The tragic situation of the hero is that in order to fight evil effectively he has to use his enemy's methods. Gary never forgot that in fighting the war he not only overcame a hideous, abstract enemy but also killed innocent people. He talks about it under the cover of irony and derision in *Pseudo*, in the third person: "During the war he was an airman and slaughtered civilians from on high" (26). In a short essay written in the year of his death, Gary was a little more explicit: "The bombs I dropped on Germany between 1940 and 1944 maybe killed a Rilke or a Goethe or a Hölderlin in his cradle. And yes, of course, if it had to be done over, I would do it again. Hitler had condemned us to kill. Not even the most just causes are ever innocent" (*Catalogue*).

Gary was on the side of weak against the strong (he called himself "a congenital underdog") and felt spontaneous sympathy for victims. But just as he never wanted to play the role of the real hero that he had been, he also refused to present himself in the role of victim, though as a Jew he could easily have done so. So we need to define what he meant by sympathy for the victim.

It was alien to Gary's nature to treat one group of victims as more worthy than another. Gary was aware of being Jewish through his mother, even though she had had him baptized, but he never claimed that Jewish suffering was unique. The whole plot of *Tulipe* plays on the equivalence between Jews and blacks as victims, even though the persecutions they had suffered were of quite different kinds. "*Black*, or *nigger*. Alternative name: *Jew*. General designation of lower orders descended from the apes" (*Tulipe*, 20, footnote). The basis for the persecution of blacks is said to be "The Protocols of the Elders of Harlem" (78), and in the desert where the characters wander, signs saying "No entry to Jews" stand alongside notices saying "Negroes Keep Out" (141). Gary keeps the muddle going in other novels

too: in *Gros-Câlin*, he gives a black prostitute from French
Guyana the canonically Jewish name of "Mlle Dreyfus." And in
Momo, the Algerian father of the boy Mohammed (Momo for
short), declares: "Madame, I can be persecuted without being a
Jew. You have no monopoly. The Jewish monopoly is finished,
Madame" (129). In the last part of his autobiography, *La Nuit
sera calme*, Gary describes what it was like to grow up as a for-
eigner in the 1930s: "What I was then in the south of France
was equivalent to what an Algerian immigrant is today" (26),
and throughout the book he refers to himself frequently as "the
Algerian." And it is obviously significant that the hero of his
masterpiece, *Momo*, is an Arab boy of fourteen — the age at
which Gary arrived in France.

In the second place, we should have pity on victims and give
succor in the time of their suffering, but victimhood does not
make people immune to doing evil themselves at a later stage.
Suffering supplies no long-term increase in the virtuousness of
victims, and Gary gives lots of examples of this throughout his
work. In *Tulipe*, the "Prayer for the Victors" movement spawns
a "Zionist" branch, which distorts the original intention, calling
for "the immediate opening of the African continent to resettle-
ment by its Black children" so as to prevent "any further attempt at destroying the Black race by progressive assimilation."
A modern army would be established and each of its officers
would have to prove "that he had not a drop of Aryan blood in
his veins" (63–64).

Racism, in Gary's world, is not the prerogative of any particular group. In *Tulipe*, we are offered a set of headlines from
American newspapers: "Are Japs human beings?" "Harry Truman says Racism will be rooted out in Germany and Japan"
"Racist Riots in Detroit. Some Dead" (22). There's also a touching letter from a girl in St. Louis who can't manage to marry
her boyfriend, Billy Rabinovich. "He wants to marry me, but
his parents won't give their consent, because I have some black
blood. I come from a good family, my brother was killed in the
Pacific by the Yellow Dogs. Didn't we fight this war to put an
end to all racial discrimination?" (83). Twenty years after, Gary
came to the conclusion, in *White Dog*, that "it's pretty sad
when Jews dream of having a Jewish Gestapo and when Blacks
push for a Black Ku Klux Klan" (218). Or as he put it in an interview: "Let me tell you something awful. Being a Jew or a

Black really doesn't protect you from [becoming] Germans, Nazis" (Jelenski, 4).

In *White Dog*, an autobiographical sequel to *Promise at Dawn*, Gary explores the issue of victims imitating the worst features of their oppressors through the story of a stray dog that he picked up in Beverly Hills. The dog had been trained to attack blacks, and so the narrator has it put in a kennel where a black dog-trainer tries to undo the training. By the end, the dog only attacks whites. The dog plot is the narrative support for a clearheaded account of racial tensions in the United States in 1968, before and after the assassination of Martin Luther King, Jr., and it deals equally with white and black racism, with original violence, and with violent retaliation, which Gary sees as equally lamentable even if it has fewer weapons at its disposal.

Things are not much different in the developing world as it emerges from colonial rule and from European or American oppression. Waitari, the African revolutionary leader in *The Roots of Heaven*, comes very close to his European models. "This Black was no different from all the other revolutionary tub-thumpers who put words like 'liberty' 'justice' and 'progress' on their banners whilst throwing millions of men into forced labor camps to die under the yoke" (*Racines*, 382). The reference here is to Communism, but the comparison could be generalized. In Africa, black skin doesn't make politicians different from "our home-grown variety." Unfortunately, racists are wrong about blacks being a different kind of people. The same point is made in *The Talent Scout*, set in Latin America, where local dictators, including native Americans, outdo the ousted colonial tyrants at their own game, and thereby perpetuate them. "Black- and yellow-skinned generals with their tanks, their palaces and their machine-guns would go on for many years repeating the lessons they had learned from their masters. From the Congo to Vietnam, they would go on performing the murkiest rites they had learned from civilized men: hanging, torturing, and oppressing others in the name of liberty, progress, and faith" (*Mangeur d'étoiles*, 418). But they hadn't really needed to be taught in any case; everyone belongs to the same species. That is not where hope lies.

Lastly, real victims, once they are out of actual danger, sometimes find themselves being spoken for by "professional" victims, self-appointed stalwarts who draw their raison-d'être from the historic sufferings of others. In *White Dog* Gary invents (or reports) hilarious scenes where wealthy Hollywood celebrities vie to become the most generous supporters of the black cause. Their real motives are not at all generous, however, as they are acting primarily in their own interests. What is even more sinister is that their enthusiastic support of distant causes allows them to mask their utter indifference to what is close at hand. "There's a new kind of casuistry abroad nowadays which means that because of Biafra, because of Vietnam, because of the poverty of the developing world, you don't have to help a blind man across the street any more" (*White Dog*, 23). Similarly the "S.O.S Volunteers," in *King Solomon*, give up their time to charity work mainly for their own personal satisfaction. The victim may be innocent but the uses to which his or her victimhood is put are not necessarily so. "The beginning and the end of all great movements in history is always: a victim" (*Tulipe*, 79).

Let us now look at characters that can be immediately identified as executioners, aggressors, and perpetrators of evil. Gary is not on the lookout for excuses, and he never preaches resignation or nonresistance to evil. But he believes that evil acts teach the rest of humanity a lesson — they tell it what it means to be human. Tulipe is an enemy of evil, and he begins by writing an "ideological treatise" entitled *My Struggle* (not "Mein Kampf") demonstrating that all the ills of our society come from whites. Therefore, "The criminal element of the German is the White that is in him" (85), and this allows him to put two categories of perpetrators (and their victims) into the same basket. But Tulipe's friend Uncle Nat, a black from Harlem, corrects him: "The criminal element in the German is Man." A "terrible suspicion" overcomes the narrator: "How German are we?" (90).

The main character of Gary's next novel, *The Company of Men*, is a despicable collaborator called Vanderputte. Reflecting on the novel in later years, Gary said that he discovered that "the character of the old [Vanderputte] represented humanity for me" (Jelenski, 9). In the stage play he adapted from this novel, another character, Raton the Algerian, says to his friend Luc: "You know how many Krauts there are on the planet? Three thousand million!" (*Bonne moitié*, 141). Luc is the fourteen-year-old son of a dead Compagnon de la Libération, and he gives up trying to be different from other people. Before he shoots Vanderputte, he says: "There seemed nothing left for me but to submit at last and to fall back on a cowardly complicity, on the welcoming embrace of guilt" (*Vestiaire*, 303; see also Huston). Nobody in Gary's world is entitled to everlasting innocence.

The same idea comes back to haunt Gary's subsequent works. "The Nazis and Stalin did in the end make us see that maybe it was they and not the playing fields of Eton that told the truth about people" (*Racines*, 95). And one of the main themes of *The Kites* is that it would be too easy to treat Germany as the sum of its crimes, France as the sum of its heroes. "I suddenly grasped that the Germans and even the Nazis were often used to provide cover. A long time ago an idea got into my head that was hard to get rid of, and maybe will never be got rid of entirely. The Nazis were *human*. And what was human about them was their inhumanity" (*Les cerfs-volants*, 278). Unless we recognize the inhumanity in humans and accept our complicity in evil, we remain no more than hypocrites. But Gary was not a hypocrite, he never managed to hate his enemies, and so he could never really become a "political animal."

All the same, there should be no confusion between executioners and their victims. Each action must be judged on its own terms. But there is no unbridgeable abyss between the human beings involved. And we cannot even take comfort by saying that we have not done any evil ourselves, for we have all been present while evil was done, and we failed to prevent it happening. We deplore the Germans who got on with their daily tasks around the edges of the concentration camps, but, in our own ways, we are all living "in the village next to a camp . . . and so what if the rest of the world is really a huge camp that kills people, slowly" (*Tulipe*, 30). There are degrees of suffering; nonetheless "we are always guilty of failing to come to the aid of people in need" (*King Solomon*, 24–25).

Good and evil coexist in everyone. Gary plays with the idea of his own duality; he claimed he was Jewish through his mother and a Cossack through his (unknown) father, so he was the offspring of both the perpetrators and the victims of the pogroms. The same idea gave him the paradoxical name of "Gengis Cohn" — half ghetto Jew, half Mongol conqueror — for the hero of one of his key books. The two sides can also be figured by a couple such as Solomon, the Jewish "rag-trade king," and Cora, a music-hall singer who had collaborated with the Germans (*King Solomon*).

By refusing to adopt either the hero or the victim role, by abandoning the idea that evil is the prerogative of only one kind of person, and that the good belongs to another kind, Gary inevitably condemned himself to write tragic tales. Tragedy echoes throughout his œuvre. He knows that men's faces are marked with hatred and scorn, he knows he is an ordinary man; and this prompted in him neither hatred of the world nor resignation to it, but anger. "Such rage, such shame rise in my heart that it no longer deserves its name. Rage against them, against you, against us, against myself" (*Catalogue*). But Gary's anger can't always produce any action, because no specific act will change human identity. "For the main part, there is no answer" (*La Nuit*, 13). So how can you hope, rather than despair of everything? Well, some days you can't, and it was probably on just such a day that Gary put a gun in his mouth (even if Gary's suicide, like all others, had many causes). But there was some kind of logic to it. As early as 1946 Gary wrote that "the most disrespectful act anyone can commit is to stay alive" (*Tulipe*, 162). Might that mean that the most respectful thing you can do is to end it all?

But that is certainly not what Romain Gary's works say to us. They are tragic, to be sure, but they also pulsate with joy and life. Gary refrained from singing the praise of his heroes, he refrained from weeping on behalf of his victim characters, and he held back from castigating his criminals, but he found ways of expressing his love of the world through other characters and other emotions. That is actually what marks him off most clearly from those many other French writers of his generation who did no more than describe the absurdity of the world and the turpitude of human beings. "I told you so, I told you so: just because it's the end of the world, it don't mean there's no more courage!" he wrote in *Tulipe* (105). But how did Gary himself manage to keep his head up for so long?

Gary the novelist and some of his fictional characters have an immense capacity for understanding and for loving even the humblest and most despicable beings. In *The Company of Men* (*Le Grand Vestiaire*), Luc's father, who had been a Resistance hero and was killed by the Nazis, leaves the lesson for his son, and for us, in these words: "No greater peril lies in ambush for us than the strange difficulty we have in recognizing humanity in men, and there are times when compassion is the only light which reveals the presence of humanity around us. Mercy rises higher than all doubt, is sheltered from all error and all truth; mercy is our deepest self" (237). People don't deserve to be admired, but they all need love. That's why Gary promises, in an unforgettable passage in *Promise at Dawn*, to mention the name of the utterly insignificant Mr. Piekielny to every important personage he ever meets. "All that I've written," Gary said later, "is made out of respect for weakness" (*La Nuit*, 102).

Dignity for an individual comes not only from the love and compassion that others may grant but also from inside. People may be all cut from the same cloth, but they are not made of only one piece. There's pride, and stupidity, and fear, and pettiness in us all; but there is also something else. Everyone somehow aspires toward something for which Gary uses metaphors relating the low to the high, such as "the roots of heaven" or "kites": and this aspiration is simply the capacity that people have to rise above themselves for an ideal—to be free. "Islam calls that 'the roots of heaven'; for native Mexicans, 'the tree of life' is what makes them kneel, raise their eyes, and beat their breasts in agony. They try to settle things amongst themselves, to satisfy their need of justice, freedom and love from their own resources" (*Racines*, 222). Without this aspiration, human beings would be no different from other animals. "If you take poetry and imagination away from people, all you're left with are hunks of meat" (*La Nuit*, 229).

The human need for justice and freedom can take many forms, including the heroic. Gary was well aware of the pitfalls of that role. He didn't give up fighting and bombing enemy territory, but he had a greater preference for a different form of humanity, love. That is why Gary tried to promote what he called "feminine" values, initially materialized for us all in a mother's love. "Man—I mean to say, civilization—begins with the mother-child relationship" (*La Nuit*, 104). In *Promise at Dawn*, Gary gave an unforgettable portrait of his own mother. A child first learns to love its mother; and that's how it will grow up into a human being capable of love—or maybe just into a human being. What Gary thinks of as "feminine" values—sweetness, affection, compassion, nonviolence, respect for the weak — match those that were put forward by Vasily Grossman. Both writers give maternal love much the same role and treat it as an emblem of what is most human about human beings.

Christianity espoused the same values — or, rather, attached them to the figure of a man, Jesus Christ; and that is why Gary, despite being a firm agnostic, treasures the person of Jesus. Not a God but a mere mortal, Jesus gave the first and highest form to those values. "Christianity is femininity, pity, sweetness, forgiveness, tolerance, maternity, respect for the weak: Jesus is weakness" (*La Nuit*, 228). Or, at least, that's what the Christian idea was to begin with, before it became an excuse for crusades, inquisitions, persecutions, prudery, and pogroms. Gary's Jesus goes back to the initial idea: "It was the first time in the history of the West that anyone had dared to talk as if motherhood actually existed" (*La Nuit*, 230). That is why allusions to Jesus run through the whole of *Tulipe* — "It was suspected that Tulipe's real name was Jesus Christ, or Kri, from the archaic expression *cry*, to call for help" (17) — and why Gengis Cohn's last appearance has him bent under the weight of a huge cross.

Does love have a place in wartime? Gary says he framed a letter that his mother wrote to him in Russian when he was in England, to say adieu and to urge him to be ever *sil'ny i krepky*, "strong and solid," to which Gary gives the meaning "resistant" (*La Nuit*, 231; see also Larat, 46). The weak can be strong by *resisting*, which is Gary's favored form of struggle — and it's no coincidence that he wrote two novels about the Resistance, and none about the war itself. He also transposed the theme of active resistance to a quite different context in *The Roots of Heaven*. Its hero Morel is a former member of the French Resistance who discovered in the camp to which he had been deported that the ground of humanity is love — love for the humblest among men, but also for animals and even for maybugs! He makes the discovery when he's worn out and exhausted, and kneels down to put a bug that had fallen over back on its feet. By a significant coincidence, Gary wrote *The Roots of Heaven* in 1955, the same year that Vasily Grossman wrote a story called *Zoo*, about a man who moves earthworms out of the road where they might get run over during the shelling of Berlin. When Morel gets out of the camp, he swears never to fail to respect all living things, be they dogs or, years later, African elephants. The novel's plot deals with Morel's fight to save the elephants — a struggle that requires him to be a doughty fighter but not hard of heart. He must be *krepky*, a resister aware of his own weakness.

Gary interprets the figure of Charles de Gaulle, to whom he remained unwaveringly loyal, in the same way. He saw de Gaulle not as a man of steel, but as someone who assumed his own weakness. "De Gaulle in 1940 and today," Gary wrote, "is in his own way a bit like Morel and his elephants" (*Racines*, 162). Why were they like each other? What Gary found attractive in de Gaulle was a kind of curious and desperate eccentricity. After all, he was a virtually unknown soldier when he turned up in London in June 1940 and claimed that he was thenceforth the incarnation of France! "For me, de Gaulle was weakness saying 'no!' to force, and his complete lack of strength made him the representative of all mankind" (*La Nuit*, 20). The de Gaulle that Gary admired was a courageous Don Quixote, practicing civil disobedience in the service of a higher authority. Or, to take a different image of the same thing, he was like Solzhenitsyn in the 1970s, a calf trying to knock over a great oak.

In *The Kites*, Gary attaches André Trocmé, the pastor of Le Chambon-sur-Lignon, his wife Magda and all the other inhabitants of the village, to the same set. During the Second World War they did not fight but devoted themselves to another task, the protection of Jews from persecution. They managed to save several thousand from certain death. That was the action more worthy than all others that makes Gary write "You can't do better than that." They represent the resistance of the weak, the militancy of love.

It was not only because people have the ability to look upward, to love and to resist alongside their capacity for inhumanity that Gary could keep despair at bay for most of the time. It was also because, irrespective of reasons and justifications, he loved the world and he loved life. He was much like anyone else in this respect, but he differed from many of his contemporaries by knowing it. He was not among those who, seeing only gloom and human frailty around them, fail to stand back from suffering and evil and thereby burden their readers with more of it.

That was what Gary held against some of the French writers of his time. The problem with the "literature of misery," Gary wrote, was that "by focusing exclusively on 'becoming aware' of pain, it rejects *total* literature and sides with *totalitarian* writing." What he meant was that some contemporary writers had closed their eyes to the variety of human experience so as to present only one of its facets. "It is false to restrict the masses to suffering in this way"; what is more, it can only serve to increase their suffering. What the existentialist lie leaves out is "the most important experience of being, which allows life to go on and civilizations to be maintained, and that is the joy of existing." We should not forget that the most downtrodden and humiliated of men, even in the worst misery that life has to offer, experience "sparks of joy and countless communions with the joy of being" (*Pour Sganarelle*, 324–25).

The true generosity of Romain Gary can be measured by his capacity for admiring the signals of humanity in every kind of human being, including those who rarely look up to the sky or encounter spiritual ecstasy. Because he kept in touch with this truth of the human condition, he was able to keep despair at bay, and his novels are full of humor and lightness that allow us to share in the joy of being. Although most of Gary's novels deal with dreadful and depressing subjects, they are shot through with the love of life, and we benefit from it. The stories are well told, the characters are captivating and funny, and they engage our emotions most effectively. Gary gave his readers a gift of life — until he could no longer feel any joy in being for himself, and withdrew. That is why people who claim that poetry should not exist after Auschwitz are wrong. To accept such a notion is to step into the debilitating logic of totalitarianism itself. Total man — let us say, humankind itself — will always need poetry and music, stories and songs. Gary dedicated *Gros-Câlin* to André Malraux with the words: "The novel is alive and well."[1]

So what is the "Memory" to which Gary's last novel is dedicated? Gary never tried to intimidate people with a "duty to remember," which others have insisted on being a universal burden. We can't remember everything, nor can we forget it either. Painful memories exist even if we would like to be free of them; on the other hand, there's not much merit in keeping the

---

[1] The dedication is characteristically two-edged. The French word for novel, *roman*, is identical to Gary's original Polish forename. "Roman pas mort" thus also means that the author Romain Gary is alive and well.

memories we cherish and which give us pleasure. The past should not be allowed to overshadow the present: "I can't stand people who live off being veterans. Life is made for starting afresh. I don't go to reunions, I don't go to memorial services, I don't rekindle the flame" (*La Nuit*, 108). Nor did Gary like sanctified images even of men he regarded as great. "I hate relics. I think that relics are always harmful, whether they're Marx's or Lenin's, Freud's, de Gaulle's or Mao Tse Tung's" (155). But that does not mean that the past has to be jettisoned. "It is in me and it is *me*" (108).

In *The Kites*, the theme of memory recurs several times. The family of the narrator is endowed with a phenomenal ability to remember — a "historic" memory — which makes Ludo able to perform mind-boggling feats of mental arithmetic and to memorize the railway timetable. But it's not that kind of quiz-champion memory that the book's dedication intends to honor. The memory that is offered for admiration in this novel is a selective one, and it involves retaining from the past those elements that help us live in the present.

Ludo's great-grandfather also suffered from "historic memory" and knew the Declaration of the Rights of Man by heart. To have a good memory is a way of implementing the motto of Ludo's schoolteacher: Hang On to Your *Raison d'Etre*. To remember is to remain worthy of your ideal and to keep your honor. For Ludo, during the war, keeping memory meant joining the Resistance. He was not alone at that time: someone else was living as he was "entirely from memory," and that was de Gaulle in London. But does he mean fidelity to an ideal, or fidelity to a person? Both: all through the many trials of war, Ludo never forgot Lila, and he remained faithful to her, not just because she was his only love (Lila slept with many other men, but remained faithful to Ludo all the same) but because he kept his faith in her intact. The two kinds of faithfulness, to persons and to principles, merge into each other by the end, and the village of Le Chambon serves as the model, because its inhabitants saved the lives of individuals. As Gary says, it is a place of "high fidelity" (*Les cerfs-volants*, 207).

Memory thus connects with the highest human virtues — justice and love. That is why it rightly figures in the place of honor that Gary gave it.

The Perils of Democracy

> And the young mother with her son in her arms
> will walk toward her fate; and when the next
> human generation comes, she will see a strong
> blinding light in the sky — the first explosion of
> the hydrogen bomb, signaling the start of the
> next war, which will be total.
> — *Vasily Grossman,* "The Sistine Madonna"

The Hiroshima and Nagasaki Bombs

The end of the Second World War was signaled by two events
with different meanings. On the one hand, the most hideous and
excessive form of totalitarianism, the Nazi regime, was overcome
and destroyed. On the other hand, the United States, the leader of
the coalition of democratic states, made use at the very end of the
war of a new and terrifying weapon of incomparable destructive
power, the atomic bomb.

When Ernest Renan, in the 1870s, tried to imagine what a state
based on scientism would be like, in his anticipation of a totalitarian state, he foresaw that terror would supplant domestic politics, while foreign policy would be transformed by the invention
of an absolute weapon capable of "destroying the planet." It is
true that the totalitarian states, the Soviet Union and Nazi Germany, ruled by terror; but no less true that it was the land of
democracy par excellence, the United States, that developed the
absolute weapon and decided to use it straight away. The execution of internal enemies in Germany and Russia required only
primitive and unsophisticated tools that had been available for
decades, if not centuries — shooting, gassing, and exhausting people through hunger and cold. But the execution of the enemies of
democracy involved contributions from the greatest minds of the
planet and was based on stunning technological exploits. The totalitarian regimes killed because of their scientistic foundations;

the democratic regimes killed with the help of the practice of science.

The comparison may seem inappropriate. There were deaths on both sides, to be sure, but their meaning was entirely different. In the Soviet Union people were put to death as "enemies of the people" so that they should conform to the laws of history and also to shore up the power of the party and its leader. In Germany people were murdered so as to cleanse the human race of its parasites and also to reinforce the power of the party and its Führer. But as every school student knows, atomic bombs were dropped on Nagasaki and Hiroshima in order to end the war, to bring peace, and to overthrow a regime that was, if not totalitarian, then certainly militaristic, repressive, and aggressive. On one side, the killing was done in the name of what seems to us to be the very incarnation of injustice; on the other side, it was done in the name of justice. The difference ought to be huge. In addition, the atomic bombs worked as they were intended: a few days after the attack, Japan surrendered unconditionally and the Second World War came to an end.

To be more precise, the interpretation that dominated in the U.S. and allied countries in the wake of the Second World War was as follows. The political imperative was clear: in order to bring the war to a close, Japan had to be defeated. Japan was guilty not only of having waged war, but also of having tortured, mistreated, and oppressed the peoples it had conquered, and of having caused innumerable deaths outside of the battlefield; therefore mere victory over Japan would not have been enough. Japan had to be not just beaten but also punished; the structures of the state and its military hierarchy had to be dismantled. To achieve this the United States demanded not just cessation of hostilities but unconditional surrender. And it was on that point that negotiations stumbled. Japan agreed to surrender, but not unconditionally, because it wished to retain its traditional structures and, in particular, the fundamental institution of the monarchy. Because it rejected U.S. demands, Japanese military authorities were left with only one option, to fight to the death. Although it could only result in the annihilation of the Japanese army, it would cause heavy losses to the enemy, as the Americans knew only too well after the bloody battle of Okinawa.

It was widely believed in the years after the war that the drop-

229

ping of the atomic bombs caused the deaths of many Japanese (about 140,000 on 6 August 1945 in Hiroshima and 70,000 on 9 August at Nagasaki; the figures were later revised to 180,000 and 140,000, respectively), but saved many American lives that would have been lost in the assault on Japan — 1.5 million was the most commonly used estimate. In 1981 Paul Fussell, a well-known American historian, who had been serving in the U.S. Army in Europe in 1945, knowing he was likely to be transferred to the Pacific for the bloody onslaught on Japan, wrote an essay entitled *Thank God for the Atomic Bomb*, and it's easy to grasp his point: he owes his life to the nuclear explosions.

In truth, the argument from the avoidance of probable deaths does not seem entirely convincing. It would require us to believe that history proceeds mechanically, which it manifestly does not. Virtual deaths can't really be entered into the accounting: events could easily have taken a different course. Paul Touvier, one of the leaders of the *milice* in Lyons during the Vichy regime used the same kind of argument in his own defense during his trial for crimes against humanity. The Gestapo had asked for thirty hostages to be executed in reprisal for the murder of a *milice* minister, Philippe Henriot; but he, Touvier, had got the number down to seven. So, far from being prosecuted for crimes against humanity, he should be hailed as a benefactor of the human race, and thanked for having saved twenty-three people from certain death! But once you start arguing this way, there's no reason to stop: why keep to twenty-three in one case, a million in the other? The as yet unborn children of those spared also owe their lives to Touvier's noble gesture; and had it not been for the atomic bombs, several million Americans would never have been born! But alas, by the same kind of arithmetic, the Americans killed untold millions of virtual human beings (admittedly Japanese). This kind of reckoning quickly becomes absurd.

A second question has undermined the certainties of the traditional account of the use of the atomic bomb. It is perfectly possible to ask whether unconditional surrender was really necessary. And if it was indispensable, was the only way to achieve it to drop atomic bombs on Japanese cities? The first question is worth asking because, once Japan capitulated, the United States decided in the end to maintain the monarchy, which was what the Japanese government had requested as a condition of surrender.

230

If the United States was prepared to accept the arrangement, why did it need the bombs? There was another side to it as well. Unconditional surrender was likely to come about because of a separate major development. In early August 1945, the Soviet Union, which had remained neutral in the Pacific conflict up to that point, declared war on Japan (the official announcement was made on 8 August), putting the empire of the sun in a truly desperate position. Notwithstanding, the U.S. high command did not leave the Japanese time to absorb the new situation and bombed Hiroshima and Nagasaki forthwith. It seems as if the Americans were intent on winning the war by their own efforts, and not with the help of the Soviets.

Unconditional surrender could also have been achieved by an experimental nuclear blast, far from civilian targets, and in the presence of Japanese military and scientific personnel. We can imagine that the mere demonstration of the bomb's power would have been sufficient. Along the same lines, we might observe that even if Hiroshima were considered necessary, nothing justified the Nagasaki bomb. The demonstration had already been performed, all that was needed was to wait for its effects to become clear.

But if the bombs were not necessary to end the war or to obtain unconditional surrender, and if we cannot grant them the generous role of having saved American lives, why were they dropped? There must have been a reason for wiping out three hundred thousand Japanese lives at a stroke. American historians like Gal Alperovitz have been asking this question for forty years and they have come up with answers that are far from simple but seem nearer to the truth than the myth that was current in the immediate postwar years. Indeed, the reasons were not one, but many.

President Truman and his advisers were human beings like any others and they acted under the pressure of a whole range of factors, whose respective weights are difficult to judge; and it was the combination of all these factors that led to the decision. The weightiest consideration, in all probability, was not related to Japan but to the recent change in U.S. relations with the Soviet Union. Even before final victory over Germany, the antifascist coalition was not in perfect harmony, and once the victory was won, the conflict of the future quickly loomed: the Allies would be rivals in the new division of the world. Roosevelt had remained well-inclined toward the Soviets and even wanted to share with them the secret of the new weapon. Truman, who had only just taken Roosevelt's place, came from a different political background and was much more subject to pressure from his advisers, who saw the Soviet Union as the greatest threat to the United States. It was time to impress Uncle Joe and to show him where real power lay. That would be a way to rein back Stalin's ambitions to expand his empire and to make him think twice before sending the Red Army's tanks to conquer Western Europe. The desired effect was indeed achieved, since there was no Soviet aggression in the later 1940s. But we know what happened next. Stalin was impressed, as intended, and put everything into building a Soviet atomic bomb. When he finally succeeded, mutual dissuasion ensued, of which we could say, along the lines of the preceding argument, that it saved millions of lives (so the Hiroshima bomb turns out to have been even more beneficial for humanity than we could have guessed). That would still mean that the inhabitants of Hiroshima and Nagasaki were sacrificed for the sake of New Yorkers, Parisians, and Londoners.

There was another set of reasons, however, which were closely related to Japan and to recent U.S. history. The United States experienced Pearl Harbor as a humiliation and an affront that had to be avenged. (At the time nobody knew that Roosevelt had *wanted* Pearl Harbor to happen so as to sway the isolationist — sometimes even pro-Hitlerian — attitudes of many Americans toward support for entering the war on the Allied side.) However much people may invoke justice, punitive expeditions are pretty close to revenge. Punishing the Japanese seemed easy to justify when the atrocities they committed in occupied countries were widely known; combined with revelations about Nazi crimes, they created a climate that favored "teaching lessons." But that does not make the punishment legitimate. As Grossman remarked in his story about Hiroshima, "Neither the little boy nor his grandma, nor hundreds of others with their mothers and grannies, understood why it fell to them to pay for Pearl Harbor and Auschwitz" ("Avel," 18).

From the point of view of humanity, if such an expression is permitted, it would perhaps have been better to find a solution to the conflict that did not involve increasing the number of its victims. But from the point of view of humbled American honor, nothing was better than a real drubbing — let the killers be killed! Even today, many U.S. states continue to base their penal system on this barbaric principle. That is no doubt why Truman and his cabinet dismissed a showcase nuclear explosion and chose instead to destroy two cities. In addition, Tokyo had already been hit particularly heavily with conventional bombs on 10 March 1945 (100,000 dead), and was even bombed again after Nagasaki, on 14 August 1945, when Japanese capitulation was only a few hours away.

A third explanation can be found in the anti-Japanese racism that was current in the United States — a kind of racism, as we have seen, that Romain Gary commented on as early as 1946 and which has been studied in detail since then by historians (see Dower, *War without Mercy*). Anti-Japanese racism flourished not only in the popular press but also among Washington decision makers, who always referred to the enemy by the pejorative term of "the Japs." American propaganda depicted them as mad dogs, pigs, or monkeys, who deserved only to be put down. Truman defended himself against accusations of having killed civilians at Nagasaki in these words: "When you're dealing with a beast, you have to treat it like a beast" (quoted in Linenthal and Engelhardt, 86). The fact that the bomb was used against non-European nonwhites did not escape the notice of the black community in the United States, which was particularly alert to the question of racism. The poet Langston Hughes wrote on 18 August 1945: "Why wasn't the bomb used against Germany? They simply didn't want to use it against white people. The Germans are white. So they waited for the war in Europe to be over to try it out on people of color. Japs are people of color" (quoted in Linenthal and Engelhardt, 272).

A fourth group of reasons for the use of the atomic bomb has nothing to do with Japan and the Japanese, or with geopolitics and competition with the Russians, but comes from the dynamic of the very building of the bomb itself. It is well known that the original decision to try to make an atomic bomb came from fear that Hitler might make one first. But around 1943 allied intelligence ascertained that Germany had put the project on hold and was pushing ahead instead with rocket development. However, research on nuclear fission was not halted in the United States. Physicists put the question of ultimate justification for what they were doing to the back of their minds and threw themselves into solving an extraordinarily complex technical problem. As Robert Oppenheimer, the director of the Manhattan Project, said some years later: "It is my judgment in these things that when you see something technically sweet you go ahead and do it and you argue about what to do about it only after you have had your technical success. That's the way it was with the atomic bomb" (quoted in Glover, 106).

Instrumental thinking, nicely illustrated by Oppenheimer's words, makes the following sequence inevitable: if it can be made, it must be made; and if it's been made, it must be used. Ultimate ends — the reasons for doing things — are never questioned. Technology seems to make the decision for us; we do what technology makes possible instead of using technology to do what we think useful.

A similar drift is characteristic of all bureaucracies and most especially, in this case, of military bureaucracy. As the bomb had been originally conceived as a shield against Hitler, you might expect it would have been shelved after Hitler's defeat. But that is not the way that instrumental and bureaucratic thinking works. Since the project was under way, it had to go on, to its end. As Oppenheimer testified after the war: "I don't think there was any time where we worked harder at the speed-up than in the period after the German surrender" (quoted in Linenthal and Engelhardt, 82). They were indeed in a hurry, because they were afraid the war might be over before they had got their fine invention to work properly. The military high command, for its part, preferred the war to end not by negotiation but in an exclusively military triumph.

In the modern world, whether under democratic or totalitarian rule, an act of the magnitude of a nuclear bombing requires the involvement of many actors, and responsibility for it is necessarily divided between numerous cogs in the machine. As a result no single individual feels directly responsible for whatever negative consequences may ensue. All involved act under the pressure of circumstance and the demands of the community. They all think in terms of means, not ends. The pilots who dropped the bombs obviously did not consider themselves responsible, as they were only obeying orders, and, anyway, they reckoned they were right to do what they did, saving a million American lives! Any remorse that arose at the time of the bombing was quickly stifled with magic formulas and amusing nicknames: the bomb dropped on Hiroshima was called "Little Boy," and the Nagasaki bomb was known as "Fat Man." The physicists who perfected the device were delighted with their achievement. The president and the cabinet did what was recommended by competent military chiefs — and they, for their part, were swayed by the logic of a process that they had not initiated themselves. The politicians had asked the military to solve the crisis by waging war, and they pursued it with the means at their disposal — incendiary and then atomic bombs.

In the West, in whose name Hiroshima and Nagasaki were bombed, it is still generally believed that these acts of war were utterly legitimate ones. Jonathan Glover recalls a significant incident that took place at Oxford University in 1956. At a meeting of Hebdomadal Council it was proposed to award an honorary degree to Harry S. Truman. Elizabeth Anscombe, the philosopher, rose to object, on the grounds that exterminating civilians could not easily be counted a meritorious action. But when put to the vote, the proposal passed unanimously, save for one vote against, Anscombe's (Glover, 106).

What can we call these bombings nowadays, better informed as we are on the military situation than people were at the time? The term that seems to fit the best is that of war crime. The Geneva Convention of 12 August 1949 defines attacks on or the bombing of civilian populations in undefended areas which are not military targets as war crimes. The military aim that was being pursued could in fact have been achieved by other means, which would have produced far fewer victims. In addition, those who died at Hiroshima and Nagasaki were predominantly civilians (in a ratio of 6 to 1). It was the clear intention of the military high command to strike a city, not a military asset, and preferably an undamaged city, to effect the highest possible number of deaths and the greatest possible psychological impact.

These legalistic definitions, based on a clear distinction between civilians and soldiers, hark back to an era of military history that disappeared with the Second World War. The development of total warfare makes them almost entirely irrelevant. People on the home front were no less part of the war effort than those on the other fronts. Without "Rosie the Riveter" the U.S. army would have come to a halt, and British forces would have starved if civilians hadn't responded to all those posters calling on them to "dig for victory." Conversely, it was thought that victory — and thus peace — could be gained more rapidly by terrorizing the enemy population. The tactic was first used by Hitler in the London blitz, but it was soon copied by the Allies. Far from being fringe events, bombings of civilian targets became the most efficient and the most widespread means used to bring the war to a victorious conclusion. Total warfare rubs out the distinction between an act of war and a war crime. Does that mean that the notion of war crime is obsolete? Or that all acts of war are war crimes?

The lessons of the Hiroshima and Nagasaki bombs are many and various, and I focus only on those that concern us directly. First, totalitarian regimes are not the only ones to engage in evil: even if the genocides of Ukrainian peasants and European Jews were the greater crimes, a crime does not cease to be a crime just because a worse one has been committed elsewhere. Nonetheless, this new form of evil was done in the name of good — not only a good that was by definition equivalent to the desire of those who performed it, but a good to which we all always aspire, peace and democracy. This form of evil arose by a different means; it did not derive from the ideology of scientism, nor was it a tool for the conquest of absolute power. It was the infinitely painful by-product of the struggle against an even greater evil. It was only a means, we are told, a maybe regrettable but nonetheless unavoidable means toward an end that remains a noble one. It was also the effect of a kind of thinking that fails to coordinate means and ends.

Atomic bombs killed fewer people than the famine in Ukraine, fewer than the Nazis slaughtered in Ukraine and Poland. But what the bombs and the slaughters have in common is that their perpetrators all thought they were but a means to achieve a good. However, the bombs have another feature: they are a source of pride for those who made and dropped them (and who deserve recognition from the University of Oxford and many other institutions, as benefactors of humanity), whereas totalitarian crimes, even if they were considered by their perpetrators to be useful and even praiseworthy political acts, were kept secret. Stalin never got a medal for wiping out the peasantry, and even Himmler grumbled that his achievement, the extermination of the Jews, could never be celebrated openly. Both the Soviet and the Nazi leadership knew full well that the world would damn them if it knew exactly what they had done. They were not wrong, because as soon as their crimes were revealed, they were treated as the emblems of absolute evil. Things are quite different in the case of the atomic bombs, and for that very reason, even if the crime is less grave, the moral mistake of the people who killed in the name of democracy is greater. It helps us to understand why Romain Gary asserted that when a "war is won, it's the losers, not the winners, who are liberated" (*Tulipe*, 25). The defeated are liberated from the illusion that they are identical to the good, whereas the victors are ready to begin all over again.

Totalitarianism may sometimes rightly seem to us to be the empire of evil. But it does not follow that democracy invariably embodies the realm of good.

Kosovo: The Political Context

It has often been noted that the twentieth century ended as it began with a Balkan war (which would make the century start in 1912). What is the meaning of this conflict of the 1990s, in light of the struggle between totalitarianism and democracy, a struggle that dominated the history of the whole century? Do the lessons of the past help us understand the present? In this chapter I try to test the lessons of history by bringing them to bear on events we all saw recently and which remain alive in our memories, paying particular attention to the last phase of the conflict, the Kosovo war.

The very closeness of these events is a problem. The passing of time helps to create at least a basic consensus. Even if there still are divergent interpretations and evaluations of the Second World War, there is at least agreement about the facts—who, what, where, and how many. But that cannot be said about the conflict of 1999. The truth of the facts is far from certain, for a very good reason: establishing the facts is part of the war. As in any interpretive effort we are unsure which information is pertinent, but in this case we are not even sure what the information really is. The meanings that have been attributed to these events and to judgments made of them are wildly divergent, even among people sharing similar democratic values and similar ideals of peace and justice. The complete fragmentation of opinion on the Kosovo campaign, even inside one country, is really depressing for anyone who would rather believe in the intellect. It makes it seem as if our opinions depended not at all on the information that we have, on our ability to reason, or on the values we adhere to, but on murkier grounds — on our infinitely variable identities as individuals, on our life histories, and on unconscious allegiances. Information and reasoned argument seem to serve only to give a rational shell to choices made deeper down.

I cannot claim to be entirely unmoved by such factors, nor can I hope to persuade people whose mind is already made up to accept my own interpretation. But all the same I would prefer not to imitate in all respects the contestants in the passionate debate that arose in France over the military intervention in Kosovo. I do not discredit any opinion on grounds of where it comes from, or because of what use might be made of it. It is not because Göbbels accused the Soviets of the Katyn massacre that the Soviets are any less responsible for it. Nor should we mask the truth about Communist regimes just because it might discourage the workers or because the far right still stalks the streets. In public debate, anything that is true is worth a hearing. Nor am I going to make my task easier by formulating leading questions: are you for barbarism or for civilization? For war or for peace? Do you want to save children in danger or let them be murdered? Do you prefer murderers or their victims? To do so would be to ape Lenin, who sought only victory in argument, not the truth, according to Grossman. It is perhaps now time to reflect on this recent episode in European history in a calmer frame of mind, without being carried away by emotion. At least I hope so.

The events of 1999 in Kosovo occurred in a specific historical and geographical context, which needs to be outlined. To begin with, let us recall an apparently separate episode, but which was in many ways a warning of what was to come. Nearby Bulgaria has a large Turkish-speaking and Islamic minority — about 10 percent of its population. There had long been endemic discrimination against the "Turks," but there were no major conflicts between the two communities until a campaign for the "Bulgarianization" of names (and life-styles) was launched in the 1980s. The result was foreseeable — protests, taken in some cases as far as collective suicides, and the expulsion to Turkey of large numbers of people who had never been there in their lives. The meaning of the campaign was also quite clear. The Communist authorities had realized that their ideology no longer held any sway over the people, but to stay in power they needed to rely not just on discipline but on some emotional loyalty, or a collective passion. To do this they decided to re-awaken nationalist feelings by making the diversity of languages (and cultures) within Bulgaria's geographic boundaries seem like an anomaly.

However, the campaign, which caused great suffering to the Turkish minority, backfired. It gave rise to an open opposition within the ruling majority, an unprecedented event in the history of Bulgarian totalitarianism. As a result, the "Bulgarianization" program contributed to the fall of a Communist regime deeply compromised by its attempt to manipulate anti-Turkish feelings.

Let us now move back to next door Yugoslavia and try to recall all the facts we need to understand the conflict. This federal state comprised six republics, and the largest of them, Serbia, had two autonomous regions, Vojvodina, primarily inhabited by Hungarian speakers, and Kosovo, dominated by speakers of Albanian. Until 1980 strict control by the Communist regime stifled nationalist temptations and maintained peace in the state. That year saw the death of Marshal Tito, the head of state, a hero of the Second World War. His successors did not have his prestige, and the repressive power of the Communist Party grew less effective. That was when Yugoslavia's Communist leaders turned themselves into nationalist leaders, in a transformation that the Bulgarian Communists had been unable to pull off. It shows once again how easily one form of totalitarianism may slip into another: "nation" is substituted for "proletariat" and takes on all the privileges associated with the former "leading class." Slobodan Milosević, the strong man of Serbia (and for the first few years, of Yugoslavia), embodied that mutation. Because (Communist) ideological passion was now in a terminal slumber, Milosević played with great skill on many Serbians' feelings of being the victims of past injustice.

He hit upon the right pretext in 1987. In Kosovo, there were only about 200,000 Serbs among maybe 2 million overall, and, as often happens, this minority suffered discrimination and minor violence at the hands of the Albanian majority. Milosević promised to right this wrong, and appealed to memory. In 1389, at the battle of Kosovo Polje, the Serbs had been defeated by Muslim Turks. There could be no question of yielding a second time: memory was enlisted in support of the reconquest of (Muslim) Kosovo. In 1989 Milosevic suspended the autonomy of the Kosovo region and launched a reverse persecution of Yugoslavia's Albanian minority.

This repressive measure had the effect of an alarm bell elsewhere in the federation. One after another, fearing Serbian hegemony, the former republics that made up Yugoslavia left the federation (save for Montenegro, which shares both its language and the Eastern Orthodox religion with Serbia). These changes seemed to fit the principle that each culturally distinct population should have its own autonomous state. But outside observers do not find it easy to grasp just what the cultural entities are. Sometimes religious traditions are alleged to be the dividing principle (Orthodox, Catholic, and Muslims live side by side), but we must not forget that after forty years of Communism most of the people are atheists. At other times, linguistic differences are said to be paramount. While it is true that Hungarian and Albanian are quite unrelated to Slavic languages (and to each other), Serbian, Croatian, and Bosniak are basically the same language (written in different alphabets), and if you can speak any one of these, you can understand Macedonian and Slovenian as well. In addition, because Yugoslavia has been a unitary state since 1918, the populations have become mixed up, through moving around and through intermarriage, to such an extent that you can't really call them "mixed marriages" any more.

The independence of the constituent republics created foreseeable friction since the new frontiers were now national and not merely regional ones. Many Serbs found themselves living in Croatia, and many Croatians were now inside Serbia. Wars broke out between Slovenia and Serbia, between Croatia and Serbia. New resentments and reasons for revenge piled up. The leaders of all these new states seemed to be working according to the principle of one country for one people. This led to movements of populations, known as "ethnic cleansing," not unlike the displacements that occurred at the end of the Second World War, when Poles were forced to leave territory ceded to the Soviet Union and Germans were expelled from areas that had become part of Poland, and so on.

We have to stress the fact that the concept of "one people, one country" is a highly contentious one, for two separate sets of reasons. The first is that the "right to self-determination," which was so often invoked in the Yugoslavian crisis, has no determinate meaning, save for implying quite wrongly that "peoples" exist prior to their organization in a state. Ethnic groups — however we might define such a term — do not automatically constitute "peoples." We should remember that there are approximately two hundred states in the world today, and that six thousand separate language communities and about five thousand clearly distinct ethnic groupings live in them. And we all know full well that cultural boundaries do not match any other frontiers: religious traditions are distributed as differently from languages as they are from physical features. Shared history — or a shared enemy — sometimes creates stronger links than the bonds of language and religion. In short, the dream (which some consider a nightmare) of a perfect fit between a territory, a people, and a state is unfeasible.

In addition, this dream is contrary to the spirit of democracy. It limits the individual to an identity determined by ascendancy and the circumstances of birth, instead of allowing him or her to exercise autonomy of judgment. The ethnic state claims to be a state *by nature*, whereas a democratic state has to be thought of as a state *by contract*, whose citizens are subjects in the exercise of their free will, and not merely representatives of a community determined by physical or cultural identity.

Indeed, a democratic state is not just a community linked by blood or origin. It gives all its members the opportunity to exercise their freedom and to break free of the determining forces to which they are subject. Such a state can absorb diverse communities and regulate differences between them by contractual arrangement, which may be based on tolerance and secularism (in modern democracies, religion is a private matter; all religions may be practiced, or none at all), or else on a concept of unity (many nations have a single official language). Democratic regimes never aim to achieve ethnic or cultural homogeneity but only to preserve the rights of individuals, which include the right to belong to a cultural minority. That is why there has to be a constant struggle against degrading stereotypes of minority groups, who must be allowed to use their languages and to maintain their faiths and traditions. By pursuing this struggle we recognize that populations have been on the move since the dawn of history and we abandon all claim to reserve a particular geographical space for any specific population.

The principle of ethnic purity, therefore, unlike the rights of the individual or respect for minorities, has nothing to do with a democratic state — yet that was what guided the ruling teams in all the states that came out of the breakup of Yugoslavia. The most catastrophic consequences of this choice occurred in Bosnia. And it is not hard to see why. This former republic of the federation had always been extremely mixed. According to a census taken in the early 1990s, 43 percent of the population were Muslim Bosnians, 31 percent were Serbian Orthodox, and 17 percent counted themselves as Croatian Catholics. What the census does not say is that until they were forced to choose between these designations many Bosnians, especially city dwellers, identified with none of these labels. A small but significant number even entered "Toshiba" or "Panasonic" under "religion" in their census returns! They thought of themselves simply as inhabitants of Bosnia, or as Yugoslavian; we should remember that they all spoke the same language, and that all of them were more or less atheist.

As the leaders of all three communities within Bosnia adopted the principle of "one people, one country," the drift toward the separation of Bosnia into three self-governing statelets became irresistible, and it led to a foreseeable outcome: "foreigners" had to be expelled to keep the area "pure." All the parties involved obeyed the same principle: expulsion of minorities and the assertion of self-governing status have a common denominator, which is the demand for culturally homogenous territorial entities. So the Bosnian conflict came not from an ideological clash, but from disagreements on how to divide the area. The Bosnian war turned out to be particularly long-drawn-out and bloody; Serbian politicians and military played the most active role in it. They carry the heaviest responsibility for the massacres, gang rapes and acts of pillage that occurred; nevertheless, some of the Bosnian Serbs were themselves displaced in the name of ethnic cleansing.

At this point a new player entered the field — "the West," that is to say, a number of European Union countries plus the United States. The West's involvement took two forms. First, it accepted the principle of ethnic homogeneity that the various conflicting parties had tried to implement, and it thus abandoned the idea of a state based on contract. It has to be said that the West had quite specific reasons for doing so. The "contractual state" of the federal republic had fallen into the hands of the heirs of the Communist regime — Milosević and his henchmen — whereas the emerging, ethnically pure, "natural" states of Slovenia, Croatia, and Bosnia seemed likely to break with their Communist past and join the Western alliance. We've seen it happen before! It's only too easy to believe that the nationalist feelings of subject populations should be encouraged in order to help them throw off the yoke of foreign oppression. But there's no guarantee that the next generation of "native" leaders will be any less oppressive — not to mention the fact that to achieve this dubious aim we will have upheld the nondemocratic principles of national homogeneity and of the state by nature.

Support for nondemocratic principles by the democratic West can therefore be explained, but it was regrettable nonetheless. Then came the second and no less paradoxical form of Western involvement: physical presence on the ground, but without engagement. What happened was that the UN, under pressure from the West, sent military observers to Yugoslavia and particularly to Bosnia, but under rules of engagement that forbade them to use their weapons, even under duress. The outcome is sadly famous. Bosnian Muslims, believing they were under the protection of the UN, took refuge in the vicinity of its camps, at Srbrenica for instance, but the peace-keepers were unable to prevent Serbian troops and paramilitaries from seizing and murdering the refugees. The paroxysm of violence at Srbrenica in 1995 seemed to summarize the whole set of conflicts in Yugoslavia, which by then had dragged on for several years. The same script had been played out the year before in Rwanda, where hundreds of thousands of people belonging to the Tutsi minority had been slaughtered under the eyes of powerless UN representatives. These episodes surely did nothing to improve the standing of the United Nations.

Parallel to the doctrine of peace-keeping without engagement, and as if to counter the impression of inactivity that it produced, there arose a movement of moral outrage. It took the form of intensive appeals to memory, and of thoroughgoing trivialization of the past. Quite implausibly, people began to liken Yugoslavia's ethnic conflicts to the Second World War, with Milosević in the role of Hitler. On television we saw the emaciated faces of Bosnian Muslims behind barbed wire. "It looked like the Holocaust," said a senior Bush administration official (quoted by Bass, 210), who probably knew no other outrage in history. During the 1992 presidential campaign, Clinton declared: "If the horrors of the Holocaust taught us anything, it is the high cost of remaining silent and paralyzed in the face of genocide" (quoted, 214). In 1995 the State Department's special envoy to Yugoslavia, Richard Holbrooke, assured us that he was prepared to stifle his moral qualms and to negotiate with the Yugoslav authorities even though he considered them to be criminals; he consoled himself by likening his role to that of Raoul Wallenberg, who hadn't shirked from talking to Nazi murders in order to save persecuted Jews from death (234). And did not humanitarian organizations attempt at that time to negotiate with Himmler? Holbrooke's historical parallel suppresses the fact that he represented the greatest military power on earth, whereas Wallenberg, who was an attaché at the Swedish Embassy in Budapest during the Nazi occupation of Hungary, was risking his own life (which he lost, by a cruel irony of history, in the prisons of the other totalitarian state, the Soviet Union).

These men must be put on trial, another White House official insisted; not to do so would be like letting Göring and Göbbels go free after the defeat of the Third Reich (Bass, 249). Madeleine Albright, who became secretary of state in 1996, saw the Balkan wars through the mirror of her own childhood memories (as a little girl she had fled Czechoslovakia with her family at the start of the Second World War). The Bosnian conflict reminded her of Nazism, and the attitude of the governments of the West looked too much like the position of the British and the French at Munich, in 1938, when Czechoslovakia was abandoned. She had already stated in a speech she made in 1994 at the U.S. Holocaust Memorial Museum in Washington (while she was U.S. Ambassador to the United Nations), entitled "Bosnia in the Light of the Holocaust": "Bosnian Serb leaders have sought a 'final solution' of extermination or expulsion to the problem of non-Serb populations under their control" (quoted in Bass, 262). It's as if everybody nowadays wants to be able to say they have prevented another Holocaust.

The breakdown of Yugoslavia ended where it had begun in the late 1980s, in Kosovo. We should remember that until 1912 the whole of this area belonged to Turkey. Albania emerged as an independent nation after and as a result of the Balkan Wars and the First World War, but many speakers of Albanian were left out of the new state, notably in Macedonia and in Serbia (in Kosovo); there are, moreover, alien minorities inside Albania. The original population mix of Kosovo was altered over the course of years. Italy invaded not only Albania in 1940 but also Kosovo, and Mussolini threw 200,000 Serbians out of the area. The Serbs came back after the end of the war, but the population imbalance with the Albanians continued to increase, since the Albanian Kosovars had larger families than the Serbs. Kosovo also remained the poorest part of the federal republic and by far the most backward. These then were the conditions in which the reversal of 1989 took place.

The history of Kosovo over the past twenty years resembles a pendulum moving in an ever widening arc. Each push by one of the parties produces a swing in the other direction, in a seemingly unstoppable sequence of action and reaction. Between 1974 and 1989, the Serbian Kosovars were persecuted by the Albanians; from 1989 on, the Albanians were hounded even more cruelly by the Serbs. The Serbians feared that Kosovo might demand independence, or even, in the name of its ethnic specificity, ask to become part of Albania proper. So they tried to smother Albanian identity and incited Albanian-speakers to emigrate: the Kosovars were given the choice between assimilation and exile. The use of Albanian was banned, teaching in Albanian was made impossible, Albanian speakers in senior positions were sacked, and all sorts of other insults were heaped on them. Nonviolent opposition sprang up, with its own clandestine institutions and schools, and elected its own president, the moderate Ibrahim Rugova. At the same time a more radical group, the UCK (or KLA, Kosovo Liberation Army), also arose and from 1996 began armed attacks on Serbian positions.

Despite appearances there was nothing preordained about this almost mechanical escalation toward violence. The looming crisis

245

could have been averted by maintaining provincial autonomy for Kosovo, or even by giving it stronger self-government within the federal state. Well-treated and protected minorities do not try to secede. But Milosević had a completely different strategy. The mood of the Albanian Kosovars, a small minority within the Yugoslav whole, mattered little to him; but he could beat his rivals for power in Belgrade if he could get the support of the Serbian majority by tempting it with the imaginary *reconquista* of a province whose very name strikes a chord with the national past.

It was the suppression of provincial autonomy that gave birth to a radical group like the KLA. To begin with the KLA was a Maoist organization, sharing the Communist ideology of Albania proper, but after the fall of Ramiz Alia and the Communist regime in Tirana, it became a purely nationalist movement. The fall of the Communist regime in Albania was a particularly stark demonstration of the prior collapse of the state, and it gave instant birth to ungovernable areas ruled over by Mafia-type bandits who seized army weapons dumps. The KLA set up its bases in the border areas of Albania and began armed struggle. It struck at representatives of Serbian authority — soldiers and policemen — and killed a number; it also executed moderate Albanian speakers for alleged collaboration with the enemy. Belgrade welcomed the opportunity thus given it to heighten repressive measures in Kosovo; it slaughtered KLA fighters and persecuted villagers suspected of favoring them.

It was not an even fight. The federal army was far bigger, far better armed and trained than the KLA. So the KLA decided to play a different hand, one that would get the international community (or, rather, the West) on its side, so as to turn the tables to its advantage. That hand consisted in presenting themselves as victims. Romain Gary had seen it all before: "The beginning and the end of all great movements in history is always: a victim" (*Tulipe*, 79). The Yugoslav leadership was equally aware of the sympathy that can be won by a victim, but it had used its own victim story in a more limited way. Serbians had been victims in the past — victims of the Turks at the battle of Kosovo Polje in 1389, and for the following four hundred years; victims of Austro-Hungary during the First World War, then of Nazi Germany during the Second; victims of Soviet threats from 1947 until Stalin's death in 1953. Having been the subjects of a victim story for so long, the Serbians decided that the time had come to change tack, and to begin their own heroic and triumphal narrative. Milosević will lead his people to victory! Past suffering was supposed to fire Milosević's Serbian audience with enthusiasm and to turn them, at last, into victors.

To counter a psychological strategy calling for revenge on the past, the KLA had something simpler — the present suffering of a victim. It just had to change the frame of reference and appeal not to Belgrade, which was quite indifferent to the Albanian Kosovars' suffering, but to an outside party — the West — which would end up feeling concerned and thus get involved in the conflict. It worked like magic, with the (presumably unwitting) cooperation of the Yugoslav authorities, who failed to see the trap ahead and believed they were engaged in a straightforward battle for supremacy, which they were bound to win. So in 1998 Belgrade undertook a campaign of violent repression of all hostile activity in Kosovo; KLA fighters and civilians suspected of complicity with them were executed, and all suspects were expelled from the country. The KLA had no problem with violence, but its means were far more limited; but we are still too close to the events to know whether this or that massacre was a response to a clever provocation by the KLA, or an arbitrary act by the federal army; nor do we really know if the corpses we saw were those of armed Albanian fighters, or of civilians who just happened to be in the wrong place at the wrong time.

All the same, in 1998 Western political leaders chose their camp, and they decided to back the Albanian independence movement, and more specifically the KLA (even though the U.S. government had described it only two years previously as a "terrorist organization"), rather than the nonviolent movement of Ibrahim Rugova, who was cut out of the debate. The West's new commitment led to the Rambouillet conference in early 1999.

Let us just take a look at the two sides present at Rambouillet. Each can claim victim status: the Serbs as past victims, the KLA as present victims (which counts for more). Each side is fully certain of being in the right. The principles they invoke are different, but both belong to the commonplaces of the modern world.

The Serbian position was quite close to the nationalist doctrines expressed in the early twentieth century by Charles Péguy, a French theoretician with a pithy turn of phrase. For example,

"The Republic is one and indivisible" (Péguy, 145), and its corollary, that "in time of war there is only one rule, and it is the rule of the Jacobins" (meaning central control of all the state's functions) (116). They also heeded Péguy's warning, "woe betide the party that does not eliminate its internal enemies" (131). The Serbians did not want to give up a part of the territory of their state on the grounds that its inhabitants spoke a different language and had a different religion — that would be to recognize implicitly that the state is based on "blood," that it is a natural and not a contractual entity. But they forgot the corollary of this principle, which is to protect the rights of the individual, which include the right to use whatever language and to follow whatever creed or tradition the individual so chooses. The Albanian-speaking Kosovars, for their part, could identify with the right to self-determination, an extension of the requirement of autonomy to the collectivity. But in asserting that the Albanians needed to be freed from Serbian oppression, they acted as if it were not possible for a people to be oppressed by its own members, which is altogether quite common. The Albanians' own situation in the 1970s was an illustration of that paradox. Albanians inside Enver Hoxha's Communist Albania were poorer and more oppressed than the Albanian minority living in what was then Tito's Yugoslavia. Supporters of independence for Kosovo, in their turn, left to one side the question of the status of minority populations within their own envisaged state.

The KLA, a "terrorist group" not so long before, has to be admired for its skill in obtaining the support of the world's most powerful military organization, NATO. It is also quite surprising that the West made such a firm choice in favor of one of the parties against the other, seeing that both held positions that were simultaneously defensible and open to criticism. But you could only really talk of a balance between them on the ideological level; on the ground, the more powerful Serbian army and its paramilitary wings exercised far more violence, destruction and persecution than their opponents. Nor had anyone forgotten the crimes of the Serbs in Bosnia. All the same, it is rather strange that the West, which with one hand rejected policies of ethnic cleansing — that is to say, all attempts to make state boundaries coincide with ethnic ones — ended up falling in with the very same policy of ethnic cleansing by supporting those who were fighting exclusively for the "right to self-determination" and by favoring the creation of a multitude of "ethnically pure" mini-states. Of course, the West used very different methods. It did not deport people or terrorize them; it just sent its diplomats to set up embassies in the new capitals and shipped in humanitarian aid.

What was also surprising, seen from Paris or London or New York, was the extreme passion with which the different parties defended their respective choices. That community leaders should be vociferous on their own account is perfectly comprehensible, since everyone prefers to be in charge rather than to have to obey stupid or offensive orders. But it is far less obvious why ordinary people were so passionately committed. Why were they so fanatically involved in the status of a territory and the definition of the state, when their personal lives would hardly be affected by such issues? During the negotiations on the partition of Bosnia, in 1995, the French news media carried the following story: "On Sunday, 26 November, in a cemetery at Illidza, mothers whose sons had died in the fighting swore to commit collective suicide if their district is handed back to Bosnian government troops" (*Le Monde*, 28 November 1995). Had these mothers been driven mad by the loss of their sons? How else can you explain they would rather die than see a change in the administration of their district? It is as if the cruelty of the still recent war had condemned the losers to turn the violence on themselves, in despair.

We are obliged to accept that after the end of totalitarianism passions have changed their content but not changed in intensity. People have always needed recognition of their social being, in the absence of which they begin to doubt their very existence. Such recognition has two levels: personal recognition, granted, for example, to the child by its parents and family; and public recognition, granted by the community to which the individual belongs. In traditional societies public recognition proceeds along well-established lines; each person has his or her place and fits into a well-signed system. We have seen the role that collective memory plays in such societies. Totalitarian states broke the traditional linkages, but at least in their utopian phase they offered new ones in their place; everybody was part of a single ideological community. The countries of Western Europe that never had a totalitarian regime or eradicated it long ago have a similar problem, now that traditional links have worn away and old faiths no

249

longer play much role. The remedy (not always entirely successful) has taken the form of overvaluing the private domain and
building new communities on the ruins of the old; at the same
time, the stability of the state institutions of Western Europe have
fostered individual integration.

No such remedy is really available to the citizens of former
Yugoslavia, and the same could be said, in different degrees, of
many other countries in Central and Eastern Europe. Totalitarianism destroyed all the old structures; we should not be deluded
by current appeals to religious traditions, which are being manip-
ulated for directly political purposes. The state as such was fa-
tally weakened by the totalitarian experiment, which robbed it of
all autonomy; and the fall of the Communist regimes laid bare
just how puny the state had become. Power passed into the hands
of various kinds of mafia, unscrupulous profiteers, special interest
groups, and lobbies. The old state-run economies collapsed as
soon as they came into contact with market economies, causing
general impoverishment. In such circumstances it was not possible to take refuge in the idea of personal success and fulfillment.
And that was when people found their last asylum in the sense of
belonging to a half-imaginary identity—a language community, a
religion that they had long ceased to practice, a history tidied up
to suit (for one side, "the battle of Kosovo Polje in 1389"; for the
other side, the call to establish an Albanian nation at Pristina in
1878), and a territory symbolically identified with "us" ("I'll kill
myself if this district becomes Bosnian, or Serbian, or Albanian").
Taking shelter in an imaginary identity was the only alternative to
despair.

In February 1999 the international conference at Rambouillet
attempted to reach a solution to the Kosovo conflict. The U.S.
delegation had a hard time persuading its European allies that it
would be a good idea to bomb Yugoslavia. James Rubin, Madeleine Albright's second-in-command, later admitted that the attitude adopted by the French and Italians could have been fatal to
the administration's efforts to unite NATO against Belgrade (*Le
Monde diplomatique*, March 2000, 3). But the supporters of the
"all-NATO" option prevailed. In concrete terms, the West, which
wished above all to "avoid another Munich," asked the Albanian
Kosovars to put off declaring independence for three years; and it
requested the Yugoslav government to give up sovereignty over a

part of the country by putting it under international control, with permission for NATO forces to move freely about the entire country. After many changes of mind, the Kosovar delegation, now dominated by the armed faction of the KLA at the expense of the legitimately elected moderate group, agreed to wait for three years. But the Yugoslav government rejected the terms and the negotiations broke down. The only way forward appeared to be war.

MILITARY INTERVENTION

What happened in Yugoslavia between 24 March and 10 June 1999 does not entirely deserve to be called a war. War requires two belligerent parties to strike at each other. In the case of Yugoslavia, what happened was more like a punitive expedition, and Western governments preferred it to be seen in that way, so they would not have to obtain parliamentary approval for a dec-laration of war. Yugoslavia was bombed for two and a half months, during which time the Yugoslav army attacked no for-eign target at all. Nor is it entirely clear who precisely was in charge of the operation against Yugoslavia. The announcement of hostilities was made by Javier Solana, the NATO secretary-gen-eral; but NATO is a military organization, not a state. Thirteen of the thirty-nine countries in the Atlantic Alliance took part in the operation. Toward the end of the hostilities, another player en-tered the scene, G8, the club of the world's seven most indus-trialized nations plus Russia. The peace settlement was signed on terms laid out by G8. The UN, the EU as such, and the OCSE took no part in the conflict.

The ostensible purpose of the intervention was to prevent human rights abuses in the province of Kosovo, specifically mur-der, torture, and rape, as well as ethnic cleansing. Is it true that such crimes against humanity were perpetrated in the months prior to the bombings? A lot depends on the answer to this ques-tion; but the sources of information all belong to one or another of the belligerents, and the figures they published may well have been intended to justify their own policies. In the days following the start of the bombing, the U.S. Department of State announced that 500,000 Albanian Kosovars were "missing," which, if true, would have been a genocide. That word was often used by Western politicians. A few weeks later, the estimate was lowered to 100,000 "disappeared." By the end of the intervention, the figure claimed had fallen to 11,000. One year later, it was lowered again (thank goodness). The ICC, which could hardly be suspected of pro-Serbian sympathies, managed to identify, for the entire duration of the conflict, 2,108 Albanian civilian victims, to which must be added 4,266 persons still missing (Lévy, *Le Débat*).

So what is the truth about violence prior to the start of the military operation? The OCSE report of December 1999 is probably the fullest study of the question, and it says that most of the conflict's victims fell in spring 1999. Prior to this, it says, "Yugoslav and Serbian military and security forces directed their attention primarily to communities in Kosovo located in areas crossed by KLA transit routes or where KLA bases were situated" (*Le Monde diplomatique*, March 2000, 13). In 1997–98, there had been a civil war in Kosovo pitting Yugoslav military, police and paramilitary forces against the KLA, and Albanian casualties were much higher than Yugoslav losses. But these were individual murders, not mass slayings, with the exception of the Racak massacre in January 1999 (45 dead, in circumstances still not entirely explained; see *Le Figaro*, 20 January 1999; *Le Monde* and *Libération*, 21 January 1999). So there was no genocide, and nothing remotely like one. And just as we cannot take pride in having saved a million American lives in Japan, so we cannot congratulate ourselves on having saved 500,000 from genocide in Kosovo. Virtual massacres cannot be entered into the accounting.

Nonetheless the situation of the Albanian Kosovars before the intervention was not a happy one, subject to an escalating series of persecutions, bullying, humiliations, and sporadic outbreaks of torture and murder. These were indeed serious violations of human rights. But were they crimes against humanity?

These violations were the reason for the military intervention, but the aim of the latter was to halt ethnic cleansing, the displacement of populations, and the separation of communities. What needed doing, it was said, was to reestablish the autonomy of Kosovo within the Yugoslav federation so that Serbs and Albanians could live in peace with each other and with full guarantees for the rights of the minorities (Serbians in Kosovo, Albanians in

Yugoslavia) — the opposite result, in brief, from what Milosević had achieved.

On 24 March Javier Solana declared that the military intervention would last only "a few days." Belgrade was clearly expected to come to its senses as soon as the bombing started and accept the terms of the previous ultimatum. But things took a different turn. From the start of the military action, Yugoslav military and paramilitary forces began to empty Kosovo of its Albanian population by laying waste their houses. Over the following weeks, up to nine hundred thousand people, many robbed of their identity papers, were pushed over the frontier into Albania and Macedonia. Was that foreseeable? Maybe not by military officers. But for politicians it really should have been obvious. Given the adoption of the principle of the natural state (the matching of state and ethnicity), leaders wishing to maintain the integrity of the former state knew what they have to do — expel the population in whose name the enemy wished to seize their territory! The KLA and Milosević were following an identical ideal of ethnic purity; and NATO, by adopting the attitude of one of the belligerents, followed suit.

By declaring war on Belgrade in the name of the Albanian-speaking minority, NATO turned the Kosovars from a pest into a fifth column in Serbian eyes. Serbs were now getting killed by an enemy acting in the name of their fellow citizens, the Albanians. The Kosovars, moreover, cheered the bombs that were supposed to bring them freedom, and the most active even helped to direct Western aircraft toward their targets. In such circumstances the "internal enemy" had to be "beaten down," as Charles Péguy had recommended, thinking of war conditions. That was even more imperative given that the Albanians were the only enemy that the Yugoslavs could get at — NATO aircraft flew high, out of range of antiaircraft fire, and the cruise missiles came in from god knows where. On the other hand the people for whom the attack was being conducted lived round the corner, and you don't have to have a crystal ball to divine that they would become the focus of Serbian resentment. But apparently it had not occurred to the generals conducting the campaign that their moves would turn the 1.8-million-strong Albanian minority into 1.8 million hostages.

During the first days of the bombing campaign there was a frightening escalation of violence. There had been OSCE ob-

253

servers in the area prior to hostilities, and their presence alone
had put a lid on criminal violence. But they were withdrawn
ahead of the air strikes, and so lawbreaking became that much
easier. In any case, the state of war suspends or upturns the rule
of law, because what had previously been prohibited — killing —
now becomes a meritorious act.

The bombings had catastrophic effects on the ground in Kosovo, and in addition they had effects in surrounding territories
that one has to believe were not sought or wanted by NATO or
by the heads of state of its member nations. In Yugoslavia itself,
reactions were, once again, easily foreseeable. Shared danger stifles dissent. The democratic opposition was thus forced to moderate its criticisms of Milosević to avoid being seen as allied with
the enemy. Ordinary Serbian people, who were the main victims
of the bombing, could not abandon their government in a moment of danger. Thus the effect of the war was not to weaken
Milosević's hold on power but to strengthen it. In neighboring
countries the results were just as bad from the West's point of
view. Most of the governments involved were either non-Communist or anti-Communist and had hopes of eventually joining
NATO, to provide the only real protection against the possibility
that Russia would once again try to expand its empire to the
south, as it had during the Communist era. Therefore they supported the bombing of Yugoslavia. But the people were mostly
against it. They did not believe that the region's endemic ethnic
conflicts could be solved by bombing; nor did they like to see
their own fates decided in the distant capitals of the West, for
that brought back too many bad old memories. The result of this
gap between governmental position and popular sentiment was a
resurgence of the formerly Communist parties of the nations in
the Balkan region, for they were opposed to the intervention.

Russia was an impotent observer of Western involvement in a
part of Europe to which it feels closely attached for cultural as
well as geographical reasons. The military intervention thus
fueled anti-Western sentiment as well as nationalist and militaristic language in Russia. But in the West, the same events produced
an unforeseen secondary effect: an increase in the sense of moral
triumph in governments and public opinion alike. Not only were
they resisting evil; they were in the process of becoming the incarnation of good. But if you look a little harder at what was actu-

ally happening, the West was supporting ethnic cleansing and the formation of ethnically homogenous states. Such had indeed been the paradoxical result of all the Yugoslav wars of the 1990s: Croatia has ended up as a country for Croats only, Slovenia as a purely Slovenian land, Bosnia as a state divided into three republics — Republika Srpska, inhabited by "Orthodox" Serbs; Herzegovina, with its "Catholic Croats; and "Muslim" Bosnia — and the Kosovars (i.e., Albanians) are in Kosovo. Although it wished to fight evil, the West got itself drawn into ethnic conflicts. Can we really be proud of what happened?

One year later, what is the current result? Albanian refugees have returned to their houses, many of them wrecked — but since it was the war that made most of them leave, we can hardly praise the war for having helped them back. The balance of power in Kosovo is now the reverse of what it was. In the days that elapsed between the withdrawal of the Yugoslav army and the arrival of NATO forces, many scores were settled. The region, which is now a kind of UN protectorate policed by NATO forces, is in practice run by the KLA. So it is the Serbians, and whoever is seen as friendly to them, who are now persecuted. An anecdote: some youngsters ask the time of day from a Bulgarian UN official, who answers in Serbo-Croat; so they beat him up and then kill him with a gunshot to the head. The Romi (gypsies) were accused of collaboration, then expelled or mistreated, and their districts were demolished. Individual Serbians and small groups of them have been murdered too. An OSCE report written in October 2000 made the sorry observation that the UN had failed to enforce human rights in Kosovo and that ethnic discrimination continued to be practiced even toward prisoners. "Albania (or Kosovo) for the Albanians" is no more democratic a slogan than "Serbia for the Serbians."

An Albanian Kosavar journalist, Veton Surroi, has denounced the "new Fascism" in his reporting. "After being the victims of the worst persecutions in Europe at the end of the twentieth century, we are turning into persecutors ourselves" (*Le Monde*, 31 August, 1999). The answer from Kosovapress, the official press agency controlled by the KLA, was to slur Surroi as a man "who stinks of the Slav," and to warn him of the "perfectly comprehensible revenge" that might be visited on him by people who feel offended by his articles. One year after the end of hostilities, between a half and two-thirds of the non-Albanian population of Kosovo has left the province, which looks very much like ethnic cleansing. Those remaining have regrouped into wholly Serbian enclaves, which they do not dare leave. The violence is certainly less widespread and less harsh than what Albanian Kosovars suffered before the NATO intervention; that is because the Albanians and the Serbs hardly see each other any more, and, in addition, the presence of foreign troops inhibits any large-scale persecution.

We can hardly be surprised by the wave of acts of revenge. The Albanians suffered many humiliations before the offensive, and were persecuted during the war, and it will not be easy to have these offenses forgotten. We can safely predict that peaceful coexistence between these two distinct peoples won't be possible in the same land for decades, if not centuries. Hatred has taken deep root in Kosovo. Each side considers the other responsible for its misfortune. How can you forgive the people for whom you were bombed? How can you forgive those who forced you into months of penurious exile in a refugee camp? If the West had aimed to make coexistence between Serbs and Albanians impossible, it could not have gone about it in a better way. "The air strikes created a greater tragedy; they heightened the hatred and resentment between Serbs and Albanian Kosovars. So how can we call that humanitarian action?" asked a Japanese columnist, Kazumoto Momose (*Asahi Shimbun*, 10 May 1999). Not to mention the anarchy that followed the destruction of preexisting structures, which favored all kinds of criminal deeds under cover of nationalist score-settling.

Ethnic cleansing has won. The logical conclusion of this policy — and the sole means of ensuring a more durable peace — would be to accept the splitting-up of the province into homogenous Albanian and Serbian cantons, and possibly also the unification of the Albanian cantons with Albania proper. But would that really solve all the problems arising from ethnic tensions? Not really. The peoples of the Balkans, in all their linguistic, cultural, and religious diversity, are scattered like the pieces of an unsolved jigsaw puzzle, and it will take more than one war to make them fit into the principle of "one state for one people." The KLA has lost its raison d'être, but a new set of freedom fighters has arisen to "liberate" Precevo, Medvedja, and Bujanovac, three largely Albanian villages inside Serbia.

The next step might well be Macedonia, with an Albanian minority comprising up to 23 percent of the population. Or Bulgaria, with its large Turkish minority. Or Romania, Serbia, and Slovakia, with their Magyar minorities. Or else the Romi, present but unintegrated throughout the Balkans. Or else the Russian minorities living in the Baltic republics — and so on. Merely mentioning the percentages of "nonethnic" inhabitants signals a retreat of democracy.

In Serbia the main victims of NATO's punitive expedition were ordinary people. About five hundred died, but thousands more suffered because power stations, water storage facilities, bridges, and railways were destroyed. The army took much less punishment — it knew how to protect itself. One year after the end of the campaign, *Newsweek* revealed that Yugoslav military losses totaled only fourteen tanks and twenty artillery pieces. The political regime suffered not a bit; it was even strengthened by the events. That became evident during the electoral campaign in summer 2000. Evocation of the military intervention remained a powerful argument in Milosević's hands, to such an extent that he thought (wrongly) that it would ensure a walkover. Any attack on him by the democratic opposition could be made to seem like support for the bombing and thus an act of treason. Opposition leaders for their part took great care during and after the air strikes to dissociate themselves from NATO's position and to shun the support of the more trigger-happy of the Western governments.

When confronted with an outcome so very different from what was allegedly being sought, we can explore two different interpretations. First, that the whole affair was a dismal failure or, second, that the real aims were not the stated ones. If it was just a failure, then we would have a vivid illustration of the difference between what Max Weber called "the ethics of conviction" and "the ethics of responsibility." An individual acting on his personal convictions alone is concerned primarily with the moral profit to be drawn from his or her action. A politician, who may also be defending his own convictions but does not forget his responsibilities, is concerned primarily with the benefits that may be derived from his action by others, that is to say, by the group on whose behalf the politician is acting. In this latter case, results count for more than intentions. Western leaders were revolted by repeated human rights violations, their moral convictions prompted them to act, and they decided to bomb the enemy. But they had simply not foreseen the exodus of 900,000 people, the increase in hatred between the two populations, the bad example set for future ethnic tensions, and the brake on the democratization of Yugoslavia. They wanted to counter ethnic cleansing but failed to realize that their intervention would only foster it.

This interpretation could be supported by quoting Javier Solana's many declarations, including a statement made as late as 18 April 1999, that air strikes would help to "guarantee a multiethnic Kosovo." So Western leaders were pursuing worthy ends with unworthy means, and in ignorance of their real effects. Well, if that were really true, any honorable person aware of being responsible for these acts of war should long ago have made a public admission of his or her mistakes and resigned. That, of course, presupposes a democratic environment. Milosević, as the head of an authoritarian regime, has never admitted to any mistakes and has not given up power of his own free will, despite the countless miseries he has inflicted on his own people and on the rest of former Yugoslavia.

But maybe the aims of NATO or of the coalition of countries that used NATO were altogether different. If so, what were they? Yugoslavia has no oil or uranium or diamonds. Therefore the military intervention had to be humanitarian, many commentators argued, including Vaclav Havel, president of the Czech Republic, whose long record as a stalwart antitotalitarian lends his words a particular weight: "In the NATO intervention in Kosovo, I think there is an element that cannot be denied: the raids and the bombs are not the result of any material interest. Their character is exclusively humanitarian" (*Le Monde*, 29 April 1999). It is embarrassing to hear someone as distinguished as Havel inventing the idea of "humanitarian bombs," which echoes the slogans of Orwell's *1984*: "War is Peace," "Freedom is Slavery." It is also very strange to think that whatever is not a matter of self-interest must be humanitarian. Whatever happened to purely political objectives?

Contemporary analysts have come up with several other explanations for the military intervention, which are neither humanitarian nor self-interested. By some accounts, the real aim, as at Hiroshima, was to scare off the Russians; by other accounts, to give the Europeans a show of force. Some commentators noted the U.S. need to set up bases in the Balkans that would be free of EU involvement; and yet others stress the U.S. need to show goodwill toward Muslims to increase their credibility with Israel's Arab neighbors; and so forth.

There is no lack of explanations of this kind, but I've no way of proving or disproving them. Still I am sure that a different kind of explanation also needs to be considered. Power needs no justification outside of itself—it is an aim in itself, not a means. Two hundred years ago, Immanuel Kant wrote that war needs no specific motive, since the prestige that it brings to the victor is quite sufficient. Demonstrating its own power was one of the main purposes of the United States when it dropped atomic bombs on Japan. Once the conduct of the war was handed over entirely to the military, there was nothing surprising about the following events. The military must first prove the tools of its power, its weapons, in combat; then it cannot stop until it reaches victory (or defeat, but that was ruled out on this occasion). Zbigniew Brzezinski, a former White House aide who still had some influence, made no bones about the aim of the war in Yugoslavia being to demonstrate the political and military superiority of the Atlantic Alliance. "A failure to prevail would precipitate a fundamental crisis of unity within NATO and a more anarchic state of global affairs" (*Washington Post*, 31 March 1999).

A modern army is very expensive. Since it had been asked to intervene, it had to prove it was effective. It quickly became apparent that despite the obvious undesirable side effects and despite the military ineffectiveness of the air strikes, it was imperative to carry on, simply because the war was under way. General Wesley Clark, commander in chief of Allied Forces, said after the end of the hostilities: "Once the threshold is crossed and you are going to use force, that force has to be as decisive as possible in attaining your military objectives" (AFPN Wire Service, 28 October 1999). As at the time of the war against Japan, the initiation of the campaign became a sufficient reason for pursuing it to its end, without any review of its ultimate justification being possible meanwhile. Power has to show that it is powerful.

The idea of "humanitarian bombs" and of "ethical war" is profoundly shocking. Some wars are just, for example, those undertaken in self-defense against aggression, or to avert the deaths of millions of people. But no war, not even a just war, is merciful.

259

Only a particularly docile public, or one that is keen to preserve its good conscience, can dismiss what the other side calls "crimes against humanity" (civilian deaths) as "collateral damage." Vaclav Havel wasn't in Serbia to tell the civilians to rejoice that they were being hit by humanitarian bombs and not aggressive ones. All wars are cruel and bring death and suffering to innocent people. We do not have the right to forget this, and we have even less right to be proud of it.

What's more, the collateral damage in Yugoslavia was not at all random. Public opinion in the West, and particularly in the United States, has low tolerance for military casualties on its own side; and the declared aim was to fight the war without incurring any losses. The effect of such reluctance to put our own soldiers at risk was a strategy of remote warfare, using missiles launched from far away and very high-flying aircraft. Obviously, the further away you are from the target, the less accurate the strike. Avoiding the risk of dying entails the risk of killing. So, by minimizing the risk to its own forces, NATO magnified the risk of killing "enemy" civilians and established a prior ranking in the value of human lives.

Modern war makers have discovered that it can be of more use to hit the civilian population than to hit the army: that is indeed the official explanation of why the two cities of Hiroshima and Nagasaki, and not the Japanese army, was bombed. Is it a war crime to choose to bomb reservoirs, fuel depots, electricity facilities, factories, and even hospitals, as has been done in Iraq and Yugoslavia? The aim of the West's military planners was not just to destroy military targets but also to cause "discomfort" (a euphemism) to the civilian population, so as to inspire it to turn against its own government. Air Force Lieutenant General Michael Short imagined the average Yugoslav getting more and more fed up with the bombing and saying to his leader "Hey, Slobo, what's this all about? How much more of this do we have to withstand?" (*Washington Post*, 24 May 1999, 1), whereby he showed that generals still have a lot to learn not only about human psychology but also about international law. That kind of "pressure" on civilians is considered a criminal act.

The Kosovo conflict also showed the extent to which the use of memory can become pernicious through excessive trivialization of the past. Each of the parties involved scoured the past for justifications for their present conduct, identifying themselves and each other with the archetypical roles of hero, victim, or evildoer. Parallels were not hard to find. The Serbs harked back to the heroic defeat of their King Lazar in 1389 — as an example they would never repeat. The West brandished the soiled flag of Munich, as it had during the Bosnian conflict — never again would it capitulate to a bloodthirsty dictator. The Albanians had more recent persecutions to recall. History is rich enough to provide convincing models for everyone. For some, U.S. intervention was necessarily a good thing, since the 1944 landings had been a good thing; for others, it was necessarily bad, just like the extermination of Native Americans and the Vietnam War. Each historical episode, moreover, has several sides that fit it for every purpose: some think you just have to fight the good fight, as against Franco in 1936; others remember that the facade of generosity may mask less speakable purposes, and that the same Spanish Civil War gave Stalin's secret services the opportunity to liquidate their antifascist rivals.

But the historical reference that was touted around the most, by a wide margin, was Hitler. There have rarely been so many valiant soldiers fighting Hitler as in 1999. During the Kosovo campaign, Yugoslav propaganda never failed to remind us that the last military aggression against Serbia had been carried out by Hitler; therefore Clinton = Hitler. Even more amazing was Clinton's own use of such a flimsy comparison to justify military intervention. "What if someone had listened to Winston Churchill and stood up to Adolf Hitler earlier? How many people's lives would have been saved?" (AFP wire report, 24 March 1999). It certainly would have been better if action against Hitler had begun earlier. But how can the theoretical undead of the Second World War legitimate the bombing of Yugoslavia? Was it possible, seriously, to think that Milosević was a danger to Europe and to the world, as Hitler was in 1936? Is a reminder of the past enough to justify anything and everything?

The NATO strikes on Yugoslavia are far from constituting an example of a virtuous action carried out by the international community to ensure the triumph of good over evil. A further question remains. If we assume that the human rights violations in Kosovo had broken the threshold of tolerance, were air strikes the only means available for putting an end to them? That was

261

Javier Solana's position at the start of the operation, on 23 March 1999: "All efforts to achieve a negotiated political solution to the Kosovo crisis have failed, and no alternative is open but to take military action" (AP Wire Service, 23 March 1999). But was that true?

Doubts arise if we recall what caused the Rambouillet conference to break down. The Yugoslav delegation accepted substantial autonomy for Kosovo, but balked at giving NATO forces free passage throughout Yugoslav territory and limited policing rights. However, after three months of bombing, the result achieved was this: substantial autonomy for Kosovo, but NATO forces still didn't have the right to move about on Yugoslav soil. In other words, the war produced no supplementary benefit — the final compromise is exactly what the Yugoslav delegation would have accepted at Rambouillet, before the start of operations. As with Japan in 1945, the end result after military action is pretty much what would have been achieved without military action.

It looks as though the NATO delegation did not want Rambouillet to produce an agreement, so it made an unacceptable demand, which in the end was abandoned — but not before thousands of tons of high explosive had been poured onto Yugoslavia. Might the war have been deemed necessary in order to punish Milosević and his countrymen, and to show the military strength of the Alliance? This sounds quite like the strategy that led up to Hiroshima (another dubious historical parallel?): the United States insisted on a condition that it knew could not be accepted — unconditional surrender, and the right to depose the emperor — in order to be able to drop its bombs; but once surrender had happened, it abandoned this humiliating requirement and left Hirohito on his throne (though stripped of some of his prerogatives, it has to be said).

Contrary to the statement by Javier Solana, even at the very last minute of the Rambouillet conference, the end result could still have been achieved by other means. But more important is the fact that the Western powers had had many earlier opportunities to solve the crisis, if only they had really been concerned about the fate of the Balkan peoples. At the time of the military intervention, Western leaders tried to reduce the situation to a simple dilemma: either we do nothing (as we did at Munich!), or else we bomb. But politics is only rarely a matter of such stark choices, and it is not true that the only choice is between coward-ice and indifference, on the one hand, and the chaos of bombing, on the other. Only if you make a prior decision that "action" means "military action" can you reach such a conclusion. In fact, there are many forms of intervention other than military strikes. Just because there is agreement on the ends to be reached does not mean there has to be agreement on the means to reach them. Otherwise you have to accept the reasoning of the Communists during the Hitler period, that anyone who was antifascist was automatically pro-Communist.

Why do the people of the West overwhelmingly choose demo-cratic regimes that protect the rights of individuals and of minor-ities? Because they gain advantages from living in democracies. But things only have to turn a little to the worse for them also to begin looking for a scapegoat to account for their misfortunes. The ideal candidate for the scapegoat role is a minority living among them but easily identified by some perceptible feature, such as a different language, different customs, or skin color. Without being intrinsically evil, even people living in democracies may then be prepared to listen to fanatical and manipulative leaders.

The Balkan countries—Yugoslavia, Macedonia, Albania, Bul-garia, and Romania—are in a disastrous economic and social po-sition. They never have been rich; in addition, Communism lasted longer there than in Central Europe and dug an even deeper eco-nomic hole. If the European Union and the United States wish their sisters and brethren in this part of the world to suffer less, or, even, more selfishly, if they just want to prevent some other corner of the Balkans from flaring up (as well they might, given the potentially catastrophic consequences of another Balkan cri-sis), then they should help this region out of its economic and social mess. A new Marshall Plan, as people say in such cases, should be launched to allow the Balkan peoples to see light at the end of the tunnel, and to find meaning in their lives. Carrots can be more effective than sticks. Fanatical and cynical leaders would be turned into absurd anachronisms and just fade away.

Milosević's fall took place in October 2000 as the result of elections that he himself called early because he was so confident of victory. It demonstrated the greater effectiveness of nonviolent policies. Some Western leaders who had realized that military action had been a failure on so many levels visibly woke up to the fact that they had other means at their disposal. The U.S. government is reported to have released $22 million for steps to promote democracy in Serbia (small change compared with the cost of military operation). The EU established confidential relations with opposition leaders inside Serbia, promising them the immediate lifting of sanctions and financial aid if they won (the EU kept its promise). It's a sure bet that the promise did not remain secret during the election campaign! Norway took in Serbian students, and other exchange programs were launched. We can only regret that the country had had to be destroyed a little bit more before we began to help it rebuild. It was poor enough to begin with.

Using the carrot instead of the stick (actually, the carrot *after* the stick) proved adequate to swing the scales and to prompt Serbian citizens to use their free judgment. Like citizens of democracies often do, they chose the solution that served their best interests. Once they had a real choice, they stopped seeming like monsters drunk on the blood of others, yearning only to rape Muslim women, and they opted for a promise of peace and prosperity. It wasn't a "miracle," just proof that you can count on the cornerstone of democracy, the autonomous judgment of a people allowed to exercise it freely. A local elected representative was justifiably proud to say: "The most important thing is that these changes came about by our own efforts, our own and no one else's, by the people. It wasn't done by the United States or by Russia" (*Le Monde*, 21 October 2000).

Economic assistance to poor countries is expensive, people say. It is, but the West has spent fabulous amounts building planes, nuclear submarines, missiles, and bombs with which to arm its fighters, and then in helping refugees. Would it be better to drop dollars instead of bombs — since bombs cost dollars, too? Confronted with situations like the Kosovo crisis, we usually argue in terms of a binary choice: activism or conservatism, idealism or realism, left or right, military action or indifference. What has to be rejected is not one or another of these terms, but that way of formulating the problem. An ethics of responsibility keeps to noble aims, but does not stop there: it also tries to foresee the consequences of each action undertaken in its name. Idealism and realism are both bad if they are separated; but taken together they make good policy possible.

The disadvantage of this solution is that it does not permit us to carry on seeing ourselves as triumphing over absolute evil, the devil, and monsters in human disguise; nor would we be able to feel proud of being the embodiment of rightness and strength. But frankly, wouldn't that be a step in the right direction?

HUMANITARIAN ACTION AND THE LAW

Humanitarian action has an enviable place in Western public opinion. People no longer believe in political utopias promising a radiant future, but they are not entirely content with their personal comfort and leisure alone. In this context, humanitarianism seems to provide an expression of solidarity with the human race. Relieving the suffering and indigence of others is a commitment that gives meaning to life. Humanitarian action seems to steer successfully between the twin dangers of political activism without morality and the ineffectiveness of morality alone, and to provide an exemplary equilibrium between idealism and realism. So it is not all surprising that it enjoys such high standing, especially with the young and the young of heart.

Humanitarian action arises most often on the international arena in times of war, conflict, or crisis where two opposing forces meet head-on. Humanitarian activists necessarily have a relation with politics. Originally, the relation could be described as voluntary ignorance: the Red Cross succored the wounded and the starving without reference to their political affiliation. Humanitarianism aimed to avoid becoming political in itself. But it quickly became apparent that the requirement of ignorance or indifference to the political dimension was inadequate.

When they intervene in a political confrontation, humanitarian workers acquire a political role whether they like it or not. Let's say a dictator decides to displace a population inside state boundaries, or to expel it, so as to grab its land. When humanitarian NGOs come onto the scene to relieve the suffering of the refugees, they become the unwilling allies of the dictator: by removing one reason for indignation, they allow him to consolidate his

265

position. But if they should decide not to intervene, or even to denounce the aggression, then the refugees die of starvation or sickness. In either case humanitarian workers cannot easily feel proud of what they have done. It's a Faustian trap: the price of effectiveness is a degree of complicity with the "devil" (the wicked dictator). If they refuse to compromise with evil, they are paralyzed, but following the orders of the powerful robs them of their soul and gives a depressing message to the world: victims have to abandon the hope of justice if they want to have something to eat.

Cruel dilemmas of that kind are not rare and there is no overall solution. That is why some NGOs like Doctors Without Borders (MSF) have decided to stop pretending to be ignorant of politics and to base their actions on as full a political analysis of each situation as is possible. Deciding between compromise and indignation will thus be not a question of principle but a matter of practicality. In some cases, protest is essential, even if it means failing to intervene; in others, assistance to the suffering comes first, despite the assistance it also gives to those who caused the suffering in the first place. But there are limits that cannot be crossed. Humanitarian action seeks to restore a state of (human) rights; it must never become a tool of (political) might.

Politicians have found subtle ways of making use of humanitarian aid workers. In France, the government calls on NGOs to fulfill roles too burdensome or thankless to be dealt with by normal bureaucratic structures, such as the relief of poverty and the treatment of drug addicts. In other cases, charitable bodies took on such tasks before politicians even noticed them. State-based solutions to such problems can be strategically and financially costly, so getting NGOs to do the work is a way of not tackling the roots of the problem. Once again, aid workers do not have to refuse on principle to replace or to assist political action, but they must try to be aware of the ways in which they are being used; otherwise they run the risk of being rejected by the very people they are trying to help on grounds of their being tools of unacceptable policies. This is what happened in colonial times.

Rarely has the vulnerability of humanitarian workers in the midst of a political conflict been so visible as during the Yugoslav war; and in the Kosovo crisis their very identity came under threat. What happened was that the West, where the NGOs raise their funds, gave them a new role of which they were barely aware—that of what Jean-Christophe Rufin, a leading NGO activist, called "triggers for the use of force" (399). In the weeks and months prior to military intervention, aid workers were often the only observers on the ground. They would have been the first to know of any disaster or outrage. But that meant that the interpretation they put upon current events and the information that they relayed back could start a war. "In the run-up to the crisis," Rufin writes, "the whole world, and especially NATO, was just waiting for an outrage to happen and to be witnessed by aid workers. So any protest at a human rights abuse could easily have the immediate effect of . . . unleashing a massive bombing of Belgrade and Pristina" (Rufin, 401). Can aid workers accept being used as triggers? Can they agree to abandon their original neutrality and to become the cause of more deaths?

Once hostilities began humanitarian action remained deeply ambiguous. Various NGOs and sometimes the various national branches of the same NGO adopted contradictory positions. Some organizations approved of the bombing and requested land-based intervention; some other NGOs agreed to staff military hospitals for KLA fighters only. At the same time, MSF-Greece set up in bomb-damaged Pristina and declared that it was able "to work freely" there (Rufin, 417). Armies need medical services, to be sure, but can we still call it humanitarian action when a medical facility is put at the exclusive disposal of one group that is trying to beat another?

The confusion between humanitarian and military action was fostered by NATO itself, because that military organization wanted to be seen as carrying out an essentially humanitarian mission. That is presumably what Havel meant to say with his "humanitarian bombs"—their primary aim, apparently, was to help women and children! Given the huge size of the job, what could be better organized and equipped than an army to deal with the hundreds of thousands of refugees? So a "humanitarian" wing of NATO was officially inaugurated, alongside its fighting wing, and it took charge of assistance to the population. Thus the reversal—or rather the confusion—of roles was complete. Humanitarian NGOs were at the service of NATO, while NATO cast itself as a humanitarian super-NGO.

Should we rejoice at the conversion of the military into a caring body? Verbal sophistry aside, war is never a humanitarian act. And even if any assistance to aid workers is in principle welcome, a take-over of humanitarian action by one of the parties to the conflict is hardly likely to reassure people that aid is impartial. Quite the opposite, in fact: as the directors of MSF noted at the time, putting states and NGOs on the same footing and binding them together through mutual obligations put the latter under legitimate suspicion. By seeking effectiveness at any cost, humanitarian workers risked losing their identity, together with what gives their work value, namely its universalist inspiration. Aid that is not impartial would not deserve to be called "humanitarian."

The same could be said of international law. It is a deep satisfaction for the mind, and a great comfort to our idea of humanity, if we can say that right preexists its expression as law, that law only codifies notions of right and wrong that are common to all people. We don't want to believe that what is right in this country is wrong once you cross the border. Humanist thought, in its universalist ambition, is based on the opposite postulate. "To say that there is nothing right or wrong save for what positive laws command or forbid is to say that before the circle has been drawn its radii are not equal," wrote Montesquieu (*Spirit of Laws*, I.1). It is this kind of justice — natural, universal, and absolute — that we aspire to find in international legal institutions, because they are free of the constraints of any national traditions. The most celebrated example of such an institution in modern times was the Nuremberg Tribunal, which, even if it was not a perfect incarnation of international law, showed that it was possible to rise above national boundaries. The Nazi top brass had not broken any laws of its own country, and yet the Nazis were criminals in everybody's eyes. The international war crimes tribunal was a plausible incarnation of universal justice.

The establishment in 1993, nearly fifty years after Nuremberg, of an International Criminal Tribunal for Yugoslavia (ICTY) in The Hague understandably raised great expectations: it was intended to make rulings over and above national boundaries. But the way it arose was rather more prosaic. War had been tearing Yugoslavia apart for three years, and images of the battered country and of murdered and maltreated people were seen repeatedly on our television screens. The weakest party, the potential victims — that is, Bosnian Muslims — appealed to the West. Two kinds of action were possible as a response to the war and to its horrors: military, or legal. The latter was thought of by all as an alternative to the first. For most members of the governments, the creation of ICTY would *avert* the need for military engagement; it offered a less costly and less risky way of discharging international responsibilities. For Bosnian Muslims and a few Western personalities such as Madeleine Albright, ICTY was a first step that should *lead to* the second step of military intervention. At this point, therefore, justice became a tool of politics, for both sides. These contradictory expectations also explain why ICTY, once it got going, ran into all kinds of resistance, from the governments that wished it into existence as well as from international organizations, the UN, and the Security Council.

International justice may satisfy a deep aspiration that we all feel, but it runs into all sorts of problems with respect to national politics. The two are not governed by the same principles; they do not share the same priorities. Leaders of democratic states draw their legitimacy from the will of the people who brought them to power, and they must first defend the interests of their electorate, which means putting their own citizens' interests above the interests of those of other countries. Nobody takes exception to Clinton or any other U.S. president putting the protection of American lives first. A president's duty is to strengthen his own country — but the consequences of choices made in pursuit of this objective may appear criminal in the light of international law.

International law is not set up by universal will, it has to be said, but by the ruling powers of the day; and yet it seeks to disregard national interests, which are the first priority for political leaders. However, actions that break abstract international law may be necessities, or even exploits, in the context of national policy. The same is true within each country. Killing is a crime, but if the slaughter is called war, then killing is a matter for glorification — the political view trumps the legal view. On the one hand, international law must resist utopian temptations, and that is why it does not aim to make all war a crime (to force humanity to become peaceful); so it allows some slaughter when it has been ennobled by being called war. It aims to punish only

269

war crimes; but, as we have seen, in an era of total war, war crimes are hard to separate clearly from ordinary acts of war. On the other hand, international law tries to ward off accusations of partiality and political subservience; and that is why it avoids holding political trials. It is obviously far from easy to make these two quite separate sets of requirements work together.

Several significant differences between Nuremberg and The Hague have become clear. First, there was almost complete consensus about Nazi crimes; everyone had a clear mental picture of the murder and violence committed, and of the death camps. Second, the war was over, and the Allies were not using the court to pursue a military objective. Finally, all the top Nazis were behind bars and arresting them was not an issue.

Things are different in Yugoslavia. The war is still going on (in late 2000), legal action is taking place during and not after the conflict, and with the aim of influencing its outcome; and for that reason ICTY has a political and even military significance that Nuremberg did not possess. The door is wide open to manipulation: accusations are thrown back and forth of inventing imaginary victims, and ploys are designed to show up the adversary as the guilty party. Also there is far less consensus about the current trials. Not just one of the parties, but several, may have committed crimes — Serbs, Croats, Bosnians, and Kosovars. Finally, arresting the suspects is a dangerous business, since we are dealing with high-ranking military and political figures who are well protected. Because they are well aware that their electorate would not appreciate actions that might result in their own soldiers being killed, Western leaders are reluctant to attempt these arrests. Nuremberg dealt with a fait accompli. The Hague is trying to judge a current, unfinished business, the nature of which is not at all clear to everybody.

The transformation of the law into a tool of policy became a material fact when on 27 May 1999 Louise Arbour, the prosecutor at The Hague, charged the entire Yugoslav leadership, and Milosević first and foremost, with crimes against humanity committed in Kosovo. Nothing could have brought the impartiality of the court into greater doubt than this gesture; and nothing could have served NATO better. A court set up and supported by one of the belligerents accuses the other belligerent of being criminal: how can you believe that the court is maintaining neutrality? You might have thought that in order to avoid accusations of partiality and also so as to conduct investigations in proper detail, the court would have waited for the end of hostilities and would have appointed independent investigators. None of these elementary precautions was thought necessary. (It had happened once before, when U.S. president George Bush and British prime minister Margaret Thatcher threatened Saddam Hussein — who was certainly guilty of having invaded Kuwait — with a trial for crimes against humanity while the Gulf War was still in progress. And of course they compared him to Hitler.) NATO leaders could not hide their satisfaction at seeing a theoretically impartial international institution giving legitimacy to the military action they had undertaken; Milosević ought to feel his back was really against the wall and surrender.

In its early years, when it was concerned with crimes committed in Bosnia, ICTY took care to lay charges against members of all the warring factions — the Serbs, the Croats, and the Bosnians (though the largest number of cases was against Serbs) — so as to maintain visibly its impartiality. In the Kosovo conflict, however, no such thing happened. All the same, accusations of illegality had also been made against some of NATO's actions, not just by the Yugoslav government, which had little credibility, but also by international humanitarian bodies. On 13 May 1999, Human Rights Watch wrote to NATO secretary-general Javier Solana informing him of several violations of international law committed by NATO. International law allows the use of military force against military targets but forbids it use against civilian ones.

The answer came on 16 May from Jamie Shea, NATO's spokesman: "NATO member-states provided the funding for the establishment of ICTY, and we are the majority stakeholders." So there was nothing to worry about there. It is hard to imagine a more cynical answer or a balder admission that law is just one of the tools of might, in this case financial might. A few days later, ICTY charged Yugoslav leaders with war crimes and crimes against humanity. A few months later, the incoming prosecutor confirmed Shea's interpretation and abandoned any prosecution of Western leaders.

Another humanitarian organization, Amnesty International, entered the fray on 6 June 2000, when it stated that NATO's bombing of civilian targets such as the Yugoslav radio and television

271

buildings (so this is not about "collateral damage") contravened international law. In a report entitled "Collateral Damage or Illegal Homicide?" Amnesty pointed out that political and military chiefs had intentionally picked these targets in full knowledge that bombing them would endanger civilians. Tony Blair, the British prime minister, had said: "It's very, very important people realise that these television stations are part of the apparatus of dictatorship and power of Milosević, and that apparatus is the apparatus he has used to do this ethnic cleansing in Kosovo — it's the apparatus that keeps him in power. And we are entirely justified as the NATO alliance in damaging and taking on these targets, and the responsibility for every single part of this action lies with the man who has engaged in this policy of ethnic cleansing and must be stopped" (AP Wire service, 24 April 1999).

General Wesley Clark added that because the television service supported Milosevic's aims it had become a "legitimate war target," validated moreover by ICTY (another proof of its harmonious collaboration with NATO forces). Amnesty International's report also pointed out that instructions to pilots to remain above fifteen thousand feet so as to avoid all risk to themselves was incompatible with the spirit of war crimes legislation, which required all efforts to be made to avoid risk to civilians. Carla Del Ponte responded only by saying that an inquiry was not justified. George Robertson, who took over Solana's position at NATO, was his usual laconic self when he merely declared that the accusations were groundless.

If it were possible to draw up a balance sheet of offenses against international humanitarian legislation, it is very probable that that the Yugoslav army's tally would be much higher than NATO's. But the partiality of ICTY and its manifest intention of serving the military objectives of its funding sources seriously undermine the credibility of its judgments. Human justice is by definition imperfect, fallible, and inadequate. But unless a court tries to show that it has done its best, it ceases to be an instrument of justice and becomes just another tool of military and political will. The envisaged ICC (International Criminal Court) provides another example of the same danger. The United States has refused to sign up to a convention that would have allowed U.S. citizens to be charged without the agreement of their government. In other words, the United States was in favor of international justice on condition that its own citizens were exempted. Can that be called justice? Even the best policy in the world cannot justify denigrating the idea of justice itself. Once again, the Bosnian precedent was quite different from what went on during the Kosovo campaign, because the Western governments funding the tribunal were not simultaneously taking military action against one of the countries involved. The International Criminal Tribunal for Yugoslavia at The Hague did a disservice to the international community: it jeopardized the concept of universal justice, which must be free of all political supervision. War is the opposite of justice, which functions under the rule of law; whereas war is used when there is no shared law, in order to impose a cause by force. To make the law a means of war is to betray the very spirit of justice.

Humanitarian and charitable bodies as well as legal institutions have to be financed. Are there any occasions when they should turn on their funders and bite the hands that feed them? The answer must be yes. Their standing and the transparency of their deeds as well as their ease of access to the media should protect them from political involvement. Moreover, it is their bound duty to maintain their independence. If they allow themselves to become tools in the hands of political power, then they give up their vocation and undermine the very idea of universality that they claim to implement. Even if the risk of losing their funding is real, it would be better for them to take that risk.

Humanitarian aid organizations are in a less difficult position than international legal institutions, because they have private sources of funding as well as public ones; and the very spirit of their commitment is to refrain from taking sides in any conflict. They can thus avoid the tension. On the other hand, international justice depends entirely on the governments that grant them their funds and staff the police forces that they need. In addition, they are not above the scrum; they have to say what is just and what is unjust, and thus identify the innocent and the guilty. But that does not relive them of the duty to obey only the dictates of justice.

The question thus arises whether, outside of truly special circumstances, such as those of the Nuremberg trial, it would not be wiser to soft-pedal international institutions in favor of increasing support for the international application of national legal systems.

To take another recent example: those responsible for the Rwandan genocide can be tried in national courts — not just in Rwanda, obviously, but also in France and Belgium, where trials have indeed been held. A French (or any other) court, not being a participant in a military conflict scarring some other country, is in principle likely to be impartial. It can also request cooperation of foreign governments, which, if they refuse, may incur sanctions. It can not make justice reign upon the face of the earth; but "international courts" are not doing that either. In any case, are we really prepared to pay the price of world government?

THE RIGHT TO INTERFERE VERSUS THE OBLIGATION TO AID

The military campaign in Kosovo was presented as the effect of a new doctrine expressed by the phrase "the right to interfere." It means that a group of states — for example, the member states of NATO — have the right to take military action anywhere in the world where massive and systematic human rights abuses are taking place. The doctrine has been defended by Kofi Annan, the UN secretary-general; by Bill Clinton ("If somebody comes after innocent civilians and tries to kill them en masse because of their race, their ethnic background or their religion, and it is within our power to stop it, we will stop it," he said on 22 June 1999 to NATO troops serving in Macedonia); and by other public figures who have become spokesmen for the doctrine — Vaclav Havel, for instance, once again talking about Kosovo: "But there is one thing no reasonable person can deny: this is probably the first war that has not been waged in the name of 'national interests' but rather in the name of principles and values. If one can say of any war that it is ethical, or that is being waged for ethical reasons, then it is true of this war" (Havel, 6). We could argue with the application of the principle to Yugoslavia, since the situation there prior to military intervention was not genocide, but a slow-burning civil war and ensuing massacres, and still agree with the idea of the right to intervene. There are less dubious cases that would support the principle more clearly. Wouldn't it have been wiser to intervene against Hitler in 1938? Or in Cambodia, as early as 1976, to avert the genocide? Or at the very start of the massacre of the Tutsis in Rwanda in 1994?

Objections were raised to the right of interference as soon as it was formulated. They are based on a variety of arguments. The most widespread objection is that the doctrine involves abandoning the principle of national sovereignty, which up to now has been the basis of international relations, and that to do so has many more dangers than it has advantages. What is the truth of the matter?

We first have to make an exception for countries that are part of a larger federal or confederal entity, and which by definition have themselves given up part of their sovereignty. The member states of the EU are in that kind of a position. That is why it was not at all surprising when some EU member states blamed Austria for allowing an extreme right-wing party to join its government (in 2000). The EU seeks to be not just a single economic and financial area, but also a community of nations with shared political values, such as opposition to racism and xenophobia. The Austrian far right had a legitimacy granted by its electoral success; but if the country wishes to continue to benefit from membership of the EU, it has to be prepared to accept limitations on its sovereignty. Or else it can maintain full sovereignty and abandon the union, together with all the benefits it derives from membership. The contract was clear from the start.

But there is a difference in other cases, where a country has made no prior commitment. Resistance to the doctrine of the right of intervention was particularly sharp in countries located outside of Western Europe and North America — countries in the Southern Hemisphere, in Africa, South America, and Asia. This geographical distribution is not haphazard, and it derives from the difference in historical memory. Contrary to what Vaclav Havel thinks, the theory of the right of intervention is not at all new. At least twice in their history European nations have invoked "principles and values" rather than national interest to justify actions taken outside their borders. And on both occasions they acted out of the conviction that they were the proprietors of the good, whereas distant countries, on other continents, were allowing evil to flourish on their soil. So the Europeans sent off their armies to try to impose good on others.

275

The first wave of interference was conducted in the name of the superiority of the Christian religion, so as to give all people on earth access to the true God, or else to rescue Christians living among infidels. The Crusaders, in the eleventh to thirteenth centuries, were no less sure of the justice of their cause than we are today, and they were just as inspired by the universalist ("humanitarian") ambition to allow all peoples to profit from an unarguable good — that is, to impose Christianity over Islam. Then the conquest of America, in the fifteenth to sixteenth centuries, was in turn legitimated by the expansion of Christianity. In any case, Columbus set off in search of a "western route" to Asia so as to obtain the means for a new crusade, which aimed to liberate Jerusalem once and for all. It is of course true that Native Americans did not have states, in the proper sense, and that interference in the New World had a different profile.

The second great wave of interference happened in the nineteenth and twentieth centuries, not so much in the name of Christian values as those of secular European civilization — progress, industry, hygiene, and, even then, human rights. France and Britain, at that time the most advanced democracies of Europe, led this new wave of colonization. It is said that on the day after the (particularly bloody) conquest of Indochina, the first thing that was done by Paul Bert, representing the government of the French Republic, was to post the Declaration of Human Rights on the walls of Hanoi (Saussure, 8). But whatever the handbills said, the reality was something else. Let us recall, to take a later but comparable example, that in 1947 the French authorities in Madagascar set fire to railcars in which they had imprisoned Malagasy rebels; and tested the rebels' sturdiness by pushing them out of aircraft in flight (a technique that was taken up again in Argentina).

We might add that Soviet Russian imperialism also always clothed itself in the most generous of intentions. When the Red Army invaded Poland in 1920, General Tukhachevsky, commander of the front, sent out a flyer saying: "On the tips of our bayonets we bring peace and happiness to the working people!" (quoted from Buber-Neumann, *La Révolution mondiale*, 24). Twenty years later, in September 1939, when thanks to the Ribbentrop-Molotov pact, the Russian army once again occupied the eastern part of Poland, the Soviet prime minister used the same argument:

"The army of freedom . . . whose banner bears the sublime words of *fraternity among peoples*, *socialism*, and *peace*, has begun the most just campaign in the history of humankind" (*La Révolution mondiale*, 394). Conquests on behalf of Communist ideology thus also portray themselves as the triumph of the good.

An objection could be made: the values connected to human rights are theoretically accepted nowadays almost everywhere, even in places where they are violated as a matter of course; but that was not the position of Christianity at the time of the Crusades or of the merits of European civilization in the period of colonization. Universal acceptance of human rights is a fact, and we should be grateful. But that's not the issue. The Christian doctrine of love for one's fellow and the European belief in the power of reason in the nineteenth century were also universal values that were worth defending. Simply, there was no reason to suppose that they would prevail as a result of military action undertaken to impose them. Jerusalem overrun by Crusaders does not embody the triumph of love. Hanoi overrun by the French army is not an illustration of human rights. Even if we grant that the proponents of these campaigns were sincere, the means they used undermined the ends they pursued. War against their country's government is not the only way to help people in need: negotiation, pressure, and seduction can be much more effective tools.

The wariness of non-European countries is perfectly understandable given that they have not forgotten prior interference in their affairs in the name of good. Stated good intentions are never guarantees — and are often just a clever mask. In any case, good imposed by force is not unambiguously good. If a country has to be conquered to be brought into line, then it's not likely that its citizens will feel gratitude (as Kazumoto Momose wrote in *Asahi Shimbun*, the Kosovo intervention became "an unstoppable operation of destruction and violence that claimed many lives in the name of 'humanity,' 'Justice' and 'national integrity'" [*Asahi News Service*, 10 May 1999]). Finally, before we inflict our universal values on others, we really ought to ask them their opinion. If we grant them the same human status as we grant ourselves, then their opinions should have no less weight than our own. We may think that their governments are worthy of condemnation, but should we simply dismiss the people's will as null and void (in circumstances where it has been freely expressed)? History is full of examples where what were taken for universal values were but reflections of our own traditions and desires; it would not be unseemly to be more modest and cautious in this domain.

Does this mean we have to abandon universalism altogether and give up the idea that human rights are the same for everyone everywhere, irrespective of race, culture, creed, gender, or age? Not at all. Classical humanists taught us that tyranny is a curse at every latitude. We certainly do not have to establish any alternative value structures such as the rights of God, the rights of nature, or the rights of a group specific to other traditions ("Asian values") parallel to "Western" human rights and of equal weight. The issue here is not the universality of rights and values, but their practical implementation in real societies — not ends, but means. Instead of contrasting fine theories with messy practice, hoping that next time it will work out fine (Christianity failed, to be sure, as did Communism, but why not try liberal democracy this time round?), we should question the meaning of the history that we are living through.

There is another reason that might incline us more toward national sovereignty than to the right of interference. Sovereignty builds the institutions of the state; interference destroys the nation-state. However, people have far more rights as citizens of a state — even of an undemocratic one — than they do as members of the human race. Human rights not backed up by the laws of the land and the machinery of a state are very flimsy indeed. So destroying a state in defense of human rights is always problematic and may lead us to throw out the baby with the bath water. Anarchy can be worse than tyranny, since anarchy replaces the tyranny of one man by the tyranny of many; and even unjust laws have the advantage of stability. The fall of the Communist regimes in East and Central Europe offered an illustration of that. In several countries it uncovered the crumbling, if not the complete collapse, of the structures of the state. Power thus fell into the hands of mafia-like groups on the fringe of organized crime who imposed the rule of the strongest. The UN protectorates that now exist in Bosnia and Kosovo (strange new versions of our colonial past) run into the same problem: how can international civil servants make up for the absent structures of a failed nation-state? If we agree that this is a real problem, then we might argue that interference would be legitimate in a country already facing anarchy. It is certainly worth fighting anarchy, but it is not clear that order imposed by an outside force can ever seem legitimate to the people on the ground. Once again, negotiation and indirect pressure may be more effective than war.

Let us now turn from the issue of national sovereignty to the principles that justify intervention—universal values and equal justice for all. What is immediately striking is that the right to interfere has been exercised very selectively, in some places but not in others. The variability is easily explained by the fact that some countries suspected of evil actions are just too powerful to touch. Whatever newspapers may tell us about human rights violations by China in Tibet, or about the Indian occupation of Kashmir, or about Russia's violence in Chechnya, nobody suggests we bomb China, India, or Russia so as to put a stop to their crimes, as there would be too high a price to pay. There should therefore be a restrictive clause on the right to interfere, saying that it applies only against countries significantly weaker than those who do the interfering. It all reminds me of Charles Péguy's mocking words to Francis de Pressensé, the president of the Human Rights League in the early years of the twentieth century: "Pressensé is in favor of right over might as long as might can't put up much of a fight" (Péguy, 143).

That's not anything to be proud of, but, let's face it, we have to take reality into account. There are other instances we could mention that can't be accounted for solely by the military strength of the guilty parties. Keeping to the Mediterranean area, we could set alongside Yugoslavia (where the original crime was persecution, deportation, or expulsion of a minority) the treatment of Palestinians by Israel, and of the Kurds by Turkey. Each case is different, of course, and calls for balanced judgment, but why has there been intervention in one case and not in the other two? Is justice for some and not others worthy of the name of justice? As we understand it today, either justice is universal, or it is not justice. If some are sentenced but not others for similar misdeeds, then a choice is being made in the name of some other principle. You could object that we have to start somewhere, and the fact that we cannot bring the rule of justice to the whole world at once does not mean that we should fail to apply it where we are able to do so. But human rights violations in Israel and Turkey go back much further than they do in Yugoslavia, and it is hard to see what has prevented the Western powers from interfering, if only with political and economic sanctions rather than military measures.

Actually, though, we can see very clearly what stands in the way of intervention in Israel and Turkey — and it has nothing to do with justice. The two countries are essential to NATO strategy and to the United States especially, with which they share military and political interests. The lesson of recent history is thus less glorious than the UN secretary-general, the former president of the United States, or Vaclav Havel would have us believe: human rights violations will be prevented but only in countries with which the West has no alliance; allied countries can do what they like with their minorities. In other words, the message is this: you had better be on the side of might. So the cynical reading of the situation is that Yugoslavia's great mistake was not to persecute its minorities but to overestimate its strength, or to believe that Russia was still able and willing to help it. It's a very familiar lesson from the annals of international politics. So there is then a second restrictive clause to the right of interference: it does not apply to strategic allies of the West.

The Rwandan genocide was a different kind of case. Let me go over the facts surrounding the West's failure to intervene. In 1993 the UN sent in a corps of 2,500 observers headed by a Canadian general, Roméo Dallaire. From early 1994 on, he sent ever more alarming reports back to his superiors: interethnic hatred, fanned by Hutu propaganda, was rising to dangerous levels, he observed, but he had woefully inadequate means of intervention. Dallaire's dispatches just sat on the desk. In early April the genocide began; ten Belgian UN soldiers were murdered; but Dallaire was just a powerless onlooker. His horrified reports continued to evoke no response — save for the Security Council's decision to cut back the number of troops under his command, since they were in danger of sustaining casualties. In the following three months an un-known number of Tutsis were slaughtered — best estimates put the figure around 800,000. In addition, tens or maybe hundreds of thousands of Hutus also perished, killed by Tutsi soldiers in reprisal after the end of the genocide, or else from untreated injuries.

A report entitled "An Avoidable Genocide" commissioned by the Organization for African Unity (OAU) and written by a panel of international experts stated, in July 2000, that the Security Council deliberately chose not to intervene. What were the reasons for the UN's attitude? The lack of political will among the most directly concerned of its member states. The United States was fully informed of the dramatic situation as it unfolded, but President Clinton or his ambassador to the UN, Madeleine Albright, knew that intervention in Rwanda would be very unpopular within the United States: people had not forgotten the Somalia disaster, when eighteen soldiers died in an aid relief operation. U.S. leaders therefore avoided using the word "genocide" in reference to Rwanda, because international obligations would then have obliged it to intervene; instead they referred more modestly to "acts resembling" acts of genocide. However, when the Security Council resolved to send a new mission into Rwanda, "American delaying tactics resulted in not a single extra soldier nor a single extra gun getting to the country before the genocide was over" (see http://www.how.org/reports/1999/rwanda). The US wasn't taking sides between Hutu murderers and Tutsi victims; simply, domestic political concerns trumped humanitarian ones. There have been other examples of the same thing: Clinton always opposed official recognition by Congress of the Turkish genocide of the Armenians because it would not be in the national interest.

So the right to interfere has yet another restriction on it: you don't exercise it if you have nothing to gain by it, materially, politically, or in terms of international prestige. The noninterference of the international community in other African conflicts, for example, in the very serious situation in Sudan, seems to correspond to this third exception to the general rule.

France has not behaved in a fundamentally different way. So as to maintain its good relations with Hutu authorities and other African states before the start of the genocide, it refrained from denouncing the racist propaganda that was rife in Rwanda. No intervention was contemplated during the genocide, although this part of Africa belongs to the traditional "French zone of influence." Only when the slaughter was petering out and the army of the Tutsi Patriotic Front (RPF) was rolling back into the country did France launch "Operation Turquoise," supposedly to hold the two warring parties apart from each other. But in practice the operation allowed the Hutu murderers to make their getaway over the border into the Congo (Zaïre). Since then, Washington has expressed its regrets at not having acted more vigorously at the time; Paris has set up a parliamentary commission of inquiry into the affair. General Dallaire, who has spoken many times about what he saw, has attempted suicide twice and suffered long bouts of depression.

All these events belong to the very recent past; they do not date from before the Second World War or even from before the "just war" against Iraq. We could see the Rwandan genocide coming; we could have intervened militarily straightaway; and if enough resources had been put into the operation, it could have been effective. The international community knew it was a genocide and did nothing to stop it. So how can we go on trusting political leaders who acted in this way?

Countries that get involved in military intervention, if they wish to preserve their credibility, must ensure that their own human rights records are beyond reproach. The United States is unquestionably more democratic than Yugoslavia, but just how clean is it? Without going back as far as Hiroshima and Nagasaki, are we sure that all U.S. military interventions have been entirely untainted by war crimes? The way the United States has "tidied up" its own backyard in Central and Southern America looks very much like the infamous "Brezhnev doctrine" cooked up in 1968 to justify the invasion of Czechoslovakia by Warsaw Pact armies. The doctrine granted only limited sovereignty to the immediate neighbors of the USSR, which reserved the right to intervene as the "protector" of the region. Second, we could hardly approve if the United States exports its use of capital punishment — which is itself a violation of human rights and is regularly criticized by Amnesty International and other human rights organizations. France and the United Kingdom, which have strong traditions of interference in other countries' affairs, are less involved nowadays and so run fewer risks of violations, although that is not because they have higher moral standards in international affairs but simply because they have less ability to do so. So we have to accept that no country can claim to be an exemplary incarnation of good; no country has automatic legitimacy in these matters.

We have raised objections to the right of interference based on national sovereignty and on the universality of law, but these are not objections to the right of interference itself, only to the un-evenness of its application (why here and not there) or to its un-intended consequences (anarchy or the return of colonial rule instead of the restoration of human rights). But we have to go one step further. Let us assume that the right of interference could be exercised faultlessly. Would that be truly desirable? Would we want to live in such a world?

The first reason why we might balk at the universal application of the right of interference is that human rights violations, not to mention mere violations of law, are far too widespread, and if we had to put a stop to every single one of them, then war would be a permanent state of affairs. No continent, no state is immune to criticism. Charles Péguy did not retreat from the consequences of such a principle and wrote that "The Declaration of the Rights of Man provides reasons . . . for making war on everyone in the world as long as there are people in the world" (139). We might well stop short of accepting such a commitment; a heap of evil would have to happen before we reach the good! The impossibility of generalizing the principle does not mean that there cannot be legitimate cases for intervention; but it does mean that appealing to the doctrine of human rights is not enough to justify an intervention.

In addition, the means used to conduct interventions is not the only issue: the aims may also be doubted. To seek to eradicate injustice (or even just human rights violations) from the planet so as to inaugurate a new world order free of war and violence is a project which harks back to those totalitarian utopias that dreamed of improving the human race and creating paradise on earth. It also implies that we be convinced that we are the sole incarnation of good on earth, just like in the wars of religion. Those wars came to an end only when it was allowed that different concepts of the good could coexist. On the other hand, evil is no acciden-tal addition to human history that could easily be got rid of; it is tied to our very identity, and to dispense with it we would have to belong to a different species.

The promotion of universal justice calls for building a world state. That is because you need a police force to find the guilty and to prepare the cases against them if the law is to be applied.

283

So to apply universal law, you need a universal police force. Policing answers to government, and so a universal police also implies something like a united world government. This was, of course, a central element in "scientistic" plans for humanity: since the ends that suited all people had been correctly identified, since the best possible form of government had been designed, the benefits of these discoveries had to be extended to all by having a single set of laws and institutions and a single police force. But would a universal state be perfect? Absolutely not. It would have far more drawbacks than advantages.

World Government is not much talked about these days, but there are plenty of signs that we are moving in that direction. What we do hear more and more are medical metaphors applied to social issues — you would have thought they would have been discarded after being so widely used by totalitarian regimes. We hear terms like "surgical strikes" and adages like "prevention is better than cure," as if social ills could be treated like diseases. The image of the body only works if you think of humanity as a single entity, with a head and heart and arms to swing (always the same ones) and patches of sick and corrupt flesh that need to be countered, if necessary by excision. Thinking of prevention in that way obviously justifies intervention to halt possible genocides and potential crimes, but it also legitimates any preventive action — even if it turns out in retrospect that there was no real danger at all.

It is not just because totalitarian regimes inherited the idea of universal government from their scientistic predecessors that we should be very wary of developments that might lead toward it. In the eighteenth century Condorcet and Montesquieu engaged in a famous argument on the subject. Montesquieu looked at the laws of various countries and reached the conclusion that the same broad principles of justice lay behind them all. Nonetheless, he argued, the differences between national histories, cultural traditions, geographical features, and natural resources meant that it would be better for each country to keep its own laws, forms of government, and religion. The crime of the conquistadors was not to disregard the law or to abandon the pursuit of good, but to behave as if all nations in the world were but one. "The peak of idiocy," Montesquieu wrote of the trial of Inca emperor Atahualpa, "was that he was judged not by the laws of his own land, but by the laws of the conquistadors' country" (*Spirit of Laws*, XXVI.22). If there were five religions into which the world were divided, then they would have been better than one, even the best one, since otherwise it would become oppressive; recognizing the plurality of religions helps each keep the others in check. Pluralism is a good in itself, in Montesquieu's view, irrespective of the value of the various views that constitute it, both in the domestic sphere (separation of powers) and in relations between countries.

Thirty years later Condorcet wrote a critique of *The Spirit of Laws* and protested against Montesquieu's insistence on plurality. If the best solution, or the best law, or the best government has been discovered, why should we not get rid of inferior ones? If politics were a scientific activity, then the choices it made would be true — and truth does not sit well with pluralism, because only errors are many, and truth is one. "A good law ought to be good for all men, just as a true proposition is true for all" (Condorcet, *Œuvres*, 1:318). Once laws had been unified, then institutions and trade would be united too, and ultimately the languages of the most enlightened nations — English and French — would become universal as well. Guided by reason, men would ultimately "form a single entity and strive toward a single goal" (Condorcet, *Esquisse*, 248).

Why is Montesquieu's pluralist ideal preferable to Condorcet's unitary ideal, and why is the humanist project preferable to one derived from the cult of science? Because human knowledge will always be incomplete, and because knowledge does not produce values in any case; and that is why politics will never be a science. So the balance of powers, mutual tolerance, and multilateralism will always be better than unity, even if the latter is imposed by the country enjoying the best form of government of its time. Plurality ensures freedom and the possibility of seeking freedom, whereas unity stifles both. Translated into international relations, that means that it is better for peace that there should be several alliances or superpowers exercising mutual dissuasion than a single dominant world power that would be tempted to become the world's policeman and to impose its own rules on everyone. We are very happy to have seen the totalitarian empire of the Soviet Union collapse, but that does not mean that the domination of the United States alone is desirable in itself. The risk is not diminished when the superpower realizes it does not have the means to keep the peace in every corner of the world and must restrict its interventions to situations where its own vital interests are at stake. For all these reasons, balance is preferable to unity. The globalization of the economy must not lead to a globalization of politics: on the contrary, we need separate states or alliances of states to counter the negative effects of the drift toward unification.

If we want to avoid a world state, if we want to steer clear of the temptation of creating paradise on earth, then we would be well advised not to take on the task of curing humanity of all its ills. So should we look on the misfortunes that befall others with passive indifference? Once again I have to insist that what we must resist are precisely these kinds of sterile oppositions, as if the only choice were between cowardly indifference and intensive bombing campaigns. We can resist evil without falling into the trap of trying to do too much good.

Military interference in a foreign country that flouts national sovereignty can be justified in extreme cases (by the ethics of conviction) provided it does not risk creating more casualties than it seeks to avoid (in the name of the ethics of responsibility). The extreme case has been called *genocide* for some decades. Not potential genocide calling for preventative action, nor civil war, however horrible the associated slaughter may be. That was why it would have been illegitimate to declare war on Nazi Germany in 1936: the genocide had not yet begun. But that would not have prevented other forms of action — commercial pressure, diplomatic sanctions, political propaganda, and generous treatment of refugees. On another front, even if sufficient information about the genocide of Ukrainian and Kazakh peasants had been available in 1933, it would not have justified military intervention, since war with the USSR would have produced even higher numbers of casualties. The crushing of Hungary by Soviet tanks in 1956 was not a genocide, but it aroused immense moral indignation in the West and in the East; I remember dreaming, together with many other East European adolescents, of American tanks coming to rescue us. In a gesture of solidarity, David Rousset asked the West to "enter the fray." With hindsight I think intervention would have been a terrible mistake, because it would have unleashed the Third World War.

Intervening in a case of real genocide is no less risky than other forms of interference. But these risks have to be taken, since the stakes are so high. Can we calculate in advance how many additional casualties will be caused by steps intended to rescue the prior victims? We can't. Can we draw a firm line between collective murders and budding genocide? We can't. How can we be sure that by intervening only when potential genocide becomes real we are not leaving things until it is too late, until real people have already been turned into virtual beings, that is to say, into corpses? We can't. All we can do is accept that human existence will never be as elegant as a mathematical proof, or as unambiguous as an insurance policy; that it is closer to Montaigne's "imperfect garden"; and that facing the extreme, we must resist. Mistakes will be made; but if we adopt as a principle that only genocide justifies intervention, then we can hope to keep mistakes to a minimum.

The two genocides that have occurred since the Second World War, in Cambodia from 1976 and in Rwanda in 1994, prompted not the slightest interference by the international community. Both were brought to a tardy stop by a local army — by the Vietnamese army in Cambodia, and by the RPF, based in Uganda, in the case of Rwanda. These precedents might suggest that the most effective reaction to crises of this kind is not the UN. The world body is forever wracked by the conflicting interests of its member states, which bring it close to paralysis; the United States, despite justifying its own policies on moral grounds, is understandably reluctant to pay its UN dues. UN bureaucracy is extremely ponderous. Furthermore, the UN has no army of its own — and that is a good thing, since it could otherwise turn into a world government. But the countries that border on a land where genocide is taking place have every reason to intervene. Their information comes not just from television news but from the refugees flowing across their borders. And proximity favors identification, which justifies the risks that have to be taken. It is much harder to risk your life for people living at the other end of the earth than for the people next door. This solution is not a cure-all, and it may well bolster regional powers, to the detriment of universal principles; all the same, it seems to me a better way of putting a stop to genocide.

From this point of view the EU and the OCSE were well placed to take care of events in Kosovo. What was going on there was not genocide, which would have justified military intervention; it was "only" a civil war (the "only" admittedly includes thousands of victims) involving mass murders, irreconcilable nationalist passions, and the misdeeds of Milosević's corrupt and authoritarian regime. The military intervention that took place almost caused a genocide by turning nearly two million Albanian-speaking inhabitants of Yugoslavia into hostages if not into enemy soldiers. It was not thanks to NATO that the genocide was averted.

The "right to interfere" can itself be questioned, from two perspectives. First, where does this right come from? Havel suggests that it comes from God, but we will let that drop. I mentioned earlier that the rights we have derive from being the citizens of a state, but that clearly does not apply to the right to interfere. We also speak of human rights, which everyone has by simple fact of being human. But it would be an abusive extension of the meaning of this phrase to use it as a reason for interfering in the business of others. If we take on such a responsibility, then we are not talking about a right, but about a duty that we freely assume. Next, this duty cannot be determined by the form that intervention takes (military involvement), but must respond to the needs of whoever requests it. A sufferer has an (unwritten, human) right to be helped, but those who are prepared to help have only a *duty of assistance*.

This implies that we all also share a *duty of presence* — a duty to be aware of what is going on, to be conscious witnesses of our own times. Without this, the duty of assistance that the more active among us will take on could hardly ever be exercised.

The duty of assistance, which serves victims, cannot include military intervention, because even "ethical" wars rarely bring benefits to victims but tend to produce advantages for some at a price paid by others. This does not make military intervention necessarily illegitimate: only the Red Army could have opened the gates of Auschwitz, and we cannot but be grateful for what it did. But its main aim was not humanitarian. It is imperative to maintain a clear distinction between military intervention and humanitarian assistance. Nor does the duty of assistance urge us to impose economic sanctions on a country because we do not approve of its policies: that country's leadership will still find ways of obtaining supplies, and all the shortages and black marketeering that result from sanctions will affect ordinary people already burdened by bad government. (That is the dreadful situation in Iraq today.) All the same, assistance can take many different forms. They may be political (pressure brought to bear on governments), they may be legal, humanitarian, and economic. It seems obvious that if the West had invested in the economies of the Balkan countries instead of financing ever more effective and costly weapons, many conflicts would never have occurred. A further advantage of assistance as compared to interference is that it is offered, not imposed. Because recipients are free to reject it, assistance is less tainted by associations with colonialism.

The duty of assistance is not the same thing as trying to establish the reign of good and cure humanity of its chronic diseases — and it resembles even less attempts to prevent evil from happening by dropping humanitarian bombs. Our fulfillment of this duty may turn out to be as selective as the exercise of the right to interfere, for reasons that include self-interest, maybe more than anything else; but we will not have made use of force and will not bear responsibility for any additional casualties. The duty of assistance is no miracle cure for the world's ills. Aid will often be blocked by governments; and anyway, even if we carried out the duty of assistance to the hilt, the world would still not be a perfect place. You cannot root out evil; but you can cut it back. The dream of universal goodness is itself evil, for it puts abstract aim in the place of real people. Loving kindness, which for Grossman was the opposite of universal good, is always directed toward a specific individual; it cannot be used as the means toward an end, even a sublimely good one.

We have learned bitter lessons from Western military action in Yugoslavia. The persecution of a minority — the Albanian Kosovars — by an unjust and repressive government has been halted, and we should be thankful for that. But we have paid a very high price indeed. NATO soldiers will eventually go back home, but the local people will have to live for decades if not for centuries with the hatred that bombs have planted in their memories. The minorities within the minority, the Serbian and Romi inhabitants of Kosovo, have now become the victims' victims; and the Albanian Kosovars have inherited a devastated country that will have to be subsidized by the UN. The economy of Yugoslavia lies in ruins, its ecology has been damaged and its political situation has

289

been frozen for the year that followed the bombing campaign. The moral self-satisfaction of Western governments has inflated, while other countries reckon that their mistrust of the West has been confirmed by the mess they made in Yugoslavia. And it is a mess. A waste of good intentions, which could have been applied in so many better ways; a waste of passions, now irremediably fixed in resentment and revenge; and a waste of money, since the cost of the weapons and troops deployed exceeded by far the national budgets of the countries in the area.

The military intervention in Yugoslavia was a mistake not because Milosević's policies should have been supported, or because Europe was made to tag along behind the United States, nor even because it occurred outside any legal framework. It was a mistake because the desired results could have been obtained by other means, by means which would not have caused suffering to some in order to mitigate the suffering of others.

Democracy does not have the same effects as totalitarianism; but murdered children can't tell the difference between totalitarian bombs and those humanitarian ones, atomic or not, which are supposed to save numerous lives and bring about a reign of justice and morality. In international relations the difference between totalitarianism and democracy is not as clear as in the domestic sphere, since both types of regime seek world hegemony. In the world as it really is, international relations cannot be separated from the balance of power. All the same, we do not need to be deluded when power pretends to shower free gifts on all, just like at the time of the crusades and the colonial adventure. Nor should we confuse the defense of national interests — a legitimate objective for any government — with the struggle for universal justice. We should choose right over might; but where might faces might, our preference goes to the one that dares say its name rather than to one that hides behind a mask of virtue.

The Achievement of Germaine Tillion

If I had to choose a single episode in the amazing life of Germaine Tillion as an emblem of her existence, it would be this one. It's October 1944 and Germaine Tillion had been interned for nearly a year in Ravensbrück concentration camp. Each day prisoners are sent off in groups to do manual labor outside the camp, but some are exempted, and remain "available" (*verfügbar*) for camp chores. Tillion usually gets to be "available," and today her camp job is unloading and sorting the booty in the rail cars arriving at the camp. But instead of working she decides to hide in a big packing case, where she cooks up an idea. She'll write a comic opera, *The* Verfügbar *in Hell*. Set to music from Offenbach, the plot tells of a naturalist trying to describe the previously unknown species of the *Verfügbar*, and its work-avoidance tactics. The libretto is full of echoes of the fables of La Fontaine and other well-known, lighthearted and popular poems, but the crazy humor of the piece is distinctly black:

> *Choir*: That's enough from you, now! You've earned your pink card and black transport. . . .
> *Nénette*: I don't mind. . . . I'll be going to a model camp with all mod. cons., running water, electricity, and gas.
> *Choir*: Especially gas . . .
>
> (*Ravensbrück* [1988], 230)

Tillion wrote the whole five-act operetta in her cardboard hideaway, and a comrade who had been among those entertained by it brought the manuscript out when the inmates were liberated. It had made them all laugh but had also given a very clear picture of the situation in the camps. A remarkable combination of wit, clearheadedness, and affection.

Germaine Tillion was born in 1907 and after studying psychology and archaeology, she took up ethnology, as a disciple of the great French anthropologist, Marcel Mauss. In the early 1930s even people with no special interest in politics grasped how serious the prospects were. In 1933 she spent three months on a study visit to Königsberg (then in Germany, now Kaliningrad in Russia). She thought that the Nazi students were ridiculous and reckoned that "racism was an utterly execrable idiocy" (*Ethnographie*, 39). But she had no illusions about Communism, either. "Marcel Mauss had the great merit of seeing through Bolshevism as early as 1920. I remember him telling us about Stalin killing people in the Ukraine through organized famine" (*A la recherche*, 52). But politics was not her principal interest: what she really wanted to do was to set off to distant places and to get to know exotic and, best of all, "primitive" peoples. The opportunity arose in 1934 when she won a scholarship to study the Berber population in the Aurès mountains, in the far south of Algeria. Between 1934 and 1940 she made four extended trips to the area, focusing on the social organization of Berber communities.

She got back to Paris in June 1940 as France collapsed in defeat. The terms Pétain proposed for an armistice prompted her immediate decision not to stand idly by. What made her do that was not so much political commitment as instinctive patriotism and faith in the idea of the republic. She came to play a key role in a small Resistance group that gradually formed among a group of intransigent individuals, some of who were connected to the Museum of Mankind. The group, later known as the *Réseau du Musée de l'Homme*, collected information and organized escapes for Allied airmen. In August 1942 a traitor gave Tillion away. She was arrested and imprisoned. The case against her dragged on for over a year, but she was eventually deported to Ravensbrück, a concentration camp for female political prisoners, where she arrived in October 1943. She survived until April 1945 when she was freed in a group rescued by the Swedish Red Cross.

When she got back to France, all her field work notes had disappeared. What also made her reluctant to go back into ethnology was that her mind was now exclusively focused on her camp experience. So she transferred to the modern history section of the newly established national research council, the CNRS, to work on the history of the Resistance and the Deportation. She turned herself from a witness into a professional researcher, putting memory in the service of history. She wrote about the *Réseau du Musée de l'Homme* and about Ravensbrück. But she took a new turn in 1954, when Louis Massignon, one of her former teachers, asked her to go to Algeria, where the troubles had already begun, to investigate what was happening to the civilian population in the colony. Tillion accepted the mission and spent the following eight years in the eye of the storm that turned by stages into the Algerian War.

Germaine Tillion came back to her first avocation in 1962, after a gap of twenty-two years. She threw herself into it and in 1966 brought out *The Republic of Cousins* (*Le Harem et les cousins*), her magnum opus, a study of the social, economic, and family structures of the Mediterranean world dealing primarily with the place of women. Since then, Germaine Tillion has continued writing as an activist, a historian, and an ethnologist.

Despite the apparent diversity and fragmentation of Tillion's different lives, a common thread runs through all her achievements: in the words of Anise Postel-Vinay, who was in Ravensbrück with her, Tillion's twin characteristics are a passion for understanding and affection for other people (Postel-Vinay 133). Two virtues we could certainly do with in the twenty-first century — which is why it is worth looking at them more closely.

At the broadest level there is no need to justify the feeling that makes us want to understand the world; after all, it's something produced by our very identity as human beings. Germaine Tillion says it is "exhilarating in itself" because "awareness and comprehension are the more profound vocations of the human species and one of the goals of humanity's place on the evolutionary scale" (*Ravensbrück* [1975], 164). For our own fulfillment, we need to find meaning in an existence situated in the inexorable flow of time, and we need also to find an order in the world to which we can relate — and only through understanding can we reach any kind of meaning. Which explains Germaine Tillion's choices. "All my life I've wanted to understand human nature and the world in which I lived" (*A la recherche*, 58).

But the need to understand is not the only reason for seeking meaning. We don't live in a vacuum but in concrete situations, which may also bring us suffering, oppression, and violence. If we understand how they work, we acquire the means to act on them; and even before we take any action, using the mind to get a grip on an event may provide relief. Outside her professional activities (ethnology, in effect, can be seen as an attempt to understand others) Germaine Tillion had the opportunity to observe the benefits of understanding during her imprisonment at Ravensbrück and in her time in Algeria. "I was in a position, in two different circumstances, to take the measure of people's bewilderment when confronted with the world they had made, and on both occasions I saw what real succor the crushed may draw from understanding — that is to say, from analyzing — the mechanisms that are crushing them" (*Harem*, 20). The same thing happens with mourning. When we learn that a loved one has died, we are paralyzed, struck dumb; but when we are able to relate this unheralded event into a series of preceding, concomitant, and subsequent facts, we can begin to mourn.

Knowledge of humankind starts with the discovery of the existence of another human being who seems similar but also completely different; the wish to interpret the nature of this (dis)similarity is expressed through contact, questions and answers. The gradual uncovering of the identity of the other gives the subject new light on his or her own identity, and the ability to distinguish between what is universal and what is singular. This never-finished process lies at the heart of all dialogue. Ethnology, Tillion says, has a role in the mutual knowledge of different peoples that is analogous to the role that dialogue has between individuals: an exchange of thought corrected by constant feedback. The other allows me to discover what I did not know about myself, even if the other never has access to what I alone know; and the pattern repeats, reciprocally. You do not have "human nature" on one side and "the primitive" on the other; you just have two varieties of the same human nature. The journey through otherness can lift each of us away from our own singularity and teach us what humanity is, in a way that naive egocentricity never can. Ethnology is therefore in the first place a dialogue with another culture. Then it is a questioning of the difference between "self" and "other." Then, if possible, it becomes a confrontation transcending the distinction of self and other.

The academic discipline of ethnology does not consist exclusively in knowledge of the other, as you might suppose, but also in putting "us" and "them" into relationship. That was the lesson Tillion originally learned from Mauss, who, she said, was just as interested in his contemporaries and neighbors as in exotic peoples. Whence comes her only apparently surprising conclusion: "To understand one civilization properly, one must know at least two—and deeply" (*France and Algeria*, 177). There is no knowledge of the human world except through comparison: which is why there will always be an element of subjectivity in it.

The tool of the ethnographer's trade, understanding, stood the camp inmate in good stead. Looking at the horror of the world around you was a better way of surviving than feeling sorry for yourself. And if you were strong enough to do that, then you could be tempted to share your understanding with others. At Ravensbrück Germaine Tillion was the prisoner who tried to bring her comrades a little clarity about their own situation, even while fear and suffering prompted them to bury their heads in the sand. She found out as much as she could and shared what she knew, in a variety of ways—in the operetta, and in a tough sociology lecture she gave in March 1944, in the walkway between two blocks in the camp. "Nothing is more frightening than the absurd. In trying to get rid of stupid gossip I was aware that I was giving moral support to the best of us" (*Ravensbrück* [1988], 200). The lecture, which described the way in which the Nazis' extermination-through-labor system worked, was not exactly lighthearted, but it nonetheless gave comfort to its inmate audience. Knowledge, in this instance, contributed directly to self-preservation.

Straight after she was freed, still in Sweden and still numbed by the murder of her mother, who had also been at Ravensbrück, Germaine Tillion began a study of what had just come to an end. She conducted detailed interviews of every one of the camp survivors. She entitled the first article that came out of this research "In Search of the Truth" "because this anguished quest for the truth about Ravensbrück gave me the courage to make all the necessary inquiries" (*Ravensbrück* [1975], viii). Shortly after, she decided to change profession—to drop ethnology for history—because it seemed vital to collect as much information as possible so as to try to understand the horror. She saw her task as a double one. First, she was, so to speak, obligated to her comrades from the Resistance and the camps to establish the facts and record the actions. Second, she needed to try to understand how the perpetrators of evil had ended up doing what they had done. It was a painful but necessary decision to "interrupt my studies of North African civilization . . . to devote myself to an examination of the 'decivilization' in Europe" (*Ravensbrück* [1975], xiii). "I'd decided to abandon ethnology and to put all my efforts into understanding how a European people with a higher than average level of education had managed to sink into such lunacy" (*A la recherche*, 58). For anyone brought up in the Enlightenment tradition, that was indeed a mystery that needed solving.

Contemporary history is not an easy discipline to pursue. The search for the truth, in the factual or the deeper sense, can be blocked by the protagonists, who are by definition biased. Since the good and the evil sides are already identified and beyond dispute, former perpetrators seek to exculpate themselves and justify their actions, whereas former victims strive to blacken their names as much as they can. "In circles affected by the camp murders, people are extremely touchy: anything that serves to increase the guilt of the perpetrators is accepted without question, and the slightest reservation unleashes great indignation" (*Ravensbrück* [1988], 282). Germaine Tillion knew that she was not and never would be an impartial witness; she was quite scrupulous in gathering and checking facts but perfectly aware of the choices that controlled the way she understood them. This is not something we should regret. The human world is shot through with values, and it cannot be understood in their absence. "Living and acting without taking sides is inconceivable" (*Ravensbrück* [1988], 283), and the best you can do is to be fully aware of the side you have taken. But you also have to avoid the regular pitfalls of research work and resist being brilliant when the truth is just dull. The documentary film, *The Sorrow and the Pity*, she said, exploited the "shocking quartertruth" of outright collaboration to the detriment of the other, less spectacular three-quarters of the truth, namely the fact that the majority were hostile to the German occupation (*A la recherche*, 134).

Knowledge may be one of the vocations of the human race, and that would be enough to justify it, but it can also be of use to men and women. That is something Germaine Tillion never forgot. In her ethnological work she wanted her writings to be of some use to the people they dealt with, and for that reason she took care to write in clear, everyday language that everyone can understand. She did not hesitate to accept the mission that Massignon offered her in 1954 because it was an opportunity to use ethnological research to ease tensions between French and Algerians. Knowledge is not there just to be piled ever higher; it also ought to make a contribution to action whenever it can. "I considered my professional obligations as an ethnologist to be similar to those of a barrister, except that they obliged me to defend a people, not a person" (*Afrique*, 18–19).

If that is true of academic knowledge garnered disinterestedly, how much truer must it be of knowledge acquired through physical suffering, through the privations and torture of camp life. Camp survivors have rights, but also duties. They must use their experience and their prestige to fight all future manifestations of evil—which will necessarily look different and yet be comparable. Not long after she got out of Ravensbrück, Germaine Tillion became a prison visitor (admittedly, none of the inmates were Resistance fighters any longer). She was particularly proud of having helped to introduce prison education in France in 1959. Since then it has been possible to go to prison as an illiterate and to come out with a university degree. This campaign is characteristic of Tillion's kind of commitment. She didn't aim to create paradise on earth or to cure humankind of its criminal instincts, for human life will always be an "imperfect garden." What she did was to make a small but real difference for the better, by giving prisoners access to culture. It is not the only example of such action. In 1950 David Rousset set up his International Commission on Concentration Camps (which led to a split between the Communists and non-Communists among camp survivors), and Tillion served on the panel at the Brussels tribunal in 1951. It was as a delegate of Rousset's commission that Tillion went back to Algeria in 1957 to investigate allegations of torture in French prisons and camps.

So when Germaine Tillion decided to work on Algeria again, she did so not just as a former ethnologist but also as a camp survivor. Her first book on Algeria, as it happens, came out of a report she wrote on "the Algerian events" at the request of the Association of Ex-Deportees to which she belonged. "In 1956 I insisted on dedicating what I knew about the extreme poverty of what we call the Third World to my comrades from the camps, because of their personal experience of extreme suffering" (*Afrique*, 63). Like David Rousset, who saw the camp survivors as those best qualified to research concentration camps still in existence, Tillion thought that ex-inmates should have something to say on the misfortunes of colonized peoples.

Throughout her activity in Algeria (not just in her investigation of torture in prison) Tillion kept her experience in the Resistance and at Ravensbrück in mind. When she got back to the Aurès in 1954 after fourteen years absence, she saw French soldiers searching an old shepherd. "The terrified peasant put up his hands in the now universal manner of the arrested. It was a scene I'd often observed on the streets of Paris between 1940 and 1942, but I had never seen it in Algeria between 1934 and 1940" (*Afrique*, 21). The executions of Algerian freedom fighters hit her hard, because they reminded her of the ten members of the *Réseau du Musée de l'Homme* who were shot by the Germans in February 1942, despite all her attempts to intervene on their behalf (and which made her own case all the worse). "For several months, and several times a week, I then had occasion to say farewell to comrades who were taken to the execution stake, and the indignation, the fury and the grief I felt then are still alive in me today," she wrote in 1957 (*France and Algeria*, 43). At the time, her comparison of the glorious era of the Resistance with the "terrorist" actions of the Algerian independence fighters met with little understanding and provoked a great deal of indignation.

Memories are not enough: you have to see what uses are to be made of them. Memories of past defeats can fire patriotism, and memories of past victories can feed pacifism — both of which can lead to war. Unforgotten pain is not necessarily a good counselor. "Humiliation is never forgotten and can always easily turn into violence or betrayal," she wrote, to explain Pétain's attitude in 1940 (*A la recherche*, 64). Some former members of the Resistance joined the infamously violent parachute troops in Algeria, seeking compensation for the defeat of 1940 — this time, they would succeed in defending France! Germaine Tillion, for her part, saw in her past experience a reason for campaigning against the death penalty.

The principle underlying the action of people like Germaine

Tillion is to keep faith with justice, not with a group. "In 1957, in Algeria, there was behavior identical to that of the Nazis. And I hated Nazism, and fought it with all my heart" (*Traversée*, 110). And that is why she joined battle—not on the side of the FLN, the military wing of the Algerian independence movement, but on the side of humanity, against war, torture, and summary execution.

The Algerian War was not Germaine Tillion's last struggle. After it ended, she worked for international bodies seeking to eradicate slavery and hunger, and to defend the rights of minorities. She also campaigned for the abolition of clitoridectomy, "that barbarous torture"; and all these actions were undertaken in the name of principles that had been strengthened and clarified by her wartime experience. Her close acquaintance with colonial life served her well when she launched herself into the fearsomely difficult task of decolonizing women. "At a time of widespread decolonization, the huge world of women seems in many respects to be a colony," she wrote (*Harem*, 199). She also wrote about recent conflicts in Yugoslavia and Rwanda, where majorities and minorities have fought over the ownership of territory. She continued to be revolted by the poverty of the developing world and protested against its descent into chaos through pauperization combined with the destruction of traditional social and family structures. The same disastrous trend can be seen in the shantytowns, *favelas, barrios*, and housing schemes on the peripheries of major cities. In retrospect, the concentration camp system looks like pauperization taken to "a rational extreme" in the attempt to extract every last drop of advantage from it (*Afrique*, 85)—an instance of the constant feedback between different fields of knowledge, which makes it possible to bridge the gap between knowledge and action.

The "passion for understanding" is, after all, not surprising. More baffling is the other unchanging theme of Tillion's existence, her affection for her fellow beings. A large part of her life's experience could be summed up as a journey through hell (which is the title she used for a book of conversations with her biographer, Jean Lacouture). Tillion suggests that two tiny groups of people can be distinguished from the rest of humanity: the utter brutes, including venal traitors and methodical sadists; and "people of great courage and great selflessness"

(*France and Algeria*, 130) who do not abuse power even when they hold it, but put it instead in the service of good. The rest of us, the vast majority, are in neither of these two groups; we are ordinary folk, harmless in times of peace and prosperity, but liable to turn "quite disagreeable" once threatened.

The individual Nazis Tillion encountered at Ravensbrück and even those in the higher echelons beyond it were not monsters; they were, rather, mediocre people trained in such a way as to be able to carry out monstrous acts. Nothing in them or in their lives up to that point marked them out as different from the civilized average. The prisoners played a sad game among themselves, placing bets on how long it would take for a new female guard to be transformed from her initially shy and likeable self into a brute who takes pleasure in beatings (average time taken: one to two weeks). Tillion saw the same process happening among French soldiers in Algeria. "I have known mild and silent men whom the four hours in the plane was enough to transform into crude fanatics" (*France and Algeria*, 159). The French colonists in Algeria were also unexceptional people. As at Ravensbrück, the only folk you came across were plain and ordinary. Even Himmler, the supreme commander of the empire of the camps, was, in Tillion's estimation, "an opportunist pen-pusher, with an obsessive and blinkered mind, who by accident acquired means out of all proportion to his mediocre abilities" (*Ravensbrück* [1988], 95). (The chapter on Himmler is called "Monsters Are Men.") These observations should not be taken as reassuring, they should rather disturb us. "It is enough to make you really scared, because the womb that gives birth to ordinary people is even more fertile than that of the Beast" (*Ravensbrück* [1988], 98).

The same may be said of groups and, in particular, of nationalities. After her release Tillion went on resenting the Polish women who had abused their positions of power in the camp, and she said so. In the second edition of *Ravensbrück*, however, she changed her position and confessed that she regretted her earlier stand. "I hasten today to say that I am ashamed of this judgment, for I am convinced that in a similar situation any other national group would have committed similar abuses" (*Ravensbrück* [1975], 28). It is obviously very tempting to treat the Germans as intrinsically evil, but doing so only demonstrates our fear of coming too close to evil ourselves. "I have heard a great deal said about the cruelty and depravity of the 'German race.' How reassuring it would be to simply think in these terms, and thus limit the responsibility for all the calamities! The truth is, however, that racism and Nazism are phenomena whose causes can be neither 'racial' nor 'national'" (*Ravensbrück* [1975], 63).

Having understood that perpetrators of evil are people like any other, Tillion strove to maintain the distinction between the doer and the deed, that is to say, to avoid essentializing crime. "One dreams of a justice pitiless to the crime and pitying to the criminal," she wrote (*France and Algeria*, 149), not knowing that she was paraphrasing something that Grossman wrote about the same time, quoting in his turn "a truth spoken by a sixth-century Syrian Christian: condemn the sin and pardon the sinner" (*Life and Fate*, Bk 1, Ch. 4). A dream, maybe, but one that sometimes comes true. In 1950 Tillion took the trouble to go to Germany to testify *for the defense* at the trial of two former Ravensbrück guards charged with imaginary crimes. She had taken part in the trial of her own prison guards in 1947 and, though she was satisfied to see their acts punished by the court, she could not help feeling "alarm and pity" even for people such as them (*Traversée*, 88); and the same feeling was aroused in her by the trial of Pétain, which she also attended.

During the Algerian War everyone in France had to decide whether they were for keeping Algeria French or for letting go of the colony. What options were there for people who refused to divide the world into black and white, or who believed that "no human lineage has a monopoly on intelligence or fairness, and all have an equal and overwhelming proportion of scoundrels and imbeciles among their forebears" (*Afrique*, 69)? Inevitably, the extremists of both camps detested Tillion. Jacques Vergès, the FLN's defense lawyer, and his sworn enemies, the fanatical supporters of *Algérie française*, hated Tillion equally; and even dogmatic Parisian intellectuals who thought they knew what the truth was and where good and bad were to be found looked down on her with disdain. From Simone de Beauvoir's diary-novel, *La Force des choses*: "We all had dinner at Marie-Claire's place and tore Germaine Tillion's article to pieces. Bost,

301

Lanzmann, and I think it is a piece of shit" (quoted in *A la re-cherche*, 257).

If the causes of racism and Nazism were neither racial nor national, what were they? Tillion's *Ravensbrück* contains a great wealth of descriptive material and psychological analysis, but it hardly touches on the deeper roots of the European catastrophe. On the other hand, Tillion has a clearer view of the causes of the Algerian War and of the pauperization of the developing world: they are to be found in the uncoordinated rhythms of historical evolution and in the fact that contact occurred between peoples at different stages of development. Evil, for Tillion, is not endemic to the human condition but the product of particular situations — of which there are unfortunately very many. "There are good men and bad men, and situations in which, furthermore, all fools are bad. Unfortunately, fools are legion" (*France and Algeria*, 153).

Tillion's affection for her fellow beings does not involve turning a blind eye to what she sometimes calls "the proclivities of the human species" (*Ravensbrück* [1988], 188) or, more bluntly, "the horrific dimension of humanity" (*Afrique*, 12). She has no illusions about the human race, but she does not believe that its bad sides are its only characteristics. The outcome is always open. "There are no truly 'mediocre' individuals in the moral sense, only people who never meet circumstances which could reveal their full potential," she wrote at the end of the 1988 edition of *Ravensbrück* (283). Human beings are morally indeterminate; they are both good and bad; their field of action is unlimited.

How does good arise? Like Romain Gary and Vasily Grossman, Tillion saw the love and care given the infant by its mother and father as the *fons et origo* of moral goodness. In normal circumstances parental love instills in the infant "a disposition to happiness" (*Traversée*, 34) and the capacity for reciprocating love. For writers like Gary and Tillion, a child's love and joy at the existence of others serves as a recurrent symbol of what can give a sense to a human life. Gary, for example, when speculating on the nature of happiness, recalls a memory from earliest childhood: "I was in bed, I was listening, listening hard, then I heard the turn of the key . . . I kept quiet, smiling, waiting, and I was happy" (*La Nuit*, 362). In the dedication of

302

one of her books to her teacher Massignon, Tillion tries to sum up his exemplary life "given to others"—and expresses herself in almost exactly the same way. She had visited the ailing Massignon a few weeks before his death, and as she sat with him, he "suddenly stood up, transfigured by the youthful and luminous joy in his eyes." What had happened? "He had heard the faint noise of a key turning in the landing door. 'I know that key!' he must have thought. It was indeed his daughter coming in to see him" (*Afrique*, 14). Human beings are also capable of love and for that reason you cannot banish love from your heart. That was the meaning Tillion saw in the "surge of youthful paternal affection [in Massignon's aged eyes] more powerful than the greed of death and the exhaustion of a life that had run its course" (*Afrique*, 14).

Ravensbrück strengthened Tillion's respect for the individual, because good was not absent from that place of ubiquitous evil. Selfishness and selflessness flowered side by side, as if the camp soil prompted people to grow into selves that had up to then been overshadowed by social conventions. Goodness came out in very ordinary virtues—in maintaining your own personal dignity, in looking after others, whether they be close comrades or complete strangers (nobody survived the camps without help from others), and in using your mind (for example, in Tillion's own efforts to understand that "other kingdom" and to share her understanding with her comrades).

From the moment she was released and out of immediate danger, Tillion did not cease offering help to strangers—not through party politics or by trying to build a new Jerusalem, but by tackling and trying to solve specific problems. For example, she helped make education accessible to all—to Algerian peasants, in 1955, and French prison inmates, in 1959; and, uninterruptedly, to women everywhere (a cause that was particularly dear to her heart). Her book on *The Republic of Cousins* (*Le Harem et les cousins*) was a searching analysis of the condition of women, but academic scholarship led Tillion toward action: women needed education if they were to emerge from subjection.

Tillion certainly chose the right path: but travel in the right direction does not necessarily get you to your destination. Tillion learned that the hard way in Algeria in the 1950s. When she got back there in 1954, after fourteen years away, she tried to diagnose what had changed. What struck her most were not the political and military issues but the degradation of the social and economic situation of the Muslim population. The Algerians were stranded in midstream: their traditional structures had collapsed on contact with European industrial civilization, but they had not yet acquired the skills and qualifications they needed to build new structures for themselves. The peasant population had grown at a staggering rate and could no longer live off the land; so people were flocking to the shantytowns, which condemned them to pauperization. Evil, in this case, was the product of demography and technology, and so the remedy had to be found in demography and technology too. Since the clock could not be turned back, the important thing was to give former peasants the means to acquire the kinds of knowledge necessary for survival in a modern society. Tillion worked hard to set up a network of "Social Centers," designed to provide the Algerians with appropriate training and education. "My dream was to give a professional skill to every Algerian who could no longer live off the land. To achieve that we had to set up an Algerian education system equivalent to what we had in France" (*Ethnographie*, 20).

It could have worked, given time; but time was in short supply in Algeria in 1955. The most energetic among the Muslims aspired to an immediate solution called independence; but France, with its one million *colons* living in Algeria, was understandably reluctant to agree to letting go. So independence could only be gained by force. Tillion's preferred solution had support from none of the parties involved in the conflict. It did not suit the independence movement, since the recipe implied continuing formal links between France and Algeria (the French were to be the Algerians' teachers); and it did not suit the anti-independence movement either, since it involved giving Algerians the means to run their own affairs. By the time Tillion published *Algeria: The Realities* in 1957, where she gives her diagnosis and her proposed cure, it was already too late. Guns were already talking, and nobody could hear the teachers any more. Algeria had more urgent matters to attend to than Tillion's ideas; but her economic analysis, which has been proved accurate by subsequent history, was turned into a supporting argument by those

who wanted to keep Algeria French. The "Social Centers" were
swept away by the storm, and staff members were persecuted
and murdered by the OAS.

As we've seen, Tillion went back to Algeria in 1957, when the
war was at its height, to investigate the use of torture in prisons.
The panel on which she sat made its report public, but that did
not stop the parachute troops under the command of General
Massu from using torture ever more widely so as to win the
Battle of Algiers. Something extraordinary then happened.
"Someone" wanted to meet Germaine Tillion. She later learned
that the "someone" was Saâdi Yacef and Ali La Pointe, the head
and the second-in-command of military operations for the Algiers region, that is to say, the two most sought-after "terrorists" of the day. Tillion decided to seize the opportunity to
speak with the "enemy." She had a wide network of Algerian
friends and was in good standing in the Muslim community; on
the French side, where she had no official position, several of
her former Resistance comrades were now in government, and
she still had access to them.

On 4 July 1957 Germaine Tillion was taken by an unknown
guide through the Algiers casbah to a room where two women
and two men — Yacef and Ali — were waiting for her. They
talked for the whole afternoon. Tillion tried to negotiate a truce.
She knew full well that each act of violence provoked an even
more violent response from the other side. If she could get one
of the sides to make a gesture, then maybe she could halt this
mortal escalation. What disgusted the French settlers more than
anything were the attacks on civilians; what provoked the FLN's
violence most of all were executions of its members. Since she
had two senior FLN fighters in front of her, why not give it a
go? She spoke at length and with conviction and after a few
hours Yacef, with tears in his eyes, burst out: "I promise you
we'll not hit civilians ever again!" That was what she was after.
As she left the room, Germaine Tillion turned to Ali La Pointe,
took hold of his collar and shook him a bit by the scruff the
neck, saying: "Have you really understood what I said?" The
cowed terrorist answered "Yes, ma'am." And off she went.

When she got back to Paris she reported on the conversation
to her contacts in government. There was a condition to Yacef's
promise: France had to promise to stop executing FLN mem-

305

bers. The agreement held for two weeks, and there was a dramatic decline in acts of violence. But on 24 July the truce was broken by the French with three executions in the prison of Algiers. The FLN broke the truce on its side in September when Yacef was arrested. The war would go on for another four years, leaving many victims in its wake and ineradicable memories in people's minds (memories that are not unrelated to the current violence in Algeria). Tillion tried but failed. Whose fault was that? Some of the blame must lie with those who considered Tillion's intervention to be "a piece of shit," or an act of deception and treason (General Massu, for example, who gave his own version of these events in 1971). Tillion's reply to these accusations asserted that it was Massu who, by using torture to win the Battle of Algiers, had lost the war. Summing up, she said: "The disastrous result was the fruit of unacceptable means" (*A la recherche*, 263).

Tillion saw the armed conflict as a confrontation of two groups of "reciprocal terrorists," the FLN and the French *colons* backed by the army, who had forgotten that they were in truth complementary to each other. They reminded her of brainless Canadian moose who lock their antlers in combat, fail to disentangle themselves, and die in pairs. Both sides lose in fights of that kind. Torture and terrorism justify each other. Peace can only come from mutual trust, but trust can only come from peace. So war goes on.

Germaine Tillion could not accept the heroic versions of the Algerian war: "We (the French, or the Algerians, no matter) were the stronger, and so we won." Nor did she accept the victim versions: "We had right on our side but we were betrayed, so we now deserve reparations." Only the third way remains open: the tragic narrative, which sees the positions of both parties to the conflict and attends to the damage done to both. She was not alone in adopting the tragic view. Louis Massignon, she wrote, also suffered through every minute of the Algerian war. "With his clear mind and his numerous sources of information, he could not help but know everything; nor could he turn a blind eye to any of the victims, since he felt a fraternal bond and a shared responsibility with the guilty men on both sides" (*Afrique*, 13). What makes a tragedy is precisely identification not only with the victims but also with the perpetrators of evil on both sides of the dilemma. Albert Camus (one of Tillion's few consistent backers; he wrote the preface to the English translation of her book on *Algeria: The Realities*) put himself in a very similar position. When he said that he understood the Muslim position as well as he understood the French, and that he always supported the underdog of the day, extremists on both sides of the Algerian conflict called for him to be strung from the nearest lamppost.

Germaine Tillion knew full well that she had not chosen the easiest path. She knew she had sentenced herself to grief (sympathy for the victims) and to shame (feeling responsible). She took on dangerous missions during the war because she could identify with both sides, "partly out of patriotism and partly because of the extreme compassion I felt for the miseries of the Algerian people" (*France and Algeria*, 41). What can you do if you understand both sides and won't sacrifice any part of the truth? "Nothing was more alarming than to listen to the echoes of two worlds so close and so distinct" (*France and Algeria*, 172). All she could do was accept the tragic plight of humanity. In 1956 she wrote: "The Algerian tragedy, as I see it, has many victims and few traitors — but its possible solutions all look like starting points for more tragedies" (*Afrique*, 66). Sadly, that has turned out to be a fair prediction.

Since then, the world has not grown better. Fate did not spare Germaine Tillion the unbearable grief of losing a loved one, which produces only ineffectual anger. Her mother, like Grossman's, died at the hand of Nazi barbarians. Yet she managed to "journey through hell" without being contaminated by evil, and she even passed on to us a feeling of exhilaration. Again like Grossman, Tillion found the heart of her message in the image of a mother sacrificed and made all the more worthy of love for having been a victim of ghastly brutality. Both of them felt they had a mission — to bring to life the teaching of a mother who died in silence. How did Tillion succeed in this act of transfiguration? What concatenation of forces allowed her to do so?

When you read what she wrote, you often feel as though you are looking at a split personality. But the two sides of the split do not contradict each other; they complement each other harmoniously. She is both a woman of action moved by affections for her fellow beings and an observer of events with a passion for knowledge. Each side of Tillion constantly serves the other.

The observer can relax tension at the most dramatic moments in the life of the woman of action, by offering a more distant view in which unintentionally comical aspects come to the fore. For example, Tillion was arrested by the German military police, on information received, for participating in the Resistance. "There then occurred a rather amusing scene," she says in her memoirs. How so, amusing? Well, her outwardly desperate situation reminded her of a Fulani folk tale that says, God can be just as kind to a man trying to swim across a river as He can be to a hungry crocodile. The thought of that story, and the ability to see her own plight in those terms, kept Germaine Tillion calm and collected. "I thought, sadly but not in panic, today God has been kind to the crocodile" (*Traversée*, 63–64). Some months later, the prison commissar told her she was to be shot next morning. There was something funny about the situation, Tillion writes: and this time the drollery was that the commissar was even more surprised by her calmness than she was.

Tillion's capacity to be "outside" and "inside" at the same time was not a secondary elaboration, but a capacity she enjoyed in the thick of action. Everyone should read — to themselves, and then to their children — the amazing letter Tillion wrote from her prison cell to the magistrate who had charged her with offenses punishable by death. A masterpiece of sly humor and barely masked irony ("I would be deeply hurt to be accused of irony"), it gives a clear account of her activities, with the help of quotations from popular songs. She confesses to having practiced witchcraft in Africa but adds that her powers are not infinite. "If the gentlemen of the German police really have lost their innocence, then I'm afraid I am unable to get it back for them" (*Ravensbrück* [1988], 35–36). It's as if the sheer joy of writing witty and stylish French almost allowed her to forget the ghastly situation she was in. Something similar occurred in the train taking her to the concentration camp, a circumstance you would not think particularly conducive to joking. When she had been a junior research scientist in the Aurès region of Algeria, she used to go around with a tiny desert fox sitting on her shoulder, on a leash made of a watch chain. On the train to Germany, she found a photograph of the fox in her pocket and went up to the SS guard. Her comrades were terrified, but she said, "I'll show you how to tame a wild animal." "Carefully, patiently, and very sweetly she put the photo in front of the guard's eyes, and finally tugged on his sleeve. They ended up having a kind of conversation" (Postel-Vinay, "Une ethnologue," 126).

Without her long practice as an observer Tillion would never have been able to maintain the distance that allowed her to behave with such a calm and clever sense of *à propos*. Conversely her research publications never obscure the fact that they were written by a particular person and are marked by the faults, qualities, habits, and quirks of that person. When she was asked how she wrote *Il était une fois l'ethnographie* (Once upon a time, ethnography . . .) she answered "By cutting half of it because I wanted to get away on holiday without it hanging over me." This scholarly book's dedication is as astounding as the ironical letter she wrote to the magistrate from prison. It's addressed to the reader — in Ogden Nash–style rhyming verse! Even when she was doing field work, she never tried to be a scholar pure and simple. "When I first encountered Africa I imagined rather stupidly that the 'human sciences' were like a chemical suspension which ethnologists had to leave undisturbed, for fear of clouding the mineral deposits. Very fortunately, my sympathies led me on various occasions to disregard my theories" (from the introduction to another story included in *Once upon a time*, and which should be in every anthology, *Ethnographie*, 129). *Once upon a time* . . . is perhaps the most unfettered academic book ever written; you can feel that its author has reached a position where she no longer needs conventions and is seeking only to recount her own experience as precisely as possible. It creates an exhilarating impression on every reader, myself included.

Germaine Tillion is an old lady now, but she remains one of the most luminous public personalities to have glowed in the darkness of the twentieth century. Let's hope that with the privilege of her vast experience she can take the human race by the scruff of its neck, shake it around for a bit, and ask: "Are you sure you've understood what I said?" And let's hope that humankind hangs down its head before answering: "Yes, ma'am."

The Next Hundred Years

THE twentieth century may have ended but it has not ceased to haunt our memories. What I have tried to do in this book is explore those memories in two complementary ways, through conceptual analyses of events and through narratives of individual lives. What remains is to bring together some of the lessons that I think I have drawn and to wonder what they might teach us about the century to come.

A lesson about memory, first of all. The choice that we have is not between remembering and forgetting; because forgetting can't be done by an act of the will, it is not something we can choose to do. The choice is between different ways of remembering. There is no such thing as a "duty of memory"; remembering may serve good ends and bad ones, it may be used to further self-interest just as it may be used for the good of others. Memories do not always bear fruit and may even lead us astray. If we treat the past as holy, we exclude it from the world of meaning and prevent it from teaching lessons that might apply to other times and places, to other agents of history. But we do just as much damage through the opposite approach: making the past trivial by likening present events to past ones too easily, trawling it for facile solutions to current issues, betrays history, distorts the present, and opens the door to injustice. An obsession with analogies is just as deplorable as blind attachment to literal facts. Auschwitz and Hitler do have lessons to teach us, but there is nothing to be seen in the world today that is at all like Hitler or Auschwitz. The past is only fertile if we grant that it has to be passed through the filter of abstraction and become part of current debates about justice and injustice.

We may like to appeal to "memory," but our behavior does not show greater wisdom than that of our forebears. We may condemn the racism and violence of our neighbors and grandparents, without ceasing to be racist and violent in our own way: for we learn little from others' mistakes. We take a harsh view of the ignorance and credulity of others, but we are just the same when we put our faith in statements made by presidents and prime ministers broadcast by uncritical media organs.

Our relationship to time has certainly changed. Traditional societies with stable, immobile populations and rituals repeated year after year have gone forever. The world around us is in flux, and we need different information all the time; preservation of the past is under threat. We have also come to prefer not to notice how time passes. We pretend we are living in a perpetual present, without transitional phases (childhood, old age), and death itself is put out of sight in the geriatric ward.

Modern individuals seek to defend themselves against this kind of assault (for it is an assault), against this amputation of identity. It is as if we are aware, and terrified, of the acceleration of time, and are doing all we can to apply the brakes. But the remedy is part of the illness. The destruction of traditional markers prompts new commemorations. We cling to the singularity of individual memory or else make a great show of the past, treating it as a universal key for explaining the present. Will we manage to avoid falling into these opposite and equally lamentable traps? Can we accept both the passing of time and the need to live in the present, while acknowledging that the present is also made, substantially and morally, by the past?

I have spent the longest portion of this book dealing with a central development in the history of Europe in the twentieth century, the opposition of totalitarianism and democracy. An opposition that played itself out not only in military and economic conflict but also between the major moral and political principles that lie at the root of the two regimes. The totalitarian attack on democracy made the elements of humanist thought that underlie democracy that much clearer. Totalitarianism promises happiness for all — but only when all who are not worthy of it (enemy classes, inferior races) have been wiped out. It denies the autonomy of individual subjects, it denies them the right to choose the norms by which they live, even while asserting that society as a whole should have no limit set on its freedom — by God, nature, moral universals, or human rights. It gives human action transindividual ends, such as the party, the nation, or the regime; and it accepts the sacrifice of the individual in the service of revolution, ideal society, or cleansed humanity. Democracy, on the other hand, adheres to the finality of *thou*, which makes the *other person* the legitimate aim of an individual's action, just as it asserts the autonomy of the *I*, the individual subject with the right to "acquiesce or resist," as well as the universality of *they*, which is any member of the human species, endowed with the same dignity as all others. Democracy is thus founded on humanist thought.

Modern humanism — critical humanism — has two distinctive features, neither very special, but which draw force from their conjunction. The first is recognition of the horrific evil that people can do. This kind of humanism is not at all a cult of humankind, in general or in particular; it does not cling to the basic nobility of human nature. On the contrary, Auschwitz and Kolyma, the greatest proofs ever given in the twentieth century of the evil people can do to each other, are where critical humanism begins. Its second characteristic is to affirm the possibility of good. Not the universal triumph of goodness, or the coming of paradise on earth, but a good that leads us to take people in their concrete individuality as the ultimate ends of all action and as objects worthy of love and affection. Humanism does not put a supernatural being, or subhuman natural forces, or abstract values invented by man (prosperity, revolution, purity, the laws of history) in place of humankind. How is it possible to reconcile this disillusioned view of humanity with the assertion that human beings must be the ultimate beneficiary of human action? That is the challenge faced by modern humanists who come after Kolyma and Auschwitz.

Knowing the history of the twentieth century makes us want to know whether in the foreseeable future we face the threat of a return of totalitarianism, as a way of life or even just as a mental model. But the future is not foreseeable. There's a story about a clairvoyant who stunned audiences with his ability to see other times and places. "What is the pope doing right now?" The clairvoyant knew the answer. "What will our city be like a hundred years in the future?" He could answer that one too, in every detail. Then a little boy stood up and asked: "What am I holding behind my back?" That floored the performer, and he left the stage in ridicule and shame. The moral of the tale is that it is safer to foretell what will happen in the next millennium or in the wide world than to guess what might happen here, tomorrow, or even to try to see what features of the present might be indicators of what the future holds. But now I will cast safety aside to speculate on what my analysis of the past suggests about the future course of events.

In Europe, the material and psychological damage done by the totalitarian experiment has been, I think, far too profound for totalitarian doctrines to be at all attractive in the near future. Of course there are neo-Nazi groups as well as small sections of the population still dreaming of a Communist utopia, but their chances of taking power are negligible. But the evaporation of that threat does not signal the start of a "post-historical" idyll. The defeat of totalitarianism does not remove democracy from all peril.

What we have seen in the preceding chapters suggests that there are three main risks for democracy. These risks are difficult to resist because they arise from the hypertrophy, or overinflation, of features of democratic life, which in small doses are positively useful to it. And they challenge the very basic postulates of humanist doctrine.

The first danger is *an excess of identity politics*. Individual and collective identities are essential to social existence, as we remarked; memory, in particular, serves to construct and consolidate such identities. But this legitimate demand becomes improper when keeping faith with a collective identity overrides the essential democratic values of the individual and of universality. Democracy tolerates intermediate bodies (communities within the broad entity of a society) but does not give them a privileged role; it requires all individuals within a state to have the same rights, but does not allow any individual to abandon either his free will or her reason for the benefit of the ethnic, linguistic, religious, racial, or sexual community to which he or she belongs. A democratic state is not a "state by nature" and does not require all its citizens to possess common cultural or physical characteristics or to come from the same background; it only requires them all to subscribe tacitly to the same contract.

The situation creates its own frustrations, which themselves give rise to nostalgia for old-style community — whence the rise of all those "us-isms" that Levi wrote about. Collective self-seeking is an increasing trend at the present, in Western democracies as elsewhere, and one of its aims is to extort collective privileges from the state for members of identity-based communities. Individuals have the right to belong to a community, to be sure, but

314

they are not obliged to do so. Communities are welcome in a democracy, on the condition that they do not foster inequalities or intolerance.

The second danger, less familiar but no less damaging, is *moral correctness*. A fundamental rule of democratic states is to recognize the plurality and diversity of their citizens, and for that reason they ensure the plurality of their institutions. The ground floor of pluralism is the separation of the political and religious domains. Mixing the two is no less serious when the religious is restricted to the moral. (Religions can be turned into simply moral codes, just as they can be used as the mortar that binds a community.) Democracy is not a "state of virtue"; it allows each individual to define the supreme good in his or her own fashion; it defines at most the means to achieve it, ruling out violence, for instance. That does not mean that democracy is hostile to morality, only that it restricts it to the private sphere. However, moral correctness seeks to put morality and politics back together, at least in the social sphere if not at the level of the state. The difference with totalitarianism is that moral correctness would make politics dependent on morality. Domestically, this trend increases the exclusion of nonconformers, the stridency of sermonizing, and spreads a mood of self-righteousness. In international relations, such do-goodery takes us right back to crusades and colonial wars undertaken in the name of good. Here, again, the recognition of plurality yields to the temptation of imposing our good intentions on others.

What is jettisoned by moral correctness is the autonomy of the thinking subject. Domestically, individuals are prevented from exercising their judgment in society because infringements of moral correctness are decried. Internationally, peoples and states are deprived of sovereignty when another, militarily more powerful, state or coalition of states, seeing itself as the incarnation of moral good, claims a right of interference that allows it to impose its good intentions on others by force. Good intentions can lead to hell, as we all know: they are responsible for the Hiroshima and Nagasaki bombs as well as for the witch-hunts that took place in countries that were not at all totalitarian. Let's not forget Grossman's warning that "the dawn of an eternal good" is a sure sign that blood will soon be spilled. It is not the vocation of a democratic state, or of the world order, to embody goodness; it is better to leave aspirations to sainthood to the private sphere.

315

An excess of identity politics and the inflation of moral correctness are both fed by nostalgia for a lost world in which communities were more bonded and where each had its own public morality. The same is not true of the third perversion, specific to democratic societies, and which I shall call *overinstrumentalization*. Once again we are dealing with something that is unexceptional when it is restricted to its proper field. Overinstrumentalization consists of focusing exclusively on the means and instruments for achieving a goal without stopping to think whether the goal is a legitimate one or not. Obviously, there are lots of occasions where you do not need to reflect on the legitimacy of goals; you only need to find the best solution to a technical problem. But it is very dangerous to generalize this observation into a principle. You could easily end up like the inventors of the atomic bomb, who were fascinated exclusively by the technical difficulty of making such a thing—and some of them spent the rest of their days pondering the dreadful results of their invention. The same mental blindfold makes soldiers of all nations examine the objectives they are given solely from a technical point of view, with no thought about the ultimate justification of their acts.

Overinstrumentalization is specific to democratic countries precisely because democracy gives no prior definition of the ultimate good and allows all its citizens to pursue their own ideals as long as they do not try to impose them on others by force. From this perspective, overinstrumentalization is the symmetrical obverse of moral do-goodery, which is but an overinflated bid to fill the void created by the refusal to set an ultimate and overarching end. Instrumental thinking is based on the untenable anthropological hypothesis that the agent-means-ends model can account for all human practices. The hypothesis leaves out of account a large part of human existence, namely intersubjective relations, which it would be difficult to account for in terms of the model. To take a simple example, when two friends meet, you can not separate ends from means. You do not call on your friend in order to get her to do you a favor but to have the pleasure of her company; in addition, and this is fundamental, there is not one single agent-subject involved, but two, *I* and *thou*, and each talks and listens, gives and receives, in turn.

Instrumental thinking goes counter to humanist doctrine which insists that the benefit of human action be only for human beings themselves. Modern societies in thrall to the logic of instrumental thinking tend to neglect this dimension of human existence and to look for purely technical solutions to all our problems — for example, "market economics." In this way they are mulching the ground of identity politics and moral correctness, if not of totalitarian revolution.

Every society needs to assert its identity, defend its ideals, and solve the problems facing it. But if the ways it does these things are transformed into ultimate principles, they become serious obstacles. There is no doubt that the three perversions I have sketched are alive and well among us today. All three came into the open during the Kosovo campaign. Identity politics ruled supreme over Serbs and Albanian-speaking Kosovars; moral correctness, in a paradoxical alliance with instrumentalization, dominated Western nations. Will we see one of these perversions triumph over democracy in the twenty-first century? Or will democracy find the vigor to fight back and defend itself? That is a forecast I don't dare call. It depends on what we do: the future is in our hands.

Let me add that defeating moral correctness, identity politics, and overinstrumentalization is only a necessary condition for individual fulfillment, not a guaranteed recipe. In like manner, the defeat of totalitarianism by democracy has not brought about universal self-fulfillment to the inhabitants of formerly totalitarian states. In modern societies fulfillment is not made by good politics and morality, but by lives filled with love and spirituality, in the guise of religion, art or thought. That is how people acquire the feeling that their lives have meaning. Morality and politics are not enough; and yet they are essential. The boundary between public and private life is not watertight: totalitarian societies do not allow you to cultivate spirituality on your own, nor do they allow you to love freely. Only democracy guarantees these conditions for personal fulfillment.

The twentieth century was an age of great confrontations and monumental battles, between democracy and totalitarianism, between Nazism and Communism. However, I would like us also to remember the individuals who managed to remain human in the midst of the tempest. As a last example, let us consider the story of a woman named Lila, or so the French press called her (*Le Monde*, 20, 22, and 23 June 2000). In 1957 she was a young

Algerian, and a member of a military cell of the FLN. She fell into the hands of the French army after a terrorist action and underwent torture for three months, without respite, until December 1957. She was released from her torturers by a military doctor who took a look at her one evening and said: "Dear child, you've been tortured!" Lila reminded the doctor of his own daughter, so he said. And thanks to him Lila was transferred to a prison in Algeria, and then to France. There, Germaine Tillion, who was working for the Education Ministry's prisoner-education project, was in a position to facilitate the release of many detainees. Lila was moved to house arrest in Corsica and then eventually escaped.

Let us take into the twenty-first century not an image of the French bringing civilization to Africa nor an image of Algerians fighting for national liberation, but a memory of these two simple, good individuals, Dr. Richaud ("Dear child!") and Germaine Tillion, two beings for whom people were much more than mere categories — enemies or prisoners. They were infinitely fragile, infinitely precious human beings.

Bibliography

Dates of first publication are given where relevant in parentheses after the title. Publication details refer to the editions used for quotations.

Alperovitz, Gal. *Atomic Diplomacy.* New York: Simon and Schuster, 1965.

——. *The Decision to Use the Atomic Bomb — and the Architecture of an American Myth.* New York: Knopf, 1995.

Arendt, Hannah. *Origins of Totalitarianism.* New York: Harcourt Brace Jovanovich, 1973.

Aron, Raymond. *Democracy and Totalitarianism.* Translated by Valence Ionescu. London: Weidenfeld & Nicolson, 1968.

——. *Fifty Years of Political Reflection: Memoirs.* Translated by George Holoch. New York: Homes and Meier, 1990.

Barrès, Maurice. *Scènes et doctrines du nationalisme* (1902). Paris: Trident, 1987.

Bass, Gary J. *Stay the Hand of Vengeance.* Princeton: Princeton University Press, 2000.

Beauvoir, Simone de. "La Pensée de droite aujourd'hui." *Les Temps modernes.* 1955.

Béguin, Albert. "Postface." In Margarete Buber-Neumann, *Déportée en Sibérie.* Paris: Seuil, 1949.

Bénichou, Paul. *The Consecration of the Writer, 1750–1830* (1973). Translated by Mark K. Jensen. Lincoln: Nebraska University Press, 1999.

Bensaïd, D. "La raison des déraisons." *Lignes*, May 2000.

Bensoussan, Georges. "Pour une lecture politique de la shoah." In C. Coquiot, ed., *Parler des camps, penser le génocide.* Paris: Albin Michell, 1999.

Berzer, Anna. "Proshchanie." In S. I. Lipkin, *Zhizn' I Sud'ba Vasiliia Grossmana.* Moscow: Kniga, 1990.

Besançon, Alain. *The Rise of the Gulag: Intellectual Origins of Leninism.* Translated by Sarah Matthews. New York: Continuum, 1981.

Bona, Dominique. *Romain Gary.* Paris: Mercure de France, 1987.

Brauman, Rony. "Mémoire, savoir, pensée." *Le Débat* 96 (1977).

Brauman, Rony, with E. Sivan. *Éloge de la désobéissance.* Paris: Le Pommier, 1999.

Brossat, Alain. *Margarete Buber-Neumann. Témoin absolu du XXe siècle.* Lyon: Horlieu, 1999.

Buber-Neumann, Margarete. *Déportée à Ravensbrück*. Paris: Seuil, 1988.

——. *Die Erloschene Flamme, Schicksale meiner Zeit*. Munich: Langen Müller, 1976.

——. *Freiheit du bist wieder mein . . . Die Kraft zu überleben*. Munich: Langen Müller, 1978.

——. *Kreigsschauplätze der Weltrevolution. Ein Bericht aus der Praxis der Komintern, 1919–1943*. Stuttgart: Seewald, 1967. Quoted here from its French translation, *Révolution mondiale* (Paris: Casterman, 1971).

——. *Mistress to Kafka: The Life and Death of Milena*. Translated by Ralph Manheim. London: Secker and Warburg, 1966. Published in the United States as *Milena* (New York: Seaver Books, 1988).

——. *Plädoyer für Freiheit und Menschlichkeit. Vorträge aus 35 Jahren*. Berlin: Hentrich, 2000.

——. "Qui est pire, Satan ou Belzébuth?" (1950). *Commentaire* 81 (1998).

——. *Under Two Dictators*. Translated by Edward Fitzgerald. London: Gollancz, 1949.

——. *Von Potsdam nach Moskau. Stationen eines Irrwegs*. Berlin: Ullstein, 1990.

Camus, Albert. *Actuelles. Chroniques 1944–1948*. Paris: Gallimard, 1950.

Camus, Albert, with Arthur Koestler. *Réflexions sur la peine capitale*. Paris: Calmann-Lévy, 1979.

Castoriadis, Cornelius. *Devant la guerre*. Paris: Fayard, 1981.

Chaumont, Jean-Michel. *La Concurrence des victimes*. Paris: La Découverte, 1997.

Chernyshevsky, Nikolai Gavrilovoch. *Das Anthropologische Prinzip*. Translated by A. Kurella. Berlin: Aufbau-Verlag, 1956.

——. *What Is to Be Done?* Translated by Michael R. Katz. Ithaca: Cornell University Press, 1989.

Cohen, Stephen E. *Bukharin and the Bolshevik Revolution: A Political Biography, 1888–1938*. New York: Knopf, 1973.

Condorcet, Marie Jean, Marquis de. *Esquisse d'un tableau historique des progrès de l'esprit humain*. Paris: Editions sociales, 1971.

——. "Observations sur le vingt-neuvième livre de *l'Esprit des lois*." In *Œuvres*, vol. 1, 1847.

Constant, Benjamin. *Œuvres complètes*. Tübingen: Niemeyer, 1995. Vol. III, part 1.

——. *Principes de politique*. Paris: Hachette, 1997.

——. *De la religion*. Arles: Actes Sud, 1999.

Copfermann, E. *David Rousset*. Paris: Plon, 1991.

Cottret, B. *L'Edit de Nantes*. Paris: Perrin, 1997.

Courtois, Stéphane, ed. *The Black Book of Communism*. Translated by Jonathan Murphy and Mark Kramer. Cambridge, Mass.: Harvard University Press, 1999.

Culver, John C., and John Hyde. *American Dreamer: A Life of Henry A. Wallace*. New York: Norton, 2000.

Descartes, René. *The Meditations and Selections from the Principles*. Translated by John Veitch. Chicago: Open Court, 1920.

————. *Selected Philosophical Writings*. Translated by J. Cottingham, R. Stoothoff, and D. Murdoch. Cambridge: Cambridge University Press, 1988.

Dower, John W. "Three Narratives of Our Humanity." In: Edward T. Linenthal and Tom Engelhardt, *History Wars. The* Enola Gay *and Other Battles for the American Past*, pp. 63–96. New York: Holt, 1996.

————. *War without Mercy: Race and Power in the Pacific War*. New York: Pantheon, 1986.

Finkielkraut, Alain. *The Imaginary Jew*. Translated by Kevin O'Neill and David Suchoff. Lincoln: University of Nebraska Press, 1994.

Frank, Semyon Liudvigovich. *Po tu storonu pravogo i levogo*. Paris: YMCA Press, 1972.

Fussell, Paul. *Thank God for the Atomic Bomb*. New York: Summit Books, 1988.

Garrard, John, and Carol Garrard. *The Bones of Berdichev: The Life and Fate of Vasily Grossman*. New York: Free Press, 1996.

Gary, Romain. *La Bonne moitié*. Paris: Gallimard, 1979.

————. *Catalogue de l'exposition* Résistance et Déportation. 1980.

————. *Les cerfs-volants*. Paris: Mercure de France, 1980.

————. *Éducation européenne* (1945). Translated as *A European Education*. New York: Simon and Schuster, 1960.

————. *Le Grand Vestiaire* (1950). Translated as *The Company of Men* by Joseph Barnes. New York: Simon and Schuster, 1950.

————. *King Solomon* (1978). Translated by Barbara Wright. New York: Harper, 1982.

————. *Le Mangeur d'étoiles* (1961). Translated as *The Talent Scout* by John Markham Beach. New York: Harper, 1966.

————. *Momo* (1975). Translated by Ralph Manheim. New York: Doubleday, 1978. Reissued as *Life before Us* (New York: Doubleday, 1986).

————. *La Nuit sera calme*. Paris: Gallimard, 1974.

————. *Pour Sganarelle*. Paris: Gallimard, 1965.

————. *La Promesse de l'aube* (1960). Translated as *Promise at Dawn* by John Markham Beach. New York: Harper, 1961.

————. *Pseudo*. Paris: Mercure de France, 1976.

321

———. *Les Racines du Ciel* (1956). Translated as *The Roots of Heaven* by Jonathan Griffin. New York: Simon and Schuster, 1958.

———. *Tulipe* (1946). Paris: Folio, 1970.

———. *Vie et mort d'Emile Ajar*. Paris: Mercure de France, 1981.

———. *White Dog*. New York: World Publishing, 1970.

Ginzburg, Evgenia. *Journey into the Whirlwind*. Trans. P. Stevenson and M. Hayward. New York: Harcourt, 1967.

———. *Within the Whirlwind*. Trans. Ian Boland. New York: Harcourt, 1982.

Gliksman, Jerzy. *Tell the West*. New York: National Committee for a Free Europe, 1948.

Glover, J. *Humanity*. London: Cape, 1999.

Gourevitch, Philip. "Behold Now Behemoth." *Harper's*, July 1993.

———. *We Wish to Inform You That Tomorrow We Will Be Killed with Our Families*. New York: Farrar Straus Giroux, 1998.

Grosser, Alfred. *Le Crime et la mémoire*. Paris: Flammarion, 1989.

———. *Les Identités difficiles*. Paris: Presses de la FNSP, 1996.

Grossman, Vasily. "Dobro Vam!" and "Avel." In *Povest. Rasskazi. Ocherki*, 4:5–20, 150–221. Moscow: Agraf, 1998.

———. *Forever Flowing*. Translated by Thomas P. Whitney. New York: Harper and Row, 1972.

———. *Life and Fate: A Novel*. Translated by Robert Chandler. London: Collins Harvill, 1985.

———. "The Treblinka Hell." in *The Years of War*, translated by Elizabeth Donnelly and Rose Prokoviev. Moscow: Foreign Language Publishing House, 1946.

Grossman, Vasily, with Ilya Ehrenburg. *Chernaia Kniga*. Jerusalem: Tarbut, 1980. Translated as *The Black Book: The Ruthless Murder of Jews by German-Fascist Invaders throughout the Temporarily-Occupied Regions of the Soviet Union and in the Death Camps of Poland during the War of 1941–1945*, by John Gland and James Levine (New York: Schocken Books, 1981).

Havel, Vaclav. "Kosovo and the End of the Nation State" *New York Review of Books* 46:10, 10 June 1999.

Herling, Gustav. *A World Apart*. Translated by Andrzej Ciozkosz (Joseph Marek). New York: Arbor House, 1986.

Huston, Nancy. *Tombeau de Romain Gary*. Arles: Actes Sud, 1995.

Jelenski, K. A. "Entretien avec Romain Gary." *Biblio*, March 1967.

Jelev, Jeliou. *Le Fascisme*. Geneva: Rousseau, 1993.

Kahan, Stuart. *The Wolf in the Kremlin*. New York: Morrow, 1987.

Kersnovskaïa, Euphrosinia. *Coupable de rien*. Paris: Plon, 1994.

Klarsfeld, Serge. *Memorial of the Deportation*. New York: YIVO, 1978.

Klemperer, Victor. *The Language of the Third Reich: LTI, Lingua Tertii*

Imperii. A Philologist's Notebook. Translated by Martin Brady. London: Athlone Press, 2000.

Kogon, Eugen, Hermann Langbein, and Adalbert Rückerl. *Nazi Mass Murder: A Documentary History of the Use of Poison Gas*. Translated by May Scott and Caroline Lloyd-Morris. New Haven: Yale University Press, 1993.

Krall, Hanna, *Shielding the Flame: An Intimate Conversation with Dr. Marek Edelman*. Translated by Joanna Stasinska and Lawrence Weschler. New York: Henry Holt, 1986.

Lacouture, Jean. *Le Témoignage est un combat. Une biographie de Germaine Tillion*. Paris: Seuil, 2000.

Larat, F. *Romain Gary, un itinéraire européen*. Chêne-Bourg: Georg, 1999.

Le Goff, Jacques. *Histoire et mémoire*. Paris: Gallimard, 1988.

Lenin, Vladimir Ilich. *Polnoe Sobranie Sochinenii*. Moscow, 1958–65.

Levi, Primo. *Conversazioni e interviste, 1963–1987*. Turin: Einaudi, 1997.

———. *The Drowned and the Saved*. Translated by Raymond Rosenthal. New York: Simon and Schuster, 1988.

———. *If This Is a Man*. Translated by Stuart Wolf. New York: Vintage, 1996.

———. *Moments of Reprieve*. Translated by Ruth Feldman. New York: Summit Books, 1986.

———. *The Voice of Memory: Interviews, 1961–1987*. Translated by Robert Gordon. New York: New Press, 2001.

Levinas, Emmanuel. *Entre nous: Thinking-of-the-other*. Translated by Michael B. Smith and Barbara Harshav. New York: Columbia University Press, 1998.

Lévy, E. "Kosovo: l'insoutenable légèreté de l'information." *Le Débat* 109 (2000).

Linenthal, Edward T., and Tom Engelhardt, eds., *History Wars: The Enola Gay and other Battles for the American Past*. New York: Holt, 1996.

Lipkin, S. I. *Le destin de Vassili Grossman*. Lausanne: L'Âge d'homme, 1990.

Locke, John. "An Essay Concerning the True Original Extent and End of Civil Society." In *Two Treatises on Civil Government*, ed. Carpenter. New York: Everyman, 1924.

London, Artur. *The Confession*. Translated by Alastair Hamilton. New York: Morrow, 1970. Published in the United Kingdom as *On Trial* (London: Macmillan, 1970).

Marchenko, Anatolii. *My Testimony*. Translated by Michael Scammel. New York: Dutton, 1969.

323

Marx, Karl. *Basic Writings on Politics and Philosophy*. Edited by Lewis S. Feuer. New York: Anchor Books, 1959.

Montaigne, Michel de. *The Complete Essays*. Translated by M. A. Screech. London: Penguin, 1987.

Montesquieu, Charles de. *Persian Letters*. Translated by John Davidson. London: Routledge, 1891.

———. *The Spirit of Laws*. Edited by David Carrithers. Berkeley: University of California Press, 1977.

Mukagasana, Yolande. *La Mort ne veut pas de moi*. Paris: Fixot, 1997.

Oe, Kenzaburo. *Hiroshima Notes*. Translated by David Swain and Toshi Yonegawa. New York: Marion Boyars, 1995.

Péguy, Charles. *L'Argent. Suite*. Paris: Cahiers de la Quinzaine, 1913.

Pikhoia, R. G., and A. Geishtor. *Katyn. Plenniki neobyavlyonnoi voiny*. Moscow: Demokratiia, 1997.

Pomian, Krzysztof. "Post-scriptum sur la notion de totalitarisme." In H. Rousso, ed., *Stalinisme et nazisme*, pp. 371–82. Bruxelles: Complexe, 1999.

———. "Qu'est-ce que le totalitarisme?" (1995). In M. Ferro, ed., *Nazisme et communisme*. Paris: Hachette-Pluriel, 1999.

Postel-Vinay, Anise. "Une ethnologue en camp de concentration." *Esprit* 261 (2000).

Procès des grands criminels de guerre devant le tribunal militaire international. Nuremberg, 1947. Vol. III.

Renan, Ernest. *Dialogues philosophiques*. Paris: CNRS Editions, 1992.

———. *The Future of Science*. Boston: Roberts, 1891.

Ricœur, Paul, "L'Écriture de l'histoire et la représentation du passé." *Le Monde*, 15 June 1990.

———. *La Mémoire, l'histoire, l'oubli*. Paris: Seuil, 2000.

Rousseau, Jean-Jacques. *Émile*. Translated by A. Bloom. New York: Basic Books, 1979.

———. "Lettre sur la vertu, l'individu et la société." *Annales de la Société Jean-Jacques Rousseau* 41 (1997).

———. *Œuvres complètes*. Vol. 3. Bibliothèque de la Pléiade. Paris: Gallimard, 1964.

———. *The Social Contract*. Translated by V. Gourevitch. Cambridge University Press, 1997.

Rousset, David. *Les Jours de notre mort*. 2 vols. Paris: Hachette, 1992.

———. *The Legacy of the Bolshevik Revolution*. Vol. 1 of *A Critical History of the USSR*. Translated by Alan Freeman. New York: St Martin's Press, 1982.

———. *The Other Kingdom* (1946). Translated by Ramon Guthrie. New York: Reynal & Hitchcock, 1947.

———. "Le sens de notre combat" (1959). *Lignes*, May 2000.

———. *Sur la guerre. Sommes-nous en danger de guerre nucéaire?* Paris: Ramsay, 1987.

Rousset, David, et al. *Pour la vérité sur les camps concentrationnaires.* Paris: Ramsay, 1990.

Rousso, Henry. *La Hantise du passé.* Paris: Textuel, 1998.

Rufin, Jean-Christophe. "Les humanitaires et la guerre du Kosovo: échec ou espoir?" In *Des Choix difficiles. Les dilemmes moraux de l'humanitaire.* Paris: Gallimard, 1999.

Sadowska-Guillon, I. "Heiner Müller à Verdun." *Bulletin de la lettre internationale* 5 (1996): 106–9.

Sartre, Jean-Paul. *Situations V.* Paris: Gallimard, 1964.

Saussure, Léopold de. *Psychologie de la colonisation française.* Paris: Alcan, 1899.

Schafraneck, Hans. *Zwischen NKVD und Gestapo. Die Auslieferung deutscher und österreichischer Anti-Fascisten aus der Sowjetunion an Nazideutschland, 1937–1941.* Frankfurt/M: ISP Verlag, 1990.

Sereny, Gitta. *Into that Darkness: From Mercy Killing to Mass Murder.* New York: McGraw-Hill, 1974.

Sojcher, Jacques. *Jeanclos.* Paris: Cercle d'art, 2000.

Steele, Shelby. *The Content of Our Character.* New York: Harper, 1991.

Tagueiff, Pierre-André. "Les écrans de la vigilance." *Panoramiques* 35 (1998): 65–78.

Taine, Hippolyte. *Derniers essais de critique et d'histoire.* Paris: Hachette, 1894.

Tillion, Germaine. *L'Afrique bascule vers l'avenir.* Paris: Tirésias — M. Reynaud, 1999.

———. *Algeria: The Realities* (1957). Translated by Ronald Mathews. New York: Knopf, 1958.

———. *A la recherché du vrai et du juste. A propos rompus avec le siècle.* Paris: Seuil, 2001.

———. *France and Algeria: Complementary Enemies* (1960). Translated by Richard Howard. New York: Knopf, 1961.

———. *Il était une fois l'ethnographie.* Paris: Seuil, 1999.

———. *Le Harem et les cousins* (1966). Paris: Seuil, 1982. Translated as *The Republic of Cousins: Women's Oppression in Mediterranean Society* by Quintin Hoare (London: Al Saqi Books, 1983).

———. *Ravensbrück.* 2d ed., 1973. Translated by Gerald Satterwhite. Garden City, N.Y.: Anchor Press, 1975.

———. *Ravensbrück.* 3d ed. Paris: Seuil, 1988.

———. *La Traversée du mal. Entretiens avec Jean Lacouture.* Paris: Arléa, 1997.

Tocqueville, Alexis de. *The European Revolution and Correspondence with Gobineau.* Translated by John Lukacs. Westport, Conn.: Greenwood Press, 1974.

Todorov, Tzvetan. *Facing the Extreme: Moral Life in the Concentration Camps.* Translated by Arthur Denner and Abigail Pollak. New York: Henry Holt, 1996.

———. *The Fragilty of Goodness: Why Bulgaria's Jews Survived the Holocaust.* Translated by Arthur Denner. Princeton: Princeton University Press, 2001.

Todorov, Tzvetan, and Annick Jacquet. *Guerre et paix sous l'Occupation.* Paris: Arléa, 1996.

Vespucci, Amerigo. *Letters from a New World.* Translated by David Jacobson. New York: Marsilio, 1992.

Wallace, Henry Agard, and Andrew Steiger. *Soviet Asia Mission.* New York: Reynal & Hitchcock, 1945.

Weber, Max. "Ideal-Type Constructs." In *Sociological Writings,* edited by Wolf Heydebrand, pp. 262–76. New York: Continuum, 1994.

Weinrich, Harald. *Lethe, Kunst und Kritik des Vergessens.* Munich: Beck, 1997.

Werfel, Franz. *The Forty Days of Musa Dagh.* New York: Viking, 1934.

Zhelev, see under Jelev.

Index

Achberg, Olof, 102
Afghanistan, xiv–xvi, xx
African Americans, 143, 233
Africans, enslavement of, 161
Albania or Albanians, 239–240, 245–246, 248, 251–253, 255–256, 261
Albright, Madeleine, 244, 269, 281
Algeria, xii, xvi–xvii, 145, 152, 166–168, 170, 297–298, 301, 303–307
Alleg, Henri, 166
Allen, Woody, 161
Alperovitz, Gal, 231
Al Qaeda, xiv–xv, xvii
American Revolution, 8, 13
Améry, Jean, 184
Amnesty International, 271–272
anarchy, 47, 278–279
Annan, Kofi, 210, 274
Anscombe, Elizabeth, 235
antifascisim, 190–191
anti-Semitism, 54–55, 89, 190, 191
Arafat, Yasser, 164
Aragon, Louis, 107
Arbour, Louise, 270
Arendt, Hannah, 14, 33, 125
Armenia and Armenians, 5, 56–57, 134, 166, 281
Aron, Raymond, 35–38, 42, 79, 81–82
artificial selection, 20, 33, 105
associations and organizations, public, 12, 15
Athens, 8
Atlantic Alliance. See North Atlantic Treaty Organization (NATO)
atomic bomb: building of, 233–234, 316; use of, xvi, 145–147, 161, 212, 228–237
Aubrac, Lucie and Raymond, 203–204
Auschwitz, 33, 75, 88, 105, 118, 142, 151, 163
Austria, 275

autonomy: collective, 7–10, 16–17, 45, 96, 248; individual, 7–11, 14, 16, 45, 61, 69, 85, 96, 158, 172, 241, 248; of judgment, 121–122, 264; political, 7–9
Azéma, Jean-Pierre, 204–205
Aztecs, 113

Babel, Isaak, 49
Barak, Ehud, 164
Barbie, Klaus, 160, 206, 208
Barrès, Maurice, 135–136, 199
Bartosek, Karel, 198–199, 201–203
Basque separatists, xvii
Baudelaire, Charles-Pierre, 13
Beauvoir, Simone de, 35, 301
Bédarida, François, 204
Béguin, Albert, 110
Belgium, 274
Benda, Julien, 193
Berdichev (Ukraine), 51, 54
Bert, Paul, 276
Besançon, Alain, 20, 33
"best of intentions" principle, xv, 70–71, 79–80, 94–95, 140, 196–197. See also "right of interference" principle
Bin Laden, Osama, xii–xiv
biological determinism, 135–136
Blair, Tony, 272
Bolsheviks, 15, 50, 64, 67, 166
Bonald, Louis-Gabriel-Ambroise, vicomte de, 85
Borges, Jorge Luis, 127
Bosnia, 242–244, 249, 255, 269, 278
Brauman, Rony, 79–80, 126, 140
Brecht, Bertolt, 191
Brezhnev, Leonid, 43, 45, 282
Brossat, Alain, 110, 191
Brossolette, Pierre, 216
Brzezinski, Zbigniew, 259
Buber, Rafel, 97
Buber-Neumann, Margarete, 4, 83, 93–112, 149, 166

327

history, 129–134; comparison as tool of, 76, 151–152; establishing the facts of, 120–122, 144, 149, 237–238, 251–252; law and, 205–212; moral correctness and, 198–205; revisionism and, 133; as sanctification of the past, 133, 161–164, 176, 311; as trivialization of the past, 161–164, 176, 243–244, 260–261, 311; truth and, 204, 296

Hitler, Adolf, 27; on Armenian genocide, 134, 166; Darwinian ideas and, 33; name/likeness of, invoked as representation of evil, 163–164, 244, 261, 271; Night of the Long Knives and, 65n, 104; power and, 16, 32; rationality of, 78–82. See also Jews: extermination of

HIV-contaminated blood, 170–171

Holbrooke, Richard, 244

Holocaust denial, 91, 122

Holocaust Memorial Museum (Washington, D.C.), 160, 164

Hughes, Langston, 233

humanism, xx, 4, 24–26, 39, 139, 211, 268, 313

humanitarian action, 265–274, 288

"humanitarian bombs," 258–260, 267

Human Rights Watch, 271

humility, xxii, 180–181

Hungary, xix, 286

Hussein, Saddam, 163, 271

Hutus. See Rwanda

ideal-type constructs, 6–7

identification, 165–167; with perpetrators, 124; with victims, 144, 167

identity, 164–165, 174, 241, 249–250, 312

identity politics, xiv, 165, 314–315, 317

Ikonnikov, 71

India, xx, 279

individual autonomy, 158, 248; democracy and, 7–11, 172, 241, 264; National Socialism and, 16; pluralism and, 10; right/left political alignments and, 85; totalitarianism and, 14, 16, 45, 61, 69, 96

individualism, 13, 39, 42, 173

individuals, stateless, x–xi, xiv, xvi

Indochina, 276

information services, xi, 12, 15, 192–193

Inka (Buber-Neumann friend), 101, 107–108

instrumentalism, 153, 234, 316–317

International Commission against Concentration Camp Regimes, 149–150, 152, 297

International Criminal Court (ICC), 210, 272–273

International Criminal Tribunal for Yugoslavia at the Hague (ICTY), 268–273

internationalism, 38, 43, 63

international relations. See foreign policy

intersubjectivity, 80, 123, 138–139, 316

Iraq, xii–xiii, xv, xvii–xviii, xx, 289

Islam, xiii

Israel, xiii, xvi–xvii, xx, 167, 170, 191, 279–280

Italy, 159, 245

Itzcoatl, 113

Japan. See Hiroshima, bombing of

Jeanclos, Georges, 174–175

Jesenská, Milena, 101–102, 110

Jesus Christ, 18, 32, 138, 143, 195–196, 224

Jews: in Bulgaria, 173; extermination of, 36–37, 66–67, 78–82, 87–89, 161–163; in Hungary, 118; memorials to, 115, 121; in Soviet Union, 51–56, 64, 69, 72n

justice, 9, 227, 268–269, 272–273; deindividualization and, 173; democracy and, 9, 11; revenge and, 170–171, 232; "right of interference" and, xx–xxi, 279; totalitarianism and, 14, 73

Kaganovich, Lazar Moiseyevich, 37

Kant, Immanuel, 18, 26, 139, 195, 259

Karaganda camp, 100

Katyn massacre (Poland), 89, 121–122, 200, 238

Kazakhstan and Kazakhs, 37, 286

Kersnovskaïa, Euphrosinia, 168